# MAD

# BLOOD

Daemon Fairless

# STIRRING

## THE INNER LIVES OF VIOLENT MEN

RANDOM HOUSE CANADA

PUBLISHED BY RANDOM HOUSE CANADA

www.penguinrandomhouse.ca

LIBRARY AND ARCHIVES CANADA CATALOGUING IN PUBLICATION

Fairless, Daemon, 1974–, author
Mad blood stirring : the inner lives of violent men / Daemon Fairless.
Includes bibliographical references and index.
Issued in print and electronic formats.

(trade paperback) ISBN 978-0-345-81292-6
(hardcover) ISBN 978-0-7352-7600-0
eBook ISBN 978-0-345-81294-0

1. Violence in men.  2. Men—Psychology.  3. Violence—Psychological aspects.
I. Title.

HQ1090.F34 2018              303.60811              C2016-906048-9

Cover design by Terri Nimmo
Cover art: Original artwork by STEV'NN HALL,
"Red James" / oil painting / 28x28 / 2012

Printed and bound in the United States of America

2 4 6 8 9 7 5 3 1

Penguin
Random House
RANDOM HOUSE CANADA

*For Lyana and Simone*

Benvolio. I pray thee, good Mercutio, let's retire:
The day is hot, the Capulets abroad,
And, if we meet, we shall not 'scape a brawl;
For now, these hot days, is the mad blood stirring.

WILLIAM SHAKESPEARE, *Romeo and Juliet* (3.1.1-4)

# CONTENTS

# THE DANGEROUS DESIRE

A FEW YEARS AGO, on New Year's Eve, I head-butted a man on the subway. Here's the version I generally tell people:

My wife and I were on an eastbound train. We had been skating at an outdoor rink near our downtown apartment. We were on our way to the suburbs, to ring in the New Year with my in-laws, when a man—a big, thick guy in his early twenties—decided to pick a fight with me.

He was loud and obnoxious and extremely drunk, and he was showing off in front of his two friends by prying open the sliding doors of the subway car and sticking his head out into the tunnel. I got up because he was dangerously close to dashing his brains out on the concrete pillars whizzing past his head. I told him to sit down. He exploded and challenged me to a fight. I told him I wasn't going to fight him and I sat back down.

The long and the short of it is that, after he yelled at me, after he threw a bottle at me, spat on me and then, finally, threatened to hit my wife, I stood up again and head-butted him in the face. A brawl erupted and at least a dozen other men jumped in and tried to pull us apart. The police came. They arrested the guy and took my statement.

I was sober and the other guy wasn't; I was the victim and he was the aggressor. The police gave me a subtle nod of approval for defending myself, even as they pointed out the obvious risks. One of the cops took my statement. "You're lucky," he said. "What if he'd had a knife or a gun?" But there was an understanding between us—I'd taken the risk to protect my wife.

Directly after the fight, while I was still a little stunned, a man came up to me. He was short and slight and wearing a well-cut suit. "You did the right thing," he said, dabbing his bleeding nose with a napkin. He had a gift bag with him, champagne decorated with pearlescent ribbons; he was on his way to a friend's party. I hadn't seen him on the train, but apparently he had been watching and, as soon as the fight started, had tried to break it up. I apologized for ruining his night. "Don't worry about it," he said. "That guy had it coming." He shook my hand. "Plus, now I've got an amazing story to tell my friends."

This is generally the reaction I get. Most people understand why I did it. And, to be honest, I like telling this story, too, in the way I've just told it. It makes me feel like a stand-up guy.

The real story is more complicated.

I'm in a bad mood even before I get on the subway. I hate crowds, and the Bloor station is a downright zoo. It's packed with cliques of tipsy revellers on their way to parties. I have to push through people to get anywhere. A girl trying to get her friend's attention screams in my ear. My skates bang against my shin.

We take the escalator down to the platform. It stinks. Some kid has just sprayed his tag on the wall and the whole place reeks of propellant and paint. The kid—he's maybe fourteen—dashes past me, followed by a gang of tittering friends. It irks me that no one has the guts to say anything, that an entire crowd of onlookers can stand by without intervening. For a moment I consider grabbing the kid by his jacket, pulling the can out of his pocket and spraying his chest. Then I consider the consequences: I'd be charged with assaulting a minor. I let it go. This pisses me off further.

On the train, I rant to Lyana, my wife, about the bovine complacency of crowds. I bring up the case of Kitty Genovese, the New York woman murdered in the 1960s in front of thirty-some witnesses, none of whom intervened. It's not the first time I've brought up Kitty Genovese. She's standard fare when I'm in one of these moods.

Now I'm having trouble concentrating on what I'm saying because of some drunk idiot behind us. He's so loud. His voice—he's got the kind of ignorant, belching yawp that's hard to ignore. He bellows like a one-man argument, all *fucks* and *shits* and *bitches*. It sets me further on edge. I can feel my jaw clenching. The train lurches from stop to stop. More and more people get on. The loud guy grows louder and more belligerent. I'm not entirely sure who he's talking to. Everyone on board has given up trying to hold their own conversations.

I turn around to get a look at him. He's younger than me by at least ten years. A big white kid in baggy pants and an oversized hoodie. He talks like a wannabe gangsta. He probably lives in the suburbs with mom and dad. He looks like such an idiot, standing in the aisle like that, legs spread wide, rocking back and forth with the motion of the train. He saunters over to a set of sliding doors and tries prying them open. He jams his fingers into the rubber seal and cracks the doors a few inches. In an exquisite manoeuvre of stupidity—we're talking Darwin Award nominee here—he pops his head outside, into the tunnel, where the concrete support pillars are zipping by in a complete blur just beyond his meaty cranium. *Whoosh!* I have a brief vision of his headless body falling back into the car. *Whoosh!* Worse things have happened. *Whoosh!* He's a subhuman moron.

The guy pulls his head back into the car. He says something boastful and obnoxious—I can't hear what exactly. I realize he's with two guys. His friends look uneasy. One of them tells him to chill. He interprets this as a challenge. He's back at the doors. This time he pries them apart, his back arched, chest out like Superman pulling apart prison bars. He grunts. He gets the doors open most of the way. Cold, stale air rushes into the car. The effervescent cheer of the holiday crowd has gone flat, replaced by a nervous hush. This guy needs a talking-to.

All this time, I'm contemplating him, whoever he is—it doesn't cross my mind to care. I take him in. I observe and calculate: he's big— six foot something, somewhere north of two hundred pounds—but he's not that big, not bigger than me, and not in particularly good shape, either. That's an advantage. He's drunk. Another advantage.

Along with this conscious consideration of detail, there's something else: a building surge on the horizon, moving towards me quickly, an impending wave, a deep, seductive swell. He's a piece of trash. There's a lapping coolness between my temples. People all around me are scared, nervous. They feel threatened. Not me. It's different in me, it's a growing itch, a form of lust. A predatory hard-on. I want him on his knees. Subjugated. Scared. I'm out of my seat. I'm standing beside him.

I should point out that I'm not an especially skilled fighter. I've spent enough time around people who know what they're doing—professional boxers, MMA fighters, martial artists—to know I score pretty low on the badass scale. But I'm six three and a solid 250 pounds, and when I'm pissed off and physically aggressive, I can be a considerable problem.

"You need to sit the fuck down," I tell the guy. My face feels tense. I'm baring my teeth, grimacing weirdly.

He looks up, genuinely surprised. He sizes me up and then cocks his head. "Who the fuck're you?" he yells. His breath is hot.

Time opens up like an accordion. The minutes have more seconds; the seconds expand and reveal details I haven't noticed before. I smell the sour tang of Gatorade and alcohol on his breath.

I lean in, almost whispering in his ear. "I'm the guy," I hiss, "who can *make* you sit down."

His friends hear this and tell him to take a seat. They're saying something to me too, but I can't make it out. My ability to make sense of language is drowned in the thrum of my own pulse. The wave has crashed. Any coherent thoughts have been dashed apart. They're flotsam and jetsam, swirling in a froth of emotion. Everything is about feeling now. His friends aren't a threat. Whatever they're saying, their tone is conciliatory. They're irrelevant. They're so distant, so far away, they barely exist.

I'm waiting for him to strike, waiting for him to push me. Waiting for a flinch or a lunge. I've been waiting for hours, it seems, watching his diaphragm. You can see the slightest movement of the legs and arms if you watch the diaphragm. Don't look at the eyes. The eyes are a distraction. Look at the diaphragm. Never mind that he's in your face, yelling. Bits of spittle land on my cheek. But nothing. Nothing's happening. He's not making a move. It's all posturing. The wave recedes a bit. The thrum in my ears subsides. My inner voice returns. *You're not going to have to fight this guy*, it says. *If he was going to get violent, you'd already know.*

I walk back to my seat. The train has stopped. Someone has pushed the yellow emergency strip. The police will be here in a moment. Or the transit authority. They'll take care of him.

"How the fuck you gonna make me sit down?" he yells. He's following me back to my seat. "How the fuck are you gonna do that?" He's saying it over and over again.

I turn around. "I'm not going to fight you." I can't tell if I sound calm or not.

"I want to know how you're going to make me sit down."

"The police are going to be here any second, guy."

"You think I give a fuck about the cops?" he barks. "Fuck them! I want to see you make me sit down." He's doing some gangster shit with his hands, waving them around.

"We're not going to fight," I say. I sit down next to Lyana. I'd told myself I wasn't going to get in this kind of situation again.

He's in the middle of the aisle, standing close to me. Too close to Lyana. The wave is welling up again. I look at my feet. Lyana's hand is on my thigh.

He throws his Gatorade bottle at me. It misses and bounces off a post, spraying me. I smell it on my jacket. I wonder whether it's spiked with gin or vodka. I can't tell. Either way, it's a terrible drink. He won't go away. He's too close to my wife.

A sprite-like South Asian man in a transit uniform appears, *deus ex machina*, from behind the guy. The transit man grabs buddy's arm and tells him to leave. The transit man is unbelievably small next to this guy.

"Get the fuck off me!" He shakes the transit man off his arm. "Get the fuck away from me! I want this guy to make me leave!" He's pointing at me. If he hits the transit man or pushes him, I will destroy him. I will pull his fucking throat out.

The transit man takes the guy's arm again and leads him out the door onto the platform. It's like watching someone pull an obstinate mule from the middle of a road. Buddy doesn't break eye contact with me, not for a second. On the way out the door, he makes a face like he's just bitten into something rotten and fires a glob of mucus at me. I lurch forward reflexively, but I catch myself and sit back down.

From somewhere beyond me, I hear someone say, "Don't do it, man! He's not worth the trouble."

Transit man has managed to coax the guy onto the platform. But then the guy starts pounding the window next to Lyana's head. He's looking directly at me through the glass.

"Get off the train, you fucking asshole!" he screams.

"Don't," Lyana says.

The doors of the subway car are still open. They stay like this in an emergency. The transit man is blocking the nearest exit, but the guy walks down the platform and re-enters the car through another set of doors. He marches directly to where we're sitting and towers over me. I can't remember what he says—something with *bitch* in it. His fist is raised over his head. He is way the fuck too close to Lyana.

I'm standing. We're chest to chest.

"You keep talking," I say, "but you haven't thrown a fucking punch. You're a fucking pussy. Throw a fucking punch. Otherwise sit the fuck down."

I can feel the heat coming off him. The tiny transit man is behind him again. The transit man looks at me imploringly and says, "I can't keep him off the train—he's too big."

The wave crashes. Everything is suddenly clear and simple. The solution is obvious. I'm relieved by the simplicity of it.

I bring my forehead down like a hammer. I aim for the bridge of his nose, but evidently he turns his head. I see stars—literally, cartoon stars. The guy reels back, but he's still standing.

*Attack!* The voice in my head is screaming. *Attack! Attack!*

I bob, ducking low, my chin tucked, fists up, protecting my head. I try to fire a hard left hook into his ribs while he's still off balance, but I can't move my arm. My arm won't move. It's like a dream, like I'm underwater. I can't understand why I can't move my arm. Then I realize there are people all around us, pulling us apart. Someone is holding my arm. I am surrounded by faceless men. I don't understand why they've gotten involved. They've formed a thicket of briars that catch my limbs. They're holding me back, and I can only think about one thing: getting at the guy, ripping into him, cutting his flesh with my knuckles. Mashing his nose. Crushing his windpipe.

The crowd shifts. I fall backwards over a seat. He's on top of me. I find his eye with my thumb and press. I hesitate for a moment and then push harder. I feel his eyeball, like a grape beneath my thumb, giving way, but before I can rip it from its socket, we're pulled apart again.

I'm shoved into a seat. I try to stand. Several people are holding me down. A fist comes at me through a gap in the crowd. My hands are trapped by my side. The fist hits me in the eye. It doesn't hurt at all.

I break away and lunge at the guy. He's encased in other people's arms, all straining to hold him. I'm pulled backwards again. Someone's arm is around my throat. I desperately, furiously, want to reach this guy. I want to kill him. I am wildly, viciously, frustrated. I need to get on top, I want to beat his head against the subway floor until his brains leak out his ears. I want to paint my face in his blood.

The police arrive. They're wearing yellow rain jackets.

"He threatened my wife." I'm yelling.

"Get the fuck off me!" the guy shouts as the cops pull him off the train. "Get the fuck off me, you motherfuckers!" A constable leads Lyana and me onto the platform. We pass the guy. He's already in handcuffs. He sees us and screams at me over the shoulder of the arresting officer: "I'm going to fucking end you! You fucking understand? I'm going to fucking kill you!" His eyes are puffy and red and his cheekbone is cut.

I want to smile at him, let him know I see how fucked he is, yelling death threats in front of the cops like that. But I keep my composure.

That night, I barely sleep. I stare at the ceiling wishing I had been able to do more damage. I think about what I'll do to him if I ever see him again. I resolve to track him down, to punch him, to pluck out his eye properly, to claw him, bite him. Beat him senseless. I can't control the recurring images reeling through my head. When I do finally fall asleep, I dream of slaughter.

I'm an unusual candidate for this sort of thing. I buck a lot of the expectations people have about the kind of man who gets into fist fights. I am, by common standards, a gentleman, with the emphasis most of the time on the word *gentle*. This is probably pretty hard to swallow after what I've just told you, but I'm confident that, were we to meet, I wouldn't fit your template for the kind of guy who starts public brawls. And I'm definitely not the kind of guy you'd imagine having fantasies about painting his face in the blood of his enemy. That's warlord stuff — it's not me.

I'm sort of a hippie kid. My parents moved to Canada from the United States in the early seventies. My dad was against the Vietnam

War; my mother was highly involved in both the peace movement and the women's movement. She took me to anti-nuke marches and Quaker meetings. When I was in grade school, I was made an honorary member of the feminist group Voice of Women. I still think that's pretty cool.

When I was eight or so, I sent a drawing to Pierre Trudeau, who was then the prime minister, asking him to "Keep Canada Nuclear Free." The slogan was my mom's; the drawing—an ICBM whizzing by a sad-looking sun listening to a Sony Walkman—was mine. I wasn't allowed to play with toy guns or G.I. Joe figures. Other than *The Muppet Show* and Disney, I wasn't really allowed to watch TV.

I should mention here, to silence the kumbayas that may have started playing in your head, that there *are* family dynamics that help explain my behaviour—stuff I'll get to shortly. Despite this, however, both my parents were committed to teaching me to question rigid gender roles and the social mores of violence. And I, on the whole, think I've been pretty successful at such questioning.

When I was eleven or twelve, for instance, my dad and I found a stash of *Playboys* and *Hustlers* hidden in the ceiling tiles of the home we had just moved into and were renovating—hidden there, presumably, by the teenaged son of the previous family. In an act of supreme coolness, my dad, sensing my poorly disguised interest in them, handed me a couple. A few days later, he knocked—twice, loudly—on my bedroom door and presented me with a book of literary erotica written by women, because, as he explained, the way women think about sex is different from the way men think about it and, although it was completely normal for me to find those girlie magazines exciting, he wanted to make sure I understood that they didn't represent the way most women feel about "lovemaking."

I was discouraged from participating in competitive sports and games. In high school, I hated gym class and team sports. I was a year younger than the other kids in my year, and the larger, more developed boys intimidated me. I hated the tribalism of jocks. I liked art, drama and English. Later, when other guys began going out at night, crossing the river into Hull, a city in the neighbouring province of Quebec, where it was easy to get into bars without ID—going there to get laid and start fights—I was at home, smoking pot, painting giant murals on my walls and reading the highly implausible books of the Peruvian-born anthropologist Carlos Castaneda.

For a brief period in my early teens, self-conscious and overly intro-spective, I worried from time to time that maybe I was gay or some-thing. Not that I found other boys attractive; it was just, as I understood it, straight guys weren't this sensitive—or as intimidated by the opposite sex. When I eventually overcame my shyness and discovered women, I took to courting them by cooking elaborate meals and expressing my feelings in saccharine and quasi-mystical terms.

On the home front, I'm highly domestic. I proudly supported Lyana through medical school and her gruelling surgical residency by doing the lion's share of the cooking, cleaning and laundry. I like holding babies. I don't really watch sports on TV. I suspect I cry more easily than many men, and I know for a fact I'm more adept and more com-fortable discussing my emotions than most. In some very important ways, I'm a successful example of what the women's movement sought to achieve. What I'm about to say may be the most ironic form male braggadocio has ever taken, but, insomuch as a single individual can represent such a thing, I *am* the post-patriarchal man.

So, what about the fight on the train? What about my alpha-male aggression and wanting to paint my face in the dude's blood? Those things don't really mesh with my granola upbringing. Maybe, know-ing a bit more about me, you're tempted to give me a pass. We all do uncharacteristic things from time to time, right? Then consider this:

One night, about six months after the run-in on the subway, I chased a man down an alley into the parking lot of an abattoir, close to where Lyana and I lived in downtown Toronto. I tackled him, jumped on top of him, punched him in the face four or five times, rolled him over onto his stomach and held him on the ground until the police arrived.

Moments before, I'd heard a woman screaming in the shadowy court-yard behind our building. I mean *really* screaming—screaming like her life was in danger. I heard this from our fourth-storey flat, where we were lying in bed, watching TV. Lyana called the police as I bolted out of our place, bounded down the stairs and sprinted onto the street, pulling a shirt on over my head as I ran. I hadn't bothered with shoes. I was afraid—Lyana and I both were—that this woman, whoever she was, was being beaten or raped.

It turned out some crackhead had run off with her purse. By the time I caught up with him, two guys had already chased him into the abattoir loading yard and were gingerly trying to corner him. I snuck up from behind. The man turned and saw me, his eyes bugging out of his head. He tried to slip past me, but I was too close; he panicked, lost his footing and skidded in the gravel. I took advantage of his misstep and brought him down. The cops came and arrested him and gave me the standard warning: *What if he'd had a weapon?* But the constable who took my statement clearly thought the whole thing was pretty fantastic.

"You just did our job for us," he said. "Half the time, these guys run off before we can get there." And when he saw I wasn't wearing shoes, he laughed. "Who are you, buddy, the barefoot bandit?" He gave me a lift back to my building and shook my hand.

But Lyana found the whole thing exasperating. "You could have been killed!" she said.

I protested. "I'd rather be dead than let a woman get raped while I listen to it from my apartment." I was jacked-up, totally wired, and I was about to launch into my Kitty Genovese spiel, but Lyana interrupted me.

"She *wasn't* being raped!" she cried. "He stole her purse. You didn't have to go after him."

She seemed to be missing the fact that I had just potentially saved a woman's life. I felt pretty fucking good about the whole thing, and it bothered me she didn't get it. I left our apartment and went up to the building's gym and got on one of the treadmills. I needed to burn off some adrenalin. My legs felt like steel cables, lashing the track beneath me. I bounced along to the whir of the machine in a weird state of endorphin-induced hypnosis.

Okay, so Lyana had a point; I get why she was upset. Me potentially getting killed was part of it. But there was something else she was attempting to remind me of, a pattern that's been there since my late teens.

A brief synopsis: In my final year of high school, I chased after two men who had broken into the junior high next door to my home. They were hauling computers out of the school library. A psychotically amusing detail: I ran after them in the dark wearing nothing but a pair of ratty underwear, waving my younger brother's souvenir Maori war club over my head. They jumped in their Jeep and drove off. I got their licence plate and the police later caught them. When I was in my early twenties, I threatened to beat up a skinhead who was harassing a woman at a house party. I taunted an aggressive cab driver out of his car by spitting on him and then, as he stepped onto the pavement, slammed the door on him. I mean *on* him, on his body. I threatened to sodomize a construction worker with his own shovel—a shovel he pulled from the back of his pickup truck and threatened to beat my friend with. I can't remember precisely what I said, but it was heavy-duty enough that he put the shovel down and his chin began to quiver. I successfully stopped a knife fight between two teenagers in the parking lot of a shopping mall. At another shopping mall, I chased after a guy who had pulled a gun on my friend. I'm pretty sure the gun was a fake because, when I started after the guy, he kicked it into high gear and ran rather than standing his ground.

A little impulsive, sure. Macho and aggressive, even. But these instances represent a minuscule fraction of my life, and every time it's been about protecting someone, being a good guy, standing up to the assholes other people can't or won't or are too afraid to confront. After all, were Lyana to find herself behind some dark building, calling for help, she'd be delighted—as she admits—to see a guy like me, ready to take out the trash. If that means an aggressive meth-head gets a bloody nose and a couple of loose teeth, so what?

But that wasn't what bothered her. What bothered her was the thing I wasn't fully admitting to myself.

On the treadmill, I replayed the scene in my head: the takedown, the look on the man's face, the surprised little O of his mouth, the greying stubble around his lips. It was like my own private action movie. I played it over in my head a few times, coaxing a fresh bolus of endorphins from my adrenal glands. I punched the button on the treadmill and picked up the pace. I had been running hard for half an hour already, and I felt great. I pictured what I would have done if the guy had been carrying a knife: I would have wrestled it away from him and dug it into his thigh. Or maybe I would have pulled back his greasy forelock and held the blade to his hairline, counting coup like an Apache warrior. I ended the run in a sprint. I felt fucking fantastic.

Ah. That was it, the thing that worried Lyana. The *Clockwork Orange* bit, the fact that I enjoyed the ol' ultra-violence a little too much.

You'd think having this type of insight would be pretty great. Especially for a guy like me, someone who values self-awareness and emotional maturity. From there, it's a simple syllogistic endeavour:

A) Violence is bad.
B) I get a kick out of violence.
C) I don't want to be bad.
D) Therefore, I must quit getting a kick out of violence.
E) Problem solved.

It's tidy on paper, but the thing is, I had already done this—agreed to quit being violent. I mean *formally* agreed, with signatures and hand-shakes and everything. What I mean—what I haven't mentioned yet—is that, a few months after I head-butted the guy on the subway, I came face to face with him again. This was about two months before the whole purse-snatching thing. Let's call the subway guy Brad. Brad was winding his way through the justice system. Other than our fight, he had no criminal history, and so the Crown, showing some judicious leniency, decided he would be less inclined to get into a fight again if he went through a mediation process as opposed to serving time. Mediation con-sisted of a supervised meeting with me in which he would issue a formal apology, providing I was willing to take part. The alternative was that he'd have to go through the courts. I hesitated at first. I still had a hate-on for him. It's small of me, but I took malicious pleasure in the thought of him doing time. Also, I had paranoid thoughts that maybe he'd bring a gun or a knife to the meeting. Remember that, as I was leaving the scene, he'd threatened to kill me.

Eventually, after a couple of persuasive phone calls from one of the volunteer mediators who helped run the programme, a diminutive and tireless retiree named Esther, I agreed to the meeting because it struck me that denying someone the opportunity to apologize was a shitty thing to do. And putting someone in jail for getting in a brawl is kind of like punishing someone for getting drunk by locking them up with a case of whisky. More to the point, it would give me an opportunity to make amends for my own shabby behaviour.

I met Brad at a community centre in Kensington Market. We were chaperoned by Esther and a young guy with blondish dreadlocks who was a week away from moving to India to do volunteer work some-where in the destitute state of Bihar. I felt as if I belonged to a different species, a morally inferior one. Anyway, Brad and I sat across from one another at a big boardroom table. He was younger than I had imag-ined him, or maybe just more boyish. He came off as a bit sullen, but I think it was embarrassment. I remember thinking I wouldn't have been able to pick him out of a crowd. It was funny, because just as I was thinking this—we were only a couple of minutes into the meeting; Esther and Josh were still doing all the talking—Brad looked up and across the table at me, obviously perplexed. "Wait—" he said. "*You're* the guy? I thought you had a goatee or something." He didn't recog-nize me either. It was a bit like waking up hungover and finding a stranger in your bed. *We did what? Oh. Weird.*

Brad was in his early twenties and, from what I gathered, still lived at home. I might be wrong about that. Either way, his family was deeply ashamed of what he had done. It was obvious this weighed on him. I found myself thinking that if we had met under different circum-stances, we might have hit it off. Not best friends or anything, but defi-nitely not enemies. Clichéd, I know, but true.

We drew up a memorandum of understanding, a contract intended to keep Brad on the straight and narrow and to mollify the Crown. He agreed to take an anger management course, to avoid excessive drink-ing and to do several hours of community service. Because I was the victim, at least as a matter of public record, I wasn't required to do anything. But after meeting the sober and peaceable version of Brad, I wrote a letter suggesting the Crown drop the charges. I told Brad, as Esther and Josh nodded in quiet approval, that I felt equally responsible for the fight. I told him I shouldn't have talked to him the way I did, and I apologized—and really meant it. We acknowledged that we had a mutual responsibility to avoid violent confrontations in the future. We wrote this into the agreement. We signed it and shook hands. The moment was full of self-conscious solemnity; I think we both took it quite seriously.

As far as I know, Brad met all the terms of our agreement. And yet, a couple of months later, there I was, kneeling on the purse snatcher, doing what the mixed martial arts guys call a "ground-and-pound"—holding him down and punching him in the face.

You'd think my failure to live up to my promise to Brad would have galvanized some change. But then, a few days before writing this, on a busy Saturday night, I was standing outside a restaurant with Lyana and her family; the sidewalk was crowded and a guy pushed me out of his way—I mean a full shoulder-to-shoulder shove. Without thinking, I kicked him as he passed. Not terribly forcefully—I just gave him a nudge in the butt with my Doc Marten. He glanced over his shoulder but didn't take the bait. He was with his girlfriend (who I don't think noticed the exchange) and I suspect he didn't want to risk losing face in front of her. It seems these urges get the best of me no matter how self-aware I am. More and more, I've been wondering why.

There's a line of Freud's I stumbled upon as an undergrad, in *Civilization and Its Discontents*:

> *Civilization . . . obtains mastery over the individual's dangerous desire for aggression by setting up an agency within him to watch over it, like a garrison in a conquered city.*

It's the term "dangerous desire" that's stuck with me. The dangerous part is self-evident: bloodshed, bodily harm, the nasty business of human brutality. But the really scary stuff—and the really interesting stuff—lies in the desire.

To put it bluntly—and I know I'm stating the obvious here—there's a part of me that craves violence. Or if not craves it, weirdly gets off on it. The other part of me (the larger, better part, I'd like to think) always regrets it after it's over, as soon as my logic and empathy come back online. But when I'm in the midst of it, violence feels right—appropriate somehow, and justified. Weirder still, and embarrassing, now that I'm putting it down on paper, is how important this capacity for violence is to me. It's part of how I define myself. Even if I were never to fight again, I'd still want to be large and powerful, and to be perceived this way. It makes me feel confident, attractive and inexplicably optimistic. It makes me whole. Take it away and it sort of feels like an amputation.

So why? Why am I this way? And what am I supposed to do about it? Broadly speaking, that's what this book is about: my own dangerous desire, but also *the* dangerous desire. Male violence in general.

My own stupidity troubles me, and fascinates me. I find it worrisome that my emotions grab the wheel from time to time—and that at some level I let them. But here's what really concerns me: what if the urges to rape, beat and murder are, in some men, as powerful as my own urge to use violence in order to protect people? What if those men are drawn to it the way I'm drawn to my own righteous anger? There's a lot of evidence suggesting this is true, that these emotions are present in many men and potentially dormant in a great many more. I find this pretty unsettling. How similar are these urges to the ones I have? What's the relationship? Could my urge to beat up the guy who threatens my wife somehow curdle into the urge to beat *her*, to rape *her*? Or some other woman? Could my hateful ability to view some idiot on the subway as subhuman twist itself in such a way that I begin to see an office rival as not really human, not worthy of my empathy? What about a political rival? Or members of a particular religious or ethnic group? How far down do these desires go? Where do they come from? And what does it mean that a man like me, someone who is self-aware, pro-social, educated, gainfully employed, who questions socially defined gender roles, who is otherwise well-adjusted, has trouble resisting the urge to be violent? What then? What do I do about it? More importantly, what do we do about all those men out there who aren't especially self-aware, or who simply don't care? Or who just plain revel in the nastiness of it all?

*Mad Blood Stirring* is about these people and the violent acts they commit. More specifically, it's about the emotions that precede violence, the urges that influence our thoughts and weaken our resolution, the undercurrents that run against our better intentions and lead us to do horrible things. This means, in addition to talking about my own, relatively limited history of violence, we'll be getting close to people you'd probably rather avoid: tough guys, ex-cons, rapists, killers and psychopaths.

There's more to this than voyeurism. It's not really acceptable to talk about this stuff—at least not as openly or as honestly as I think we ought to. We're touchy about violence the way Victorian society was touchy about sex. These urges are crude and unacceptable. We feel naughty when we admit to having them, so we often don't. Especially since accepting that these emotions are real and extremely common might be mistaken for condoning them. Understandably, we've erected strong moral sanctions against these feelings. It makes sense to do so because, quite clearly, violence *is* a moral issue. But it's easy to fall into a trap by convincing ourselves that as long as people understand and agree that violence is immoral, they won't do it; by insisting that what we really need to do is re-educate men in order to buttress their sense of morality. If we do this properly, we presume, violent men will become more pacific. This hasn't been my experience. I think the whole thing is a lot more complicated than that. I'm struggling with the *how* of it all.

As I see it, the problem with trying to contain vice by moral sanction alone is that you never get close enough to the thing you're trying to keep at bay to understand it. At least, that's how it's been with me. I'm a nice guy until, suddenly, I'm not. Part of it is that moral sanctions, the notion that we simply shouldn't act violently, prevent us from fully acknowledging these feelings. And this makes it easy to be caught off guard when they quietly work their insidious little tentacles under our feet and unexpectedly yank us over to the dark side. If you really want to understand something, if you want to dissect it and name its parts, you need a certain intimacy with it. You need to touch and feel and grope around in the dark and get your hands dirty. With violence, this is particularly distasteful, but it's important because, as with any human behaviour, what we keep from ourselves, we can't understand. And what we don't understand, we can't control. And that's kind of the point, isn't it?

Having an honest conversation about violence is uncomfortable. I think we all get that it's emotionally uncomfortable. But it's also *intellectually* uncomfortable. It's hard to talk about human violence without suddenly finding yourself in either the Nature camp or the Nurture camp. Even if you're not one for carrying banners, you'll find yourself handed one, often by people with ideological axes to grind.

Before I began my career in journalism, I studied neuroscience and psychology; I've spent a sizeable chunk of my journalistic career reporting on science. As a result, one of the ways I view human behaviour is through the lens of science, especially neuroscience and evolutionary biology. It's not the only way to view human behaviour, nor necessarily the best way. But the past few hundred years of logical inquiry make it clear that the brain is the source of human behaviour and that the brain, like the rest of our body, has been shaped by the evolutionary process. Violence is a moral concern, but issuing forth, as it does, from one of our bodily organs, it's also a scientific one. There's a lot of compelling research suggesting that my violent tendencies can be partially understood as a product of our evolutionary past and our biological makeup.

So, clearly, I'm a Hobbesian, right? A hawk. A biological determinist who believes humans are a bunch of meat-robots programmed with the cold logic of genetic propagation. It figures that a guy like me would glom on to whatever explanation allows him to rationalize his desire to be nasty and brutish.

That's not my position at all. But people often go there when I express my interest in the biology of human violence. Likewise, if you tend to champion the environmental causes of violence—economics, education, role models, cultural influences, those sorts of things— people will assume you're waving the flag for Jean-Jacques Rousseau; that, in addition to being naive and wearing hemp and listening to the Grateful Dead, you believe that humans are inherently sweet and that the world would still be peachy and wholesome if our natural goodness hadn't been corrupted by the patriarchy.

That's what I mean about being assigned a position. Start talking about the causes of violence and, invariably, it becomes not just an intellectual discussion, but a political one.

Violence is too complex, too multifaceted and protean, to have a single cause. We can begin to wrap our heads around it only once we let go of reductionism—both biological *and* environmental. Violence, like all other forms of human behaviour, is a complex interaction of nature *and* nurture. I'm less interested in finding the root cause, *the* ideal factor that best explains it all, than in understanding how all the various contributing factors interact. Oh, and how to fiddle with those interactions so I can prevent myself from going thermonuclear.

I have to be clear from the outset that I'm going to have some challenges with objectivity, and I know, as a journalist, this is a liability. I feel a bit like Marlow, travelling upriver into the heart of darkness. Part of my role is to catalogue what I find there, but there's a catch: I'm also my own Kurtz. The emotions that motivate me to be violent do so, in part, by distorting my perception, making it easy to rationalize and justify these urges. I'm confident I can get us upriver, but I can't guarantee I won't get tangled up once I'm there. And so, to compensate for this, I'm going to occasionally rely on people who are committed to the objective study of violence, researchers on both sides of the nature–nurture debate, who will help me triangulate my findings. My challenge is to be two journalists at once: the guy on the inside, the gonzo reporter, as well as the impartial observer, the science journalist aiming, as Doris Lessing put it, to see humans as "a visitor from another planet might see us."[1]

This is a book primarily, although not exclusively, about men. This is because men are responsible for the vast majority of violent acts. They—we—commit nearly all of the assaults and beatings and the lion's share of homicides. We're specialists in rape, gang killings, torture, serial predation, acts of terror and warfare.[2] That said, while this book is largely *about* men, it's certainly not meant exclusively *for* men. It's important to me that women find it accessible. After all, male violence is a women's issue, if not *the* women's issue. Hopefully, this book serves as something of a guide to regions of the male psyche that aren't particularly well mapped out.

One of the central arguments of this book is that the emotions that motivate us to act violently—the emotions I'm so familiar with—*are* inherent. They're part of who we are as a species. Now, before you start freaking out about biological determinism, let me clarify something. What I'm saying is that we have an inherent *emotional* capacity for violence, which makes it extraordinarily easy for us to resort to violence in particular circumstances. The better we control those circumstances, the better we control the emotions that lead to violence. That's the inherent part—the *emotions*, the urge, not the behaviour. Evolution doesn't determine our behaviour, but it *has* shaped our emotions. They are like fossilized success strategies, motivations that paid off in the past. Those creatures that *felt* a strong urge to breed, that *felt* compelled to explore the environment for food, that *felt* a fierce need to protect themselves and their kin from predators and competitors, were more likely to act on those feelings and, in turn, survive to pass on those drives to subsequent generations.

This might not sound like good news, but it is. The word *biological* is often confused with *fixed, unchangeable* and *automatic*. But these emotions are modifiable. We can learn to control them, just as we can learn to amplify them. But because they're part of our evolutionary inheritance, we cannot choose to get rid of them; they're here to stay. And we need to deal with that.

The other point I want to make here is that a biological understanding of human behaviour doesn't condone gender essentialism—the idea that certain behaviours are exclusively male while others are female. Biology is, among other things, the study of diversity within a population. And humans are, if nothing else, profoundly diverse creatures; our physiology, behaviour and predispositions span countless continuums. You can be fairly certain that anyone who uses biology to argue that humans *ought* to behave in a particular way has a pretty weak grasp of Biology 101. There are a lot of women out there who feel—and act on—the emotions I'm discussing in this book—just as there a lot of men out there who aren't especially given to them. But I suspect there are more men than women, especially young men, who find themselves carrying an explosive charge they're not entirely willing or sure how to defuse. And so, because of this and because men clearly do most of the harmful and truly terrible things, I've focused here, at the risk of seeming exclusive, on the inner lives of violent men.

The people I know who are prone to these emotions, both men and women, tend to take the inherent bit as given. I think once you've experienced the emotions of violence, it's difficult to see them as anything other than the awakening of some dark and untended corner of our mammalian cortex.

If you aren't especially prone to these urges, you might find it tough to sympathize. Try articulating these emotions to someone who's especially phlegmatic and the reaction you get ranges from the recommendation of a good therapist to outright denial—an insistence that these emotions are somehow not your own, that you're a patsy who thoughtlessly helps perpetuate a culture of male violence. There might be something to that, the perpetuating part at least, but why—and how—do cultures of violence get started in the first place? Part of it is that violence can be compelling and exciting. The emotions that lead to violence have the pull of a riptide and, far from being a sign of a personality disorder or mental illness, they are normal.

There's that old trope that men think about sex every eight seconds. That particular figure is an overestimate,[3] but the larger point is spot-on. The majority of men *do* tend to think about sex a lot. And it makes sense. Sex is fascinating and exciting and inherently pleasurable. It makes for a rich fantasy life. The same is true of violence.[4] Men spend a lot of time entertaining aggressive fantasies, thinking, for instance, about whether they could win a fight against another guy they know.[5] I definitely do a lot of this: daydreaming in line at the corner store, pondering how I might wrestle a gun away from a robber or entertaining ridiculous scenarios about pulling an aggressive driver out of his car and shoving his keys in his mouth:

> Me: *"Know what a BMW and a pair of underwear have in common?"*
> Driver [gagging on his keys]: *"NN-nnn."*
> Me: *"There's always an asshole inside."*

Like me, a lot of men find satisfaction and pleasure in thinking violent thoughts, even men who aren't necessarily given to acting on them. My friend Neil is a good example. He has devoted his journalistic career to covering parliamentary politics and civil society. Anyone who knows him will vouch for him as a kind and gentle man. Several years ago, when Neil's partner, Jill, was pregnant with their first child, he began having some awfully grisly fantasies. Jill was in her third trimester and was really beginning to show. Neil found himself growing more and more preoccupied with the impending responsibilities of parenthood, and also more vigilant and protective of Jill. In the moments before sleep, lying next to her in bed, somewhere in that hazy place between thinking and dreaming, Neil would hear a noise—the creak of a floorboard, the house settling on its foundation. In this semi-conscious state, the noise became something else, something sinister, someone breaking into the house, sneaking up the stairs, a psychotic killer preying on the young family-to-be. And from there, the fantasy would take on a life of its own.

Neil told me about these fantasies, over drinks. "I'd plot in my mind how I would allow them to get close," he explained. "I'd hide behind the bedroom door and I'd allow them to come closer and I'd leap on them and—I'm not kidding—in this fantasy I would leap on them and take their eyes out." Here he made the motion of digging his thumbs into invisible eye sockets.

Another of his fantasies went like this:

1) Wait silently behind the bedroom door with the heavy lamp from the bedside table.
2) Let the intruder enter.
3) Brain him with the lamp.

In this gruesome headspace, Neil would resort to the most animal of manoeuvres: "My teeth would lunge into them and I'd pull their throat out!" The fantasies went on night after night, fantasies of "utterly destroying" faceless home invaders. "The craziest thing," Neil said, leaning forward and lowering his voice—we were in a pub and he didn't want the couple at the next table to overhear—"was that it was a rich, deeply satisfying, almost erotic fantasy. That's the thing—I enjoyed it! I wanted it to keep going. What the fuck is that about?"

Neil was so unsettled by all this that he eventually brought it up with a close friend of his, a guy he describes as "about as big of a peacenik as you can possibly imagine." Neil divulged his fantasies to his friend, how vicious and gory they were, how irresistible, how he had to will himself *not* to think about them. Neil's friend, the peacenik—who was, coincidentally, a new father at the time—was taken aback, but only because he knew precisely what Neil was talking about. The two of them were walking down the street together. His friend stopped and turned to Neil and said: "I've been having the exact same thing!"

As I mentioned earlier, I was a sensitive kid. I was also a particularly gentle boy. Into my late teens, the idea of fighting terrified me. Being aggressive back then was about as realistic as unaided flight or invisibility. I've been trying to remember when that changed, and why.

After high school, I didn't really have a plan. I had mediocre grades and hadn't applied to university. I left Ottawa and drove to rural Alberta, where I found work on farms and feedlots—baling hay, weeding orchards and cleaning up people's junk piles. One night, there was a social in town, a dance at a local hall. Because of my size, I was hired to work one of the doors. I was given a T-shirt with *Security* emblazoned on the back and I stood there awkwardly, not really sure what I should be doing.

Towards the end of the night, as things were winding down, someone told me there was a fight in the parking lot. I stuck my head outside. There was a pack of young guys, the kind of crowd that makes me nervous—loud, bawling for action, actively looking for an enemy. They were standing in a circle, silhouetted against the blaze of pickup headlights. The pack broke apart and I saw him: a large boy crouched over the inert body of another guy. He moved like a predator, this boy. I say "boy" because he was about my age, but really he was a man, solid and powerful. He looked like an animal that had taken down a kill. The muscles in his arms and chest jumped and twitched as he repositioned himself over the other kid. He looked up at the crowd, assessing it, tense, electric. His eyes were silver coins in the headlights. The moment passed. The boy on the ground stirred and the other boy, the predator, started punching him like some steam-driven thing put into gear, a machine designed to drive railway spikes into the ground.

My bowels tightened up. My mouth went dry. My legs felt rubbery and awkward. I was worried I would be expected to go out there and break it up, and I knew facing that boy would be like walking into the blades of a threshing machine. But I think the crowd scared me more. It was as though it had the power to call me out somehow, that it knew, despite my size, I wasn't really a man. I closed the door and stood perfectly still in a corner of the gymnasium. As soon as the dance ended, I peeled off my *Security* shirt. I didn't want to be caught on the way to my car wearing such an obvious target.

A year later, things started to change. My chest broadened out, my shoulders thickened. My beard came in. Muscle took the place of fat—the biochemical cascades that mark the final phase of male puberty.

And something shifted inside, too, emotionally I mean; a growing tension, like a giant coil spring, had come to life inside my chest.

I had trouble sleeping. I took long runs at night through the suburbs where I was living with my father and stepmother. One night, I was crossing the street. A pickup truck with tinted windows was idling at a stop sign. I had the right of way, so I crossed in front of it. The engine growled and the truck lurched forward, into the crosswalk. It was clearly a taunt, or at least I took it that way. The truck peeled out and took off—and I took off after it, sprinting, intent on catching up, jumping into the flatbed, reaching through the window into the cab and grabbing the driver by the throat. All fantasy, of course. I stood in the middle of the street barking profanities as the tail lights faded into the sleeping subdivision.

That same year, at a house party, I did something even weirder. There was a guy there who rubbed me the wrong way. He strutted around in a Polo Ralph Lauren shirt, scoffing at everyone, like a princeling displeased with his subjects. I had put back two, maybe three beers. I was by no means out-of-my-head drunk, just a little disinhibited. I was standing in the doorway between the living room and the kitchen, talking to some friends, when the Crown Prince of House Parties tried to squeeze by me. He said something, I can't remember what, something fairly innocuous. Certainly not an insult or a threat, but something that confirmed my suspicion that he was a snotty little prick. Suddenly, out of the corner of my eye, this hand reaches out and grabs him by the throat. It takes me a second to realize it's my hand, that I'm trying to strangle him. Guys around us begin chiming in: "Whoa, big guy! Easy, now." I realize they're talking to me, talking me down. As soon as I clue in, I ease my grip. I remember being genuinely puzzled. It was like something you'd do sleepwalking. The little prince stood there, my thumb resting on his Adam's apple, looking at me, wide-eyed, frozen, unsure how to react. Someone separated us. I remember smiling at him, but not saying anything. I couldn't think of anything to say. There was nothing in my head, only a fury that was simultaneously thrilling and nauseating.

It's common to talk about the emotional changes girls experience as they grow into women. I wonder if we might be missing out on an analogous process in boys, because we tend to focus on the physical changes, ignoring some of the emotional complexities.

Despite my parents' guidance, despite the granola upbringing, there are some things about my family that may help explain this. My mother comes from a family of pacifists. She didn't even like me playing competitive board games. But there are some issues there, things I'll explore later in this book. My dad comes from a different place. He was born in Idaho, into a frontier culture of cowboys and ranchers, where it was hard to consider yourself a man unless you were willing to use your fists from time to time.

My granddad was this kind of man when he was younger, and to the extent you can be like that in your nineties, he still is. As a boy, he was an exceptional athlete. He was a good-enough shortstop that the Phillies signed him to their farm team for a season. But where he really excelled was in a fight.

When he entered high school, in the late 1930s, he was tall and slim. For whatever reason, the school tough guy targeted him. One day, the two boys passed each other on the stairs. The tough boy taunted my grandfather. Without saying anything, my grandfather hit him, quick as lightning. The boy crumpled and slid down the stairs.

The next day, before class, my granddad saw that someone had scrawled on the blackboard:

*Mike Fairless is a dirty fighter!*

He walked to the front of the class, erased it, picked up a piece of chalk and wrote: *Who won the fight?*

That sealed his reputation. As a friend, Mike was gregarious and warm; as an enemy, he was brutal and efficient. Mike's brother-in-law, John, recalls having to hold my grandfather's jacket from time to time when they were younger so Mike could take care of a couple of guys in the parking lot of some restaurant or roadside tavern. My granddad is one of the sweetest, most affectionate men I know. Still, there's a loaded .38 Special in the glove compartment of his minivan. "For carjackers," he says. Even in his early nineties, he can't stand the idea of being pushed around.

Because standing up for yourself and for those who can't stand up for themselves has always been important to Mike, he gave his two boys plenty of advice. "It was largely about how to get a fight over with in a hurry," my dad recalls. Speed was key, and so was straight-up nastiness. Forget the bravado, the talking, the posturing. If you know you're going to have to fight a guy, take him by surprise. "The fundamental was really this: what matters is that you win."

That said, there *were* rules, a code of conduct you had to adhere to if you wanted to remain the good guy, the man in the white hat. You didn't pick on a smaller man; you didn't gang up on a guy. And the men you fought always deserved it—men who cursed in the company of women; men who picked on people weaker and smaller than themselves; men who were drunk, rowdy or simply ignorant sons of bitches. Most importantly, you never, ever hit a woman. Sociologists call this kind of social milieu a "culture of honour." They tend to be places with higher rates of physical violence.

My father spent his youth trying to get away from that way of thinking, psychologically but also physically. He moved north, crossed the border and headed east. He pursued an academic career and eventually a corporate one, transforming himself into what my granddad characterizes, in a ribbing sort of way—in a way that drives my father a little crazy—as a "white wine–sipping Eastern intellectual." For many years my dad was distant from his father, meaning that my granddad and the cowboy culture he's part of weren't a direct influence on me as a child. Some things change from one generation to the next, but others are harder to shake.

Once, on a business flight, my dad confronted a man seated next to him. The guy was being verbally abusive to a flight attendant. My dad turned in his seat and asked the man if his "soft, mushy stomach" was ever "a liability when trying to please a woman." This shut the guy up for the remainder of the flight. The guy put on one of those complimentary sleep masks and pretended to nap until the plane landed. More recently, my dad verbally castrated a particularly odious customer at a FedEx outlet. The guy was making xenophobic comments about the woman behind the counter; she was clearly an immigrant. My father subjected him to a good old-fashioned public shaming. The woman must have copied my dad's address from the package he was shipping, because a few days later he got a card from her, thanking him for being her "guardian angel."

All this may help explain why I feel the way I do about guys like Brad—at least the drunk, belligerent version of Brad I met on the subway—and why I feel a duty to confront them. But there's an important difference between the ol' block and the proverbial chip, a significant one. My dad has never been in a physical altercation. Not once. He uses his words, not his fists. He's a large man, exceptionally fit, and he's had plenty of opportunities to fight. But he never has. He has always backed off. Once, when we were drinking bourbon together in his basement, I asked him why.

"It would be great if it was about peace, being good, about not hurting each other," he mused. "But it's more just the impracticality of it. It's not fun to get hit."

One of my dad's favourite quotes, the one he reliably pulls out whenever we're having this kind of serious conversation about manhood, comes from Cardinal Newman:

*A gentleman is one who never inflicts pain.*

My father has never hit me or my brother. I've seen him angry and frustrated. I've seen him punch a hole in the wall once or twice when I was younger. I know there are schools of thought that argue this is a form of domestic violence. With a different man, maybe. But my father has no drive to physically harm someone. It's not part of his temperament.

Nor is my brother, Michael, physically violent. By the time he was born, nine years after me, our parents had relaxed their ideological concerns. They had also divorced, and in the domestic rubble of their breakup Michael was allowed unrestricted access to all the pop-culture indulgences I had pined for as a kid: G.I. Joe action figures, toy guns, television, action movies and shoot-'em-up video games—all of the cultural influences we assume contribute to violent attitudes. Yet, when it comes to blood lust, my brother is unquestionably more civilized than I am.

I've asked my dad why he thinks I'm different, why I'm more like his father. "I don't really know," he said. "I think it's wiring."

All this to say that while cultural values and the way we're raised are important, they don't account for everything. In those rare instances when it kicks in, my urge to be violent feels as much part of me, as fundamental, as my other basic urges—hunger, thirst, my sex drive, the need to socialize, to love. Which is part of the reason I've come to believe my violent behaviour is linked, in part, to my physiology, to the way my brain works.

If you believe, as I do, that social and environmental factors are important, what's the point of discussing biology? Especially since you can't exactly disown your evolutionary inheritance. I'm certainly not advocating, nor would I trust, some sort of technical fix—a pill or operation or implant that promises to pacify us. All those things have been suggested—and sometimes tried, with the predictable dystopian consequences that come with seeing a shitty sci-fi premise to its end.[6]

So maybe it's better to ignore the science and stick to trying to fix the social mores that amplify and perpetuate violence. But here's the problem: we don't really know how we're doing on that front. In 2009, the World Health Organization published a massive study examining the effectiveness of the various violence-prevention strategies used around the world. It found that although "interventions that attempt to alter cultural and social norms . . . are among the most widespread and prominent," rarely are these interventions evaluated, "making it currently difficult to assess their effectiveness."[7] Meanwhile, guys keep on doing nasty things.

Part of the solution, of course, is to put more funding into testing existing violence-prevention programmes. Some of them work, no doubt. Those that do are able to get men to take charge of their inner lives. Still, there are a lot of men out there who don't give a fuck about social values. How do you get to *those* guys? How do you convince them to take charge?

One way, I believe, is by first acknowledging the power of the emotions men experience. There's plenty of objective evidence that biology influences violence. But maybe more important—at least as far as violence prevention is concerned—is the subjective power of that acknowledgement. It has always struck me as ludicrous whenever anyone has suggested I'm not hard-wired for these feelings I experience.

On the other hand, there are plenty of twelve-step groups that are effective in part because they embrace objective reality—that there are inherent factors that influence addiction. One of the central tenets of successful addiction treatment is the acknowledgement that it is a behaviour you cannot just wish away, that it's part of you and always will be. Denying you have a problem is often one of the biggest parts of the problem. Accepting your inherent predisposition, on the other hand, is often a first step towards changing your behaviour.

Violence doesn't seem all that different to me. I find it easier to accept that I have some inherent emotional tendencies I need to pay attention to than to believe I can just wipe myself clean and build a new emotional life based on a more "appropriate" set of social values.

The pendulum has always swung back and forth between nature and nurture. At this moment, the biological perspective happens to be the angle a lot of people would prefer to exclude from the story we tell ourselves about ourselves. In other times, it's been different. Different eras have pinned violence and other social problems wholly on bad blood, race, breeding. Those ideas too were premised on an incomplete understanding of human behavior. I know what it's like to tell yourself an autobiography that's only partially true. In terms of bettering yourself, it doesn't get you very far.

In terms of understanding violence—my own; male violence in general—I suspect the best way forward lies in trudging out into the no man's land that lies beyond the various ideological camps.

That's usually closer to where the truth lies.

—

# CHAPTER ONE

# THE RIDE

YOU'RE LIGHTER THAN AIR. Faster than light. You are photons streaming from the sun, hot, pure and incalculably fast. You're the air as it superheats and the ozone smell of the purified atmosphere. You glide above everything.

You realize flight has always been in you and you've finally managed to make it come out, the way the voices of men have started to come out of the mouths of the slightly older boys. In your dream, you can fly as easily as you walk.

You spring out of bed with an unselfconscious joy you haven't felt since primary school. For a moment you believe you've carried flight out of the night and into the waking world. Then, as you take your first step, you remember gravity and real life and junior high. And flight retreats back into your dreams.

That moment—when you're awake but still believe you can fly, when you feel boundless, uncoupled from the anxieties that weigh you down in the schoolyard—that's what it feels like to be able to win a fight.

It's freedom.

It's spring. The snow has melted and a winter's worth of dog turds are liquefying in the weak sun. You're the new kid. You've moved here to Snob Land from a poor neighbourhood in a poor province. You do not know about Polo Ralph Lauren shirts or Levi's red tab jeans or Reebok high-tops. You're wearing generic clothing from a generic store. You're a year younger than everyone else in your grade. Your voice hasn't changed and you're still cherubic with baby fat. You lean against one of the school portables, not quite sure what to do with yourself. You try your best to look casual, but your hands are like fledglings pulling at your clothes, trying to find their way back to their nest. You don't know where to put them.

A cluster of kids comes around the corner. They're wearing Polo Ralph Lauren and red tabs and Reebok high-tops. One of the boys' voice has changed and his face is red and angry with acne. The other boy has a faint moustache. The girls do not look like the other girls. They have hips and sharp little breasts. They are some vicious new species of child whose eyes are on you.

One of the girls sniffs at the air and, staring at you, says, "Ew. It smells like dog shit!"

The boy with the faint moustache looks at you and says, "Yeah. It *looks* like it too."

You're standing near the portable again. A boy wants to talk to you. Not one of the Ralph Lauren kids but a second-tier kid, blond, beefy and big for his age. Bigger than you. Stronger. There's a girl with him, a girl who has been working hard to make herself into a first-tier girl. You're trying to figure out why he wants to talk to you, why he has that fuming, closed-up look, because until now he's been pretty nice to you. He talks to you on the bus. He tells you about books he likes. He doesn't give off snob vibes. While you're thinking about this, he has worked the situation so that your back is up against the aluminum siding of the portable.

Just as the gears click into place and you realize that he's no longer your friend, he drives his fist into your solar plexus so hard it feels like he has reached up inside you and flipped the switch that controls the in-out of your breathing. You double over and maybe he punches you once or twice more, but you can't be sure because the need to suck air is so urgent you aren't aware of anything else. You open and close your mouth like some sort of moronic fish until the switch resets and allows your diaphragm to expand. When it finally does, you take one massive, sucking gulp before busting out in wet, pathetic sobs like one of the elementary kids. The second-tier girl stands there, shaking her head at you.

It turns out the second-tier girl had told the big beefy kid that you were hitting on one of the first-tier girls in music class, the one the big kid has a crush on — *the* blond queen of the first-tier girls. What puzzles you is that you weren't hitting on her. You knew she was out of your league, like way out in the Milky Way. The only thing you've ever had the guts to say to the blond queen was, "Can I borrow a pencil?"

A few weeks later, you have ascended slightly. The lowest-ranked kid is now a boy named Allan. At this age, only the first-tier girls and boys mix with one another in the schoolyard; the rest of you still play in all-girl or all-boy packs. The pack you're with has come upon another pack of boys who are giving Allan a cherry tree. Your pack merges with this pack and joins in.

Allan is flat on his back. Between his legs is a sapling. Several boys are pulling his feet so that his crotch is pressed tight against the tree. Allan is squirming. More and more boys come over to see what all the hollering and jumping around is about. Allan is looking up at the boys, at you, and laughing the unconvincing laughter of someone trying to tell himself he's in on the joke rather than the brunt of it. The boys holding his feet come and go like flies on roadkill, but the pressure on Allan's testicles is constant. If anything, it's getting worse, because every new rotation of boys attempts to outdo the previous group by pulling harder, trying to smear Allan's future manhood into a meaty paste in his underwear. You are one of the carrion flies. You take a turn. His shoes have been pulled off. His socks are warm and sweaty. Now his nervous laughter is punctuated with quick, pleading yelps. You give up your place at his foot. Now the game is not fun at all, not even pretend fun. Allan has stopped laughing. His yelps are louder and more insistent. The flies doing the pulling have worked themselves into a fury. Allan hollers for them to stop.

One of the boys in the crowd says, "C'mon, guys. That's too much." And then another boy says, "Okay! Okay! Stop." And another. And then you. And then the circle breaks apart and Allan is left alone in the field, crying and cupping himself.

You're not sure what to make of this. Allan is a nice kid, big-hearted and friendly. You do not understand why the pack of boys settled on him in the first place. You do not understand why you felt a twinge of contempt for him yourself, watching him on his back like that, why you felt for a moment that he deserved it when you know the game was not right. You aren't sure why you and the other boys thought of it as a game when, clearly, it wasn't one.

You *are* sure of a couple of things, though. You know very well it could have been you instead of Allan. You feel somewhere inside yourself that being one of the boys doing the pulling makes it slightly less likely you'll be the next Allan.

The other thing you're certain of, the thing that's clearer than just about anything else in your life at this point, is how easily we can become prey among our own species.

The question is, what exactly can you do about that?

—

ADAM HAS BEEN TRAINING two, sometimes three times a day for weeks now, and at least once every day for years.

During the week, the gym is full of recreational athletes, sweat-soaked men and women flopping around on the rubberized floor mats like netted fish, trying to perfect the techniques of Gracie jiu-jitsu. But on Sundays, the gym is as peaceful and airy as a cathedral. Sunlight streams through tall windows. The muted sound of traffic rises up from the street below. The gym smells, not unpleasantly, of medicated muscle ointment. On Sunday mornings, the place is reserved exclusively for athletes preparing for an upcoming fight.

Overhead, painted on one of the ceiling beams, are the words BELIEVE IN YOURSELF.

Adam is five foot nine. He normally weighs 160 pounds. He is supposed to weigh 140 by Friday, the day before his fight—the second mixed martial arts bout of his professional career. He's already dropped eight pounds, but it will be a difficult five days, getting to 140, because, really, he has no more weight to drop. He's already a walking model of the human muscular system. His body fat percentage is hovering just above the single digits. In this weight class, the body of a fighter and the body of a dancer can be difficult to distinguish. There's no allowance for excess—showy pecs, biceps pumped up like dinner rolls. Those are showpieces that'll weigh you down, pull you out of the air and plunge you into a dark anoxia halfway through a round. No amount of body-building or spin class will get you such a physique. To get in this kind of shape, you must devote your days, as Adam has, to the merciless pursuit of anatomical efficiency.

He enters the gym like a warrior prince surveying his domain. Actually, he looks like a bronze statue of the warrior prince. For the past few weeks he's been training with a thick five-o'clock shadow and dark, unkempt hair, sparring in ratty T-shirts, wearing fight gloves that smell like rancid cheese. But this morning he has shaved. His hair is cut like Julius Caesar's. He's wearing a clean T-shirt. The eight pounds that have evaporated out of him over the past few days have pulled the skin closer to the bones. His cheeks and jaw and clavicles all look burnished from the inside. His eyes sit deep in his skull. They're searching the room.

"You look lean," says Oliver. Oliver is one of the fighters who will be sparring with Adam today. "Look at your face." Oliver is built like a circus strongman, with legs that could hold up the roof of the Parthenon. He's in the middle of warming up those legs with short, effortless, rib-shattering kicks to one of the massive heavy bags. A solid kick, the bread and butter of Thai kick-boxers, the kind of kick Oliver is unleashing on the bag, is a swift strike with the shin, as opposed to the foot. Done right, it's like taking a swing at someone's ribs with a baseball bat. Sometimes fighters will condition their legs by running a rolling pin up and down their shins to deaden the nerve endings, though, over time, beating the bag the way Oliver does has the same effect. His kicks reverberate off the ceiling like thunder. He stops to size up Adam more completely. "Yeah, man," he says. "You look good."

Adam doesn't feel so good, though. Not emotionally. Adam is a pre-parer. He plans. He trains. He cogitates. He worries. Late at night, he studies old UFC fights from a huge library he has amassed on his hard drive. He reviews styles. Techniques. Upsets. Strategies. All of which is a form of wrestling with himself. It's good to prepare, to perfect strengths and work on holes in your defence. But too much and you wear your-self down before you step in the cage.

"I just want to get this thing over with," Adam tells me. He has dark circles under his eyes. "It's the waiting. The anticipation is what kills you."

Not literally, of course. Though there are plenty of things that could kill you in the cage, things the other guy might do to you. In mixed martial arts, it's legal to use your knees and elbows—to the face, to the head. You can choke and kick and twist the limbs off your opponent if you're able. You can break bones and pull joints out of their sockets. You can lift him up and smash him on the mat.

Sometimes a body gets beaten raw as hamburger, or knocked out cold with a roundhouse kick to the temple, and still comes through just fine. Other times, a head hits the ground at the wrong angle; a neck goes in a funny direction; a tiny blood vessel breaks and floods a cortex; or a rib shatters and pops a lung like a lunch bag and a clot shoots north into your brain and you fall into the darkness that never ends. These are the things I'm thinking about as I watch Adam prepare for his fight. I suspect these are the thoughts he's trying his best to avoid.

"I thought your next fight was in China in a couple months," Oliver says between kicks.

Adam *is* fighting in China in a couple of months, in Zhengzhou, the capital city of Henan province. It'll be a big fight, in front of a big crowd and a lot of media. He doesn't know who he'll be up against, which is an unknown that worries him.

Adam has had only one pro fight. He won it handily. But it's hard to BELIEVE IN YOURSELF, especially if, like Adam, you're a rational creature with an education, a decent capacity for analytical thought and some understanding of statistical probability. And are prone to the jitters. If you don't BELIEVE IN YOURSELF, if you have even a momentary lapse of confidence in the ring; if, while you're in the cage dodging blows and trying to keep away from chokeholds, you're suddenly overcome by what-ifs—*What if I've been fooling myself? What if I get knocked out? What if this guy is the next big thing? What if my shin connects with his and shatters like a piece of rock candy?*— then you're in serious trouble. Like the kind where you're halfway across the Atlantic and look out the window to see an engine flaming out beneath your wing. And so Adam has taken this in-between fight hoping it will serve as a test run. A pre-flight check before Zhengzhou, to make sure all systems are go.

There's no way Adam should lose this fight. Not on paper. Adam knows this, rationally speaking. The guy he'll be fighting, a guy named Kyle, has a sorry professional record: four fights, four losses.

"He's no bum, though." That's what Adam tells Oliver. "All of the guys who beat him are good fighters."

Still, this Kyle guy is probably not a preparer the way Adam is. Word has it he works a lot and doesn't have much time to train. He's several inches shorter than Adam, too, which gives Adam the reach advantage. But Kyle is built like a tiny brick shithouse, which is both good and bad for Adam. Good because, while all that muscle looks impressive, it will probably exhaust Kyle partway through a round. Bad because it's the kind of muscle capable, before that exhaustion, of tremendous power. He apparently throws bombs—big looping punches that should be easy enough for Adam to avoid. Adam is quick and strong, light on his feet and exquisitely reactive, so, if he's paying attention, he'll be able to see those kinds of shots coming at him long before they land. But here's a significant what-if:

With almost no body fat to speak of, if Adam is to drop down to 140 pounds over the next few days, he will have to turn himself into a living mummy. In a day or two he'll start cutting fluid. Then he'll take a diuretic, which will do to him what you do to a dishrag before you hang it over the faucet. Never mind that dehydration messes up your digestion or bonks your electrolytes, which can give you nightmarish muscle cramps and do to your cardiac rhythm what a jazz drummer does to a set of Zildjians. That's all serious stuff. But what's more perilous—and Adam is perfectly aware of this—is that to dehydrate this much means shrinking the volume of your cerebrospinal fluid, the protective substance bathing your brain.

One of the functions of cerebrospinal fluid is to act as a shock absorber. When you take a blow to the head, physics sets you up for a nasty treat, the counter-coup injury. Your head gets hit and starts travelling. Your neck stops it the way a string stops a yo-yo. Your head immediately starts travelling back in the opposite direction, but momentum keeps your brain moving in the original direction, where it bounces off the inside of your skull. All of this happens in a fraction of a second.

Cerebrospinal fluid normally cushions the blow, so it's like tossing a watermelon onto a waterbed. But dehydration drains the waterbed. The watermelon lands on the bed frame.

Here's what happens if you don't BELIEVE IN YOURSELF in the cage: instead of reacting, you think. Thinking makes you a patsy by asking you, *What's he gonna do next?* And while you're considering that question, you're not paying any attention to the wide arc of a hot punch careening towards your temple like the meteorite that ended the dinosaurs.

All this is buzzing through Adam's brain. And there's a lower-voltage buzz in there too, the knowledge that while it's pretty bad to have the sort of no-win record Kyle has, you could do worse: you could be the guy who loses to the guy with a no-win record.

—

IN JUNIOR HIGH, our fathers took turns driving me and two friends out to a rundown clapboard church in the country for karate lessons. My dad wasn't super keen on it, but I begged him—though in the end I went for only a couple of months at most. The *gi* made me look, I imagined—I hoped—something like Luke Skywalker in the original *Star Wars* rather than an overheated child in fancy pyjamas. This was before there was a martial arts school in every strip mall, back when I was still nervous in the schoolyard. I hoped it would be the sort of place where a master would transmit something like the force unto us. Or the death touch—that ninja move where you strike someone, usually with just the tip of your finger, and it kills them, usually hours later.

I could tell right away it wasn't that kind of place, despite all the ceremonial bowing, the *Yes Senseis*, the black-and-white framed photo of the old Japanese guy on the wall; despite the instructor carrying a bamboo sword and cracking it against the insides of our ankles so we'd spread our legs wider during warm-ups. Even at twelve, I knew the only real power he had was the ability to intimidate a bunch of preteens. All the punches and kicks, all the talk about channelling your chi in a powerful "KIA!" as you struck your opponent, did nothing transformative, as far as I was concerned.

One of my friends stuck with it for years. He was also into Dungeons & Dragons, which I pretended to like. I wanted to like it. My buddy was skilled at creating imaginary little worlds in which he thrived and conquered. Karate class felt the same: a set of pretend powers you gave yourself in a pretend environment. Back in the schoolyard, those special powers meant nothing. It was still the domain of the larger, more aggressive kids. The only special power karate gave you was the magical ability to get your ass shoved immediately to the ground if you happened to mention you were taking martial arts.

In high school, I tried jiu-jitsu. I liked learning how to get out of a bear hug or a headlock. These things seemed applicable, at least on a theoretical level. But there was an insurmountable gap between the theoretical and the practical—partly because I could never remember all the moves, but mostly because there were always the boys who were no longer boys, the boys in the higher grades who were on the senior rugby, football and hockey teams, who lifted weights—boys whose physical strength tore through technique, no matter how perfectly you remembered it. And among them were boys who fought actual fights that weren't anything like the carefully choreographed moves you learned in the dojo, just white-eyed rage and wild, flying fists. Neither of which I had in me back then.

My parents divorced when I was fifteen, and shortly after that I tried another dojo. Again I lasted a couple of months. It was like going on successive diets: I hoped martial arts might make me into a better, stronger, more powerful me, immune to schoolyard dread. I'd do the classes and not feel any different and, disappointed, drop out.

Then puberty put its polishing touches on me and suddenly I was six-three, two hundred pounds. A man. I became lean and fit. Women started to notice me. But men started to notice me too. In a different way, for different reasons.

Being big is nice, but not as nice—and not as secure—as you might think if you're not so big. For all its advantages, it can be a serious liability, especially when you're young. Guys your age see you as competition. Older guys see you as an up-and-coming threat. The average man will think twice about provoking a big dude. But that leaves the not-so-average men—guys with chips on their shoulders, inferiority complexes, wild tempers; all the guys who have been in fights, who know how to fight and who like it. And as a rule, none of them give a rat's ass about the courtly principles of one-on-one. If a smaller man starts something and finds himself in trouble, he's almost always got backup, guys who will feel good ganging up on you because, after all, *you're* fighting a smaller guy. *You're* the prick who needs to be taught a lesson. So, yeah, being big, doing weights, being fit are all decent deterrents. But if you're a realist, you understand that a big man stands out in the forest and that a lot of angry little men with sharp little axes want to take him down.

After I got big, I couldn't go out to bars and clubs without some guy wanting to start something. My public persona changed from open and friendly to suspicious and anxious, especially when I was around men my own age. I finally figured out what to do with my hands: I crossed my arms over my chest and stood bolt straight and unsmiling in order to heighten the walls of the defensive facade I was building. But, still, it was a facade. I didn't have a clue about how to actually defend myself.

I tried martial arts again in my second year of university, tae kwon do this time. And something clicked. I got good, fast. I trained every day of the week. Within a few months I was flexible and coordinated enough that I could kick the top of a door frame. I could snap a kick to the head nearly as fast as I could throw a punch. I had endless stamina and energy. I beat everyone in the club every time I sparred—everyone except my instructor, a black belt who had trained on the national team. I went to a few competitions, little local events held in community centres. I won. My instructor introduced me to his instructor and told him to keep an eye out for me, that I had a lot of potential. By the end of the year, despite my being only a low-ranking green belt, my instructor made me the head of the club's competitive team. He ordered team track suits and surprised me by having *Captain* embroidered on the sleeve of my jacket, over my name. He invited me into his office and told me he wanted me to consider eventually trying out for the national team. He handed me a three-inch section of black belt attached to a key ring.

"That's what you're working towards," he said. "Just focus on training. Every time you do weights, do an extra rep. Every time you kick the bag, do ten extra kicks."

—

NO MORE TIME ON THE bag will help Adam now. There's not really anything he can improve upon, not less than a week before he faces Kyle. He's as physically prepared as he can get. He's got a solid arsenal of techniques: wrestling, boxing, jiu-jitsu, kick-boxing. He's in peak shape. His conditioning is probably better than that of any of the other fighters who will show up on Saturday night. It's better than any of his sparring partners'. Except maybe Seiji. But Seiji's not here today.

Seiji is one of Adam's friends. A couple of nights ago, Seiji fought his sixth professional fight and lost. It was televised nationally. As Adam will be, Seiji was paired with a power puncher, a guy who, on paper, was predicted to lose. Now he was at home with a couple of messed-up ribs. I e-mailed him to see how he was doing. He wrote back:

*Don't feel great about losing with almost everyone I know watching but not much I can do about that now.*

"I'm pretty sure that guy was on something," Adam said. He meant Seiji's opponent—he meant steroids. "He had a huge strength advantage."

Before we can sink into the what-ifs of Seiji's loss, Nelson comes charging into the gym. He kicks off his shoes, dumps his bag, hugs each of the fighters. There's a reason Adam has asked Nelson to be one of his corner men. If anyone can make you BELIEVE IN YOURSELF, it's Nelson.

"Nice haircut!" Nelson says on his way to Adam, and laughs. "You look like a twelve-year-old. That's going to make him more aggressive."

Adam says, "What is?"

"Your haircut. Your clean face," says Nelson. "It's going to make the other guy more aggressive."

"That's no good," says Adam. "I'd rather be intimidating."

Nelson realizes his mistake. The problem with Adam before a fight is that the what-ifs are like a swarm of gnats buzzing around his head. If you try to shoo them away with a joke, he's liable to think you're taking a swipe at him.

"Don't worry about it, man," Nelson says. "I'm joking."

I've heard stories about Nelson. If you hang out in the fight gyms where he trains, you'll hear conversations like this one:

"It's always the little guys you gotta watch out for."

"Yeah, a lot of guys underestimate smaller guys."

"A lot of guys have made that mistake with Nelson."

"That's a mistake you only make once."

Nelson is five-five, 160 pounds. He looks a bit like the movie star Jason Statham—if Statham were playing a character who was prone to cracking jokes. Nelson had a short pro career from 2006 to 2008. He's taught kick-boxing at several gyms across the city, including this one, which he arranges to have on Sundays, partly so up-and-coming pros like Adam have a regular stable of fighters to spar with. And partly because, even though Nelson isn't interested in fighting pro any longer, he enjoys these sessions. They keep him feeling alive. They keep him sharp too, for his job as a bouncer.

The term *pro* is misleading in the fight scene, especially in mixed martial arts. As a professional you get paid, but unless you're in the highest echelon of fighters, you can't really make a living. Adam made four hundred dollars with his first fight. He and Kyle will each earn fifteen hundred on Saturday. The fight in Zhengzhou will earn him about the same, plus plane fare and a hotel room. What *professional* really means in MMA is that you devote your life to your training, your diet, to the perpetual horizon of the next fight, to rising, fight by fight, up the ladder of badassedness. It means sacrifice. It means sometimes closing doors in other areas of your life.

Adam is twenty-seven and lives with his parents. He has a university degree and a teaching diploma but not a full-time job. He tends to take short-term, irregular work as a substitute teacher. At least once, before going into a classroom, he has had to borrow his girlfriend's concealer to cover up a black eye.

Most guys who turn pro have a few fights, realize they're not UFC material and get out of the scene. If you count gym fees, what you pay your coaches, the money you don't earn doing other work, it's definitely a losing affair. But money's not the draw for most guys.

Back when Nelson was in his late twenties and getting paid to fight, cage matches were still illegal in most provinces and throughout the majority of the United States. He'd drive all night with his buddy, Bill, to one of the few states where you could get a sanctioned fight. Most often Virginia. Or casinos on Native reserves. Usually he and Bill would fight on the same card, Nelson as a lightweight, Bill as a middle-weight. Sometimes they'd each fight two or three guys in a single night. They'd take turns cornering for each other—staunching cuts, squirting jets of water down one another's throat, telling the other guy he's a beast, a predator on the hunt. They'd make enough cash to pay for gas, split a motel room, and order a post-fight pizza while icing their faces and fists. But money wasn't the point.

"It was just something fun to do," Nelson told me. "I just wanted to go on a ride. It didn't matter where it was going. It was just fun to be on that train for a while."

A ride. Fighting is one of a whole constellation of risky and seemingly stupid things men do, apparently just for kicks. Men are about two and a half times more likely to be killed in a car accident than women—three times as likely in the highest-risk cohort, fifteen to twenty-nine years old.[1] Whatever his age, a man is more inclined than a woman to speed, drink, do drugs, have unprotected sex, gamble and risk his neck. Because of this, in industrialized nations, where avoid-able deaths have been brought down to near-utopian levels (at least compared with historical levels), men are still at the highest risk for dying young.[2]

Men are a danger to themselves and a danger to be around. Young men have the highest chance of being hurt or killed—almost always by another young man. Men are responsible for 85 percent of all homi-cides and 91 percent of all same-sex killings. Most murders are men killing other men. And the vast majority of these crimes start as trivial arguments that turn into serious altercations,[3] the kind of fights I've tended to get in. An insult, a shove, a guy throwing another guy shade, a guy thinking some dude has been hitting on his girl, one guy thinking another guy is being an asshole and needs to be taken down a notch.

On the surface of it, it's hard to understand why men get themselves into these sorts of binds—on the street, in the ring. A life-or-death situ-ation is one thing. But if you consider how little is actually at stake at the beginning of most fights, how they often become life-or-death only after men actively trip what ought to be an entirely avoidable switch— it seems straight-up insane.

I get what happens with street fights from first-hand experience. They're like train wrecks, a set of circumstances that gets away from you and can have disastrous consequences. It's easy to shrug them off as the result of "losing it." On an individual level, that's exactly what it feels like—some sort of internal glitch.

But it also feels that way to all the other guys who get in fights. So that glitch is actually the norm. Meaning fully half of the human species seems prone to "losing it" in a way that risks gambling away their future before they've peaked. We are a creature that is transiently immune to its own capacity for reason in a way that often turns deadly.

Competitive fighting isn't as risky as starting something with a random stranger. Fighters are generally well matched and know what they're getting into. And even MMA imposes enough restrictions that few fighters have died in the ring. Still, it *is* risky—if not immediately, then down the road when you start forgetting the names of your children. And you can't blame the choice to become a pro fighter on super-heated emotions; it's a perfectly sober decision. There are some bad men out there who fight because they enjoy the opportunity to hurt another human being. But that's not most fighters I've met. It's definitely not Adam.

"To be honest," he told me, "I get sick to my stomach when I see street fights. I only like controlled violence—where no one's going to get seriously hurt."

Even chasing the ride, as Nelson calls it, the ultra-stimulation of putting yourself in a risky situation, is a puzzling explanation. Winning a fight feels fantastic. But the lead-up, the weeks and months of preparation, is full of so much work, sacrifice and anxiety that it reminds me of George Orwell's description of writing a book: "a horrible exhausting struggle, like a long bout with some painful illness. One would never undertake such a thing if one were not driven on by some demon whom one can neither resist nor understand."

Let's assume that young men are not all stupid, insane or sociopathic. Whether it's a built-in predisposition to violence or a learned behaviour, fighting doesn't make a ton of sense. Presumably something that has so clearly been the cause of widespread injury and premature death throughout human history[4]—and disproportionately at the height of a man's reproductive capacity—ought to have been phased out one way or another.

The fact that it hasn't requires one hell of an explanation.

After one of his Sunday sparring sessions, I asked Adam why he fought. We were on the mats. He was stretching his hamstrings. His T-shirt was soaked with sweat and clung to his chest like saran wrap.

"I just love the sport," he said.

Adam was nine when the Ultimate Fighting Championship debuted in 1993. Back then, mixed martial arts hadn't yet gelled into what it now is: a unified form of fighting that borrows techniques from a number of disciplines. These days, UFC fighters still have different strengths and weaknesses, but they all enter the octagon with more or less the same fundamental set of skills. They can all punch and kick, wrestle, grapple and submit one another. But the early UFC matches were different. They had a campy, sideshow quality. Promoters would pair up fighters from entirely different fighting disciplines, sometimes to ridiculous effect: Elephantine Sumo Wrestler vs. Tiny Kimonoed Karate Guy; Collegiate Greco-Roman Wrestler fighting B-Movie Kung-Fu Guy; Jacked-up Steroidal Jock matched with Judo Master. The point, ostensibly, was to resolve the philosophical question that perplexes every adolescent boy at some point: which martial art is most effective in a real, no-holds-barred fight?

What captivated Adam, along with pretty much every other mixed martial artist I've met, was that these early events were consistently dominated by an unimposing, average-looking, 175-pound man named Royce Gracie. Gracie used Brazilian jiu-jitsu, a profoundly technical martial art his family had developed, to submit much larger, more powerful, more malicious fighters. He didn't rely on size or raw strength, or psychological intimidation, but intelligence and exacting technique. Watching Gracie incapacitate men twice his size was like watching a member of the debate team take down the senior football team's entire offensive line. Adam felt as though he were witnessing the birth of a real-life superhero, an everyman who had somehow made himself unconquerable. The idea of it sank into Adam's skin like a radioactive spider bite.

Adam admits he had a tendency to push other kids around when he was young. "But," he told me, "I also went through periods of being picked on by older kids, too."

"Are you trying to prove something to yourself?" I asked.

He thought about it for a moment. "Subconsciously, I think I probably am. Not everyone can do what we're doing. I like being associated with that. I think part of it, too, is that it's the ultimate form of competition. It's body against body, but also mind against mind. It takes absolutely everything you have. Physically. Mentally. Emotionally. Plus, there's something about being able to put another man under your will. He's at your mercy." He paused again. "I don't really know how to articulate this without sounding like a total jackass. But that guy's your bitch."

—

AFTER ABOUT A YEAR OF tae kwon do, martial arts started to define my thinking—and not in a Zen, open-to-the-universe kind of way. Not in a hateful, belligerent way either, mind you. But it changed how I thought and the thoughts I had. Whenever I was in a public place, I'd scan the room for guys who might present a threat—guys bigger than me, more fit, mean or arrogant. I'd think out various hypotheticals, combos of kicks and punches. I liked imagining beating several men at once. I liked the idea of impressing people around me with my prowess. I spent a lot of time in front of my bathroom mirror, flexing, practising combos, striking Bruce Lee poses, talking to an imaginary opponent like I was De Niro in *Taxi Driver*. I loved being fit and wearing a jacket with *Captain* on the arm. I loved feeling as if I could take care of myself.

One night, as I was coming out of the Student Union Building, I saw two meaty guys walking towards me. One of them said, "Look at this faggot." He meant me. I felt the old schoolyard flutter, but I walked straight at them and at the last moment they parted for me like the Red Sea.

I started calling out bullies. A guy in the line at Subway was pestering the young woman making his sandwich. I told him to quit being an asshole. He did.

A young woman was waiting for a bus. There was a pickup truck idling at the curb. The guy inside was leaning out of the driver's window, trying to convince her to get in. The woman had that frozen, open-eyed look of a cornered animal, clearly freaked out. I told the guy to get the fuck out of there. He asked me if I knew her. I told him it didn't fucking matter, to move along or I'd smash in the door of his truck. He crept off. I was afraid he'd circle back, so I drove the woman to the restaurant where she was meeting her friends. She bought me a drink.

One of my teachers, a psych prof in his early sixties, liked to invite small groups of undergrads into the faculty lounge periodically for a little salon. After a couple of drinks, he told the half-dozen of us who had joined him that his wife had had a string of affairs and that, to get back at her, he had set about trying to have sex with all of the men she had slept with. I was trying to figure out whether this was some sort of mini social-psych experiment he liked trying on his students when he asked me about my Captain's jacket. I told him about tae kwon do. He asked if I had been bullied as a kid. I didn't want to admit to it, but I did.

He said something like, "That's why you do martial arts. You never want to be treated that way again."

I told him I wasn't actually worried about being bullied.

"Yes," he said, "because you do martial arts."

I dismissed him as obviously unbalanced. Also, at the time, if felt as if he had made the observation with the arrogance of someone who feels they understand the entire human condition because they've studied some psychology. He doesn't know me, I thought. He doesn't know why I do what I do.

Except he sort of did.

—

MUHAMMAD ALI LEARNED TO FIGHT, so the legend goes, after his bike was stolen. Antonio Carvalho, a UFC featherweight fighter from Toronto, got into MMA to cope with severe bullying as a boy. And before he learned to box, Mike Tyson was a timid kid with a speech impediment who got beat up by other kids. He raised carrier pigeons on the roof of his apartment building and learned to fight only after a bigger kid tore the head off one of his birds in front of him.

I asked Nelson about growing up.

"I wasn't the kind of kid who would scrap," he told me. "I got beat up, if anything. In fact, I got beat up pretty bad in grade three by this one kid."

Nelson grew up in the 1970s and '80s in Parkdale, a working-class Toronto neighbourhood that's rapidly gentrifying. But when Nelson was a kid, it was a tough place. There was a gang of older kids who hung out in McCormick Park. All the local kids knew to avoid drawing their attention. You knew, for instance, not to be near the local arena when there was a hockey game on. The McCormick Boys would sit up in the stands, clustered together like a murder of crows.

Nelson didn't play hockey. But for several years he took figure skating lessons at the arena. One day he had a performance. He was seven or eight. He glided out onto the ice and began his routine. Partway through, he looked up and saw the McCormick Boys staring down at him.

"The look on their faces was enough," he told me. "I did my routine, sweating buckets, and the whole time I was like: 'I'm never figure skating again.' And that was it. I never skated after that."

Seiji was shy and quiet, unpopular and small as a boy. He was good at school, and because of his looks (his mother is fourth-generation Japanese-Canadian) the other kids assigned him the role of nerdy, diffident Asian kid. His brother used to give him a hard time, too—just the normal sibling poundings. But they were enough to get the point across: that his brother was the older, bigger alpha and Seiji the scrawny beta. At fourteen, Seiji took up martial arts, a fistful of them—capoeira, kung fu, wushu and tae kwon do.

Nelson calls Seiji a "real-life ninja" because of his speed and accuracy. He is impossibly quick and supple, and extraordinarily skilled at kicking and punching his opponents and then, once they're on the ground, tying them into a knot with the precision of a surgeon stitching sutures. But Seiji is also extraordinarily unassuming and quiet. He sort of melts into the shadows. Unless you're actively watching him fight, it's easier to see him as his alter ego—the Seiji who works in a lab as a post-doc in molecular biology, quietly unlocking the mysteries of *Deinococcus radiodurans*, a bacterium that thrives in extreme environments. This is the Seiji he presents to most of the world, the Seiji he presents to his in-laws. His wife is a medical resident; her parents are, as he tells it, conservative, old-school Chinese immigrants who would find it unforgivably shameful that their son-in-law spends much of his time beating on other men.

Watching him in the gym, it's hard not to make the comparison: *Deinococcus radiodurans*, the bacteria he studies, is interesting to scientists because it is an extremophile, an organism that thrives in the kind of hostile environments that kill other life forms—extreme heat or cold, radioactivity, the vacuum of space. Watching Seiji sweating it out with men bigger than him, stronger than him, watching him overtake them calmly and efficiently, it seems pretty clear that through his years of training he has made himself into an extremophile.

One afternoon in a coffee shop near his apartment, I asked him why he had decided to turn pro. He answered me softly as he looked into a paper cup of black coffee.

"What I tell myself," he said, "is that it's about competing."

I had told Seiji about my periodic blood lust, my especial hatred for bullies. I asked him if fighting was a way of channelling some inner rage.

"To be honest," he said, "I don't get that at all. I think you're a way more violent person than I am. I don't put myself in situations where I get into fights with random strangers. I mean, I've never been in an altercation—though I tend to think about them a lot."

We had also been talking about the risks of competitive fighting, especially the possibility of repetitive head injuries. Seiji's scientific career depends on keeping his grey matter in working condition.

"It's something I'm definitely cognizant of," he told me. "If I get KO'd a few times, that's it. I'll have to give it up."

"So, given the risk," I asked, "if it's just about competition, why not, say, competitive chess?"

He mulled the question but didn't answer, and we moved on to something else. Later, when I got home, I saw he had e-mailed me. He had been thinking about my question. He wrote:

*I think it definitely ties into the issue of dominance. I've never known any of my opponents before fighting them, so I've never had any feelings about them—good or bad. But in competitive fighting, we're given the opportunity to display dominance over*

*someone in front of an audience. Who the person standing in the*
*cage with us is isn't really important. I tend to put more effort in*
*when I know that people are watching. It's not something I do*
*consciously, but I find I'm more alert and more aggressive when*
*there's an audience, even to the point of showing off. I really don't*
*like that about myself. But I still do it and I know I won't stop.*

But still, why fighting? If the central issue is dominance, why *physical*
dominance? And why take the risk of violent, bloody combat? There
are a million ways to stand out in the crowd as an alpha. Careers to
pursue. Money to make. Property and belongings to accrue. Wardrobes
and garages to fill. Fame to achieve.

I think there's a lot to be said for the explanation that these guys
are—that *I* am—somehow compensating for feeling weak and vulnerable as kids. But then, who didn't? Didn't most of us—male, female;
popular, unpopular—feel the sick fear that we could slip to the bottom
of the pack if we weren't careful? Even if you weren't bullied, you knew
it was potentially waiting for you around the corner. I suspect that's why
so many bullies are bullies in the first place—it's their pre-emptive
strike, a way of avoiding becoming the Allan in the crowd.

But there's more to it than just that. There is a reason this fear sticks
around, even in adulthood. It is not just some neurotic divot pounded
into us by childhood trauma. No matter how you achieve success later in
life—money, fame, esteem—no matter how high up the social ladder
you climb, we all know that we can be shoved off that ladder by the
simple application of physical force. We never quite escape the schoolyard, because the schoolyard is a microcosmic hothouse in which a fundamental of human behaviour is provided optimal conditions in which
to thrive: a period of intense social sorting-out; limited sophistication in
how exactly to go about doing this; as-of-yet-not-fully-developed empathy;
a relative lack of supervision. Physical domination makes fewer appear-
ances as we get older. But it remains backstage, like a reliable understudy.

There is, after all, a reason why a hockey game will break out in a
fist fight but a fist fight will never break out in a hockey game; why we
have that notion that no matter the kind of contest, things get settled
once and for all, mano-a-mano, that a physical fight is the irreducible

form of male conflict. There's a reason why we feel that *that's* the way of settling something.

Men have been settling things this way among themselves since before there were, technically speaking, men to settle things. And this has shaped us—*physically* shaped us—as a species.

—

MEN, ON AVERAGE, are taller and heavier than women. A significant proportion of the weight difference is muscle mass: men, in general, have a higher proportion of muscle and a lower proportion of subcutaneous fat. Men are also correspondingly stronger and faster than women on average. They have denser bones, bigger teeth, stronger tendons, a faster metabolism, larger lung capacity, thicker skin (literally, not figuratively) and higher levels of hemoglobin in their blood. Men die earlier of natural causes than women. They hit puberty later. They remain fertile longer. There are subtle differences in brain structure and bone composition, and significant differences in the proportion of sex hormones coursing through their bodies—especially the androgen testosterone.

Of course, there's a lot of variability out there—lots of smaller, weaker men and plenty of larger, stronger women. But the largest and most physically powerful humans in a given population are certain to be men. This is not just a coincidence. Biologists refer to the physical differences between males and females as *sexual dimorphism*. It's not the result of learning or socialization, but of our physical evolution, specifically sexual selection.

The traits that, say, make tigers such formidable predators—teeth, claws, fierceness—are the result of natural selection. Natural selection is the development, over successive generations, of physical and behavioural adaptations that allow animals to thrive in specific environmental niches. In addition to environmental pressures shaping animals, we, the animals, do a considerable bit of the shaping ourselves. So, while natural selection accounts for the differences between species—say, the physical and behavioural differences between turkeys and peacocks—*sexual selection* accounts for the fact that male turkeys and male peacocks sport ornate plumage while their female counterparts are comparatively drab. Natural selection results in traits that better our chances of survival in a given niche; sexual selection results in traits that better our chances of reproductive success.

The peacock's tail is an example of a sexually selected trait that impresses and attracts the opposite sex. That's one way of doing it. Another way is to impress members of the *same* sex by being imposing and intimidating enough—or physically powerful enough—to knock them out of the running. Think stags locking horns and silverback gorillas beating their chests. Sexual selection among primates—the order we belong to—is driven largely by contests for physical dominance. Generally speaking, the bigger and more aggressive you are as a male primate, the more successful you will be at mating.

In most animals, including humans, reproduction is a high-cost affair for females: it takes a lot of time, energy and physical resources. For the most part, one high-quality male is all a female needs to fulfill her reproductive capacity. And because, ultimately, females are often the ones who do the selecting, they tend to be choosy about who they mate with; they want the best specimen they can find. Males, on the other hand, can potentially increase their reproductive capacity with every female they hook up with. And so, throughout the natural world, males tend to try to mate with multiple females and they tend to be less choosy. Which means, for any given female, there can be several competing males. Often a single dominant male will mate with several females, meaning there are always more males than females who lose out on the ability to reproduce.

Given how important reproduction is, this has resulted in an evolutionary arms race in which, over generations, males evolve traits to outdo the other guy. Hence the male peacock's tail and the stag's antlers—or simply being big, strong and aggressive.

In nature, the degree of sexual dimorphism within a given species is related to the degree of male competition within that species. There are, incidentally, species that are not sexually dimorphic, in which the males and females are difficult to tell apart. In those species, there is very little male-male competition for mates. The rule of thumb is this: the more intense the physical competition, the bigger the males and the more fierce they are towards one another.

Male gorillas and orangutans are about 50 percent bigger than females. Male chimpanzees are about 20 percent bigger. The males of all three species compete fiercely and brutally among themselves for females—and they are also fierce and brutally controlling *towards* their mates. Bonobo males are about 15 percent bigger on average than females. Bonobos aren't as violent as gorillas, chimps or orangutans, but, contrary to their reputation as hippy primates, they're not pacifists either. There's a lot of pulling, slapping, hitting and biting among bonobos, especially among young males competing to have sex with a fertile female.[5]

Human males tend to be about 15 percent bigger and heavier than human females, though lean muscle mass—the source of physical strength—is often upwards of 60 percent higher in men than women (and as much as 75 percent higher in men's arms). All of which means that men, on average, are about 90 percent physically stronger than women.[6] But does men's desire to fight one another stem from the same process? Almost certainly. It would be strange and sort of magical if every other sexually dimorphic species on the planet got that way as the result of same-sex competition—in particular all the great apes—but that human males didn't. All the evidence points to us being shaped through the millennia as a species in which males competed with one another for social dominance by means of physical intimidation and aggression.

And it stands to reason that sometimes we still do.

—

NELSON COMES TROTTING OUT of the change room, barefoot, wearing board shorts and a T-shirt. He pops in a mouthguard and pulls on his shin pads and gloves. He and the other fighters—Oliver, Julian, who is a rangy kid with a tattoo of the Ferrari logo on one of his shoulders, and Albert, a friend of Adam's who will be fighting at the same event in Zhengzhou—are all wearing big, well-padded sixteen-ounce gloves. This is to avoid cutting Adam while they spar. Gloves turn into bullwhips when they're at the end of a fast arm. Leather tears skin, especially cheeks and brows, and Adam is especially prone to cuts because of his high cheekbones—and because he's dehydrated, which literally makes him thin-skinned. A bad cut now would disqualify him. Adam is wearing the thin, fingerless gloves he and Kyle will be using during the fight. They have almost no padding, so you can grab the other guy.

Oliver is applying Vaseline to his face. The other guys have already done this as another precaution against cuts. Oliver's eyebrows are twin versions of Magnum P.I.'s moustache. He coats each of them with petroleum jelly as if he is applying wax to the hood of a '67 Corvette Sting Ray.

Nelson is bouncing impatiently on his toes, his scalp gleaming with petroleum jelly in the sunlight. He's punching himself lightly in the face with his gloves, watching Oliver. "Gotta brotec' dosh awshome eyebrowsh!" he says through his mouthguard, then grins. Addressing Julian and Albert, he says, "When you're wit' Adam, try throwing big, looping punshesh." This is to emulate what they think Kyle will be doing in the match.

They start with five consecutive five-minute rounds. Adam and Nelson pair up for the first one.

"I wanna keep it light, guysh," Nelson reminds them. "Light, 'kay?"

This is for Adam too, because usually Nelson isn't all that concerned with keeping things light. If you spar with him and stay light yourself, he'll keep a governor on things. But if you're aggressive or even if you just get nervous and start slugging him in a panic, he'll not only match your shots, he'll start raising them.

I once watched him spar with another seasoned fighter who had the same philosophy. It was supposed to be a relaxed and friendly session, but things kept escalating until it was as though they were fighting for a world title. There was no beef between them, but neither seemed capable of backing down. Afterwards, they both wandered around the gym in a way that made me worry their brain cells were dialing in an advance order for adult diapers. The other fighter told me later he couldn't remember much of the rest of that day.

When Nelson starts ratcheting things up, his punches land mercilessly and squarely between your eyes like the handle of a rake you've stepped on. He becomes less preoccupied with defence. He is highly capable of avoiding shots — ducking, weaving and slipping out of range. But when things heat up in the ring, he steps straight into the other fighter's path, the way you might step out from under an awning during a heavy downpour, thinking, *Ah, fuck it!* As the shots careen off his head, a funny thing happens: rather than slowing him down, the blows seem to speed him up. You can see it in his eyes, the way he comes alive, grunting, smiling, laughing occasionally.

Fighting wasn't Nelson's first career choice. As a kid, he was star-struck by Kiss, the Rolling Stones, everything Motown. He dropped out of high school to play in a band. He eventually moved to Manhattan to make it big. It was a hard life. Success was always around the next corner. And there always seemed to be another corner. The scramble wore him down. By his mid-twenties, his dream of musical success felt like a parade float steadily losing air. Around that time, he saw a photo of himself and realized he had grown fat, pale and soft. "I didn't recognize myself. It just depressed me. I was like, 'I've got to change this.'"

He came back to Toronto, where one of his friends invited him to take up kick-boxing. Like me, Nelson had dabbled in martial arts as a kid, but he hadn't ever trained at a real fight gym, a place where men learn to knock other men into the dark. It gave him some structure in his life, gave him back some of the confidence the New York music scene had torn out of him.

"It was full of hard men," he told me, "legendary men." The kind of men who worked as bouncers and doormen in the clubs where Nelson soon found jobs as a busboy. The kind of men other guys told stories about. "This one guy, this Irishman, he was built like a trash can. He got shot one night at the club. Just grazed, but still—shot! He was at the gym the next day, training, bleeding."

Nelson intuitively picked up combos, footwork, defence. For him it was like playing Tetris on easy: the pieces fit naturally. "Once I started training at this place," he told me, "things just flipped. I went from playing music all the time to training all the time."

He started working the door at clubs, which allowed him to test his skills in the real world. He was even better in street fights than he was in the gym. The stakes were higher. The adrenalin jacked him up. He had good instincts and a temper that welled up when guys insulted him, made fun of his size or his lack of hair, or, especially, if they threatened him.

The story you'll hear most frequently about Nelson—the story other fighters in other gyms like to tell about him—is the time he surfed a guy down a set of stairs after a brawl broke out in one of the clubs he was working. He was stationed in a stairwell. Two guys started up with him. He knocked one guy out, then punched the other guy in the stomach, tripped him, dumped him on the stairs and then, without being entirely sure what he was doing or why, hopped on the guy's back and rode him, bumpity-bump, down the flight. "Half of me was like: 'You're going to kill this guy,'" Nelson told me when I asked him about it. "The other half was like: 'Yeah!'" Surprisingly, the guy was okay.

Probably the story Nelson likes telling the most is the time he knocked a guy out just by slapping him. Or maybe the time he hit a guy so hard he crapped his pants. Once, early in his bouncing career, two guys cornered him. Nelson freaked out and hit one of them in the throat with a sharp little punch that dropped the guy to his knees. The guy knelt there, bug-eyed, clutching his larynx. The guy's pal looked at Nelson as though Nelson had just run over his puppy. Nelson ran home—literally sprinted—and holed up in his apartment, glued to the TV news for a couple of days until he was sure he hadn't inadvertently committed murder. Another time, he was working security at the Hard Rock Cafe when he saw a freakish steroidal mammoth pick up a smaller guy and smash him on the pavement like a rag doll. Nelson thought the smaller guy was dead (he wasn't) and someone called an ambulance. But the big man continued to beat on the smaller guy, which pissed Nelson off. Nelson climbed the big man like a kid on a jungle gym and worked an arm around his neck and choked him unconscious.

I once asked Nelson how many fights he had been in.

"Too many to count," he said.

His decision to turn pro literally hit him in the head one day, during an especially intense sparring session. The other guy sent a roundhouse to Nelson's skull; the guy's shin collided with Nelson's temple. "But it didn't hurt at all," Nelson recalled. It was a liberating moment because, despite being enamoured of fighting, watching Bruce Lee and Chuck Norris and WWF as a kid, fundamentally he had always found it intimidating. But there he was, his own action hero, the kind of guy who could not only give a knockout blow but take one and stay standing. "There's no bullshit when a guy hits you in the face," he told me. "It was actually fun. It was like the first kiss, you know?"

Nelson, Adam and the other fighters have worked their way through four rounds, twenty minutes of punching, kicking, kneeing, pulling one another to the ground, trying to choke and put an arm lock on one another. Adam and Nelson pair up again for the fifth and final round. The bell rings. Nelson marches straight at Adam, fists up. He swings wide and grazes Adam on the mouth. Adam returns with a kick and a couple of punches. Nelson bobs, swings at Adam, misses, pivots, circles Adam and swings wide again. Adam moves, but not fast enough. You can see that he's thinking, the gears whirring away. Nelson's fists connect with the side of his head.

"Watch your shit!" Nelson says. "I'b clipping you wit' wild punshesh."

Afterwards, Adam sits against the wall, staring straight ahead. He's covered in a slick of sweat though he's breathing easy.

Nelson comes back onto the mats after getting a drink.

Adam immediately says, "Nelly, you may need to put pressure on me before the fight."

"Yeah," says Nelson, pulling his gloves back on, "don't worry. We'll warm you up."

"No," Adam says, "I mean more than that. I mean, get me used to *pressure*. I was coming out way too laid-back. I was kind of lackadaisical."

They begin another set of rounds, with the focus on grappling. They start from the ground. Adam is on his back in guard; this is a common defensive position that looks fairly sexual. Nelson is on his knees between Adam's legs. Adam's legs are wrapped around Nelson's waist. The goal here is for Adam to transition out of the defensive posture and take a dominant one. I start the clock. In the midst of the scramble, Adam cries out. Nelson has inadvertently head-butted him.

"It's my cheek," Adam says. He paws at his face and checks his fingers.

"There's no blood," Nelson assures him. "It's okay. There's no cut."

They start up again. A couple of minutes later, Adam stops again, yelling, "Fuck." Nelson has scratched him under the eye.

"It's not bleeding, buddy," Nelson says. "Don't worry about it."

In the next round, Adam pairs up with Julian. About halfway through, Adam cracks his ankle against Julian's shin. They stop. Adam is on his back, clutching his foot and grimacing at the ceiling. "I'm going to stop," he says. "I can't afford an injury."

—

SHORTLY AFTER MY tae kwon do instructor took me into his office and gave me that motivational talk, I quit going. I just stopped. I didn't quite understand why at the time, because I loved it, truly.

The best explanation I've come up with is that the effort, all that time in the gym, meant confining myself to a sort of hyperbaric chamber, constantly turning up the pressure on myself. In that environment, a particular aspect of my personality thrived, but other parts of me asphyxiated. I quit tae kwon do and the suffocated parts came back to life. But about a year after I gave up tae kwon do, I took up boxing because the other part was once again clamouring for air. And then, about a year and a half later, the alternating anxiety—the sense I was depleting some future me of oxygen—took over and I dropped it.

It became a cycle that has continued to this day, dropping in and out of martial arts, ticking, like a metronome, back and forth between these two selves, both of them me, neither of them completely me. On balance, the me who is devoted to long-term planning and sensible career goals has come out on top, though I have to admit that *that* me often has trouble finding contentment.

The idea of devoting myself to fighting appeals to me enough that I periodically feel a twinge of disappointment that I've never developed it more fully, the way Nelson and Adam have. And I still sometimes wonder what that alternative me might have done with himself.

—

THE FIGHT WAS four hours away.

The waitress set a peanut butter and banana sandwich and a bowl of fruit salad in front of Adam. We were at a restaurant down the street from the arena.

"I'm not even hungry," Adam said. "I'm probably not going to eat anything."

"Just eat a few bites," Nelson said.

"Maybe I'll just have some of the fruit salad." He ended up just staring at it.

I had rented a minivan and made the five-hour drive north that morning with Nelson. Along the way, we picked up Adam's training partner, Albert, and Horace, Adam's boxing coach. Adam had driven up the day before in his parents' BMW with his jiu-jitsu coach and good friend, Andrew, and his wrestling coach, Luigi. Andrew and Luigi had got Adam successfully through the weigh-in. Then they'd returned to their hotel room and hooked him up to an IV line.

We met them there when we first got to town. The room looked as if a plane had gone down nearby. There were clothes and towels and empty gym bags scattered across the floor and beds, along with a couple of dozen crushed Tetra Paks of coconut water. Adam had sucked back an entire case after the weigh-in.

He showed me a photo of himself on the scale, flexing his biceps. He looked two-dimensional, like Wile E. Coyote after he's been steam-rolled. He had dropped from 152 to 139 pounds. He had a funny look in his eyes in the photo, the result of either starvation-induced psychosis or him just hamming it up. Low-level MMA events are still sideshow enough that they can be campy and slightly transgressive. Adam flipped to a shot of another fighter who had stepped on the scale wearing a Borat-style thong and aviator sunglasses.

Then he showed me another photo, of a pile of bone-white hotel towels stained dark red and piled up in the bathtub as though someone had done a shoddy job cleaning up a crime scene. It was Adam's blood. He had been so dehydrated after making weight that his blood vessels kept collapsing as Andrew tried to insert the IV. It was like trying to stick a deflated balloon. "I got blood all over my track pants too," Adam told me. "But I take it as a good omen. I spilled blood before the last fight and it went well. When Andrew started up the IV, I could hear my ears popping. It was the fluid coming back in. You sort of feel like someone brought you back from the dead."

There was another picture of Adam post-hydration in which he *was* clearly hamming it up: he had a fork in one fist and a knife in the other and a napkin tucked into his shirt and he was making googly eyes at a huge steak on the table in front of him. Overnight, he'd put on twenty-one pounds.

Back at the restaurant, the waitress came by again. Adam asked her to take away his meal.

"I'm just going to have some of my cereal," he said to no one in particular. He had brought a bag of organic muesli from home. "It's gluten-free. It's good for me." He chewed a handful without joy and then pushed the bag aside. He called the waitress over and asked her to take a photo of the group of us. He posted it on his Facebook page with the caption: "The crew before the war." And soon his friends were posting replies. "Kick some dick, brother," one read. Another read: "Good luck to one of my closest training partners as he steps into the cage for his second pro fight."

"All this shit's making me emotional," Adam said. He got up and went outside. A few minutes later, he came back to the table. "I talked to my mom," he told me. "Just to let her know I'm thinking of her. I wanted to hear her voice. She pumped me up. She told me that she wanted to pray for me." He chuckled. "But then she said the guy I'm fighting is some mother's child too."

"What's going through your head now?" I asked him.

"I'm visualizing hot spots. Places where I'm not in the most advantageous situation. Honestly, there's a little bit of anxiety there. But it keeps you sharp, right?"

There were pieces of white paper taped, crookedly, to the cinder-block walls outside the change rooms—photocopies born of a machine so low on toner I had to get within a foot to see the ghostly images. One was of a group of soldiers laying a wreath. Another was of a World War I cenotaph. There was also a copy of "In Flanders Fields," but I could barely make out the words of the poem. The photocopies were the promoter's doing. The event was billed as some sort of tribute to the armed forces, a way of commemorating the fallen dead. From what I could tell, the photocopies were the only sign of that tribute and no one but me had noticed them.

The arena started to fill up. Guys in hockey jerseys and Carhartt work pants. Young couples on dates. Families with kids. Some of the kids were freaking out because they had spotted Nate Diaz and "Big" John McCarthy in the octagon, taking pictures with some of that night's fighters. In this crowd, Diaz and McCarthy were stars of startling magnitude. The promotor had flown them in to give the whole thing an aura of the Big Time, and both men would probably be making off with cheques a full order of magnitude bigger than anything Adam would be taking home. Nate Diaz is one of the bad boys of the UFC. He got his break starring on the TV series *The Ultimate Fighter*. The night of Adam's fight, Diaz was ranked the number-five lightweight fighter in the world. He has a reputation for having a temper, for taking his bouts personally, for getting heated and emotional. Tonight, he just looked bored.

I took photos of Nelson and Adam with Diaz. It was the first time I had seen Adam smile all week. Diaz stared vacantly at the camera with raised fists and hooded eyes. It was the look of someone doing something purely for the money. "Big" John McCarthy was putting his heart into it, though. He was glad-handing like a local politician up for re-election. McCarthy is one of the original UFC referees and sort of an unofficial mascot. At six-four and 270 pounds, he's more physically imposing than most of the fighters he presides over. He officiated the very first UFC event, the one Adam watched as a kid. I took shots of Adam and Nelson holding up their fists next to him. They looked like children at Disneyland getting their photo taken with Mickey.

We'd had to take off our shoes before stepping in the ring to keep the mat pristine. It felt like moss beneath my socks, soft and spongy. I wondered how it would do at sopping up blood.

There were five fighters and their men getting ready in our change room. The opponents and their crews were in the other change room, including Adam's guy, Kyle, whom I hadn't seen yet. Nate Diaz was hanging out with our group, sitting on a bench staring at his phone, studiously not paying any attention to the fighters. There were no lockers, so gear was scattered across the floor as though a tsunami had recently receded. There was a single open shower at the far end of the room and, next to it, a small washroom that reeked of piss and cheap industrial cleaner.

There were several cases of bottled water stacked in the corner—the only thing the fighters were allowed to drink. This was supposedly to prevent them from surreptitiously downing amphetamines or painkillers before the fight, though the more serious doping happens well before a match. There were a couple of guys in the change room I suspected were on juice—men with narrow waists and wrists and incongruously thick shoulders and backs. Anabolic steroids, of course, increase muscle mass and strength. More importantly, in the context of fighting, they speed recovery, meaning you can train two or three times a day without the same risk of burnout.

"Fighting is a steroid sport," Adam told me during one of his training sessions. "Honestly, I sort of thought about it at one point, but I decided instead to go with fitness, to see where I could get on my own."

—

EVEN WITHOUT USING synthetic steroids, men sort of come pre-doped. Testosterone, the male sex hormone, is a naturally occurring steroid. And one of the fundamental differences between men and women is the amount of the hormone they produce. Men, on average, make about twenty times more of the stuff than women[7], the majority of which is produced by Leydig cells in the testicles. Men metabolize far more testosterone than women too, meaning that their cells use it to perform specific functions. Among these, it's the hormone responsible for the development of secondary sex traits during puberty: body hair, a deeper voice, increased muscle mass and bone density, decreased body fat, and the thickening of the bones of the brow and jaw. There's a reason that transgender men take testosterone in order to pass.

More fundamentally, testosterone masculinizes a male fetus during development. Without high-enough levels of the hormone during gestation, a genetic male cannot develop a male body.

Periodically, this happens. People with a condition called androgen insensitivity syndrome develop as genetic males with an X and Y chromosome. But they have a mutant version of an androgen receptor, which essentially renders all the cells in their body immune to the effects of testosterone. And so, despite having the hormone circulating through their body, it's as if they are completely devoid of testosterone. As a result, they develop female bodies. In fact, they often look like supermodels: they tend to be tall and slender, with a cinched waist and large breasts; they have lush hair, dewy, hairless skin and symmetrical, prototypically feminine facial features. Other than a genetic test, there's no way to tell that someone with androgen insensitivity is not a genetic female. In fact, a diagnosis of androgen insensitivity usually is a shock to the woman herself; it often comes after she sees a doctor sometime in adolescence because she's failed to get a period. Menstruation is impossible for women who are androgen insensitive because, while their external genitalia are all standard issue, their entire reproductive tract—the uterus, fallopian tubes and ovaries—is absent. In its place is a pair of undescended and sexually immature testicles, busily pumping out the biological signal for masculinity to which the rest of the body is deaf and blind.

This is the power of testosterone—or of its absence. Testosterone levels are the primary source of sexual dimorphism in humans, the fundamental physiological difference between the female body and the male. And because the brain is part of the body, it shouldn't come as a surprise that testosterone also has a profound effect on the way we think and feel.

While I was in the early phase of researching this book, I met a guy I'll call Mike who had worked for a man who had accidentally killed another man in a street fight. (Since his client is fairly well-known, Mike asked me not to use either of their names.) I was trying to chase down the man who had done the killing, and I explained to Mike that I wanted to write something about testosterone and alpha males and aggression.

The man wasn't game, but Mike ended up telling me a story about himself. He said that a few years earlier he had suddenly started feeling like shit: no energy, no sex drive, no interest in his considerably success-ful business. No vim, vigour or self-confidence. He told me this over drinks at his private club, the kind of place where the country's business elite mingle in expensive suits.

These were profound and sudden changes—and entirely uncharacter-istic for Mike, especially the lack of interest in work. One of the primary driving forces in his life is to be the very best at what he does for a living. Figuring he was clinically depressed, he saw a doctor, who diagnosed him, instead, with low testosterone. Mike was then in his early fifties, but he had the testosterone levels of a man in his eighties. He didn't go into detail about the cause of his hormone depletion but testosterone can spontaneously bottom out as the result of an acute illness or, in some cases, obesity. The doctor prescribed biweekly injections of testosterone to bring Mike's levels back up to normal. The effect was immediate. Mike sprang back to life, full force—greater than full force, actually. It took a while to get the dose right, and at first he was getting more testosterone than he was used to.

Mike is a measured and articulate man. He is not at all macho or physically alpha. But when he started getting testosterone injections, he found the first few days after a dose pretty wild. He was perpetually horny and perpetually impatient. He'd have fits of road rage—no fights, but plenty of swearing and gesticulating from his car. A couple of times, he caught himself yelling at his employees.

"That was extremely unusual," he told me, shaking his head. "I'm not a yeller at all. I feel terrible about that."

I asked Mike if he planned eventually to ween himself off testosterone as he got older. He is in an unusual situation: testosterone naturally declines with age, but he has the option of keeping his levels artificially high. He hadn't thought of the possibility of going off it until I asked him.

"It's a funny thing," he said. "Testosterone makes me feel edgy. You think about sex all the time. You're competitive. You're driven. You want to win, to be the best. That's not always pleasant. It's tense. Manhood is like that—it's sort of an uncomfortable space. And here I am with the key to take away that discomfort. But that sense of tension is *exactly* what I was missing when my testosterone bottomed out. It's part of what I need to be me. I think I'd miss it too much to ever give it up."

For a long time, I assumed my own fights, my temper, my obsession with being a decent fighter, had something to do with testosterone. After all, I only started feeling and acting aggressive at the end of puberty. A man's testosterone starts to peak and stays high throughout his youth. It's at its highest from about fifteen until about thirty, at which point it slowly tapers off. This mirrors the pattern of male aggression: highest in early adulthood, dropping off after thirty, and continuing to decline throughout adulthood.

If you give animals—mice, birds, monkeys—injections of testosterone, they become aggressive and violent. Castrate them—removing the primary source of testosterone—and they become docile.

Some studies have shown that men with more symmetrical physical features—markers of having been exposed to higher levels of testosterone during fetal development—tend to be more aggressive than men with asymmetrical features. And violent male prisoners tend to have higher levels of testosterone than non-violent criminals. Sometimes castration—usually chemical castration, the administration of androgen-blocking drugs—is used to reduce aggression in humans, most often violent sexual predators.

But still, the relationship between testosterone and violence is a whole lot more complex in humans than it is in other animals. Mike was getting walloping doses of the stuff. It made him edgy and impatient, but it didn't turn him into a fighter. Nor do transsexual men taking high doses of testosterone turn into thugs.

A few lab studies show that injecting men with the hormone can make them more aggressive, but the majority of studies contradict these findings. Even so-called 'roid rage—the notion that steroids can cause psychotic and violent anger—isn't so clear-cut. The common belief that steroids can make a man do nasty, shitty things may not be accurate. There's some evidence it works the other way around, that steroids make a man big and that he's more prone to acting violent *because* he's big (and knows it).[8]

People differ, too, in the amount of testosterone in their system. Men almost always have far more than women, but, within the sexes, both men and women can have inherently higher or lower levels. This is part of the natural variation among humans. People at the high end of the spectrum—men *and* women—tend to share particular behavioural and emotional traits. They tend to be fairly alpha, and motivated to maintain a high social status. If they lose that status, it feels especially bad to them. They become distracted, depressed and intent on regaining their former status. This differs from people with low testosterone, who tend to find *gaining* a high-status position stressful.[9] In short, people with naturally higher levels of testosterone tend to strive for social dominance. That said, there's not a lot of evidence that men with higher testosterone levels are any more violent than men with lower levels.

The most important thing to understand about the relationship between testosterone and violence in humans is that context, while not everything, has a lot to do with it.

Whether you naturally have higher or lower levels of testosterone, the amount you're producing at any given moment changes in accordance with what's going on around you and with what's going on in your head. Testosterone levels are naturally highest in the morning and lowest at night. The hormone spikes in a heterosexual man when he's around an attractive woman—and presumably in a gay man when he's around an attractive guy. It goes up when he has sex—but not if he masturbates. It drops significantly and for a long time when he becomes a father and is in the presence of kids. It rises before a contest or athletic competition, even if that competition is staid and civil—a chess match, a game of tennis. It definitely goes up before a competitive fight. It stays elevated if you win that competition and plummets if you don't. Strangely, it can rise or drop even if you're only competing vicariously. Male soccer fans, for instance, show a corresponding rise or drop in their testosterone depending on whether their team wins or loses. Testosterone rises if you gain social status and drops if you lose it. Eerily, a man's testosterone will rise significantly after he handles a gun. And if a man feels threatened or seems to be headed towards an altercation, it will spike and stay high if he wins that conflict and bottom out if he doesn't.

The big picture is this: aside from testosterone's role in shaping the male body, the hormone works as a biochemical signal within that body, transmitting important information about the environment. The information that testosterone concerns itself with has to do with sex, social status and threats—especially threats *to* social status. And the big picture gets even bigger: how testosterone responds to what's going on around you depends on the broadest possible context, the mores and values of the social milieu in which you live.

The American social psychologists Richard Nisbett and Dov Cohen have studied the relationship between testosterone and the environment among university undergrads. They found that when young American men from the southern states were physically provoked (for the purposes of the experiment, they were shoved), their testosterone shot up higher than it did in men from northern states in the same situation. Southern men also got angrier than northern men and were more willing to fight. Incidentally, this was true only of white subjects.

These are especially intriguing findings given that the southern and western United States have higher rates of homicide than the rest of the country—especially homicides that start as trivial arguments and then blow up into more serious fights. Violence is a more accepted part of southern and western American culture, especially as a retaliation against insults and in situations of perceived self-defence. Southern and western Americans tend to watch more violence on TV. They are more likely to subscribe to magazines such as *Guns & Ammo*, in which violence is normalized.[10]

Social milieus like this, which Nisbett and Cohen call "cultures of honour," are not exclusive to the United States. They're common across the world and throughout history—think ancient Tenochtitlán or modern-day Afghanistan. These are societies in which it's not only acceptable but expected for a man to stand up for himself, to defend himself, his friends, his family and his reputation—where being a man is tantamount to being capable of doing this.

The liberal, humanist democracy of cosmopolitan eastern Canada— the milieu in which I was raised—is not, by any stretch of the imagination, a culture of honour. But that's maybe the most interesting thing about it. Cultures are not perfectly homogeneous; they're made up of subcultures. I'd argue you'd have trouble finding a single society on Earth in which this kind of male culture is entirely absent. In Canada, you find it in hockey culture, police culture, street culture, military culture, prison culture, to name just a few examples. Wherever you have concentrations of men—especially younger men—you'll tend to find some strain of it. And so, even if you weren't raised in the deep South or northwest Pakistan, even though you may not buy into it—at least not fully—and may, in fact, find it largely repulsive and claustrophobia-inducing, a part of you may still be attracted to it.

And you may find that part of yourself actively seeking it out and looking to join in.

About six months before I began writing this book, when I was still working as a radio producer, a job that was essentially secure and comfy in a milieu in which I was surrounded by friendly and urbane colleagues, I started to feel a familiar anxiety stretching its limbs again after a long slumber—that sense that I had grown complacent and was no longer capable of taking care of myself in a fight.

There was a Brazilian jiu-jitsu gym down the street from my apartment. I joined. The first couple of months were tough. I got dizzy during the initial warm-ups and had to stop. Whenever I rolled over in bed, I woke up in pain. But that other part of me, the part I had tried to shut down when I dropped out of martial arts, came to life again. And it was happy. Sitting on the mats, breathless, in pain, drenched in sweat, focusing all my attention on the physical challenge of not getting crushed or choked or arm-locked, it all felt like opening up a room that had been shuttered for years. I felt the light and air inside me. I felt calmer and freer, more myself. I bought books on jiu-jitsu and watched instructional videos and UFC fights. I kept a notebook of the techniques I learned. I started thinking about how to apply them to random guys when I walked down the street.

I had my eyes open for this—my tendency to become monomaniacal about training. I didn't want to asphyxiate some part of myself. I wanted to learn to be both versions of me at once. So when the obsessive fight fantasies started up again, I consciously limited myself to training twice a week. I put the jiu-jitsu books back on the shelf. I reminded myself that it was only a hobby.

This worked for a while. Then I started hanging out with Adam and Nelson, going to their Sunday sessions, watching them spar. It was like watching someone beautiful smoke a cigarette or sip expensive Scotch— the crackle of tobacco as the flame touches the tip, the clink of ice against heavy crystal. It makes you crave again what you thought you had given up for good. I was nowhere near their level. But still, I secretly wanted them to ask me to join them.

—

THE ARENA WAS STILL filling up. Nobody knew exactly when the fights were going to start, which meant no one knew when to start warming up their fighters. Adam had already changed into his shorts and T-shirt and was sitting on the bench, jiggling his legs up and down, staring straight ahead. Nelson and the other guys were milling around, trying to get some intel on the schedule. I took a walk. There was a concession stand around the corner from the change room. A glut of spectators had gathered to buy nachos and hot dogs. The thought of them stuffing their faces while they watched the fights made me despise them. More than that, the whole thing made me sad—the bus-station feel of the arena, the piss smell of the change room, the anemic commemorative photocopies, the hungry crowd.

I think a lot of fighters are aware at some level that the grand events of their short careers will be limited to backwater spectacles like this, the work of some second-rate promotor—fighting in front of the hungry citizens of an unspectacular whistle-stop town.

"It sounds weird," Adam had told me during one of his Sunday sparring sessions, "but I had some slight depression before the fight." He meant his first professional match. "It was like, it's finally here, everything you've been working towards, and you're like, 'This is it?'"

Adam also told me that one of his closest friends, an experienced pro, had confided in him that he had cried before a couple of his fights. It wasn't fear or anxiety. It was, for a fleeting moment, sitting on the edge of a hotel bed, the conviction that all of it—the training, the fighting, the winning—was utterly pointless.

"Take your body to the edge and see if it flies." That's what John Updike wrote in "The Disposable Rocket," his essay on what it's like to inhabit a male body. "Men," he argued, "put their bodies at risk to experience the release from gravity."

Fighting has always been one of the riskiest things you can do with your body. And winning a fight takes you there, to the very edge of space, to that place where you are very nearly weightless. To the edge of a vast and endless void.

When I returned to the change room, a commissioner in a navy blazer and brass buttons was reading the fighters' names over the top of his glasses. He had a severe comb-over. Adam and his man Kyle were second on the card, right after the heavyweight fight.

One of the heavyweights was on the bench next to Adam, a massive red-haired guy in his mid-twenties. His coach dragged over a chair. The heavyweight got up and straddled it, cowboy-style. He hung his hands over the back of the chair. His love handles hung themselves over the waistband of his shorts. The coach began the process of wrapping the big man's hands—first in gauze, slowly and methodically, as if he was preparing china for shipping, then taping them until they were as hard and immobile as the hands of a marble statue. The commissioner took the heavyweight's hands in his, turned them over, appraised them and, when he was satisfied, signed each of them with a Sharpie.

Horace, Adam's boxing coach, had been watching this with me. He leaned over and told me fighters sometimes try to run their hands under a faucet before the fight. "That way, when it dries," he said, punching his own hand, "it's like plaster of Paris."

The heavyweight lumbered towards the toilet. The commissioner followed him and made sure the door stayed open a crack. The big man's piss hit the water and echoed off the tiles. The commissioner leaned against the doorjamb like a bored prison guard. The heavyweight trudged out into the hall to warm up. I could hear the torpid propeller spin of his plastic skipping rope and the click-clack each revolution made against the concrete floor. It sounded like a giant, clawed creature slowly pacing back and forth in tight quarters.

Andrew started wrapping Adam's hands. The commissioner stood over them, reading the rules of engagement from a clipboard.

"Elbows to the face are fine," he said. "No blows to the back of the head. No blows to the neck or spine. No strikes to the groin. Any questions?"

Adam shook his head.

"Who do you want talking to you?" Nelson asked him. During a fight it's hard to make out discrete sounds over the sound of your own breathing, over the blood in your ears, the roar of the crowd, the punches raining down on your head. It's best to have a single desig-nated voice calling commands.

"Andrew," Adam said.

"Do you want the water in your hand between rounds?" Nelson asked. "Or do you want us to feed it to you?"

"Feed it to me."

The commissioner signed Adam's hands and gave Nelson an unwrapped pair of gloves. They were flat and stiff, like fingerless driving gloves, only puffier. Adam couldn't get them on over the mound of tape encasing his hands. I put on the gloves and splayed my fingers wide a few times. I made tight fists. The leather creaked. Nelson held up a pair of focus mitts. I threw a few punches to loosen up the leather. Nelson helped Adam pull the gloves on. I could still feel the reverberation of each blow in my wrists and forearms.

We went out into the hallway towards the warm-up area. The heavyweight was still skipping. He was slightly knock-kneed. He stepped over each pass of the rope with the slow precision of an ungulate avoiding a line of electrified fence. In that moment, I was convinced I could take him, that I could step into the cage that night and come out the winner. I was in better shape, a few inches taller, a little heavier, carrying less fat, quicker and more coordinated. I felt a surge of anticipation and optimism run through me. I pictured the blows I'd give him, quick strikes to the face, kicks to the legs.

Writing this now, I'm embarrassed to admit it—not because of the fantasy, but because of my own self-delusion. I've looked the guy up since. I've watched a couple of his fights. He's no Olympian, but he's tough and strong as hell—tougher and stronger than me, I'd guess. More to the point: he had done this before. If I had gone against him that night, I think he probably would have got me up against the fence, dragged me down, crushed me under his weight and then turned my face to hamburger. It would have been like fighting an upholstered Mack truck, slow and soft but unstoppable. What's more embarrassing—and telling, I think—is that even while admitting to this, I feel compelled to add a caveat: that I still think I *could* beat him, *if* I trained properly for it. And even thinking about that distant and abstract hypothetical makes me sort of want to do it. Just for kicks. Just to prove it to myself.

Testosterone's role in human aggression isn't entirely clear, but its role in the kind of self-delusion that drives this kind of risk-taking is.

Giving people high doses of testosterone lowers their startle response to, say, the threat of an electrical shock. Animal studies show the same thing. Richard Ronay, an Australian psychologist, found that when male skateboarders are pulling tricks near a good-looking woman, their testosterone shoots up. They also try to pull off higher-risk stunts—and the skaters with naturally higher levels of testosterone take the biggest risks. They also get the biggest payoff: they look badass in front of that woman when they land a killer trick. Several other studies suggest that testosterone makes us less sensitive to punishment and more sensitive to reward. Young men with high levels of testosterone tend to worry less when given a serious medical diagnosis than men with lower testosterone levels[11]—which may explain why men so often avoid seeing a doctor, even when it's clear there's something seriously wrong.

Testosterone distorts our perception of risk. It makes us overconfident of our own physical abilities. It is, in addition to being the chemical substrate involved in social dominance, a sort of natural anaesthetic against fear. And men, especially young men, are coursing with it.

The warm-up area was sad: a couple of old blue gym mats laid out on the concrete, surrounded by blackout curtains for privacy.

Adam was standing on the mats. Nelson was kneeling in front of him, massaging his thighs. The commissioner popped his head through the curtains. "Boys," he said over his glasses, "the card starts in three minutes. Warm your man up."

Adam and Luigi, Adam's wrestling coach, ran through a series of takedowns. Adam dropped to one knee, lunged at Luigi's leg, picked it up, drove his head into Luigi's abdomen and dumped him over onto the mats, all in one quick, fluid motion.

Horace stepped in with the focus mitts and took Adam through a series of combos. Adam's hands in the light little gloves made a clean snap each time they struck, like someone tap dancing on bubble wrap.

Adam was breathing slow and easy. There was a light film of sweat on the back of his neck. He rolled his head around as if he were working sand out of the joints.

A wall of sound flooded the hallway and hit us like a storm surge. The announcer was inside, pumping up the crowd. The echo off the concrete was overwhelming. The announcer's "Are you ready?" washed over us, muddy and distorted: "AAAAOUUUUUUEEEEAAAAAADY?" The crowd roared back.

Nelson stepped onto the mats and, without warning, unleashed quick, wide hooks. Adam slipped under them perfectly, effortlessly. Nelson swung again. Adam ducked and sprang up in front of Nelson's face like a Whac-A-Mole and snapped his elbow at the bridge of Nelson's nose, pulling back at the last second. Nelson swung again. Adam ducked, side-stepped, lunged at Nelson, locked his arms around him and slid to the ground, twisting Nelson's neck so he had no choice but to follow him to the ground. Adam worked his arm tight around Nelson's neck and squeezed. Nelson went bright red and tapped the mat loudly. Adam stood and gave Nelson a hand up. Nelson was nodding.

"I like that," he said. "That's what you do in there, okay?"

The noise inside the arena receded and then a new swell of sound hit us, more intense than before. The heavyweight match was under way. We had no idea what was going on in the cage. We could only listen. The fight might last all three rounds—fifteen minutes—or it could be over in seconds.

Adam was punching himself in the face gently, as if he was trying to determine whether this was all a dream.

"You're hard," Andrew said. "You're smart."

Adam nodded.

"Just watch out for power," Nelson said. "Don't be shocked by him being aggressive. Don't be shocked by him clipping you. You're faster than him. You're better than him."

There was an enormous din from inside the arena. The bell rang three times. Albert and I ran down the hall to see what was happening. The crowd was on its feet. The red-headed heavy was sitting on the floor of the octagon, slumped against the cage, his skin pushing through the chain link like rising dough. His opponent, a sturdy black guy with love handles of his own, was doing a victory lap, arms over his head.

Albert and I ran back to the warm-up area and ducked through the curtains.

"It's done," I said. "It's over."

"So, we're up," Adam said. His voice was flat, resigned.

Nelson heard the tone. He still had gloves on. He swatted Adam lightly to break up whatever dark thoughts were beginning to swarm and forced him to do some light boxing for a few seconds.

"We're all here," Nelson said, "just like last time."

A series of apelike grunts came from the other side of the curtains. Adam cocked his head like a deer.

Andrew went over to the curtains and looked out into the hall. He rolled his eyes. "It's your guy," he told Adam. "He's being a retard."

Nelson shook his head. "All that is is aggression," he said. "He's just making noise."

"It's nothing," Adam said. "It doesn't do anything."

The commissioner pulled the curtains open and escorted us down the hall into a backstage holding area of the arena. A giant Teenage Mutant Ninja Turtle mascot walked by, waving at us.

"You serious?" said Horace, shaking his head. "For real?"

The air around us was swelling and contracting with the noise of the crowd.

"Talk to me, guys," Adam shouted over the din. "Talk to me when I'm in there."

Andrew stood square in front of Adam. He leaned in forehead to forehead and said, "He's going to pay every time he doesn't hit you."

Horace said, "It's hunting time."

"It's surgical," said Nelson. "Use your elbows. Use your knees. He's an idiot. You're going to run through him."

The commissioner led us up a short flight of stairs. We passed through two sets of enormous black curtains. For a moment everything was pitch-black. Then we were standing on a platform looking down into the arena. The octagon was spotlit in the distance, floating on a cloud of dry ice. Overhead, there was a video of Adam on the giant overhead screen. His mouth was moving. He was explaining something to the camera, but I couldn't hear what he was saying over the noise, just the *whah-whah-whah* of an adult in a Charlie Brown special. The entire place was vibrating. Adam was vibrating. I was vibrating.

We walked down the stairs and up one of the aisles towards the cage like moths drawn to a giant, incandescent lantern. The spectators were watching Adam from the dark, but we couldn't make out their faces. We walked into the fog of dry ice. Adam took off his hoodie. He stood in front of the crowd in shorts and a pair of flip-flops. Nelson smeared Vaseline on his forehead and cheeks. A referee came over and checked Adam's gloves and peered in his mouth the way a vet checks out livestock. Then the commissioner escorted Adam up the steps and suddenly he seemed very far away from us, elevated, awash in white light, on the other side of the chain-link fence.

A different commissioner brought Kyle into the cage. He was bulkier than Adam, with a more powerful build, but significantly shorter, just a touch over five feet. Adam was bouncing on his toes. Kyle was standing flat-footed on the far side of the cage, shifting his weight ever so slightly from one foot to the other, hands by his side.

Two ring girls began slow, counter-opposing circuits along the outer ledge of the octagon, carrying signs overhead that read: ROUND 1. They both wore tight, high-waisted white satin shorts and painted-on black T-shirts that exposed their stomachs. One looked bored. The other seemed angry.

The two commissioners walked out of the ring.

The ring girls finished their sullen circuit.

The announcer introduced the fighters. The crowd was yelling and hooting and cheering and booing simultaneously.

The announcer left the ring.

The cage door was shut and latched.

The referee stood in the middle of the octagon. Adam and Kyle were in their respective corners.

Nelson yelled, "Hands up."

Adam raised his fists mechanically.

Kyle stood in his corner. His hands were still by his side. From where I was standing, with Albert in front of the ringside seats, he looked like an overgrown child.

There was a pause. The crowd noise died down. Albert was recording the whole scene with his iPad so Adam could watch his performance afterwards.

The ref yelled into the mic: "ARRREEE YOOOOUUUU REAAAAADYYYYYY?"

The crowd erupted. Then there was a pause that felt like the string of a bow being drawn back, pulled tight and held there.

"FIGHT!" yelled the ref.

The bell rang. The arrow flew.

It lasted a minute and forty-six seconds.

Adam comes out of his corner and hovers in front of Kyle, who charges in with his fists up. He tries to kick Adam's thigh, but Adam glides away. Kyle tries another kick to the leg and Adam uses the opportunity to lunge in with a punch—a straight right—but Kyle backs away and the punch barely touches him. Adam follows Kyle then shoots in low and closes his arms around Kyle's waist and drives him into the fence and pulls him down to the ground. Kyle is now sitting on the mat with his legs straight in front of him. Adam is lying on top of Kyle's legs with his arms wrapped around his torso.

Albert yells out, "Yes, Adam! YES!"

From this sitting position, Kyle is more or less immobile. He can move only his arms. He pounds on Adam's back with his elbows. His elbows do nothing. Adam continues to work his way up Kyle's body, forcing Kyle into missionary position. It's like watching an anaconda subdue a deer. Kyle is now flat on his back. Adam straddles him and sits on his chest. Kyle tries to buck Adam off, but Adam grabs one of Kyle's arms and suddenly he has the arm between his knees and he's cranking it, forcing it the wrong way in the joint the way you do when you want to take apart a chicken wing and get at the last remnants of meat.

Albert is yelling: "Nice! NICE!"

The referee stops the fight.

Albert and I are both screaming, "YES! YES! ADAM!"

Adam does a victory lap around the cage. He walks over to where Kyle is now standing and gives him a hug. Kyle's arms are by his side again.

I saw the heavyweight alone in the hall, leaning against a wall, talking quietly on his cellphone. His eyes were red and bleary. He looked as though he had been crying, though it was probably from being knocked around in the cage. In that moment I felt even more certain I could beat him. Maybe it was the spike of testosterone you get from a vicarious win, but I felt the way I had as a boy, taking my turn pulling on Allan's sock foot. I had no reason at all to feel superior to him. But I did.

It's fair to think of testosterone as a biological substrate of social competition. It spikes, as I've mentioned, in situations in which someone challenges our status. It provides us with the conviction and confidence (and, often, the *over*confidence) to face the potential risk of that challenge—the public disgrace, the loss of wealth, injury. Death. If we come out on top, our testosterone stays high and provides us with a subjective sense of power and fulfillment, which spurs us to attain ever higher status. When we lose, it drops. We feel dumpy and terrible about ourselves. As shitty as this is, the reaction serves us well, signalling us to back down and hold off. To hole up, lick our wounds and maybe try again later, when circumstances are in our favour and the risk is not as high.

A weird thing happens after some fights, and it happened between Adam and Kyle. They were talking to one another like old friends. Kyle thanked Adam for the fight and Adam thanked him back. They called one another "bro." They bitched about the pains of cutting weight like old school chums. They hugged several times. There was no longer any tension between them. It had all dissipated.

I had experienced this before, in junior high. A few weeks after the big beefy kid punched me in the gut, he invited me to his thirteenth-birthday party. I went. We had a good time. There were maybe six of us. We played basketball. We ate cake and chips and watched VHS movies. I don't remember being worried about him beating me up again. What had happened behind the portables was a done deal. We knew where we stood. He knew I wasn't ever going to hit on the girl he liked. I knew he could pound me. The equation had been solved, so there was no point going back over the math. And there was no reason—within the constraints of this new understanding—not to continue along amicably.

Adam asked Kyle if his arm was good.

Kyle nodded and complimented Adam on his jiu-jitsu and asked where he was training.

Adam told him.

Nelson overheard this and said, "You should come by and train with us sometime." It was a genuine offer.

"Maybe I'll do that," Kyle said. He seemed to be genuinely consider-ing it.

I was watching all this with Horace, both of us leaning against the wall. I was taking notes. Kyle was the shortest guy in the crowd, strain-ing his neck like he was trying to keep his head above water. Horace and I had been speculating whether Kyle had it in him to fight again. This was his fifth consecutive loss.

Visit any fight gym. You'll find old fighters there—men my age, Nelson's age—guys who have been there for a couple of decades and are still convinced they can make a go of it, launch a pro career, become something. They just need one more fight, one more opportu-nity, and they'll finally break free of gravity once and for all. This yearn-ing is why old pros get back into the ring well after their prime.

Fighting is a kind of flight, a ride, sure. The problem is, the rocket goes up but then comes straight back down; it takes you to great heights without necessarily transporting you anywhere meaningful.

For some reason, I glanced down at Kyle's feet that night, while he stood there with Adam, Nelson and the other guys. He was standing, ever so slightly, on his tiptoes, trying to measure up to the other men.

As I write this now, three years later, Kyle has had three more pro fights. He's lost all three.

After Adam's fight, I started training more. It crept up on me gradually. Three, then four times a week. Nelson and I practised together. Fighting with him was like grappling with a human bear trap. Then our gym suddenly shut down. The owner turned out to be a member of a biker gang and, because he wasn't a citizen, he was deported. Nelson and I joined another gym together. We trained most days at noon. We spent hours on the mats, learning technique, practising, con-ditioning, fighting. Sometimes, on Saturdays, I'd put on gloves and do a few rounds of kick-boxing with him and the other guys there. I was sloppy, but I held my own. I was still nowhere near the level of a pro, but I was strong again and fast. And I felt like myself—at least closer to that version of myself that feels comfortable in his own body.

Often, I'd still be on the mats mid-afternoon on a weekday. Part of me felt it was where I belonged. Beneath that, the other part felt the way you do when you dream of having to write an exam for a course you don't remember enrolling in: I was guilty of some dangerous form of self-neglect. I had quit my job and was writing full-time, so I had a flexible schedule. Part of me wondered whether I was in the gym because I was writing a book on violence or whether I was writing a book on violence so I could be in the gym.

Adam's mother, Susan, ran a restaurant with her husband in the north end of Toronto. They got a lot of repeat customers, retirees from the nearby apartment buildings and assisted-living facilities who appreciated the cloth napkins and tablecloths. The food was good and abundant.

When Adam wasn't cutting weight, Susan had her cooks prepare comical quantities of food for him and his crew: linguine with scallops; spinach salad with sliced mango and goat cheese; sautéed eggplant and roasted peppers; a monstrous chocolate cake that she baked herself.

We were sitting together in the restaurant one evening a couple of weeks after the fight—me, Nelson, Adam, Adam's girlfriend, a tall, shy woman with dark, bolt-straight hair, and several of Adam's training partners, men with thick necks and cauliflower ears. Adam and his buddies were talking shop. Susan, a convivial and energetic woman in her early fifties, was running back and forth between the table, where she was trying to hang out with us, and the kitchen, where she was overseeing her staff.

She came back and sat down between me and Nelson.

"We have a very close relationship," Susan told me. She meant her and Adam. She had moved to Toronto from Shiraz, Iran, when she was younger, and a Persian accent still inflects her English. She had Adam when she was in her early twenties. "The first time Adam experimented with ganja," she said, "he told me and I cried." She threw her hands in the air. "I put him in private school to protect him from all that."

"What about sex?" Nelson asked. "Does he tell you about that?"

Susan nodded. "He told me after his first time."

From the far end of the table, one of Adam's friends fired the inevitable shot, "Last year, right?"

Nelson laughed. Adam shook his head.

"What do you think about him fighting?" Albert asked Susan.

"I feel bad for the other guy," she said. "I don't want anything to happen to him."

Nelson laughed and said to Adam, "You should get your mom to corner your fights. Whatever she tells you, just do the opposite."

"I would tell him to leave my son alone!" Susan cried in mock distress. Then she turned to me and said, "Don't ever have children."

"Why?"

"Because they'll break your heart." Susan turned to Adam and said, into a natural lull in the conversation, "Everything is good in your life except this." She turned to the entire table: "If he gives it up, I'll jump into the sky. I'll fly! I just don't understand it."

"When you were in the kitchen," Adam tried explaining, "I was saying how, when you hug your teammates and they lock the cage behind you and ask you if you're ready, it's a great feeling. It's like being at the top of the roller coaster—"

"Adam?" Susan interrupted.

"Yeah, Mom?"

"I have to drag you to a psychologist." We all laughed. Susan was smiling too, but then she got serious. "It's not just the beatings, Adam. It's the way you cut weight. You dehydrate every cell in your body."

Andrew, who up to then had been quiet, said to Susan, "It makes you a stronger person. You know what you're made of."

Susan ignored him. "Adam," she continued, "why don't you get your master's degree in education?"

"Mom," he said, "I don't want to be a principal." It was clear it wasn't their first run at this conversation.

Susan turned to me and asked, "What do you think of all this? You're a writer. You use your head. You must think it's crazy too."

That night, I drove Nelson home from Susan's restaurant. He was getting out of the car in front of his building when he sat back down in the passenger seat.

"The funny thing is," he said, "she's right. I actually agree with Adam's mom. The whole thing seems silly. We're going to agree to fight in a cage with little gloves? It's weird. Maybe I'm saying this because I'm older and ready to take the next spiritual step. Maybe it's because

I'm artistically inclined. But it just seems we could all be doing something more productive."

If you only heard the stories about Nelson and the bar fights, the cage matches, you'd miss the fact that he has—at least he did on the day I first interviewed him—the remnants of nail polish on both thumbs from where his three-year-old goddaughter painted his nails. You'd miss out on the screen shot of the two of them talking over Skype, both of them wearing Day-Glo plastic sunglasses. You'd miss the fact that he comes from a stable, loving family that gets together on Sundays for dinner; that he has no shame at all telling his father he loves him if the two of them are talking over the phone in public; that he makes fun of guys who are homophobic even if, on occasion, he himself might call you a fag; that he regularly and unselfconsciously also tells his guy friends he loves them.

You'd miss the fact that when the temperature plummets, he buys gloves and toques, granola bars and toothbrushes, and bikes around his neighbourhood handing out homemade winter survival kits to homeless people.

You'd miss out on the fact that he sings in public—that he sings extremely well—belting out Motown tunes and blues and old TV theme songs when he's browsing the aisles of a health food store, and that this makes other customers smile and, on occasion, join in. Or the fact that, while in the health food store, he tells a stranger how buying Tom's of Maine toothpaste isn't actually the best choice because it's now owned by Colgate-Palmolive, which has a questionable track record on environmental issues. You'd miss out on the fact that he doesn't consume animal products, that he is somewhere on the vegetarian-vegan continuum because why harm animals if you don't have to? And that this ethos is the result of his daily meditation practice. That for the past couple of years he has headed north of the city for an annual ten-day meditation retreat.

"It's not about mysticism or anything," he's careful to point out—he is categorically anti-religion and pro-science. "It's purely a technique." The purpose of that technique, he'll explain, is to cultivate peace and harmony through the development of self-awareness. When I asked him what prompted him to start meditating, he said, "I want to be more in control. I want to evolve. I don't want to be washed up, the fighter guy, the doorman. I want to be more essence of me."

And when I asked him about the obvious conflict between peace and harmony and, you know, surfing a guy down the stairs, he said, "Yeah, I have trouble with that too. When I was at the retreat last year, I asked one of the instructors about that. They said it was okay as long as I do it compassionately."

"What does that mean?" I asked.

"Basically, I'm still trying to figure that out."

One night a few years ago, after he had given up on being a professional fighter, an old musician friend of his ran into him in front of one of the clubs. He invited Nelson to jam. They started playing shows together. Eventually Nelson started booking solo shows at bars around the city. And songs started pouring out of him.

Nelson lives in a two-bedroom rented apartment. He used to live there with his wife until they split up. He now shares it with a buddy. There's a heavy bag hanging on the concrete balcony and a chin-up bar installed in the kitchen door frame. The first time I visited him, there was a whiteboard on the fridge on which Nelson had written a version of Edmund Burke's famous quotation: "All it takes for evil to appear in the world is for good people to do nothing." And also: "Conceive. Believe. Achieve."

His bed was sequestered behind a curtain in his room. He had transformed the rest of the space into a recording studio. There was a bay of left-handed guitars, a mic stand, a computer and a digital mixing board.

"At the meditation retreat last year," he told me, "I wrote this long list of all these things I wanted to accomplish." At the top of the list was devoting more time to songwriting. "It's what makes me the happiest," he said. "Fighting makes me happy, but it's a different beast—it's not derived *from* happiness. I don't give a fuck how spiritual a martial artist you are, it's designed to hurt another human being. You can dress it however you want—it's not made for peace and love. I think the pro fighting was a darker period in my life. And music brought me back out of that. But I had to go through it. The sun needs to go away and the moon has to come out in order to appreciate the sun."

There was a thick spiral-bound notebook on his desk. Inside were hundreds of song ideas, verses, choruses, fragments he had written down over the past year. He had worked several into rough tracks in his studio. The best of these he had fleshed out, recorded and polished. He played all the instruments, bass, rhythm and lead guitars, laying down the beat with a drum machine, doing the vocal tracks himself and then, once a month, uploading a finished track on YouTube.

One evening in early winter, I met him at his place. He was putting the finishing touches on the bridge of a song he had come up with a couple of weeks before, riding home on his bike. There was something about the dull hum of the bike's tires on the cold asphalt, something about the flat grey sky and the general sense of anxiety he had been feeling lately, about getting close to forty and not having anything resembling a normal job, about the fact he had been seeing a woman who recently broke up with him, who mentioned this as one of the reasons she didn't think they had a future together, despite telling him she loved him.

"When I date chicks," he told me, "I have, like, zero to offer."

"You really feel that way?" Nelson had more luck with women than just about any other guy I had met.

"In terms of long-term livelihood? Yeah. I don't have a pension plan. I don't have a well-paid job. I don't have long-term plans." He was picking out a melody on his guitar while he said this. There was no self-pity in it. He was just stating the facts.

He started to strum a new song.

"It's an ode to winter," he explained, tapping out the rhythm on the cold linoleum with his bare feet. "No, actually"—he laughed—"it's a fuck-you to winter. I hate winter. I'm going to be forty in two years. I was riding home thinking, 'This is miserable!' I don't know how many more winters I can go through. It's a sad song."

Nelson has a strong, warm voice, a tenor that breaks into a clear falsetto. He closed his eyes and sang:

> It's a-no-ther cold win-ter, this yee-ee-ee-ee-ee-ar,
> And the wind's al-ready gone bit-ter, I fee-ee-ee-ee-ee-ee-eel

He moved into a simple staccato chord progression.

*And I know, no mat-ter how warm your coat is*
*You'll still be fee-lin' a chi-iii-iii-iiill.*
*Oh oh oh. You'll still be fee-lin' a chiii-iii-iiill.*

He was right, it *was* a sad song. And it was simple and beautiful, the work of someone who had gone inside himself and dredged up something real. I sat there listening to him, wondering why he wasn't already famous.

Over his desk, he had taped up a handwritten schedule. Each day of the week was divided into discrete units for band rehearsals—he was playing in four at the time—recording sessions, songwriting, guitar practice, time for his personal training clients, time for himself at the gym, his work as a doorman, a few hours each night for sleep, sometimes as little as two or three. The schedule was new.

"I had to get up and write that down last night," he explained. "I couldn't sleep. I was lying in bed, tossing and turning." Work at the clubs was getting him down. It was November. His fingers and toes ached where the cold crept into his old injuries. He had plantar fasciitis, which meant standing in front of the club all night with his weight on his good foot, making sure not to let on he was in pain, that he had a weak spot.

"It's definitely not my dream job," he told me. "I fucking hate doing it. I've told myself I will not be forty years old and still working the door. No ifs, ands or buts about it. Sometimes I think I should give up going to the gym altogether and devote myself a hundred percent to music. But that's not me either."

—

I'VE THOUGHT ABOUT Susan's question—what I make of all this, MMA, fighting, putting your life on hold to pursue something that is both short-sighted and dangerous—whether it's crazy or not.

It's understandable why she and so many people—probably the majority of people I know—feel that way. There's a lot not to like about MMA. John McCain, the US senator, referred to it as "human cockfighting" during a push to get the UFC banned. He had a point. The UFC is a business built on the spectacle of human bloodshed. And it's big business—one of the, if not *the*, fastest-growing spectator sports in the world. I've talked to enough bartenders to believe the anecdotal evidence that barroom brawls go up on nights UFC fights are shown. I'm not convinced it adds anything of much value to civil society. I'd argue it brings us a little closer to reverting to a culture of honour.

Weirdly, a number of fighters I spoke with feel this way about it too.

"Not to insult it," Nelson once told me, "I love fighting, but I hate all the other stuff that goes with it: the fans, the guys who wear Tapout and No Surrender"—he was talking about two athletic-clothing companies that specialize in fight wear—"I hate the people involved in the scene. It just seems like a bunch of savages."

I think that's probably the right word for it: *savage*.

MMA isn't really a sport. Sport is a symbolic contest for physical dominance; fighting is an *actual* contest for it, something we probably developed the capacity for long before we developed the capacity for symbolism. Sport is constrained by rules—the particulars of the game—which are there, to a great extent, to limit the use of violence in achieving a particular physical goal. But with MMA—and boxing or any other form of full-contact combat—physical aggression *is* the goal. You'll never see an MMA match *devolve* into a more serious fight. It already is one.

It's worth considering why cultures of honour—that is, cultures of savage male violence—develop in the first place, how they come to define entire swaths of human society and so much of human history. They aren't just arbitrary occurrences. There are reasons they arise—reasons that help explain why so many men, even peaceable, progressive men, still find those values appealing at some level.

Todd Shackelford, a psychologist at Florida Atlantic University, argues that cultures of honour spring from a specific form of vulnerability: "when a man's resource holdings can be thieved in full by other men and when the governing body is weak or nonexistent and thus cannot prevent or punish theft."[12]

Nisbett and Cohen, the researchers who studied the difference in testosterone responses between men from the northern and southern United States, argue this helps explain, in part, what happened in the southern and western parts of the country. Both regions, the West and

the frontier South, were settled to a large extent by herding cultures—
the West by nineteenth-century cattlemen, the eighteenth-century
Southern colonies by Scots, northern English and Scots-Irish, a large
number of whom were descendants of old-country herders, as well as
"cracker" cowboys, originating from the English Midlands.

A herder's livelihood—his wealth and reputation, his capacity to
attract a mate and provide for his family—was tied up in livestock that
could be, and often were, rustled by thieves in the night. Preventing
this from happening and doling out justice when it did was up to the
men who owned the animals; there was little, if any, law enforcement,
let alone formal law, in traditional herding and frontier societies. The
best protection you could hope for was a reputation as the kind of guy
you don't mess with. And the best way of getting this reputation was by
being capable of severe retributive violence. Which, incidentally, goes
a long way towards explaining every hero in every western ever made.

But frontier America is just one manifestation. In contemporary
urban ghettos and impoverished regions of the United States, law
enforcement is also unreliable from the point of view of the people who
live there, as opposed to those who want to keep them contained. As a
result, street justice—men taking things into their own hands and settling it outside the law—thrives.

It can be hard to see past the toughness, the badassedness, of lone-
wolf gunslingers, mountain men and gangsters in order to discern
what's driving them to be that way. But their toughness is a way of pushing back against the gravity of their situation: the other men threatening to push them down. It can be hard too to understand at first glance
why cultures like this persist long after the conditions that sparked them
have changed.

I think part of the answer is that, no matter what kind of culture you
live in, being a man among other men can leave you feeling vulnerable much of the time, especially if you've experienced the crushing
misery of being physically dominated. No matter how successful you
become later in life, no matter what other skills you develop, it's normal
to crave the capacity to defend yourself from physical assault. And once
you've experienced how liberating that ability can be, how the weight
comes off you, it's hard to let it go—even if, in all likelihood, you

won't ever really need it. Even if, by investing in it, you might subtly be detracting from other ways of being successful.

—

NELSON TEXTED ME one night, shortly after he had come back from a meditation retreat. This was a couple of weeks before Adam's fight with Kyle.

COME BY IF YOU CAN!

He was working at the club down the street from my place. He had grown a beard at the retreat. He was wearing a peacoat and a black woollen cap and looked convincingly like a stevedore. When I got there, one of the men who worked with him, a huge, bulky guy who looked something like a limo driver for the Mafia, was telling a story about how he had once been fishing when a goose started pestering him, squawking and hissing. He snapped the goose's neck, took it home, plucked it, barbecued it and fed it to his dog.

One of the bartenders was outside, smoking a cigarette. "Dude," he said, "you're telling me you fucking fed it to your dog?"

"It's meat," the big man said. "I'm not going to waste meat."

"Did it ever occur to you," Nelson asked the big man, "that maybe the goose was bugging you because it was defending its children or something?"

The big guy shrugged.

"I mean, maybe not too far away," Nelson continued, "there are all these baby geese and you're sitting there fishing and it's scaring the fuck out of the mama goose and so she's telling you to get out of there, and then you go and break her neck? It's sad. What about all the little baby geese?"

The big guy looked bewildered.

Nelson smiled at me, knowing he had just done jiu-jitsu to the guy's brain.

Then he said, "I had this revelation or insight or whatever you want to call it when I was at the retreat. Basically, I realized we're enlightened animals. Or actually, scratch that—we're animals who can *choose* to become enlightened. The animal in us, all it wants to do is smash things and eat and fuck and every once in a while look at something pretty. When I was up there meditating, those were the only things the animal wanted to do: 'I'm so angry! I'm so horny! I really want to play music!' I realized after sitting there for five days that that's all the animal ever says to me—over and over and *over* again. And I think we either train him or we let him run wild. That's what you try to do with martial arts—train him. But real enlightenment isn't just about training the animal. It's about not having to deal with that animal at all.[13]

"I'm not there yet. Maybe none of us are. Maybe in a thousand years we'll have evolved to the point where we don't have to deal with the animal, we'll have moved on to a higher plane of existence. But we're definitely not there yet."

CHAPTER TWO

—

# THE MOUSE AND THE SERPENT

IN THE LIGHT OF DAY, after a couple shots of espresso, black and thick as bitumen, Mr. Douglas is the man. To the kids at school, he's *Yo! Mr. Douglas!* Walking tall, moving down the hall, tapping the top of his head and smiling when he passes a kid in a 9FIFTY Snapback—a low-key reminder to take off his lid. Telling students in an *I'm laughing but I'm also serious* voice to hustle-hustle to class, while the *William Tell* overture plays maniacally over the PA in the moments leading up to the national anthem.

He fist-bumps *his* boys, the boys who are playing football for him this season, who played for him in past seasons and have now moved on to the senior team. He's made this a thing, greeting each boy. It teaches them respect, teaches them collegiality, teaches them to acknowledge others.

Mr. Douglas has had his fill of discipline, so when a kid shows up late to his first-period physics class, some doe-eyed grade-niner, Mr. Douglas doesn't make it into a big deal the way other teachers sometimes do. He nods. He says, "Welcome!" He goes on explaining the concept of a light year.

He walks around the class, pacing the rows. He grabs an empty seat, plonks down next to a kid and keeps talking—about parsecs, astronomical units, the speed at which photons move out into the void. He slouches in the seat and looks around at them, and the look transmits a message that has nothing to do with physics, a message that says *we're all in this together* and *it's going to be okay.* He tries to get the kids to understand how absurdly far the sun is from the Earth. How, even with photons zipping along at two-hundred-and-ninety-nine-million, seven-hundred-ninety-two-thousand, four-hundred-and-fifty-eight metres per second—which is to say, fast enough to whip around the entire Earth almost seven and a half times in a single second—it still takes light leaving the sun a full eight minutes and twenty seconds to get here.

"Maybe I should just stand here," says Mr. Douglas, now back in front of the class, "and say nothing for eight and a half minutes—just to give you a sense of how incredibly long that is."

*Oh shit. He's actually going to do it.* The kids can tell. He stands stock-still, blinking at them for, like, twenty seconds. *Douglas is INSANE!* Twenty-five seconds. *He'll do it, too—just watch.* Thirty seconds. *He'll stand there for a full eight and a half minutes, boring his laser-beam eyes right at you, smiling slightly, like he actually enjoys torturing you.*

The kids get twitchy with self-consciousness. At the half-minute mark, they start giggling and tittering.

Mr. Douglas breaks his silence, as he shakes his head. "Nah. You get the point. It's a long, long time."

Two boys have been hanging out in the doorway, trying hard to look casual. The bell rings. The grade nine students leave. The two boys, larger, thicker, roll in. Their faces stone. Chins up, eyes down. Mr. Douglas shakes their hands. He asks how they're feeling.

"Good, Coach," the boys mutter.

"Good," says Mr. Douglas.

They look as though they have something more to say. Or maybe they're waiting to hear something.

So Mr. Douglas says, "*I'm* feeling good." He says it like he's got all the time in the world for them. "I have a good feeling about today."

The boys nod. "Okay, Coach," one of them says. The other boy is chewing his upper lip. The two drift back into the hall as if it was an accident they ended up in Mr. Douglas's classroom in the first place.

"They're nervous," Mr. Douglas tells me. "They're checking in with me for reassurance. They'll never admit it, but they sort of tell you without telling you."

Mr. Douglas could use some reassurance himself from time to time. He doesn't sleep much most nights, but before his boys have a game, his insomnia gets especially bad. His head is a motor he runs hard and which never fully cools down. It clicks and ticks in the dark, searching for some cog that will catch, some gear to engage. Instead, it finds the loose, unhinged things that spin in the night. Some of which, in no particular order, are:

—the fear that one of his boys will drop on the field; a ticker tapping out from some undiagnosed condition; a brain sizzling, overheated, in its pan; a vertebra cracking under a crush of adolescent bulk.

—the fear maybe he is not entirely prepared to be head coach. This is his first year, after all. If the previous coach hadn't been transferred for inappropriate behaviour—rumour is he said something tasteless about a student—Mr. Douglas would have been perfectly happy to remain assistant coach.

—the fear that his boys will pull some version of the stunt they pulled last year when they played Collegiate Heights—their main rival—tagging the visitors' change room, making themselves look like a pack of hoodlums rather than the young men Mr. Douglas is eager to see them become.

More broadly speaking, Mr. Douglas worries about the boys who will never get what being a man is all about. He worries about them entering adulthood still conflating manhood with being hard—the kind of hard that cuts you down mid-stride because you stupidly step up to the wrong guy. The hardness Mr. Douglas is trying to instill in his boys is the kind that allows you to move forward, to make your way in your own life, even if you grew up surrounded by that wrong kind of hardness.

And so he paces the laminated floor of his apartment, stopping to adjust the next day's plays on his laptop. Pacing and typing. Typing and pacing. Back and forth, into the early morning.

Mr. Douglas tells me there's a boy on the team you can hear wishing as he runs downfield.

"What do you mean?"

"Like, wishing he was faster. You can hear him pleading with himself to go faster when he runs. It breaks your heart."

There's another boy who will never be able to play senior ball because, despite being one of the most aggressive boys on the junior team, he is tiny. No amount of food or exercise will do the trick. The boy has the skeleton of a bird. If his wrists and ankles are any indicator, he's not about to bulk up. He'll be the senior kid who comes to all the games, wishing desperately he was on the field with the larger boys, the small man who lives his life wishing he was bigger.

On the team there are fat boys who wish they were thinner. Black boys who wish they were white. White boys who wish they were black. Ugly boys who wish they were handsome. Boys who wish they were safe at home. Popular boys who wish popularity made them happy. Grieving boys who wish to outrun grief.

Mr. Douglas takes it as a good sign he hasn't received any calls after first period. It means that none of the other teachers have a problem letting his boys out of class in the middle of the day.

Sometimes they do. Some teachers don't get football. They see it as giving boys, many of them unpromising students to begin with, a free pass to miss class and get props for pushing other boys to the ground.

Mr. Douglas is head of the physics department. He has a master's degree in physics, so he's not blind to the importance of academic achievement. But many of his boys *are*. In his opinion, forcing a boy to pursue something he cannot perceive as important is not only a waste of time, it's dangerously counterproductive. Push a boy to do what he's *supposed* to do when he doesn't know *why* he should be doing it—or, more importantly, that he's *capable* of doing it—and you'll eventually push him away altogether. You'll push him right out of school, push him away from academic interests entirely and, ultimately, push him beyond the reach of those internal levers that allow a boy to move himself forward into manhood, at least the kind of manhood Mr. Douglas is talking about.

Which is why you need an oblique strategy to keep him in a place where you have some influence. You need to know how to speak without talking, teach without teaching, discipline without disciplining.

"Be proud of who you are."

This is what the educational assistant is telling the boys before they launch into some pre-game yoga.

"Be proud of your teammates."

Mr. Douglas doesn't want me to use the educational assistant's name. He's asked I don't use the real names of his students either. He's protective that way.*

"Have you not accomplished great things?" the assistant asks the boys. "Have you not pushed yourself man to man?"

The boys are standing on yoga mats in shorts and T-shirts and sock feet. None of them are speaking. They are nearly as self-conscious as if they had no clothes on at all.

"What part of your body do you need to strengthen and relax?" the educational assistant asks.

The boys are silent. They shift from foot to foot. They look at the floor.

"Which parts of yourself do you want to make stronger?" the assistant asks again.

The boys say nothing.

The educational assistant waits.

Finally, one boy says in a hoarse whisper: "Core."

Another boy says, "Back."

And another says, "Legs."

"Arms," says another one.

The educational assistant takes the boys through Warrior One, Warrior Two, Downward Dog.

"Remember to breathe," he reminds the boys. "You're only as good as you feel. You can only control what you can feel."

Say a decent high school senior team is a piece of machinery—nothing as well-oiled as a college team, nothing as finely engineered as a pro team, but a mechanism that operates well enough to grind its way downfield. It's composed of boys who know each of the plays; who visualize success; who know it's attainable; who remain focused even when nagged from within by their own potential for failure; who know the expectations and limitations of their position; who know they can only succeed by working together with the other parts.

That is not at all what a high school junior football team is like.

---

* In fact, Mr. Douglas is so protective of his students, I am not using anyone's real name in this chapter and I have also changed a few identifying details.

A junior team is the workshop where those parts are first hammered, roughly, into some sort of shape. Mr. Douglas gets to work those parts for two seasons before he has to hand them over to the senior coach—that's if the boys decide they want to stick with the game.

Mr. Douglas took over as coach of the junior team several years into a bottom-of-the-heap slump. Otherwise, Downtown Standard's football programme has a reputation for excellence—the kind that occasionally leads to a professional career and makes fathers who once played for the school enrol their sons, hoping they'll be part of something excellent too.

Mr. Douglas was determined to break the slump. The previous coach had a thing for complex plays and a lot of mid-game adjustments. Mr. Douglas thought that just being on the field, just showing up and facing a dozen opposing players (who are themselves so frightened they'll run over you to escape their *own* fear), brings a boy to the edge of emotional overload. Expecting them to memorize dozens of complex plays on top of that is too much. All but the most gifted athlete shuts down in the face of that. So, at the beginning of the season, Mr. Douglas settled on a dozen bread-and-butter plays. Then he brought the number down further, to eight.

Football is about execution. That, and the confidence to execute. If you give the boys a limited number of moves to master and make them feel *good* about those moves, the parts ought to come together and start rumbling in the right direction.

He put his plan into action in August training camp, just before the school year began—around the time he and I first started talking. At the tail end of September, he sent me a text:

MY BOYS WON THEIR FIRST GAME TODAY.

37–0.

IT WAS MY FIRST GAME AS HEAD COACH.

THE FIRST JUNIOR WIN IN OVER FIVE YEARS.

Followed shortly by:

FUCKING AWESOME.

I texted back to ask if he was going to celebrate. He replied:

NOPE.
REVIEWING TAPE FOR NEXT GAME.
KEEP MOVING FORWARD.

—

GORD WILSON DIDN'T HAVE a Mr. Douglas when he was in high school. He probably could have used one. He entered high school afraid. His fear was a mouse. It crouched and twitched as long as the object of his fear was present: a boy at school, his stepdad.

Gord never knew his real dad, though he was told the man got violent sometimes. Gord was three when his mother left, with him and his infant sister.

Gord's mother eventually remarried. His stepfather had two sons, three and six years older than Gord—which meant he ended up at the bottom of rec room pile-ups and face down in snowbanks.

"I was a crier," he tells me. "I was a super-sensitive kid. I cried all the time."

Gord would dream of his real father. He'd wake up with a deep, unsettled longing. He knew very few details about the man. He knew he was an engineer, that he had his pilot's licence, that he liked boats. In his mind, Gord made his father into someone like James Bond, a mysterious figure who might one day step out of the shadows and introduce his boy to a life of glamour and mystery.

Otherwise, why wouldn't he get in touch with Gord? Why wouldn't he try, at least, to get to know his son? His stepbrothers' mother called them, so why did Gord's dad never call him?

Gord didn't play football when he was a boy. He grew up in a small town in Newfoundland where boys played baseball. He was pretty good at baseball, just didn't care much for it. He preferred exploring the woods alone, or reading. What little he knew of football came out of the *F* volume of an old set of *Encyclopaedia Britannica*, an abstract set of rules.

As a kid, Gord sort of had a thing for learning and mastering the rules of games: cards, chess, cribbage, board games. They offered him a concrete set of parameters by which to understand his place, at least in the microcosmic world of a particular game.

Many things in his life were beyond rules—and understanding. Like the things his stepfather did to him when he crept into Gord's room at night. This started when Gord was eight and tapered off as he got older and entered high school.

Just before high school, the family moved from Newfoundland to London, Ontario. The boys and girls at the new school were cliquey. Gord didn't wear the right clothes. The kids called him "Newfie." His accent was strong. The words burst out of his mouth like greyhounds lunging out of their cages after the lure, especially when he was nervous. And he was nervous a lot. The first day, a big, meaty kid shoved him in the hall. And then pretty much every day after that for the next few years.

Gord fell in with the drama kids. He was safe with them. It was okay to be a shy, sensitive guy in that crowd. It was okay to talk differently. It was okay to be a kid who got picked on. Drama kids were always getting picked on. To fit in with the drama kids, you sort of had to be an outcast.

In later grades, he and some of the other drama kids formed a troupe that worked with the city police. They'd put on shows for elementary kids about the perils of shoplifting and doing drugs. Gord liked being part of something positive.

The problem with being a drama kid—the problem, more generally, with being a sensitive, artsy guy in high school—is that you get called faggot a lot. The problem with being called a faggot, the reason it's such an effective insult at that age, is that it gives a name to an unarticulated fear.

One day, you are an unselfconscious boy; the next, you're self-conscious *because* you're a boy. You want to be a man—or at least a lot more manly—and from where you stand, that's about as realistic as ending up on the surface of Mars.

Going into puberty, I was androgynous and plump. I got mistaken for a girl a couple of times. I checked daily for armpit hair. I checked my dick for signs of growth. I heard my voice on tape and was mortified it was so high. Watching myself go through puberty was like hovering in front of the oven, waiting for a loaf of bread to rise. I worried that maybe there wasn't enough leavening agent in the mix, that I was short of some key ingredient and the whole enterprise would fall flat.

Being called a faggot at that age is like being hit with a poisoned arrow: it doesn't need to be accurate to do damage. Boys call other boys faggot not so much because they think the target is actually gay—though of course that can be part of it. Most of the time, it's about legitimacy. No man—no *real* man, if you follow the juvenile logic—would let himself be fucked by another man.

The problem is, when you're a boy, regardless of which way your budding sexuality is leaning, you're *not* a real man. And so you worry that maybe they sort of have a point.

But there's more to why being called a faggot was such a big deal for Gord—for any boy who has been sexually assaulted by a man. You can know that it isn't something you'd seek out, you can be overwhelmed, the circuitry of your emotional understanding can be shorting out— and, at the same time, the hydraulics of your body can be working just fine. To put it bluntly, fondle a dick long enough and it gets hard. It doesn't really matter who's doing the fondling.

But you don't know that as a kid. And so, when you're called a fag later, in the long purgatory between boyhood and manhood—even if you have a serious girlfriend whom you love deeply, as Gord did later on in high school—it's hard not to think, *Well, I did get a hard-on when a man was trying to fuck me.*

And that can kind of fuck you up.


What will fuck you up even more is suddenly finding out your long-lost father is dead.

In the winter of his final year of high school, Gord got a call from his dad's mother. His father had not been James Bond. There was some mystery, though. Gord and his sister were written into their father's modest will. But so was a man no one in Gord's family had heard of.

At first, the story actively promoted in the family was that Gord's dad had died of a heart attack. The truth was that he'd died of AIDS. The man was his lover.

As Gord understood it back then, AIDS was the disease gay men got. It was also, coincidentally, a time when the research that suggested there is a genetic component to homosexuality was getting play in the news.

This is something Gord remembers thinking about a lot, something that worried him at the time.

By the end of high school, Gord had transformed physically. Though he was still slender, he was over six feet tall, and he no longer got shoved in the halls.

Fear can change its appearance too. It doesn't always stay shivering and cowering. A boy can grow sick of the mouse as he gets older. He can come to hold the mouse in such contempt he sends a serpent after it. And the serpent, having engulfed the mouse, can make the boy feel better, make him believe the mouse is no longer there.

Gord's girlfriend dumped him. School ended. Somewhere out there was the capital-F Future he was supposed to be making his way towards. But it was hard to think much about it. His head buzzed like a wasps' nest. He'd go out Wednesday, Thursday, Friday, Saturday nights with buddies. He embraced the bar scene, and the bar scene embraced him back. He landed a job behind the bar himself. He moved in with a few friends. They'd watch TV, smoke up, drop acid.

Drugs helped hush the buzz of the wasps. Drinking helped too. Some guys drink and their brain gets smeared against the inside of their skull like the yoke of a juggled egg. When Gord drank, the alcohol entered him like ice water.

At the bar, when Gord wasn't working, he'd hunt.

You can tell when another guy wants to fight by the way he holds himself, the way he looks out at the crowd. You get next to him. You bump him, nudge him. Wait for him to nudge you back. Typically, a guy will start talking, start asking you if you've got a fucking problem, maybe call you a faggot. Then you say something. Then he says something. Back and forth, back and forth, until someone loses their cool and makes contact.

But Gord was done with rules of this sort. He had put up with the chirping in high school, the shoves, being called a faggot. In school, he had developed a knack for witty comebacks. Problem is, wit is lost on dimwits. Gord was done with talking in general. And so the other guy would open his mouth and, before he had finished saying whatever stupid thing he was going to say, the serpent would strike. It would strike the guy in the face, in the throat maybe, and then keep striking until he was on the floor, unable to talk at all.

"I just wanted to react," Gord told me. "I was looking to bully bullies. I was looking for violence. I had early success. It was addictive."

"How did you feel about what you were doing?"

"I had no feeling. I was going for the numbness."

"And *that* felt good?"

"At the time, very positive."

—

WE'RE SO FAMILIAR WITH the notion of violence as some sort of cycle that we take it for granted. Do bad things to a boy and he'll turn out bad, right?

Sort of.

Being treated poorly as a kid—growing up amid violence, being beaten, bullied, sexually abused, having especially harsh, punitive parents, being neglected, living in hard neighbourhoods among hard people—will almost certainly affect you. These things are all risk factors for depression, suicide and substance abuse later in life. And, in boys specifically, being mistreated when you're younger also increases the risk you'll end up a violent offender as an adult.[1]

But there's a caveat: most maltreated boys don't actually end up violent.[2] There are, after all, kids who have lived through abuse and neglect—hell, kids who have lived through wars, who were raised in gangland, in whorehouses, in concentration camps—who don't go around looking for fights.

So why Gord? And why me? How do nice, sensitive boys, criers, boys who weren't prone to bullying or violence as children, make this kind of hairpin turn as they enter adulthood? What is it about some boys that prompts the serpent to swallow the mouse?

Clearly, people differ in how they're shaped by their environment. Similar upbringings can have a drastically different effect on different people. And so, because it's *not* just the environment that determines how a kid turns out—because it also has something to do with the unique makeup of that specific kid—it's worth trying to figure out what exactly that something is.

While this is a perfectly reasonable question, it has a tendency to spark some extremely unreasonable answers. People have been making arguments for the inherence of criminality and violence forever. For nearly all of human history, we've taken it for granted that there are certain types—certain individuals, physiognomies, breeds, tribes, clans, whole countries, entire races—cut from the devil's cloth.

The early antecedents of modern psychiatry, neuroscience and anthropology let this assumption guide them in the creation of the pseudo-scientific practices of phrenology and physiognomy. The underlying idea was that you could gauge inherent dispositions—criminality, intelligence, creativity—by way of physical traits such as the circumference and shape of the cranium; the length and breadth of the nose (or other facial features); the length of, say, the forearm compared to the upper arm. Or, you know, skin colour.

Not true in any way, shape or form. Still, these theories were popular and widely viewed as sensible and valid throughout Europe and North America, especially during the first half of the nineteenth century. And, of course, long after these pseudo-sciences were discredited, they— and their bastardized offspring—were still used to rationalize racist and misogynistic policies. Not to mention eugenic ideologies, like the one that was so popular among German National Socialists.

And so, whenever you find yourself talking about inherent predispositions—especially when that predisposition is for something nasty, like violence—it's a good idea to keep in mind that we always seem to be on the lookout for some new proof that other groups of our fellow humans are dangerously—and inherently—inferior. (More on that in the last chapter of this book.)

Another part of what makes this such a touchy line of inquiry is that, despite the danger of wading unwittingly into ideologically motivated biological determinism, there *is* clear evidence that genetics play a role when it comes to male violence.

For a short time in the 1960s, researchers thought the Y chromosome—the male sex chromosome—held the answer. Guys born with an extra Y chromosome are overrepresented in prisons; XYY Syndrome occurs in about one in a thousand boys, compared with about one in four hundred male prisoners. The thinking at the time was that the root of male aggression might lie in this particular clump of genetic material. After all, men tend to be brutes, and these particular men had an extra helping of man genes. But it's not so straightforward. By the mid-1970s, it started to look as though guys with an extra Y probably weren't any more brutish than other men. There *were* more of them in jail, but they tended to be there for property offences, not violent crimes—most likely because XYY Syndrome is often associated with mild intellectual impairment. (These guys probably weren't the hardest criminals to catch.) The pendulum has swung back in the past few years, with some more recent studies suggesting men with XYY Syndrome may be slightly more prone to violent outbursts.[3] Though, because of the back and forth, I'm not convinced this theory is worth laying any money on.

In any case, the better bet to make is on the X chromosome.

In the early 1990s, a team of researchers led by the Dutch behavioural geneticist Hans Brunner came across a mutation that has since become the most compelling evidence that male violence—at least *some* male violence—might be linked to a specific gene.

I'll qualify this by pointing out that this mutation is extraordinarily—*exceedingly*—rare. It's limited, from what anyone can tell, to a handful of men who are all members of a single family in the Netherlands. But what it lacks in prevalence, it makes up for in intensity. Men carrying this gene have a tendency to become wildly, uncontrollably, sociopathically violent—especially when they're frustrated or angry.[4] These men only came to the attention of researchers when, in the late 1970s, one of the sisters in the family sought help from health care workers because several of her male relatives were so out of hand. One of these guys had attempted to rape his sister. Another had threatened his sisters with a knife and forced them to take off their clothes; another had tried to plow down his boss with a car; a couple of them had committed arson after one of their family members passed away. When researchers started to investigate, they found a pattern of behaviour that stretched back several generations in a way that made it pretty clear the men's volatility was a sex-linked trait—something that, because it is passed on from mothers to their sons on the X chromosome, only expresses itself in men. (Since women have two X chromosomes, the "abnormal" gene is masked by a functioning one.)

To get technical for a second, the mutation Brunner discovered affects the gene responsible for producing an enzyme called mono-amine oxidase A, or, in the scientific shorthand, MAOA. We all carry the gene and, correspondingly, we all produce the enzyme. And that's what's so strange about this particular mutation: people who carry it produce virtually no monoamine oxidase A, which is stunning given that it's vital for normal brain function; it regulates the breakdown of the neurotransmitters serotonin, noradrenaline and dopamine. Without the enzyme, these neurotransmitters accumulate to abnormally high levels. And because they all regulate mood and emotional states (among other things), there's good reason to believe this is why men with this mutation are so impulsively violent.

Shortly after Brunner's discovery of the gene, other researchers developed genetically engineered mice whose MAOA gene—and the enzyme it produced—could be switched on and off. With the gene on, these mice produced normal levels of the enzyme and showed normal behaviour. With the gene turned off, their MAOA plummeted and the mice became the murine equivalent of the Dutch men in Brunner's study, often killing their cage-mates.[5]

Clearly, the mutation has something to do with male violence. But it's not a universally applicable finding. The mutation is so rare it can't possibly account for the violence committed by the vast majority of men. The rest of us—murderers, rapists and thugs included—carry functioning MAOA genes, which produce normal levels of the MAOA enzyme.

That said, there *is* a range of normal MAOA levels—and this is where things start to get really interesting. People vary in the amount of MAOA enzyme they produce because there are three different versions of the normal, functioning MAOA gene. Two of these versions result in relatively high levels of the enzyme, while the third results in relatively low levels.

All things being equal, there's no evidence that simply carrying the low-MAOA version makes men any more prone to violence than carrying the versions that result in higher levels of the enzyme. But a lot of the time, things aren't equal. Some men have had a harder go of it in life than others.

In 2002, an English research team published a paper showing that men who carried the low-level version of the gene were more likely to be convicted for violent behaviour—*but only if* they had been maltreated as children. Men who carried the high-level versions seemed somehow more resistant to childhood trauma.[6] There have been studies since that show men with the low-MAOA version tend to be more aggressive when provoked or made to feel like social outcasts.[7] And there's some evidence that men who have inherently low levels of MAOA *and* inherently high levels of testosterone are more likely to be aggressive.[8]

This gene understandably got a lot of attention after it was discovered, being dubbed the "the warrior gene" by the popular press. And it's not the only so-called warrior gene. There are two other genes—one that influences the role serotonin plays in the brain, another that influences the brain's dopamine system—that show the same effect.[9]

Men don't need to carry these specific genes for abuse or childhood trauma to lead to violent behaviour later in life. But the big picture is clear: some of us require fewer hard knocks than others to respond with hardness in return—and this seems to be determined, at least to some extent, by our genetic makeup.

—

MR. DOUGLAS IS WORRIED about Samuel, but you'd never know it by looking at him. Mr. Douglas's fear is a shard of glass immersed in ice water: you don't know it's there unless you've been told.

Samuel is the same. He's as stone-faced as an Easter Island god, even though his cousin was shot earlier in the week, killed. Word is it was some sort of gang thing.

Mr. Douglas told Samuel he didn't have to show up for practice until he felt like it, didn't have to play—his position would be there waiting for him if he needed to take some time off to be with his family. Otherwise, Mr. Douglas had an unwavering policy: skip practice, skip school, and you're sidelined. Samuel said no. He didn't want to be at home. He wanted to be on the field.

Mr. Douglas was secretly relieved. Gang connections are often tangled up with family ties. Samuel being on the field meant he wasn't at home, getting snared in some sort of retaliatory counterattack. It meant he was, for the moment at least, headed in the right direction, moving forward.

Not all boys are as good at hiding their pain and fear as Samuel and Mr. Douglas are.

Before this week's game, most of them are wandering around the school's subterranean equipment room in various states of undress. They suddenly can't remember how to get their gear on, how to adjust their shoulder pads, which way the neck guard is supposed to sit. They're too self-conscious to ask anyone, so they glance at their teammates the way you look to other dinner guests when you can't remember which fork you're supposed to use. Mr. Douglas calls this the deer-in-the-headlights look. He's standing in the cinder-block hallway outside the equipment room, shaking his head. He's just called them to come take a knee for a pre-game pep talk. Exactly zero boys have heeded his call.

"What's the first rule?" he hollers.

A couple of boys hear this. The rest are still wandering around as if they've been in a car accident: wide-eyed, half-dressed, dazed, either completely mute or balls-out manic. One of the boys is pounding on a door, making the entire basement into a gigantic, offbeat kick drum.

"Yo!" another boy shouts at him. "That is *not* psyching me up. It's pissing me off!"

"TAKE A KNEE!" bellows Mr. Douglas. His voice claps off the cinder block and slaps the wandering boys to attention. They finally gather around him and settle to the floor.

"What's the first rule of football?" he asks again.

A couple of boys yell, Marine-style: "SHOW UP!"

Mr. Douglas nods. "We're in for a *big* fight today," he says. "A big, big fight. We're going up against Collegiate. We're in Collegiate's territory."

Collegiate is Downtown Standard's main rival. Collegiate is an uptown school; Standard is not, neither literally or figuratively. Collegiate's team is the Red Warriors; Downtown Standard's is the Blues. Collegiate boys are richie-riches; Standard boys are poor. Collegiate's players tend to be white; Standard's tend to be black.

One of the boys shouts, "Let's make it OUR field!"

Mr. Douglas nods again. "They don't know what's coming today. They have *no* idea. This is a brand new junior team. They have no idea who's going to show up today. *We're* going to show up today."

Some of the boys growl and nod.

"SECOND RULE," Mr. Douglas shouts. "PAY ATTENTION! Some of you *aren't* paying attention. How do the coaches know you're paying attention?"

"Stand up and look at the play!" yells one of the boys.

Mr. Douglas nods. "Watch the game. Watch. The. Game. We're going to need you. What's the third rule?"

"TELL THE TRUTH!" shout the boys.

"Yes," says Mr. Douglas.

"Fight for every inch!" yells one boy.

"Fight for every inch," repeats Mr. Douglas. "Yes. That's the truth about football. That's what we have to do today. Fight every play. This is *our* game today. All out! That's what rivalry is about. We need your best. Your best is *you* paying attention and telling the truth.

"Now," he continues, "when Tyler runs and someone illegally tackles him and brings him down to the ground, what does he do?"

"NEXT PLAY!" the boys shout together.

"Right! We move on to the next play."

Mr. Douglas has been trying to drill this into their heads all year. Boys would get hit, take it personally and then want to fight—exactly the opposite of what he's trying to teach them. Then Tyler, the team's running back, handed Mr. Douglas a textbook example.

Mr. Douglas looks around for Tyler and realizes Tyler is already standing by his side.

"Tyler is *a man*," says Mr. Douglas. "That means he gets up and goes on to the next play."

This kind of manhood has only just recently come to Tyler. Tyler, at fifteen, is the opposite of the kid who prays he can run faster; he's the answer to that prayer. When Tyler runs, you can hear the air trying to hold itself together as he rushes into it and tears it apart like Chuck Yeager breaking Mach 1. Tyler uses tape to cinch in the loose fabric of his jersey so other players can't grab him as he bolts past them. You watch him run and you think to yourself: nothing on Earth can hold back a kid who moves like that.

Anyway, last year—grade nine, Tyler's first year playing ball—he got blindsided with an illegal tackle. He got up, rattled, blood fizzing with spite, and attacked the other boy. Then he mouthed off at the ref. It cost Downtown Standard a ten-yard penalty. They lost the game.

Earlier this season, though, Tyler got laid out illegally again. He got up, blood boiling. There was a moment of *uh-oh, here we go again.* Then he took a breath, shook off the hit, went back to the line and moved on to the next play. Later that game, he made a hundred-yard run. Downtown Standard won.

On top of that, Tyler's grades are picking up nicely. His math teacher has told Mr. Douglas that Tyler is always the first kid to arrive for class.

When you've got a boy like Tyler on your team, Mr. Douglas tells me, most of your plays become some version of *get the ball to that guy.* That's how you think as a coach, anyway. The other kids on the team think: *how do I get to be like that guy?*

Then there are the ones like Ali, a big, baby-faced ninth-grader who is kneeling in front of Mr. Douglas.

"Now, when someone touches Ali inappropriately—" The boys laugh. Mr. Douglas shakes his head and smiles. "I mean *on the field.* When someone touches Ali, what do we do?"

Ali shouts, "Fuck him up!" in the most convincing impersonation of The Notorious B.I.G. you can pull off with a voice that hasn't changed.

Mr. Douglas puts a hand on Ali's shoulder. "Ali's going to keep his mouth shut. And then what is he going to do?"

"Move on to the next play!" one of the boys shouts.

Mr. Douglas leans over, his forehead almost touching Ali's. "Next play," he says softly. "Next play."

One of the kids yells at Ali: "Keep your cool this game!"

Ali shakes his head like this is all beneath him.

"When you're on the field," Mr. Douglas continues, speaking to the rest of the team again, "there are eleven other guys there with you. When you go for your tackle, keep on them. Help is coming." Mr. Douglas motions to Samuel. "In the centre." To the others, he says, "Bring it in."

"YO!" yells Samuel. "LET'S BLEED BLUE!"

The boys close around him like a sea anemone capturing prey. The anemone begins to pulse up and down. With each pulsation, it emits a short staccato grunt: "Huuuggggh!" It's the sound you make when you're dreaming that someone is holding you down. "Huuuggggh!" The huddle is tight and getting tighter. "Huuuggggh!" Moving up and down. "Huuuggggh!" In and out in time to the grunts. "Huuuggggh!" Somewhere at its core, Samuel begins his song. It is muffled at first, lost in the crush of bodies. Then the boy grows bolder, his song louder:

"I don't know about *you*
but *I'm* reppin' for the Blue!"

The boys answer, together: "Huuuggggh!"

"Cut me to the wrist
and you see I bleed blue!"

"Huuuggggh!"
They cycle through this call-and-answer maybe a dozen times. Then Samuel yells:

"Blues on *me*!
Blues on *three*!
One! Two! Three . . ."

And the boys yell, "BLUES!!!!!!!"
For a moment, charging up the stairs, out into the parking lot, onto the bus, flushed with the confidence Mr. Douglas has infused in them, taller in their helmets and cleats, broadened, thickened with pads, the boys feel the way they look: tough, strong. Fearless.

But traffic is thick. The drive uptown to Collegiate Heights takes the better part of an hour. Enough time for the adrenalin to flush out and the fear to wash back in.
One of the assistant coaches asks, "Everybody have a solid lunch?"
The boys all nod.

Still, he passes around yogurt cups and a giant bag of apples. "Got to make sure you've got good energy."

The boys eat their snacks, looking out the windows, chewing quietly, eyes wide.

—

ONE OF GORD WILSON'S buddies from the bar scene knows a guy who knows some guys in Jamaica. The guy Gord's friend knows is looking for a couple of dudes who want to make some money and are willing to travel. Gord's more than willing. He's never been anywhere. He's dying to get out of town.

There's a car waiting for them at the airport in Montego Bay. They spend a week at an all-inclusive resort, like tourists, courtesy of the men in Jamaica. Blue skies, white sand beaches, a heat that sears the worry out of your flesh. One of the Jamaicans comes by with good weed and some spending money.

At the end of the week, another man shows up and tapes four IV bags full of hash oil to Gord's legs and another four to his buddy's.

Gord is in the customs line at Mirabel when he starts to sweat like he's picked up a tropical disease. The agent eyes him and the baggy overalls he's wearing and writes a bunch of symbols on Gord's declaration card. He directs Gord to another line. Gord wonders why there are so many symbols on his card, what they mean and what happens to people sent to this new line. The person in front of him is told to open his carry-on. Gord realizes this is the line for baggage searches. The man in front of him is carrying a stack of licence plates. Or maybe something else. Gord has trouble remembering because, at this point, he is more focused on his dry mouth, his inability to swallow, to breathe, on the sensation that what's blocking his esophagus might actually be his own heart, which seems to be trying to escape via his throat. The customs agent opens Gord's bag. There's nothing there. Then the agent tells Gord to step into a room. The door closes behind him. Someone else tells him to strip. He takes off his overalls mechanically, revealing the bags of hash oil.

Gord remembers one of the agents saying, "I could tell right away."

Gord is actually sort of relieved. He reaches down and rips off one of the IV bags and hands it over to the agent.

The agents tells him to put it back. It's evidence.

The judge, looking at Gord's school records, at the letters written on his behalf by teachers attesting to his good behaviour and character, at the fact he was an active participant in anti-drug school plays, at the fact that he has recently been accepted at Memorial University, says to Gord, "You don't belong here."

What the judge means is that a middle-class white kid with good grades is not the type you expect to see in shit this deep. But Gord *does* belong here. He's guilty of importing narcotics, which means two years, plus a day. Federal time.

—

MR. DOUGLAS'S BOYS ARE laughing at the Collegiate Heights boys from the sidelines as their opponents march out onto the field for their warm-up.

"They're a bunch of skinny white kids!"

This is pure bravado, because the Collegiate boys aren't skinny at all. They look like corn-fed mules—large, solid, indistinguishable in their well-padded uniforms, red and shiny as new Ferraris.

Collegiate Heights has money. Money for uniforms. Money to keep its field well-maintained. Mr. Douglas's boys assume Collegiate kids drive to school in Mommy and Daddy's BMWs and have personal trainers who feed them protein powder off a silver spoon. Rumour has it the coach of its senior team presides over games from the roof of the school, looking down on the field like a general, communicating plays to his assistant coach via an expensive headset.

Downtown Standard's equipment—and the boys wearing it—smells slightly like vinegar and several generations of adolescent musk. The decals on their jerseys are slowly peeling off. The team looks poor and hardscrabble. Standing here surrounded by Collegiate's home-team crowd, they probably feel it too.

"Our team's different," says one of the boys.

"How?" asks the assistant coach.

"We're better!" says another boy.

Ali, the baby-faced Biggie Smalls, comes lumbering across the field at a half jog.

"Hurry up!" Mr. Douglas yells at him. He has been looking for Ali for several minutes. Kickoff is any second.

"Where've you been?" the boys yell.

Ali slows to a surly stroll. "Fuck off!"

"Don't swear at your teammates," says Mr. Douglas. "Get on the field!"

"I'm gonna . . ." Ali stutters, embarrassed at being chastised in front of the other boys. ". . . I'm gonna fuck 'em up!"

But soon it's Ali getting fucked up out there.

By the second quarter, Collegiate Heights is leading 9–0. Ali is part of a defensive line that keeps getting kicked apart by Collegiate's mules. He comes off the field between plays, winded, injured in some vague way, needing an ice pack or water or a seat in one of the lawn chairs.

He wanders off between plays towards the edge of the field. There's a middle-aged man there, watching the game from the other side of the school's chain-link fence. Ali recognizes him; the man coaches MacDonald Park, a team Downtown Standard lost to earlier this season.

"You like how we're playing," Ali says to the MacDonald Park coach. It's more a command than a question.

"I do," says the MacDonald Park coach. "But you guys really got to move your ball."

"Yeah." Ali sniffs. He turns on his heel. When he's about ten feet away, he yells over his shoulder, "You fucking bitch!"

One of Ali's teammates has been stretching near the fence, listening in. He takes a mouthful from his water bottle and spits it in the direction of the MacDonald Park coach. Mr. Douglas's assistant coach sees this.

"What's up?" he says to the kid with the water.

The boy says, "Nothing."

"That's right," says the assistant coach. "Nothing. Get back to the game."

There was a lot of confusion during the first half. Mr. Douglas's boys kept coming off the field, rattled, winded. One kid staggered off the field clutching his chest—an asthma attack that dissipated as soon as he stepped over the sideline. Another kid insisted on an ice pack for his left knee but put it on his right. A heavy kid who complained that his ankles were killing him refused to go back to the defensive line after an especially grinding series of plays. He took himself out of the game without telling Mr. Douglas or the other coaches. The play restarted with Downtown Standard a man short. Mr. Douglas realized what was happening and quickly sent in another boy, albeit one who had never played that position.

Despite all this, late in the fourth quarter, the boys began working together as a unit. They started running the ball down the field in ten- and fifteen-yard increments. Collegiate Heights's defence began to fall apart under Downtown Standard's gathering momentum, but the clock ran out before they could convert that motion into a touchdown.

Collegiate Heights won, 23–0, but Mr. Douglas's boys understood that they had put up a respectable fight against one of the most formidable teams in the city.

In the bus on the way back downtown, the boys had the grim, satisfied look of miners coming home from the seam after a long shift underground.

Mr. Douglas was satisfied too. "I don't give a shit about winning," he told me. "I'll never tell *them* that. But I don't. This is all about turning boys into men."

But then, later, after school, as Mr. Douglas and I were locking up the equipment room, he cocked his head abruptly. "You hear that?"

I didn't hear anything.

"That's the sound of paperwork," he said, and bolted out of the equipment room. He bounded up the concrete stairs to Downtown Standard's sports field, with me close behind. We saw two groups of boys across the street, just off the school property, almost all of them boys from his team. The two clusters were shouting and posturing at each other. This is what Mr. Douglas had picked up in the equipment room—the sound of an argument rounding the bend into a fist fight.

The boys saw their coach and went quiet. One of the boys raised his chin at us and said, "Douglas."

"What's up?" said Mr. Douglas.

The boys didn't say anything.

"What's going on?"

One of the boys smiled. "Uh, we were just arguing about whether we wanted to go to Subway or Popeye's."

The other boys laughed. It seemed to break the tension.

"Then you better go your separate ways," said Mr. Douglas.

We watched them go. When they were out of sight, we left too. That was on Friday. On Monday, Mr. Douglas texted me:

I DIDN'T ESCAPE THE PAPERWORK.

When I called him, he told me he had had to fill out an incident report.

The boys had found one another again a few blocks away. One of the ninth-grade players, a kid who had recently moved to the city from rural Jamaica—a kid whom the other boys teased because he spoke backcountry patois—had started trash-talking one of the grade ten kids. During the game, Mr. Douglas had substituted the younger, backcountry kid for the older player because he works hard to get all the players on the field in each game. But the younger boy took it to mean Mr. Douglas put him in because the older kid was no good, and started ridiculing the older kid. The older kid got fed up, grabbed the younger boy and put him in a chokehold. The younger kid pulled a blade, cut the older kid's arm.

The cops came. The kid with the blade was still in custody. The older kid had been suspended for fighting.

Some boys get a hard start and then things keep getting harder.

The problem is, by the time one of those boys reaches high school, that hardness has begun to do to him what a chisel does to a slab of marble. It's hard for a teacher to reverse the effect of the chisel. You can set up all the alternatives in the world—an alternative way of being tough, an alternative way of dealing with aggression and fear, an alternative way of gaining respect. You can cordon off turf you know is packed with potential land mines, try to make the surrounding territories more appealing. But then turn your back for half a second and you find a boy has wandered directly into the middle of the minefield anyway. Like he *wants* to blow himself up. Like he's magnetically attracted to trouble.

A lot of teachers—a lot of people, period—see boys like Mr. Douglas's boys—boys who, at fourteen or fifteen, swagger down the hall, avoid eye contact, don't talk much, who seem callous and aloof, who skip class, talk back to teachers, get in fights, maybe bring a blade to school—as a certain *type*. As a hard kid headed for the streets and then, let's be realistic, prison. A type that, past a certain point—let's be realistic again— probably isn't worth trying to rescue from that fate.

But Mr. Douglas doesn't believe in fate. He believes in his boys.

—

STILL, SOME PEOPLE *are* vulnerable—inherently vulnerable—to specific disorders. For instance, if you're a woman who carries one of several mutations of either the BRCA1 or the BRCA2 gene, your risk for developing breast cancer is about five times higher than that of the general population (and upwards of thirty times higher for ovarian cancer). There are several genes that increase the risk of getting Type I diabetes. Same with Type II diabetes. Genetics accounts for about 50 percent of the risk of getting coronary artery disease. There are also genetic risk factors for psychological disorders; substance abuse, depression, schizophrenia—to name just a few—all have a genetic component.

Inherited risk factors aren't a guarantee you'll get sick, but they *do* make you more vulnerable than you otherwise would be to environmental risk factors—cheeseburgers, sugar, cigarettes; trauma, abuse.

Researchers who study how genes and environmental factors interact to influence psychological disorders sometimes use the term *diathesis* (Greek for "disposition") to describe this sort of inherent vulnerability. This is sometimes called the stress-diathesis model of psychopathology. You can frame it, crudely, as:

> vulnerable gene(s)
> + bad shit happening
> ---
> = you winding up fucked in the head

The "warrior gene" tends to get thought of in this way, as a genetic vulnerability that renders men who carry it prone to breaking under specific kinds of pressure.

But the answers you get in science depend on the questions you pose. The initial interest in the warrior gene was driven by this question: what happens when men carrying the low-MAOA version of the gene are exposed to terrible circumstances?

Ask a more sophisticated question and you get a more sophisticated answer.

The American sociologist Ronald Simons wanted to know what happens when men carrying the low-MAOA gene (as well as the other two so-called warrior genes) faced a wider range of conditions—from hardknock childhoods to ones that were secure and nurturing. He found that when men with these presumed genes for violence had been raised in *optimal* circumstances, they were actually *less* prone to violent behaviour later in life—less prone even than men who don't carry any of the so-called warrior genes.[10] In other words, take two kids—one with the presumed genetic vulnerability towards violence and one with so-called normal genes—raise them both in loving, peaceful, nurturing families, and the boy with the ostensible genetic vulnerability to violence has a better chance of being *less* aggressive and more pro-social later in life than the other boy.

So, warrior genes aren't warrior genes at all. They *do* imbue the men who inherit them with a particular genetic predisposition. But it's no more a predisposition for violence than it is for peace.

Simons prefers the term "environmental sensitivity alleles"—*allele* being the technical term for a specific version of a gene. Other researchers have used "vantage sensitivity" to describe what's going on: that some of us are more responsive to a wide variety of environmental conditions than others.[11]

One of the most compelling findings about the environmental sensitivity genes is how common they are. The low-MAOA allele is carried by about a third of all men.[12] Likewise, you have a 50 percent chance of carrying each of the other two environmental sensitivity genes—the ones that influence the brain's serotonin and dopamine systems. And it's common to carry two or all three of these genes at once. What's more, the effect of these genes—the environmental sensitivity they imbue, regardless of whether that environment is good or bad—is amplified when you carry more than one of them.

These genes are widely prevalent among all races and ethnicities. And they're not just a human trait: non-human primates carry versions of these genes too—and there's good evidence they predispose them to be especially peaceable in peaceful times and especially violent in stressful times.[13]

So, what's the take-away from all this?

The take-away is what Mr. Douglas already understands through experience: often the boys who are the hardest are those who are most sensitive and adaptable; counterintuitively, hardness sometimes is an *expression* of a boy's sensitivity and adaptability. If you are extraordinarily sensitive to your surroundings, and your surroundings are extraordinarily frightening, after you have crouched and twitched for a spell, you will eventually send out the serpent.

Mr. Douglas understands that there *is*, in fact, a certain type of boy you have to look out for.

The sensitive types. The boys like Gord.

—

GORD IS IN A TEMPORARY holding facility on the outskirts of Montreal. At night, his cell is awash in the sulphurous glow of the city.

A guard takes him to the weight pit, a large cage where men throw around iron corroded over the years by the sweaty grips of murderers and thieves. The guard locks the cage behind Gord and walks away.

Some of the men are anatomically impossible: no necks, biceps bulging like the bellies of recently fed pythons. Gord has never worked out before. He's not about to start now, though he does feel a compulsive urge to pace. He resists it. He doesn't want to attract attention to himself and end up with one of those pythons wrapped around his neck.

He ends up attracting attention to himself anyway. Over the next few days, he starts playing chess with some of the other inmates. He was in the chess club at school, so he's pretty good. He's playing this old guy from the Caribbean. Gord's winning. The old guy starts, all matter-of-fact, telling Gord how he's fighting to stay in Canada, how the US is pushing for his extradition.

Gord's not paying much attention to this. He's focused on the game. He's mowing through the old guy's pieces like a fat kid attacking a bag of Oreos, knocking them back one after the next.

The old guy is saying he doesn't want to get shipped to the States because then he'll be facing the death penalty.

Gord builds his way to a two-rook lead, a considerable advantage.

The old guy says again, a little more pointedly, that in America he'd be on death row, on account of his having killed a man.

It finally strikes Gord that this isn't chess club, that it's not even chess he's really playing. It's a game that *looks* a whole lot like chess but has a whole other, unstated set of rules. Taking the guy's queen wouldn't be a win so much as a way of setting himself up for a much more serious, much more painful, loss.

Gord quits his push as subtly as he can and lets the old guy hunt down his pieces, one by one.

Gord is transported north of the city to an intake facility where inmates are given a battery of psychological tests before being transferred to the institution where they'll serve the rest of their sentence.

He soon encounters a massive no-neck who keeps blowing Gord kisses and laughing maniacally. Another guy keeps rapping on the window of Gord's cell with a bar of soap, saying the only word he seems to know in English: "Shower!"

Gord doesn't wash for three weeks.

It normally takes about six weeks to get transferred out of the intake facility. Gord's there close to three months. The prison psychologists have determined that he's exceptionally intelligent, gifted probably. This is the first time he's been told this. It should be welcome news. But, according to the prison psychologists, such intelligence makes Gord extremely adaptable to his environment—meaning he's a quick study, the kind of guy who catches on to the ins and outs of a given system pretty quickly. Meaning, with a bit of work, he stands a decent chance of coming up with a way of busting *out* of this particular system in short order. And so the authorities take their time deliberating whether he ought to be placed in a minimum- or medium-security facility.

Gord is desperate for them to make up their minds. His cellmate is a horror show. The guy has scars and tattoos up and down his face. He's serving a fourteen-year sentence. Gord doesn't know what for. Probably it's best not to know.

Crazy Face has insomnia. He stays up all night, slowly shredding his pillowcase into long, thin strips. Gord lies in his bunk trying not to think about what Crazy Face is planning to do with those shreds of cloth. Crazy Face eventually tells Gord that he's decided to protect him. Gord needs protection, because he is young and vulnerable and the men inside are like wolves circling a dying campfire. The cost for protection is a hand job.

When Gord tells me this, the muscles in his jaw and temples clench and unclench.

Shortly after the hand job, Crazy Face gets transferred. But before he leaves, he tells Gord that he has arranged for one of the other men to watch over him. Gord assumes this will involve more hand jobs. Or blow jobs. Or . . .

After Crazy Face is taken away, Gord is in the cell alone. He doesn't feel right. His heart is beating in a way that makes him worry something is seriously wrong. There is a terrible weight on his chest. He can hear his own breath coming and going too fast, and the cell seems even smaller than it was a moment ago, and now it doesn't even seem real. Can you die of a heart attack at nineteen? He's talking to himself, yelling, "What the fuck!? This is NOT going to happen again!" And he is pacing, turning in tight circles and telling himself that he's going to fucking kill everyone, that he's going to beat them to a fucking pulp, that he is done being scared, that he's going to find a way to blow everything up, destroy them all.

After a few hours of this, he's wrung out, drained. But also calmer. There's got to be a smarter way of doing this, he thinks.

Survival is a game.

Games have rules.

Find the rules; win the game.

The most obvious rule in prison is: look hard. Look like you can fuck a guy up. Short of that, hang out with guys who look like they can fuck guys up for you.

Gord makes friends with a short, stocky guy who—a penchant for armed robbery aside—turns out to be pretty nice. He's in his late twenties, fit, squat. Gord walks the yard with him. Other guys see them together. Gord is able to shower.

Rules help you survive, as long as you follow them. Sometimes, though, it's easy to fall back into old habits—outside habits—and forget which rules ought to take precedence inside.

For instance, one day there's a cribbage tournament. Gord's cleaning up and gets focused on the wrong set of rules. He mugs one of his opponents, meaning he claims the points his opponent forgot to count.

That's a legitimate ploy in cribbage. But, as far as prison is concerned, it's a solid way of winding up with your teeth kicked into the back of your throat. It's a way of publicly demonstrating that your opponent isn't just a chump at cribbage but also the kind of guy you can mess with, steal shit from, fuck with.

And so the guy Gord mugs flips over the card table and starts screaming in Gord's face, half in English, half in French. The guards march in and tell the guy to pipe down. He shuts up but then sits there giving Gord a laser-beam death stare. Gord feels himself going hot and cold simultaneously.

Over the next few days, Death Stare wanders in and out of the common room. He circulates. He stands and beams his death ray on Gord. He goes around telling the other people he's in for murder, double murder actually. He says it loud enough Gord can hear. He walks by Gord and bumps him. Later, he bumps the table Gord's chess set is sitting on, knocking the pieces on the floor.

Gord's buddy steps up to Death Stare and tells him to go to the other common room, where the other French guys are, where he fucking belongs. Death Stare backs off. But then the rumours start to fly. The French guys are going to storm the English common room, fuck them all up. There are maybe forty-five French inmates and about eight English guys.

When he hears this rumour, Gord says, out loud in the common room, "They're gonna need more guys." And suddenly the English guys are all laughing and for a moment no one's worried about getting beaten up.

That's another solid rule: jokes are good. They signal to the other men that you're not scared, and while they're laughing, they feel like they're not scared themselves.

But some rules you have to break. Like, for instance, there are two new guys who have been brought to the temporary holding facility. A big, bald, badass motherfucker—six feet four inches of solid man, old-time wrestler big—whom Gord actually ends up getting along with at first. And an American kid who, like Gord, got caught trying to smuggle drugs. Unlike Gord, this kid is always talking. Apparently, he is always listening too, because he overhears Gord calling the big bald guy Kojak, which he promptly reports to the big, bald, badass motherfucker.

Kojak is deeply fucking unhappy about this new nickname. He wants to make Gord unhappy in return. Which is highly probable, considering that Gord's buddy has recently been transferred out and so now it's just Gord.

Gord tries nice. He apologizes to Kojak, tries to explain that he meant it as a compliment because Telly Savalas was, you know, a serious badass. In Kojak's eyes, apologies are for faggots. He sits in the corner of the common room, grinding his fist into the palm of the other hand, staring at Gord in a way that makes Death Stare look like a fucking Care Bear.

Gord is saved by the proverbial bell. The authorities have decided minimum security is suitable for him after all, and he's cleared for transfer. The guards take him to a small holding room where inmates await the prison bus. They lock the door behind him.

Kojak is sitting on the bench in the transfer room like the punch-line of a joke. For a second they look at one another, wide-eyed in mutual surprise. Then Kojak comes at Gord like a Mack truck barrel-ling down on Bambi. Gord's legs refuse to take commands from his cortex. Kojak seems to grow, ballooning as his rage explodes inside him. At the last moment, Bambi jumps out of the way and rolls under one of the benches. Kojak gets down on his hands and knees and presses in on Gord, grabbing at him. Gord's hand shoots out and closes around Kojak's throat. It's enough, for the moment, to keep Kojak from tearing him apart.

The guards come in. They pull Kojak off Gord. They put Kojak in the back of the bus and Gord in the middle. The drive to the minimum-security joint is short, and Gord can feel Kojak radiating hatred like a breached nuclear reactor the whole way. Thank Christ Kojak is being transferred to another facility. Still, Gord is woozy by the time he gets off the bus. He should be participating in frosh week, buying textbooks, meeting girls on campus. Not fending off career criminals.

The new place, the minimum-security prison, looks like an ultra-austere summer camp, if you don't take into account the surrounding perimeter wall and watchtowers. There's grass and red-roofed barracks where the men work and take classes. There's a track and a ball diamond.

The guards take Gord into one of the barracks. The other inmates are still on work duty and he's alone. He lets his guard down. Soon he finds himself sobbing into the pay phone, crying like a baby, his sister on the other end. He can't catch his breath. Then he hears voices, growing louder. The men are returning to the barrack from work. He tells his sister he has to go. He quits crying. *Quits* quits. He doesn't cry for at least another twenty years. He doesn't cry even when his daughter is born. Something deep within him turns off the tap and snaps off the faucet so nothing can come out. He hangs up the phone.

By the time the other men arrive, he looks grim, impenetrable. Hard.

Another solid rule in prison is to do your own time — keep your fucking nose out of other people's business.

Gord builds a routine for himself. He signs up for a few courses. In the computer lab, he teaches himself the programming language Pascal. He tutors some of the other inmates in math. He makes friends with a guy who works in the prison gym and a goth who works in the prison library.

So he's getting by. The problem is, some of the other men don't care to do their own time. A big, aggressive kid in his mid-twenties is taking the same computer programming course as Gord. *Course* is the wrong word, really. The teacher sits with his feet on the desk, reading, while Gord and the aggro kid hunt and peck on outdated PCs. It's just the two of them, Gord and Aggro. But Aggro isn't interested in learning the Boolean commands of computer programming. He's more interested in giving Gord commands.

"Why you doing that?" he says. Or, "Why you sitting that way?" In the cafeteria, he tells Gord where he can and can't eat. He shoves Gord in the chow line. Sometimes he's just quiet, watching Gord, unblinking.

Sometimes, while staring at Gord, Aggro will run his thumb slowly across his throat like it's a blade.

Aggro has a lackey. A skinny kid who comes up to Gord in the cafeteria while Gord is talking to the goth librarian. Skinny says to Gord's friend, "Why you hanging out with this fucking goof?" He means Gord.

On the outside, the word *goof* barely registers as an insult. Inside the Canadian correctional system, it's about the worst thing you can call someone. It is, to an inmate, what *faggot* is to a high school student—and then some. It connotes pedophilia, two-faced squealing, spinelessness. When an inmate calls you a goof in front of other men, you're pretty much sunk unless you deal with it. If you let it go, it means you can be disrespected and you won't do anything about it.

A week or so later, Gord's in the cafeteria at an hour in which it's full of men. Gord sees Skinny across the floor, talking to a few guys. Gord doesn't have a plan. This isn't some sort of premeditated thing. One moment he's tingly and shaky and the numbness is coming on, and the next he's gliding across the floor like he's on casters. And now he's trying to kick Skinny's legs out from under him, but he misses and so quickly follows through with a punch to the head. The punch lands square. Skinny falls backwards and Gord drops with him. Skinny is on the hard floor. Gord is on top of Skinny, his fists attacking him like dogs that have been caged and starved. Wet, crunching crimson blows for his stepdad and Kojak and Aggro and Crazy Face and prison and the stupid fucking idea of trying to smuggle drugs into the fucking country in the first place. And now his punches aren't reaching where he's directing them, because Skinny is falling away—no, wait—it's Gord being lifted from behind as Skinny's bloody, pulpy face retreats from him. There are hands on him, pulling him, pushing him back into the crowd as the guards come running in. Gord is controlling his breath. He is smart enough to shove his hands into his pockets, to hide the blood and raw knuckles.

For a few days after, he has a quiet meltdown in his cell. He's worried about the possibility of retribution, or about getting caught. He also feels guilty. He has no idea whether Skinny has a busted face or brain damage, because Skinny either is still in the infirmary or has been shipped out to hospital or another joint.

Gord's up for parole after serving eight months because he's been on good behaviour. Destroying a guy's face is not good behaviour. He's scared sick someone's going to rat him out. He's not entirely sure what he was thinking. Doing it in front of a huge crowd was a mistake. Though maybe not. Aggro hasn't ratted. That's good. It means that, in addition to not wanting a reputation as a rat, he's looking at Gord differently.

Gord's sitting in the common room. Aggro's there. One of the other inmates gets into it with Aggro, a minor squabble. Funny thing, though—Aggro's not being so aggro. He's stepping down, cooling things off. He's saying, "I only got short time," meaning he's near the end of his sentence too, and he doesn't want to do anything to fuck that up. He says this to all the guys in the room, but Gord has the distinct impression Aggro is broadcasting at him.

Gord says to the room, "I've only got short time too."

There are no more death-ray stares from Aggro. No more shoves in the chow line. No more invisible knives across his throat.

One of the most unpleasant realities of human existence is—and always has been—that sometimes you find yourself in a position where you need to be able to physically protect yourself. The other unpleasant—and unavoidable—fact is that, in many circumstances, violence is the most effective way of doing this.

—

MR. DOUGLAS'S TEAM WAS having its best season in years. Better than anyone hoped for, including Mr. Douglas.

Midway through the season, the boys were headed for one of their away games when Downtown Standard's principal—who I'll call Cynthia Goldblum—climbed aboard the bus. The boys quieted down.

"Before you go today," said Goldblum, "I want to remind you that we're getting a reputation." She paused. The boys looked at her, resigned to the forthcoming lecture on not swearing or fighting or tagging school property or whatever. Instead, Goldblum said, "And it's a good one. You go out there and keep that up. We're depending on you."

The boys went from looking like they were being written up for speeding to looking as if they had just been tossed the keys to a Lamborghini. They started shouting, "GO BLUES!" and "BLEED BLUE!" and stomping their cleats on the floor of the bus.

One of Downtown Standard's former coaches, a retired teacher I'll call Steve Mayfield, had seen the team's standings and wanted to know who this new coach was, this Mr. Douglas who had turned around the juniors' five-year slump. Mayfield had coached the senior team throughout the 1980s, '90s and early 2000s. Downtown Standard had won more than a dozen city championships under him, and several of his students went on to play college ball in the United States. A few had CFL careers. Some of Mayfield's former students credit him as the reason they stayed in school. Mr. Douglas spoke of Mayfield the way a fan of the Chicago Bears might talk about Mike Ditka.

Mayfield showed up to Downtown Standard after school one day. He watched Mr. Douglas coach the boys for a while then asked Mr. Douglas what he had been doing differently. Mr. Douglas told Mayfield about limiting the number of plays, about making sure each of the boys got on the field during a game. Mayfield nodded. He didn't really say anything, not explicitly. He didn't have to. Mr. Douglas knows how to send a message without talking; and he knows when he's being told something without being spoken to.

Mayfield came to practices a couple more times. He threw the ball around with the boys, helped finesse the quarterbacks a little. Mr. Douglas told me it was good to have him there, that he felt he had been handed the torch.

The boys made it to the city playoffs. They were eliminated after losing their first game, but they didn't care.

"They were running around happy at the end of the game," Mr. Douglas told me. "They were excited, getting their pictures taken. Making the playoffs—the kids were proud of that."

The senior boys' team had an even better season than Mr. Douglas's squad. They made it all the way to the city championship, where they faced Collegiate Heights.

The final game was in early November. The sky was grey, the trees wrought iron. The field was hard-packed and the grass like worn-out corduroy. The bleachers were largely empty. Mr. Douglas and I sat high up behind a small cluster of parents.

A guy built like a fire hydrant was sitting a couple of rows behind us. The kind of guy who looks as though he's made of poured concrete. He was in his late thirties, I guessed, about my age, with kanji symbols tattooed down one side of his neck and a tattoo of a crown on the other side. He wore his toque low on his brow so you couldn't really make out his eyes. His goatee was trimmed to a diabolic point. I noticed a bulbous ring on one of his fingers. I immediately thought of how that ring—that fist— could stamp a hole into my cranium. At one point we heard the guy on his phone, sounding like an AK-47 going off—short, injurious bursts: "I don't give a fuck! Shut up! Where's your mother?"

At half-time, Collegiate was leading slightly. I stood to take a walk in order to warm up. I came back and was about to sit down next to Mr. Douglas when we heard shouting below us. It was the Fire Hydrant, yelling at a younger guy who was taller but not as powerfully built. I'd noticed him sitting with two women in the front row of bleachers, wearing an immaculate peacoat and a black Kangol cap.

Fire Hydrant and Kangol were now standing chest to chest, Fire Hydrant steaming like a faulty pressure cooker while Kangol was stone cold.

Fire Hydrant yelled, "Tough guy!" Then he barked at Kangol, actually growled like a dog, as if to say to Kangol *you're all bark!*

Kangol stood there, unflinching, staring straight at Fire Hydrant.

One of the women stood up and said to Fire Hydrant, exasperated, "I can't even come to support my nephew without you—"

Fire Hydrant cut her off. "Shut up, cunt!"

"I can't be talked to that way!" she yelled, looking back and forth between the two men.

Mr. Douglas and I had slowly worked our way down from our seats until we were standing on the risers a couple of rows above them. Fire Hydrant had his back to us and I was trying to gauge whether he was carrying a weapon under his baggy windbreaker. I was worried he might pull a gun. I was thinking about the kids in the stands. (Mr. Douglas told me later he was thinking the same thing.) I was trying to figure out whether

I was capable of tackling Fire Hydrant, whether it would have any effect. It was like psyching yourself up to step in front of a bus.

Then Mr. Douglas's educational assistant stepped between the two men. He was smiling and talking to Kangol as though he were a buddy of his, like there was nothing to worry about. Kangol was still staring down Fire Hydrant, but he was nodding slightly at whatever the educational assistant was saying. Then he was pursing his lips in disgruntled resignation. Then he was walking away, heading towards the parking lot.

Fire Hydrant, convinced he had won the exchange, strutted back to his seat.

During the second half, Downtown Standard was preparing for a punt. The kid kicking the ball was Fire Hydrant's son. Before the kick, Fire Hydrant left the stands and called his boy over and said something to him. The kid walked back onto the field as if his father had just slapped him in public, head down, his shoulders up near his ears. He paused before the kick. Then he ran at the ball and fired it up the field like a cannonball.

Still, Standard couldn't overcome Collegiate's lead, and were beaten 10–2. After the final whistle, Fire Hydrant came out of the stands and lit a cigar and walked onto the field towards the players. One of the refs, a slender, middle-aged guy with thinning hair, approached him and told him he couldn't smoke on school property. Fire Hydrant pushed past the ref without acknowledging him. The ref started to follow but then stopped and walked away.

The boys came off the field. Some of them had tears running down their cheeks. A couple of them were full-on sobbing.

Mr. Douglas was there to greet them, shaking their hands, congratulating them for a good game. "It's tough," Mr. Douglas was saying to them in consolation. "It's tough. For real."

Fire Hydrant's son, the kicker, came off the field. No tears. Face hard.

Later, Mr. Douglas gave me a lift to the subway. The educational assistant was in the car with us.

"You were doing some serious politicking back there," Mr. Douglas said to him.

"I think they had a beef from back in the day."

"What did you say to the younger guy?" I asked.

"I told him it would look bad for the school if something happened. He seemed to listen to that. I said they could settle their beef later."

We drove in silence for a couple of minutes.

"We'll hear about something going down later," Mr. Douglas said. He sounded tired.

—

FOR A LONG TIME after he got out of jail, Gord wasn't especially interested in feeling much. He was focused on moving forward, as far away from his past as he could get.

He returned to Newfoundland and started university. He had an uncle in the Salvation Army who helped him find an apartment. To this day, Gord will slip a hundred-dollar bill in a Sally Ann collection basket at Christmastime. His mother's family was warm. His cousins welcomed him back to the Rock, brought him into the family fold. But they gave him his space, didn't make him talk about his time in prison. He reported to his parole officer at regular intervals. He kept his distance from other students, which wasn't so hard because he had trouble being around other people. If someone sat too close to him, stood too close, he'd get twitchy and uptight. He didn't look people in the eyes. Sometimes, as he walked to campus, a cruiser would follow him for a distance like a hound.

Gord concentrated on his studies with an unholy intensity—math and then physics, the realms of pure logic. The pure rules by which we attempt to explain the world, make it a predictable, solvable place.

He eventually got friendly enough with a few other math and physics nerds. Guys who were most comfortable playing cards and games. Gord never opened up, discussed where he'd been or what prison had done to him.

One of the things it did, he says now, nearly twenty years later, was dull his empathy, harden him in some permanent way. "Before," he told me, "I used to bond with people who got picked on or hurt." He meant when he was in high school. "But I lost it at nineteen, and in my twenties. I don't think I had much in university. I think it had a lot to do with prison."

Gord had got out, but a wall remained between him and the rest of the world.

After he graduated, he focused on establishing a career. He found a girl, got married, bought a house with a fence and a garage. Had a kid. He kept moving forward, away from his past. After work, he'd drink. A couple beers, a couple fingers of whisky. A bottle of wine. Drink helped maintain the wall, the distance between him and other people. The distance between him and himself.

"How long did it take for you to take down the wall you built in prison?" I asked him. This was during our third or fourth conversation.

He looked at me, then said, "I don't know if I *can* take it down. It might just be who I am. I think it's made me think differently about how I trust people. You can lose my trust in a split second. It doesn't mean I won't talk to you or be friends with you. But I'm very selective, and almost nobody gets in."

"Who's in now?" I asked him.

"You," he said. "I would say you."

I should explain that I met Gord through his ex-wife, a former colleague of mine who knew I was working on this book. At the time, she and Gord had just separated, just sold the house with the fence and the garage, and had each bought condos within walking distance of one another so they could share custody of their daughter. My colleague thought it would be good for Gord to talk to me — I think maybe because she felt it might be good for him to open up to another guy about some of the feelings he'd been keeping in for years. Gord and I met for a beer. He told me a bit about his story. I told him I wanted to write about it. I was surprised when he agreed. And then I was surprised by just how much he opened up to me.

Once, while we were talking — this was during one of our first interviews, when he had just started to tell me about prison — he stopped abruptly and said, "I've been scared ever since."

"Are you scared right now?" I asked.

"I'm actually fucking terrified," he said. "I'm a terrified guy."

You'd never guess it. At the right angle, Gord looks a bit like the actor Timothy Olyphant playing tough-as-nails Deputy US Marshal Raylan Givens in the series *Justified*: rugged, handsome, slightly boyish — though notably more tired, a touch heavier.

"What are you afraid of?" I asked.

"I don't know," he said. "Everything—like, we're having this conversation right now and I can feel it. My ears are buzzing. I feel this every day."

"So, what—like, driving? Walking? Teaching?"

"Yeah. You think of the worst-case scenarios. Like, at school—is this going to be the day someone brings a gun? Is today the day a fight breaks out? Is this where two kids are going to get into it? Is this where I'm going to get hurt? Is this where it's going to end?"

Another time, we were sitting at his table and Gord pulled out a copy of his federal pardon. There was a photocopy of his fingerprints too.

"Usually," he said, "you only get to see this after I've slept with you."

We both laughed, but really, that's normally as close as you have to get to Gord before he'll tell you about doing time. Most of his colleagues have no idea. None of his students.

The pardon refers to him as Gord Wilson. It was the first time I realized he wasn't born Douglas.

I asked him about this.

During the period when he was seeking the pardon, after he'd done his undergrad, moved on to his master's degree in physics and was thinking about applying to teacher's college, he legally changed his name. Along the way, Gord's fingerprints had got mixed up with some other guy's, which meant he had a slew of other charges attributed to him under his birth name. The mix-up got resolved, but taking a new name was part safety precaution, part new start.

After several interviews, I still wasn't entirely sure why Gord was opening up to me, a stranger who was going to make his private life public. I brought this up the day he showed me his pardon.

"I didn't tell you why we're doing this?" he said.

I shook my head.

"Like how it relates to the breakdown of my marriage?"

"No," I said. "Tell me."

A couple of years earlier, Gord told me, his wife had mentioned his time in prison to one of their neighbours. She did it without really thinking about it. Or thinking anything of it. It was just something Gord had done when he was a kid. So long ago now, it seemed like an inert compound. And Gord had never explicitly told her *not* to talk about it. The neighbour didn't find it an especially big deal.

But Gord did. It wasn't inert to him.

"I was blindsided by how much it affected me," he told me. "It was so damaging that I still get a physical response from it. This piece of my past had a way bigger influence than I expected. It sucker-punched me. I tried to get over it, but I couldn't. I went into a brooding, downward spiral."

He quit drinking, cold turkey.

"Normally, you get drunk and *then* blow up your life," he explained. "I got sober and did it."

Sober, Gord realized he didn't trust his wife. That he no longer loved her the way you need to if you're going to spend your life with someone. Or maybe it was that he never had, and had never fully known it, having kept such a wide berth between having emotions and actually feeling them. Maybe the capacity to open up enough to fully trust someone, love someone, got left behind in that version of himself that used to be able to cry.

He had an affair. It wasn't love, but like setting off an incendiary device. His marriage, he felt, was a bridge that needed burning.

"It was a purposeful thing," he explained. "And it was fucking evil of me, really."

"And, so, what does this have to do with why you're talking to me?" I asked him.

"Basically," he said, "I ended my marriage because she told someone about my incarceration."

"Okay. And?"

"And I'm attacking the problem because the incarceration shouldn't be that powerful anymore."

"So, talking to me? Going public with your story, your past, is—what?"

"It's me taking control over my fear."

"You ever think about what you did?" I asked him once. I meant beating up Skinny.

"Every day," he said.

Early on in his teaching career, Gord was encouraged to work with gifted kids. But he pushed hard to work at an inner-city school like Downtown Standard. "This is where I belong," he told me.

"Is it a kind of penance?" I asked.

He shook his head no. "But I definitely feel like I've got a debt to repay. I fucked up pretty badly, and I don't feel like there's room for any more fuck-ups."

Because here's the thing: you beat a man in the prison cafeteria or go hunting for fights in bars, or bring a knife to school and cut someone, or smash another player who has illegally tackled you, or start a fight on a subway—whatever—you're still responsible. That's still on you. Even if you've had a few hard knocks, had your junk batted around by your stepfather or someone's funny uncle, live in a tough neighbourhood, get picked on, called faggot, or find life overwhelming because you are overwhelmingly sensitive. No matter what your particular predisposition, vantage sensitivity genes or not. Because genes don't cause you to commit violent acts unawares. Whatever their influence, they don't make you a preprogrammed automaton. Just like a hard environment, no matter how it chisels away at you, doesn't *make* you do hard shit.

*You* make you.

Gord and I got together a couple more times after we had finished all the serious interviewing. We went for wings and beer once. Gord talked football. Another time, we hung out at his place. He had bought a life-sized light sabre for his daughter, who was at her mother's that week. Gord was catching up on laundry using detergent he had made with his students, part of a class project. I told him about some of the other guys I had been spending time with for this book. When I left, Gord saw me down to the lobby and out to the street.

"Hey!" he called as I was walking away. "Be careful, all right?"

I turned around. "What do you mean?"

"I worry about you, man, with some of the guys you're talking to out there."

I smiled. "Nothing to worry about, brother."

"Yeah," he said. "Still. You know—keep your eyes open."

—

ONE OF THE GUYS I was spending a lot of time with was on the lam. I'd meet Tommy at a subway stop and then wander around with him, avoiding major streets and intersections. We trotted like stray dogs in the cold, through back alleys and parking lots, talking. Well, Tommy talked. He talked so much and smoked so many cigarettes he'd develop a slurry of yellow foam in the corners of his mouth.

He had turned thirty recently and had spent nearly half his life inside, starting with a stint in juvie at thirteen. When I met him, he had been out of jail for six or seven months. It was a personal best—the longest stretch he had spent outside the system in his adult life. He was tall, about six-two, and roughly two hundred pounds. His face and hands were covered in tiny scars. His nose was off-centre from a bad break. His eyes were hooded like a retired prizefighter's. He had tattoos—bad, roughly done ink—on his neck and arms. His hip was messed up from a time, he told me, when the guards beat him so bad they busted it. His orbital socket had been broken too. He pulled his pants down once to show me the divots in his thigh where, according to him, a bullet had entered and then exited again. He had some sort of graft on his head from—again, according to him—some sort of bullet wound.

I met Tommy through a woman who worked for the John Howard Society, the non-profit organization that helps get ex-cons on their feet. I'll call her Tina. Tommy wasn't a client, but Tina had known Tommy's dad when she was younger and had a soft spot for the old man even though he was dead now. He had been a pro bodybuilder and, before that, high up in a local bike gang, selling coke and heroin. Tommy told me that the official cause of his father's death was a heart attack but that he believed his father had been poisoned by an old gang member.

Tommy's mother had been a junkie and wasn't in the picture. Once, when he was a kid, he told me, she forgot him at a pharmacy because she was so eager to get back home and inject the painkillers she'd scored. Before he ever wound up in custody, Tommy was in and out of Children's Aid and foster homes.

Neither Tina nor I could figure out where he was living. He told me he had been kicked out of a flophouse after refusing to have sex with the landlady. He said he was living in a large military-style tent on a friend's property, but when I asked to check it out, he changed the topic. He had told Tina he was staying with friends.

"Tommy's 'friends' aren't friends," she told me. "Some of the people he knows are very dysfunctional and fully engaged in illegal activities, to say the least. I really wonder what situations he puts himself into sometimes."

Tommy was shoplifting food regularly in order to eat. It was getting cooler each day and he kept showing up to our meetings wearing two or three hoodies at a time. Tina was bringing him bags of non-perishables and clothing. When November made its turn from chilly to merciless, I gave him an old down parka.

I enjoyed hanging out with Tommy at first, as he dodged the law. According to him, the warrant for his arrest was for failing to meet with his parole officer. Tommy told me the charge was pure bullshit because his probation had ended; his parole officer had signed off on him. It was the cops at the local precinct being vindictive—they knew him, knew his reputation, and weren't willing to give him a second chance.

Tina thought this might be true, but she kept encouraging Tommy to turn himself in, get it cleared up.

"He's no angel," Tina told me, "but he's fundamentally a good kid."

I had trouble seeing what Tina saw.

When he was ten, Tommy shot an old Chinese couple with a pellet gun because he wanted to show his buddy how tough he was. Also, it pissed him off they weren't speaking English. Later, he was associated with a chapter of the Bloods, cooking and selling crack. He had been arrested for grand theft auto; as a teenager, he stole a Chrysler K-car that happened to be an undercover vehicle. He had beaten guys with his bare hands more times than he could count, and though he wouldn't come out and admit to killing anyone, that's clearly what he wanted me to believe. He told me he'd run up in the clubs and "squeeze," meaning pull a trigger. "That was part of the rush for me," he said. But when I asked him what club, who exactly he was shooting, he'd veer off topic.

When he was eighteen, Tommy was charged as an accessory to murder. A kid he knew blew the head off another boy with a shotgun. "It was over a girl," Tommy told me. The shotgun was traced to Tommy—though he insists it was stolen from under his front porch, where Tommy's old man had stowed it.

He took me to the site of the shooting, Monarch Park, a public green in the east end of the city. There was a swimming pool, drained for the winter, full of brown puddles and dead leaves, surrounded by chain-link.

"There were all these police tags along the fence," Tommy said, running his finger along it, "and about a million pieces of the guy's brain." He was like a tour guide at one of those sad roadside museums that house a single morbid curiosity—a two-headed calf, a cyclopean fetus. Tommy clearly enjoyed having the power to spook.

That time he ended up in the Don Jail and his cellmate, an older guy, tried to put the moves on him. Tommy said he stuck the guy with a toothbrush he had made into a shiv. "I stabbed him six times."

Tommy always kept us moving because he didn't want the cops to spot him. We settled for a time on a bench in front of a public school so he could smoke a joint. He pulled out a four-inch Spider-Man pocket knife and opened the blade. "It's not like in the movies when they stab someone all over," he said. "When you stab someone for real, you stab them relatively close to the same spot." Tommy jabbed the blade in my direction, a few inches from my chest. He was messing around, but I had to keep myself from flinching. "You end up with one big hole," he continued, "not just a bunch of puncture holes. The last time I stabbed him, it just opened up, and when my thumb went in, that's when I decided, 'Okay. He's probably not going to fight back now.'"

"How'd it feel," I asked, "sticking him?"

"It felt great," Tommy said.

The thing about Tommy is that he was full of shit. I was just never sure quite how much. He had done a lot of bad stuff as a minor, which I couldn't confirm because I didn't have access to his record under the Youth Criminal Justice Act. Tommy kept promising he'd bring me a copy but then wouldn't follow through.

Then there were all his tough-guy stories. Every time we met—*every* time—Tommy had a new fight story for me. How he had just got into a scrap and won, usually with a single, spectacular knockout punch. A couple of times he said these fights had taken place on his way to meet me. Once, he cold-cocked a guy because, apparently, the guy offended Tommy's sensibility by pissing in sight of a children's playground.

Tommy was a huge fan of the UFC and said he used to train seriously as a kick-boxer, that he wanted to train again—hit the bags, knock guys out in the ring the way he used to. He told me that when he was in prison, he kept guys in line, kept the range in order with his fists. When I asked him if he wanted to go to the gym, get some sparring in, he was enthusiastic, but, as with bringing me his record, he never followed through. He told me about all the guns he used to own. Engraved handguns, sawed-off shotguns. Cars, too. For a while he was staying in a new flophouse but had to leave abruptly after his landlord, mistaking him for someone else, attacked him. Tommy knocked the landlord out cold. With a single punch, of course.

He'd posture, too. We'd be walking down the street and pass a clean-cut guy minding his own business—someone who looked as though he might spend time in a gym—and Tommy would say, "Look at this fuckin' goof." He'd say it loud enough the guy would hear. And then, when the guy turned his head our way, Tommy would follow up with, "Yeah, you heard me, you fuckin' tough-guy faggot."

It was intimidating. But it *was* just talk. No guy in his right mind was going to take that kind of bait, not from two big guys. And Tommy knew it.

After a while, his tough-guy routine started to feel like reading too many Clive Cussler novels—the plots all running together, fantastical and formulaic. Still, Tommy genuinely had the power to put me on physical alert like no one else I spoke to while researching this book. There *was* the accessory-to-murder charge—that was real. I had been able to verify that.

I spent a lot of time trying to figure out who would come out on top in a fight. I felt I ought to be able to take him. I was heavier, stronger. I was training a lot. And Tommy's health was shaky. He kept getting skinnier every time I saw him. He told me on separate occasions that he had diabetes, hepatitis C, a bacterial infection, walking pneumonia and a busted foot. One time, after he told me he was starving because he was so broke, I took him out for breakfast, where he just sat, absent-mindedly dipping a triangle of cold toast in congealed egg yolk. I was pretty sure he also had a serious drug problem. He had the teeth and mouth sores of someone who hit a pipe.

All this to say that, if it were to come to a fair fight, I felt the odds should be in my favour. But I was never sure, if it ever came down to it, it *would* be a fair fight. I thought of the Spider-Man knife. I thought of Tommy getting a kick out of running into clubs and squeezing the trigger.

I eventually realized that it wasn't his physical presence that sketched me out. It was all the talk. All the tough-guy stories. I knew there was a high degree of bullshit mixed in with whatever he had really done, that he was amplifying how dangerous he really was. But it still worked.

I got a text from Tommy early in December:

> I HAVE NOWHERE TO STAY ANY MORE!!
> SO I THINK I'M JUST GOING TO GO IN 2NIGHT!!

Life on the lam was getting to him. The streets were cold and hard as iron. It had sapped Tommy, running from the cops. He told me he was going to take care of the mix-up with the warrant, try to get a job, get a place of his own.

Tommy had a son, a young kid who was somewhere in the foster system. "I want to get him back," he told me. "Bring him up right."

It sounded like a lot of wishful thinking. But, for what it's worth, I believed him—not necessarily that he'd follow through. But I believed the wish, that he *wanted* to be able to do it.

That evening, he called me from outside the police station. He had been expecting it to be a big deal when he showed up to turn himself in. But the officer at the reception desk knew nothing about the outstanding warrant and had no idea who he was. Tommy sounded mildly disappointed telling me this. He'd had to explain the whole thing to the officer. Since then, he had been waiting for a detective, someone who knew his case, killing time chain-smoking outside the station.

"I'm just going to stay out here and talk on my phone."

He reminded me of Gord's boys—he was checking in with me, telling me he was scared without telling me. We chatted awhile. He made fun of the guys being brought into the station as they walked past him. Then he got quiet. He told me he wanted to hang up so he could call his lawyer.

His lawyer didn't answer, so he called me back.

"If the fucking detectives aren't down here in the next fifteen minutes," he said, "I'm taking off."

"It's probably better to stay there," I told him. "You'll just be making life harder for yourself at this point."

"Yeah. But the waiting is killing me. I don't want to get into that mode, getting ready to go back in, get into that frame of mind."

We had talked about this frame of mind before. Life on the street was physically harder than it was inside. Inside, you got fed; you didn't freeze to death. But it required you to flip a switch.

"I go from nice guy," Tommy told me, "to don't-fucking-come-near-me. It's not a comfortable thing. It's not something you like going through. It makes you that much angrier, and you take it out on people that much more."

But he stayed.

—

THAT'S THE THING ABOUT living the kind of life Tommy was living, about living in any hard environment, really—prison, the streets, gang life: it'll change you, change the way you feel.

The Yale sociologist Elijah Anderson has spent his career studying this kind of impact in Philadelphia's inner-city neighbourhoods. Anderson is an ethnographer—he walks the neighbourhoods he studies; he talks to the guys who live there, gets to know them, where they're from, how they've been raised.

These are dangerous places, where fights happen all the time. Things escalate and go sideways quickly. Weapons are cheap and easy to get hold of. Retaliation and turf wars are part of the landscape. Dudes die, and they die young.

People who live in these places, especially young men, follow what Anderson calls "street code"—though it's equally fair to call it "prison code" or "gang code"—the belief that being able to step up and protect your own neck matters. Part of the code is making sure other men know you're a credible threat—that they are not to take you lightly. It means more than just the quiet knowledge that you can handle yourself in a serious situation. It means reacting to situations that seem trivial to outsiders — a slight, a rumour, a look — as if they are deadly serious. Taking dudes out at the slightest provocation. Starting things, posturing, amplifying your badness, broadcasting to the general public that you are not to be fucked with. Because, if you let disrespect slide, someone's liable to think you're soft, that you can be walked all over, used as a stepping stone.

The more dire the situation people find themselves in, the deeper they tend to buy into these beliefs — that being hard and acting violently are necessary. And the deeper the buy-in, the higher the likelihood of actually being hard and acting violently.[14]

The standard sociological explanation for this is that people internalize the social values of the environment they're in. Violent subcultures condone and promote toughness and violence, *ergo* people in those subcultures value toughness and violence.

But it's not a particularly satisfying explanation. Besides being a circular argument, it makes it seem as though social values are arbitrary, as though kids growing up in tough places choose violence the way you might choose to wear a porkpie hat simply because all your friends are wearing them.

There's a tendency in sociology to view social values as the cohesive element that helps bond the individuals who compose a society. There's something to this, clearly. But part of why Anderson's research has got so much attention — his work is highly regarded among his peers; he's also written about it for the lay public [15] — is that he argues that street code exists because it also serves a utilitarian purpose for the individuals who adopt it.

Street code emerges out of a particular ecosystem, a set of circumstances that are beyond the control of the men in those neighbourhoods: high levels of unemployment, low levels of education, a chronic and systemic lack of resources and opportunities. Dealing drugs and fencing stolen goods is often the only viable option for a lot of them, and even then, competition is stiff. And, importantly, these are not neighbourhoods where the cops do the same kind of serving and protecting that they do in richer, whiter neighbourhoods. Not by any measure.

So, in these circumstances, being a tough guy *is* a choice, but it's a choice you make between the devil and the deep blue sea. Maybe if you're Gandhi you have the spine to remain a pacifist in the face of terrifying circumstances. It's a noble ideal, but good luck convincing a terrified fifteen-year-old who lives in gang-riddled public housing that he's not better off carrying a weapon.

Psychologists who study violence in non-human animals sometimes refer to it as a contingent response, meaning it's a behaviour elicited under specific circumstances. Intrude on a songbird's territory, threaten a rodent, challenge the social dominance of a primate, interfere with mating or feeding, corner an animal, and they turn violent. After all, there is no survival without self-preservation. Violent behaviour in animals isn't the result of higher-order cognition—planning, tactical thinking, the adoption of abstract social values. It's the result of a particular emotional state, one underwritten by two emotions: fear and anger.

People who live in violent places, particularly kids raised in violent subcultures, have higher levels of chronic anger. They tend to view relationships in a hostile, mistrustful way. They perceive the world and the people in it as dangerous and threatening.[16] And if they also happen to be carrying one of the environmental sensitivity genes, fear and anger are amplified—all the more so if they're carrying more than one of these alleles.[17]

Humans, of course, have the capacity to make conscious decisions, an understanding of consequences, a moral code. But it's worth considering that, at an emotional level, we respond to threat just like the rest of the animal kingdom. Put us in a corner, we get scared and angry. And some of us get more scared and angry than others.

You choose being a tough guy over being a potential victim. But you have to commit to that choice, act on it. There's a lot of fronting, sure. A lot of talking and posturing. Looking hard, never smiling. Talking a mean game. But if you're in a dangerous-enough situation, a tough-guy act will only get you so far. In fact, it might just get you in deeper shit. Eventually, you'll find yourself in a position where you've got to walk the walk, bury your fear and muster some venom.

And so the serpent is a Chinese finger trap. There comes a point when you've shoved the mouse down so deep, you can't pull it back. Not without losing a sizeable chunk of who you once were.

—

THE MORNING AFTER Tommy turned himself in, I bailed him out. It was self-serving on my part: I thought maybe he would reciprocate by finally getting me a copy of his record.

As his surety, I was obliged to let the police know if he skipped town. I also had to verify that he had a fixed address. On that front, Tommy said he needed a few days to pull something together.

A couple of weeks later, I met him at a subway station in the east end and we walked to an old, dilapidated two-storey house. The front windows were draped with black garbage bags from the inside. Tommy led me down the alley to the back door. The tiny backyard was littered with broken furniture and a large trampoline that had come apart over the years and now looked like the wreck of a hot-air balloon. I thought I caught something ghoulish crawling along the ground, but it was only fabric torn from the trampoline undulating in the wind.

Tommy unlocked the side door. The smell from inside was overwhelming. Before I could even register it consciously, I broke out in goosebumps. It was the smell of death—not putrefaction, but the stale smell of life that has come to an end. Of collapse and entropy, abandon, the end of civilization; the smell that's left after everything organic has rotted and all that remains is dust and fibre, the particulate matter of a million smoked cigarettes, the tang of oxidizing metal, the blood smell of rust. Ceiling tiles falling. Wood bending and bowing as water seeps into it. Glass cracking, caulking and rubber seals withering like dying worms. Floorboards shifting and the dirt beneath them mouldering.

The kitchen was falling apart. There were empty cans of Alphagetti sitting in a sink of stagnant water. Their tops had been hacked open with a knife. Old magazines lay across the floor with their pages curled up like the wings of giant, dessicated moths. Along the walls, there were countless cigarette butts, receipts, wrappers, nameless fluff, detritus— mummified viscera pouring out of holes in the drywall.

"There are rats in the walls," Tommy said. "They pack it full of that shit and it keeps coming out."

He opened the fridge. The light was out. Inside were rumpled bags of mouldy Wonder bread, jars of corrupting mayonnaise, plates of inedible, poisonous matter heaped upon itself. Dark slime-mould coated the inner walls. Tommy pulled out a bottle of vanilla Ensure and offered it to me. I declined.

I asked him whose place it was. He gave me a vague story about a buddy of his. I had the distinct sense there had been other people here recently, that Tommy had convinced them to vacate the place for the afternoon.

His room was near the side door, where we had entered the house. He slept on a floppy, sodden, rat-gnawed foam mat. The floor was littered with old clothes and garbage. The door to his room had been hijacked from a closet, a rickety bi-fold thing that only closed halfway. Tommy had torn the screen from one of the windows and placed it on the floor across the entrance to try to keep the rats out.

He pointed to the stairs leading to the basement. "That's where they come from," he said. He meant the rats. At the bottom of the stairs was a door, which was shut. The stairwell's walls were coated in graffiti. On the overhang were two crimson palmprints, as though someone had bathed their hands in blood and high-fived the wall. I felt as if I were in a horror novel, that maybe there was something in the basement behind that door. A meth lab. Tweaked-out, pin-eyed meth zombies, skeletal and volatile, jittery and murderous. Or something worse. Some dark H.P. Lovecraft shit I was better off not knowing about.

"You can go down there if you want," Tommy said, "but I'm not going with you."

I told him I didn't need to see it.

I never ended up seeing his record either. He never came through with it, though he kept promising.

In the end, I knew all I really needed to know about him. We sleep in the safest, most secure environment we can find. The house Tommy took me to was the safest spot he had.

That night, after I visited him, I thought of him sleeping on the floor, listening to the rats moving through the walls, trying to gnaw through the screen that lay across his doorway. Listening, in all probability, to whoever else came and went in that place, transient meth-heads smoking themselves into amphetamine psychosis in the next room. Tommy's world was a scary place.

I fell asleep and dreamt I was walking down the street with a young guy. It wasn't Tommy exactly, but it felt like him. He was wearing a sling. His arm was folded against his torso in the worst, most unimaginable way—a compound fracture with multiple switchbacks. It looked like a mangled wing, twisted and wrecked and utterly unusable. The pain from a break like that would have been unbearable in real life. But in the dream, the Tommy stand-in was coping somehow, masking the pain, trying to move forward, making like it didn't bother him.

The real Tommy was good at fronting, acting the tough guy. He *was* tough. He was genuinely hard, brutal even, however much bullshit he added to the mix. The bullshit stories were like the hood of the serpent, the threat that precedes the strike. There was venom in him too, I was sure. But there was something else. I had glimpsed it for a moment, talking to him while he was waiting outside the police station, thinking about how going back to prison was going to be, and in the way he looked at the dark stairwell leading to the basement of that house of horrors. Look far enough down the throat of the serpent and you'll always find a mouse.

—

THE SCHOOL YEAR GOT CRAZY and I didn't talk to Gord for a couple of months. I got busy too. The holidays came and went. It was January. The city was cold and dark. I was in a pub with my wife and a couple of our friends when I got a text from him:

> I WOULD LIKE TO TALK TO YOU.
> CALL ME WHEN YOU GET A CHANCE.
> I CAN'T TEXT WHAT I HAVE TO SAY.
> SORRY. THANKS.

When I called, Gord sounded stuffed up, as if he had a bad cold. The words were pouring out of him like something inside had cracked open. The pub was underground. The reception wasn't great. I wasn't sure I had heard him right.

"Hold on," I said. I ran up the stairs and out onto the sidewalk. "What did you just say?"

"My running back was shot this afternoon," he said.

"What did you mean?"

"Tyler. You met him."

The kid who was the answer to the prayer for speed.

"I'm a wreck," Gord said. "I don't normally reach out."

"I'm glad you did," I said, sort of automatically. I was having trouble picturing Tyler, bringing his face to mind. It was the weirdest thing. I *knew* I knew him, but it was as if my mind, by withholding the image of the kid, was preventing itself from acknowledging what had happened.

"I saw him yesterday." Gord sobbed into the phone. "I shook his hand. He was smiling and laughing. He was a happy kid."

"Wait," I interrupted. "When you say shot, you don't mean fatally, right?" I knew the answer, but for some reason I asked anyway, as though I was looking for a loophole. "He's not dead, is he?"

"Yes," said Gord. "He was killed."

The Saturday papers ran stories about the shooting. There weren't a lot of details. Tyler was visiting a friend. The two boys were planning to play Xbox all afternoon. Somehow Tyler ended up in the stairwell of his friend's apartment building with several bullets in his chest. The elevators were out. The paramedics had to run up several storeys. Tyler bled out. The building his friend lived in was part of a public housing project that had a reputation for gang activity. The police thought Tyler was probably lured into the stairwell. They had no idea why. They were looking for two men in their twenties, a skinny white guy with bad skin and a short black guy.

Gord spent a lot of time over the weekend curled up in bed, holding his four-year-old daughter. His ex-wife came over to comfort him. He talked to his colleagues on the phone.

On Monday, there was work to do. The media were running a shot of Tyler wearing a do-rag, looking hard in football gear. Tyler wasn't a tough guy. He had nothing to do with gang stuff. The police had told this to the press. The stories mentioned this, but Gord and Cynthia Goldblum, his principal, knew how people's minds worked. You see a picture of a black kid; the headline says something about a shooting; the copy says something about public housing. You jump to the conclusion the kid's a gang-banger without reading much past paragraph two.

Gord and Cynthia held a press conference on Monday morning in the school library. The reporters set up bouquets of microphones and recorders on a folding table in front of them.

Cynthia made the opening remarks. She said the school was shaken to the core. She talked about Tyler's sister, how she had graduated from Downtown Standard and was in her third year of college on a scholarship. How Tyler had been on the same track. How he ought to be remembered in that way, as someone to emulate.

Gord wore a Blues jersey. He was thin and waxen, as if he had lost a lot of blood himself. The circles under his eyes were so dark it looked like he had been in a fist fight.

"Every now and then," he told the reporters, his voice wobbling hard to avoid falling into a sob, "you get to see a boy become a man." He stopped. "This is why I teach. This is why I coach." The features of his face started to do the thing that Dali's clocks do. He recovered. He apologized. A salvo of flashes went off. "People need to know how good he was. He had the potential to be great. And now, we'll never know. Also . . ." The words caught in Gord's throat. He was choking back tears. "Also . . . he had a really good smile." Gord held up Tyler's number-seven jersey. The reporters gathered around like fruit flies. Shutters clicked. Pieces of the tape Tyler used to cinch it in still clung to his jersey. Gord explained what the tape was for. "I couldn't bring myself to take these off," he said. "We're going to have the team sign it and give it to his mother."

That afternoon, the news sites ran stories about how Tyler was a leader on the field and in the classroom; how he was blossoming into a first-rate athlete and student; how he had the potential to get a university scholarship. There were new photos of him, too. One showed him on the field, running, looking focused but relaxed, a portrait of the man he was becoming. One was his school portrait from the year before, before he had figured out how to look tough. Smiling. Unguarded. Still a boy.

For weeks, there were teddy bears and flowers in the hallways of Downtown Standard, all for Tyler.

"I realized today," Gord told me not long after Tyler's funeral, "that we also can't build up Tyler too much."

I asked him what he meant.

"There's this kid," Gord told me—a student of his, a kid Gord worried might get himself into trouble. "He was telling me how he could end up like Tyler." The way the kid was talking about it seemed almost aspirational to Gord. "It makes Tyler's death even more weirdly morbid, like he's a kind of celebrity."

Tyler was killed at the beginning of the winter semester. Three weeks in, Gord was confident of about 90 percent of the new kids' names. Usually, he has them all memorized within the first week. "I don't want to attach," he told me.

"Because of Tyler?" I asked.

"Absolutely. I've been talking to my colleagues about this. It's good to stay aware of it. These kids, they need to know that you're invested in them, but I'm probably going to be this way for a little while."

This was all happening in the middle of a labour dispute that had been going on for some time between the teachers and the school board. The teachers' union had curtailed extracurricular activities. Gord lost sleep worrying that maybe the work-to-rule had contributed to Tyler's death, because he had skipped classes the day he was killed to hang out with his friend. "If there was basketball going on," Gord said, "maybe Tyler would have gone to school."

March break was coming up. Gord's plan was to ignore the work-to-rule and start up a junior football camp once the snow melted off the field. Usually the team doesn't start training until late summer.

"I feel like we need to come together sooner," he said. "I need to do it, because I can't sit here and not do anything. This is a big fucking hole in these kids and it's ripping through me too. We need to get the kids out there. We need to have a game of two-hand touch. I need to run and play the game, and some kids have to come and slap me on the back. It needs to happen."

The team retired Tyler's number, number seven, and changed one of its pre-game cheers from:

Blue on me!
Blue on three!
One! Two! Three! BLUES!

to:

*Seven* on me!
*Seven* on three!
One! Two! Three! SEVEN!

There was a kid on the junior team who used to play with Tyler, same grade, same age. I'll call him Sean.

Sean was well-liked by the teachers, but he skipped class—this was back when Tyler was still alive. It got him kicked off the team and expelled for a while even though he was, in Gord's estimation, profoundly talented on the field.

But Gord had faith in him, knew he could turn his academic career around if he wanted to. And he knew football was probably the best incentive the school had to offer. He approached Cynthia and suggested they continue to let Sean play, that it would be good for the kid, good for the team. She agreed.

The year after Tyler was killed, Sean made the senior team. Gord kept his eye on Sean while coaching the juniors, watched him when he was running a play. He was fast, surgical, focused. He executed every play perfectly. The kid's marks had picked up, too. He was getting seventies. Gord noticed another pattern as well. Sean was tackling some of his opponents especially hard—legally but, still, he was laying them out as though he had some personal vendetta against them.

"I'm crazy with numbers," Gord told me. "I'm always paying attention to them." So was Sean—one specific number. All the kids he was hunting down had the number seven on their jerseys.

Gord pulled Sean aside once during a game. "What's going on?" he asked him.

"There's only one number seven," Sean said.

—

# CHAPTER THREE

# THE LACUNA

ONE OF HIS EARLIEST MEMORIES is standing in a cluster of other kids, waiting for a bus. They're going on a field trip. Darrell is maybe seven or eight. He has the stale, fecal tang of a child who has gone unbathed too long, but he's not really aware that his hygiene is poor. He is standing next to a girl who would otherwise not choose to stand next to him. He is still too young to understand how poor his family is. The girl is aware, though. She looks at his feet. "With shoes like that," she says, "you should be standing in the gutter." The boys make fun of him too, but when a girl does, for some reason it cuts deeper.

That's how he remembers his childhood: a long period of shuffling from place to place in shoes that reveal his dirty socks.

Darrell is passive. He's always been passive, though he's not sure how he got this way. His mother is industrious: three jobs, three kids, strict rules, no time for teenage nonsense. When she gives Darrell a chore, she expects it to be done. If he doesn't do it, which is often, she berates him. "Why are you so lazy?" she yells. Sometimes she slaps him upside the head. She caught him stealing change from her purse and she bit his face. That happened only once. She's not to blame.

When he talks to me, some twenty years later, he wants to make that clear. There's not really any one thing, no outside source you can pin the blame on.

"It was a regular childhood," he tells me, "especially for someone with a Jamaican background. You did something wrong, you got physical beatings."

Look at the kids he grew up with: they got beatings, but they turned out fine. None of them are where he is. None of them have done the things he has. Also, his mother had a point. He *was* lazy. He didn't even follow through with the things he *wanted* to do, like running track. He had talent. The coach encouraged him, but he couldn't bring himself to care enough to make practice. Eventually the coach turfed him, and Darrell couldn't bring himself to care about that either.

Probably his passivity has to do with his tendency to avoid conflict.

"One of the things about rapists," he tells me, "is that, at some level, they're all cowards." He includes himself in this. Funny thing, though: being too passive can lead you *into* conflict.

His father was like this. He'd ignore things, tell the family everything was fine. When Darrell was twelve, he and his mother came back from the grocery store to find that the lock on their apartment had been changed. His mother knocked on a neighbour's door. The neighbour refused to let them in. Instead, she handed Darrell's mother the phone and stood there with her arms crossed, shaking her head, while his mother stood in the hallway talking to the landlord. They had been evicted. His father had been lying about paying the rent. He had been giving the money instead to some other woman he had on the side, pretending the whole time that everything was all right.

Darrell tells me he has the same tendency. He balls up his problems like a pair of dirty socks and lobs them in a neglected corner of his mind. He'd do this with household chores and social interactions, with his physical hygiene. By the time he entered high school, he had a reputation for serious body odour. He knew this, but he did nothing about it. After gym class, he wore the same sweat-moist underwear to class. He didn't shower, didn't put on deodorant. He went to class reeking of crotch and armpits.

He does this with his anger and sadness too—puts them in that place he doesn't have to think about. As a result, he never quite knows how he feels.

He remembers as a kid being surprised and a little insulted when someone, one of his mother's boyfriends maybe, told him he was showing signs of depression. Darrell thought it was a stupid thing to say. Depressed people were sad. Like, obviously sad—crying and stuff. He'd get down on himself sometimes, but he wasn't sad like that, not like *sad* sad. Not depressed.

It's growing, the neglected space within him. He is not aware of this, of course. He is the opposite of self-aware. It took him several years of seeing prison counsellors to realize the space was there at all, to understand there was something weird about how he sees the world.

Sunday evenings, he calls me collect from the common room on his range. I've had a new land line installed because the prison won't allow him to make calls to cellphones. Sunday night is shower night. The other men are off getting clean, leaving him alone. It's the only time he can speak freely about what he has done. Still, he speaks so softly I have to plug my other ear because the ambient sound of my apartment, the low hum of traffic outside, competes with the hush of his voice over the phone line.

Darrell is housed in the Special Handling Unit, the SHU; the inmates pronounce it *shoe*. It is a large, crucifix-shaped structure, one of several buildings that make up the Sainte-Anne-des-Plaines correctional centre, a sprawling complex an hour's drive northwest of Montreal. The SHU is the most secure prison in the country. It exists to keep the most intransigent, most violent prisoners from the rest of society. Bikers, killers, gangsters, sexual offenders—they all have their own segregated cellblocks. There's a rigid hierarchy. Darrell and the other sex offenders are the shit on the heel of prison society. Some of the men, the killers and gangsters, would love to get their hands on a guy like Darrell. They would see it as a form of public service. Much of the public would see it that way too.

Darrell's calls last twenty minutes. At seventeen minutes, a voice comes on and gives him a three-minute warning. On a good night, he'll call back and we can stretch the conversation to forty minutes. On a bad night, he won't call at all because the SHU is in lockdown, the inmates in their cells. On those nights, I'll wait twenty minutes. If I haven't heard from him, I know he's not able to call. The following Sunday he'll call and apologize for leaving me hanging.

—

I HAVE NO IDEA to what extent I can trust Darrell. I don't think he's lying to me, willingly withholding information or purposefully altering the facts. There's enough documentation to verify his version of events. He's given me permission to request his psychological records and case history, and I'm in touch with his lawyer. I feel he wants to be honest with me. I just don't know how honest he can be with himself.

The other complication is that Darrell's not representative of most men who rape. He's more like an airline disaster, a statistical rarity that, because it is disproportionately frightening and destructive, comes to represent our worst fears. It's entirely reasonable to be afraid of him, just as it's understandable to fear dying in a plane crash. But if you are truly afraid of dying in a flaming wreck, you should be more afraid of the ride to the airport. And if you are going to worry about rape, pay close attention to the people in the car with you. Husbands and boyfriends account for more than 50 percent of men who rape; acquaintances account for another 40 percent.[1] Like car fatalities, this kind of rape happens every day, but it often goes unreported, which leaves us to focus on the more sensational and vivid cases.[2] Darrell is one of the latter.

My original intention was to try to understand how a man, a normal, outwardly respectable, average man—the type of man who is representative of the majority of men who rape—comes to do such a thing. But in the end, I didn't have that option. I chased defence lawyers for weeks. I'd send them introductory e-mails, take them out to lunch, explain what I was looking for. None of their clients wanted to speak to me. For that matter, few of the lawyers wanted me to speak to their clients. I grew frustrated enough that I asked the lawyers to let their clients know I'd pay five hundred bucks for a series of interviews. I felt a twinge of self-disgust doing this. Besides, I knew paying them might distort what these men told me. But still there were no takers.

While I was courting defence lawyers, I also talked my way into a therapy group for men charged with sexual assault. About a dozen men attended, all of them there on court orders. The youngest had just turned eighteen; the oldest was in his late seventies or early eighties. We met on Tuesday evenings.

Several of the men were there on child-porn charges. If I'm remembering correctly, the old guy had a history of grooming underage boys. A grey, deflated man in his late fifties had fondled the thigh of a young woman with Down's syndrome. There was also a small, well-dressed professional man in his mid-thirties who lurked on pedophile chat sites. He had tried to persuade another member of the site—ostensibly the father of a little girl—to film himself having sex with his daughter. It turned out to be a sting. The "father" was an RCMP detective.

The man who ran the group is a notable forensic psychiatrist. He's often called as an expert witness in sexual assault cases across the province and, more occasionally, across the country. I wasn't allowed to take notes during these sessions or write about any of the men in any detail. My hope was that at least one of them would come to trust me and consent to being interviewed. When I first sat down, they were friendly. They assumed I was one of them. We made small talk. A couple of guys made corny jokes. Then the psychiatrist introduced me and told the men I was a writer, and they all quit looking in my direction. Still, I took something important away.

The small man who had wanted to see a father have sex with his daughter told the group he didn't really want to see it, not in a sexual way, because he found pedophilia disgusting and immoral just like everybody else. It was more that he was curious about what other people did. Like, how you can have strong principles as a vegan and not ever eat meat but still, you know, you can *watch* someone eat a hamburger without actively betraying your principles. It wasn't as if he would have found it arousing. Or, you know, beat off to it. And he would never ever, *ever* actually do anything like that—you know, to a kid. It wasn't even really fair to call it a sexual fantasy. It was more like an intellectual experiment, an observational inquiry.

There was another man in his late thirties or early forties, the kind of shapeless, thin-haired guy you see on the commuter train and forget almost immediately. He was fuming. Just being there heated him up to a simmer. I wouldn't have been surprised to see tendrils of cartoon smoke coming out of his ears. Most of the time, he refused to talk. He had been harassing a woman at work. It started with him hanging around her too much, then he began following her and calling her and eventually propositioning her. He either pushed up against her or pushed her up against a wall or grabbed her. Or maybe all three. She got a restraining order against him. He sat with his arms crossed and his chin up the whole time, the way a fighter looks into the camera before a bout. I can't remember exactly what he said, but he was furious at the woman because he hadn't done anything wrong. She had been leading him on.

"Even after she asked you to stop?" asked the psychiatrist.

The man sort of snorted. He wouldn't dignify that question with an answer.

The old man who had been grooming boys had a long history of sexual assault dating back, I think, to the late 1960s but which was only now coming to light. He sat, legs crossed, with a pasted-on smile that was so smug even the psychiatrist had trouble hiding his impatience. He asked the old man to talk about his role in the charges that had been brought against him.

"I've told you," replied the old man, as though he were a schoolmaster and the psychiatrist an especially dull student, "I'm *not* the only one responsible."

"Because you think the boy in question was a willing participant?"

"Well, he *was*," said the old man.

"Even though he was underage? Even though he couldn't make an informed decision?"

The old man shook his head contemptuously. "It *was* an informed decision."

"Can you see how this is an example of distorted thinking?" the psychiatrist asked the old man, though really he was addressing the whole group.

The old man closed his eyes and grinned. "Frankly, no. I can't."

After the session, the psychiatrist told me this is much of what his job consists of: trying to get men to see their own distorted thinking, to see how they have shaped the world around them in a way that suits their own desires. They are often not willing to acknowledge those desires precisely because those desires have shaped the world around them. He was describing a sort of *ouroboros*, the serpent that eats its own tail. The mind is like that. It has trouble looking upon itself clearly. This is true of us all, even the most self-aware. But with sexual offenders, the mind has a special tendency to run away from itself, to hide from reality by consuming a reality it fabricates.

—

IT'S DIFFICULT TO PINPOINT where things began to go wrong. And how exactly.

Darrell is twelve or thirteen when he discovers *Urotsukidoji: Legends of the Overfiend*. He has the animated series on VHS cassettes. The Japanese dialogue is subtitled in English. Sometime he puts one on for a friend. More often he watches them by himself. He is by himself a lot.

The Overfiend is a demon—a mega-demon, really. The Godzilla of demons. According to legend—a legend made up in the 1980s by the creators of the series—once every three thousand years the Overfiend awakens. He is ravenous when he arises. He craves the flesh of human females.

During hibernation, the beast hides in the body of unsuspecting mortals. In the first video we learn that the Overfiend has been stowing away in the body of Nagumo, a shy, underdog teen who hides in the girls' change room and beats off while the cheerleading squad changes out of their Lolita school uniforms into vulva-enhancing unitards. This is not especially pervy in the context of the Overfiend world. Everyone in these cartoons—men, women, the various supernatural creatures from demon realms—they all have radioactive libidos. The boys are overinflated sperm sacs, thin-skinned, ready to burst upon contact with anything vaguely female. The girls are sodden and squirmy in their short skirts and tight sweaters. Nagumo envies the popular boys their ease with the opposite sex. In one scene, Nagumo's nemesis, the captain of the basketball team, has three girls at once. They jump on him like he's a bouncy castle. In the Overfiend world, all of the characters are dying for it. Literally dying sometimes.

In the first episode, Nagumo is hit by a car. The authorities assume he's dead. He is taken to the morgue, where he transforms à *la* Incredible Hulk into the Overfiend: large and muscled and bat-winged. He has horns and gnashing teeth, and an enormous and preposterously veiny cock dripping with Day-Glo demon juices. His first act upon awakening is to claw the clothes off a buxom morgue attendant then force her to go down on him. She is freaked out about the supernatural factor, but more generally she seems okay getting freaky. After the epic blow job, he presses her up against the wall. He enters her. Her sex cries are ambiguous. It isn't clear whether she is crying out for him to stop or to continue at a more vigorous pace. (All the sex in the Overfiend world is like this: no-means-yessish.) The Overfiend has grown to ceiling height. His cock is now of equine proportions. The morgue attendant is dummy-eyed with pain and/or pleasure. Tight shot: sparkly, twinkly, My-Little-Pony goo is coming out of her animated vagina.

When the Overfiend comes, his eyes glow red and Bat Signal beams of light shoot from the eyes and ears and mouth of the morgue attendant. The nuclear reactor of her desire has gone critical inside her and she literally orgasms to death, her body exploding in an eruption of blood and guts. The Overfiend grows and grows. He towers over the hospital. Over the city. He is the king of fuck demons.

In episode after episode, demons battle one another; humans battle the demons; teenage girls get fucked by gruesome monsters. The plotting is idiotic, but analyzing the plot is missing the point. The appeal of superheroes—and supervillains for that matter—lies in the allegory: the secret powers that come on as a boy crosses into manhood; the newly discovered abilities; the uncomfortable coexistence of a mild-mannered self and a new self that is overwhelming and confusing and sometimes difficult to control and which you must keep hidden.

The choice of what you do with these new-found powers.

In the evenings, Darrell rides his bike in the parks near his home. He does figure eights on the asphalt. He does pop-a-wheelies. He watches women walk through the vast green space between concrete apartment blocks. He watches their thighs, their calves, the strong systolic contraction of their buttocks as they move away from him. He feels a flushed, uneasy excitement.

When you're older, you forget the force with which it comes on. How it appears from nowhere. One month it's not there. Or only vaguely there.

You're ambivalent about it. You're preoccupied with bikes or action fig-ures or movies, and then at some point it's all you can think about. You try to push out of your mind the terrible and embarrassing things you did to satisfy it. You forget how you gave yourself friction burns from the palm of your own hand, from the upholstered crack between couch cushions; how you experiment making holes of varying effectiveness out of hol-lowed-out melons or marrow squash, out of a cut of beef or pork; you hump warm, wet towels or banana peels or two pillows pushed together or the nozzle of a vacuum cleaner; you beat off with Crisco or butter or olive oil. You beat off in the shower. In the closet. In the backyard. You touch yourself slowly and, you hope, discreetly through a hole in the pocket of your sweatpants while your parents watch a steamy TV love scene on the couch next to you, trying not to breathe. You beat off secretly on the school bus. In public toilet stalls. You beat off until your right forearm and shoulder are as defined as a pro tennis player's, until your kidneys ache and your glans burns. You know puberty is normal, that a sex drive is normal, but you suspect you're probably a little freakish.[3] You hope it passes, though you don't entirely want it to pass. It too is an *ouro-boros*. It feeds you and it consumes you.

There's a woman who lives upstairs. She's Indian or Pakistani or some-thing. She's married. Darrell hears her arguing with her husband. He and his mother and two sisters live in the basement apartment. There is a shared laundry room on the second floor. Sometimes the Indian woman does her laundry in a thin, loose robe. He can see the contours of her body. She is thirty maybe, which is old to a fourteen-year-old boy. But still, she's sexy.

One of the movies he's into—not the Overfiend stuff, some other movie he can no longer remember—has this part in it where the main guy rescues these girls from a dangerous situation. He gets them to safety, but then he keeps them locked up in these cells and has sex with them. In Darrell's mind, it becomes the only likely scenario in which a woman will have sex with him. He masturbates to this fantasy a lot.

The strange thing is, there are actually girls who like him. On at least two occasions, a girl has asked him to hang out after school. His reaction to this is strange too. Both times he says yes but then bails at the last minute. He gets nervous. It's more than just a bad case of butterflies. He sinks into a place he can't climb out of. He thinks about his bad traits: his laziness, his dullness, his perverse sexual interests, his poverty, his shitty clothes and his repulsive, skinny body. He can't face himself. He can't face a girl. His logic is like this: *I'm not attractive. Girls like attractive boys. By definition, a girl can't be attracted to me.*

Years later, a prison psychologist will tell him this kind of thinking is typical of someone with severely low self-esteem. True, but it doesn't explain the other thinking going on in that blind spot in his mind.

You see a kid like Darrell, walking along the chalky sidewalks of his neighbourhood, passing through the grey industrial parks, skulking among the looming concrete apartment blocks in scuffed shoes and shapeless clothes, undistinguished, unnoticeable, quiet, turned inward, looking down, shuffling along in starts and stops like a plastic bag caught up in an eddy of wind. You assume his internal state matches his external state. You assume he's beaten down. And he is. But not all of him. Somewhere inside, just out of his peripheral vision, he's striving for something he thinks he can't have. Somewhere in the lacuna of his own self-awareness, in the place he refuses to see, he is telling himself there is more than one way to skin a cat.

He's heard the beautiful Indian woman crying. He's pretty sure her husband beats her. He runs into her in the laundry room and tells her he can help her. Her English is bad. She doesn't understand him. Plus, Darrell mumbles. He doesn't make eye contact. He hurries out of the laundry room feeling stupid and embarrassed.

There's this girl at school. He walks up to her. He says something like, "There are some guys after you." He thinks maybe, if she's adequately afraid, he can persuade her to come with him. "Don't be stupid," she says. She rolls her eyes like he is one of the special ed kids.

A lady is walking across the park. She's Asian. He trails her slowly on his bike. She's in her mid-thirties. He prefers petite women, women with tight waists, nice hips. He watches her from behind as she walks.

He watches the back and forth of her ass. He's not thinking about doing anything, not actively. Not that he's aware of. He has no plan per se. But if he is honest with himself, there's something in the corner of his mind. There is a feeling in his chest like the feeling you get standing at the end of a diving board, leaning out into space, the moment before you hurl yourself off. He pedals faster. He comes up behind the woman and slaps her ass and speeds away.

He's thinking more and more about the Indian lady, how he might go about saving her from her husband. In his fantasy, he takes her to his bedroom, where they would be alone. She'd be grateful. She'd cry on his shoulder and he'd hold her and then she'd get naked and they'd do it.

This time, it's a white woman he follows. He's watching her ass swinging like a pendulum. His heart is beating hard. He gets the tight feeling in his chest. He is leaning out, peering into the empty space below him. He is leaning out over his handlebars, pedalling faster. He comes up behind her quickly. He lets go of the handlebar and leans to grab one of her cheeks. She jumps and flails her arms. He is already well past her. She yells at him, her voice crackling with rage. He stops in the middle of the path feeling as though his heart is going to come out of his mouth. She charges towards him, her shoes clacking on the asphalt. She's yelling like a holy terror. She's red in the face. Darrell is frozen with fear. But he's curious. He wants to see what she'll do. He gets the feeling of leaning out over space again. She slows down as she gets closer. She stops. She turns around and walks quickly away from him.

One evening, he takes a roll of Scotch tape from his mother's cupboard. He walks upstairs, through the laundry room, towards the Indian woman's apartment. The door is open. She is in her bedroom folding laundry. Her husband is not home. She looks up and sees Darrell. Along with the tape, he is holding a hammer. There is a moment of silence before she starts screaming. In that moment, he realizes he hasn't really thought this through. It's strange when you bring a fantasy out into the world. They are like hothouse plants: they wither and fall apart outside the protective capsule of your imagination. She screams before he can do anything. She pushes past him. He raises the hammer and brings it down without conviction. He has overestimated his strength and coordination. The hammer barely grazes her head. He's panicked and confused. The woman is screaming. There are other neighbours upstairs. They come crashing down the stairs. Someone calls the cops.

—

I DON'T REALLY UNDERSTAND his motivation.

It's been a month of Sundays and I'm still not clear why Darrell has agreed to speak with me. He's told me not to bother with the money—it isn't right for him to take it. If I want, he says, I can send it to his mother. His youngest sister is now in college and his mom could use the extra cash. He has also asked me not to use his real name, which rules out one of my other concerns: that he's looking to sell himself to the public as a changed man. He doesn't seem especially concerned with redemption. He seems to know he's past that.

When he calls, he's always ready. It's usually me who avoids diving into the details. I make small talk until he politely reminds me we only have twenty minutes. I think he enjoys talking to someone, but I don't think he enjoys telling me about the things he's done. Some men, sexual predators in particular, enjoy talking about their crimes. Describing specific acts in detail can be a way of reliving them, a form of verbal onanism. Darrell says he met a lot of men like this in therapy. At first I worried that he might be this way. But listening to him talk is more like watching someone who's out of shape do laps around a track. It's work for him. It's as if he's putting himself through the paces. He sighs a lot. When he tells me something especially disturbing, he becomes even more soft-spoken. If he's faking shame, he's doing a convincing job. He's patient when I interrupt to ask questions. He interrupts himself too and asks me if he is being clear, if he is answering my questions satisfactorily.

When I ask him why he's speaking to me if he doesn't want the money, he tells me he wants to give back in some way. He knows it sounds like a cliché. He says he hopes it'll help people understand why men like him do the things he has done. He has never fully understood it himself. He says he hopes talking to me might help him figure it out a bit more. He says he knows it's hard to believe, considering what he did when he was released from prison, but he always took the therapy to heart. Or thought he did. Now that he's in the SHU, there's only one psychologist and a waiting list that's years long.

His language is interesting. He swears less than other men who've done time, less than I do. When he describes his acts, he uses words like *breasts* and *vagina* and *penis* instead of *tits* or *pussy* or *cock*. Most of the time he avoids naming body parts altogether.

I've asked him whether he still thinks about what he's done, about the attacks, in a way he finds stimulating. No, he tells me. He's taught himself not to think of them in that way.

I wonder if the language he uses is part of this conditioning. I feel that the words he chooses are like stones he's placed over the entrance of a crypt to keep the ghouls from climbing out. I wonder if the barricade would weaken if he were to use different words. I wonder how powerful those ghouls are, whether they are really dormant, what it would take to stir them.

Sometimes, when I ask him to describe a particular event with more precision, I feel a quiver of apprehension, as though I'm encouraging him to strike matches so I can get a better view inside a darkened dynamite factory.

—

HE IS FIFTEEN. He and his mother and sisters have had to move because of the incident with the woman and the hammer. The police charged him with assault—plain assault, as opposed to sexual assault, because the cops weren't aware what he had in mind. This makes it easier for Darrell to brush aside his real motivation and tell himself he was just momentarily confused, temporarily crazy. He puts it out of his mind. He doesn't really think about it again for years. The charges are eventually dropped because, despite being troubled and awkward, he's a polite kid. He's respectful towards authority. He's not the kind of kid you have to worry about.

At school, one of his classmates is dating a girl, a total knockout. Her breasts are unreal. Darrell thinks this guy is lucky to walk around with her on his arm. When his friend and this girl break up, Darrell starts thinking about her. He doesn't really know her. She spends a lot of time in the school library. He goes there and watches her. There's a rumour going around that she has brought charges against a guy Darrell knows, that he—the guy—tried to touch this girl's breasts.

Darrell thinks about this for a few days. Eventually he approaches the girl and tells her he has some information on the guy who tried to feel her up. She doesn't want to talk about it. Darrell insists. It's a pretty big deal, this information. She might freak out when she hears it. They should probably go somewhere private. She looks skeptical, but she follows him down an empty hallway.

The hallway is dark. Some of the overhead lights have burnt out. They are standing in front of a secluded washroom. Darrell tells the girl they should talk in there. She says no. Darrell insists. The girl says she doesn't care about whatever it is Darrell has to tell her. He says no, trust me, it's really important. She relents. Once she's inside, Darrell locks the door. He pulls her into one of the stalls. Darrell is holding her close. She is struggling. She is stronger than he thought. *Shit*, he thinks to himself. *This isn't going to work.* He's trying to get her shirt off, but beneath the fabric of her sweater something lets go and makes a snap. Darrell stops. He has torn her bra. She's yelling and hitting him in the face. This is definitely not going to work. *Sorry*, he says. *Sorry for tearing your bra. I'm sorry.* He lets go of her. She unlocks the door and runs.

The rugby coach comes to get him and escorts him to the office. The secretaries give him the stink eye on the way in. The girl is there, seated in a chair before the principal's desk. Her face is flushed. Her eyes are red. She wants to call the police, but the principal feels they should speak with Darrell first. Darrell starts crying, really bawling. He apologizes through his tears. "I'll never do anything like that again," he promises. He means it. "I don't know what came over me." He means that too.

The girl is upset about her bra. It's crazy expensive, some sort of bespoke medical-grade support bra. Her parents are going to kill her if they find out. Darrell says he'll pay for it. He'll get a job. They make an agreement: he'll give her cash to replace the bra if she doesn't call the cops. He quits fantasizing about this girl. For a while he gives up following women at night.

He's working a few nights a week. After school, he walks to a nondescript plaza in a nearby neighbourhood. There's an airless office attached to a warehouse. A rotating stable of sad older guys drive crews of boys Darrell's age around town. They boys get dropped off in different neighbourhoods to peddle teddy bears and chocolates and spice racks door to door.

The boys are given prepared scripts explaining how the money goes to charity. Only a small portion of it really does. One week, Darrell and the other boys carry laminated pictures of serial killer Clifford Olson's victims since one of the so-called charities is a foundation for the families of Olson's victims. Later, Darrell will be locked up in the same range of the SHU where Olson was doing his time before he died of cancer.

He picks up a flyer advertising escorts from the floor of the subway station. He's obsessed by the thought that, if you have enough money, you can just call a woman and she'll come to you and have sex. He keeps the flyer. He keeps the door-to-door job too, even though he's paid off the girl at school. He likes having money.

The girl he attacked in the washroom is still unhappy. She tells him she doesn't want him going to the same school because he creeps her out. She's angry in a way Darrell has trouble understanding. He has apologized. He has given her money for another bra. He's staying away from her. What more does she want? She tells him she'll call the cops unless he transfers to another school. He has no choice. He transfers. It's the first time he recalls being bitter towards a woman.

By now, he's back to trailing women in the park at sunset. He walks behind these women and, as they approach a shrub or a little gully or an underpass, he makes a mental note: *This is where I'd grab her. No one will see me. I'll take her over there.* They are just thoughts, he tells himself. Fantasies, but more intensely erotic than any he's had so far.

He follows women at dusk for about a year.

He's seventeen when he starts carrying a knife.

He is still a virgin.

—

THE MOST CHILLING THING about Darrell is that his fantasy life is in line with a large proportion of the male population's. I'm talking here about normal, respectable, well-educated young men.

The findings are consistent across various studies. Roughly 30 percent of college men admit there's at least some chance they'd rape a woman if they were sure they wouldn't be caught and punished. Of these men, about 11 percent say they'd be either "somewhat likely" or "extremely likely" to rape, given the chance.[4] In some studies, 50 percent of the men polled said they'd rape if they could get away with it[5] and 25 percent thought "women would enjoy being raped if no one knew about it."[6]

Of course, saying you'd do something and actually doing it are two different things. And college students aren't always representative of broader society. In this case, though, they likely are: one in five college women reports being the victim of an attempted, if not completed, rape—approximately the same proportion as in the general population. It's clear a lot of the normal, respectable, well-educated young men out there are actively following through on their fantasies.

What's even more disconcerting is that the men following through on these fantasies are often not aware that this is what they are doing. What I mean is this: If you ask the men in these studies whether they've ever raped a woman, only a tiny portion—about 3 percent—say they have. The men are guaranteed anonymity, so there's no reason to think they're withholding the truth. At the same time, about 20 percent of the men report that, although they have never raped, they have, at some point, become "so sexually aroused they could not stop themselves even though the women did not want to have sex with them."[7] Which is to say about one in five of the polled men had raped a woman, or tried to. They just didn't think of it that way.

Other studies have found the same pattern: men are more likely to admit to "having coerced somebody into intercourse by holding them down"[8] than to having raped. And it's not that they're trying to avoid the stigma of being labelled a rapist. It's weirder than that: they actually don't seem to perceive that this is what they're doing.

It's not just his fantasy life that's so common. Darrell's blind spot is common too.

How is it so many men are like this? Why are so many of us willing—eager—to violate and harm women? How is it that so many of us are this way but, at some level, are oblivious to the true nature of our desires?

These are precisely the questions that concern a lot of feminist scholars. Because much feminist scholarship is founded on the premise that human behaviour can be explained wholly by social learning, much of this research focuses on rape as a social problem. Rightfully so—it is.

Depending on the society in question and the extent to which that society encourages men to brutalize women, it can be an extreme problem. It's hard to get exact figures in many of the places where rape and sexual assault are most severe. In South Africa, a woman is raped roughly every thirty seconds; this is also a country that boasts some particularly callous and grotesque cases—the gang rape of infant girls, for instance, by men who believe sex with a virgin will cure their HIV. In some districts of the Democratic Republic of Congo, currently the rape capital of the world, sexual violence is used as a highly organized form of warfare, and it can be hard to find a woman or girl who hasn't been sexually brutalized. And in Bougainville, Papua New Guinea, 80 percent of men polled in a UN study admit to beating their partner, being sexually violent with her, or both.[9]

The point here isn't to shame specific countries (though I don't really see a problem with that) but to point out that the incidence of rape changes from place to place and from culture to culture over time. The rate of child rape in South Africa rose by 400 percent in the last decade of the millennium,[10] while the numbers of sex crimes are currently dropping across North America.[11] Point being: if rape was not strongly influenced by environmental factors, you'd expect to see a more or less static rate of sexual violence, which is not the case. Sexual violence is fluid. That fluidity is related to the nature of the society in which sexual violence occurs.

Darrell grew up without a dad; he grew up in poverty,[12] in a neighbourhood with relatively high levels of gun violence and gangs. He watched his parents physically fight. "My mom doesn't take shit," he told me. "My dad would win, but she'd give him a go." And he was raised with certain assumptions about what real men are like. He explained to me that, when he was young, "I was like: 'a man has sex with a woman.' So, to be a man, I couldn't be a virgin. Having sex would make me less of a loser, you know what I mean?" All these aspects of Darrell's life are factors associated with sexual violence and domestic abuse, influences that presumably shape the way young men think about women.

It's hard to say what the Overfiend videos did to him, encountering them, as he did, on the cusp of puberty. There's a lot of debate over porn — and a lot of conflicting findings about whether it actually makes men violent. What's more clear is that men who are sexually violent have a tendency to see sex in the same sort of depersonalized, parts-doing-things-to-other-parts way that characterizes a lot of porn. There's also a great deal of blatant hostility towards women in mainstream porn — hands around throats, feet on faces, faces being slapped, anuses being rammed, mouths being spit in. Hostility towards women is a clear correlate of sexual violence, an attitude men seem to learn from other men, especially while growing up.[13]

On the other hand, exposure to porn has gone up dramatically over the past couple of decades in North America while rates of sexual violence have been dropping. Something like 85 percent of young men look at porn at least once a week,[14] and most of them don't commit sexual assault. None of the guys Darrell grew up with are locked away in the SHU for serial rape.

As important as some of these environmental factors are, they don't explain why some men rape and others don't, despite being raised in the same shitty environment, and, conversely, why so many men who aren't exposed to these factors do rape.

Rape is not about sex, we've come to understand, but about power. Rape is absolutely about power, especially its effect on women. Rape is a way — arguably the ultimate way — of disempowering a woman. And when it's socially condoned through lax laws, poor enforcement and a tacit acceptance of the old chestnut that boys will be boys, rape is the ultimate way of disempowering women as a whole.

It would be naive to think that many men don't know this, and that some of them aren't motivated precisely by the desire to denigrate women. It would take an act of wilful blindness to dismiss the feminist argument that society—all societies, it would seem—is organized in such a way that men are encouraged to take what they want, to do it by force if necessary and, quite often, to do so with impunity. In this sense, rape is very much about power.

But that doesn't mean it's not also very much about sex.

The *effect* of rape is to disempower the victim. That's irrefutable. What's not so clear is whether that's always the primary intention of a rapist (although with many it is). I'd argue that if we dismiss sex entirely as a motivation, we fail to understand everything that's going on.

Discussing men's sexuality—their desires and frustrations especially—is an incredibly unpopular subject within most mainstream feminist discussions of rape and sexual assault. This is partly because the subject has been hijacked by so-called men's rights advocates— misogynists who claim men are under attack from a malicious and pernicious feminist cabal. The so-called logic of their argument goes something like: men are *supposed* to take what they want while women are supposed to secretly *want* to be taken. *Ergo*: deal with it, ladies.

That nonsense aside, most feminist scholarship is based on a social science model of human behavior, which assumes that we're shaped exclusively by social learning, and that male sexuality is different from women's only because men and women are taught to follow different social norms.

If you subscribe to this view and you want to do something about rape, the only thing worth concerning yourself with is changing the social norms that shape men's sexual behavior. The individuals in whom those values reside are sort of beside the point. They are palimpsests waiting to receive a new script. In this context, sexual violence is an expression of manhood, culturally mandated, rather than something that also rises out of the bodies we inhabit. Follow this train of thought to its end and rape is not about sexual gratification at all but about "the deployment of the penis as a concrete symbol of masculine social power."[15]

The thing is, women aren't the only victims of that deployment. Women *are* raped far more frequently than men (meaning, specifically, penetration is forced upon them far frequently that it is forced on men), but the number of men and women who are the victims of sexual assault in all its varied and repellant forms, is almost exactly the same.[16] And a sizable chunk of male victims—in one study around 65 percent—are the victims of other men.[17] Meaning at least some rape and a great deal of sexual assault have nothing at all to do with the patriarchal subjugation of women.[18]

That's not to say that some of the men who rape and sexually assault men and boys aren't also doing it to lord power. But my point here is that sexual violence is a lot more complex than just men raping women. Part of that complexity is that, while sometimes it *is* about using sex as a symbolic display of male power, a lot of times it's the other way around. Sometimes men use their power to get what they want most, which is sex.

Rape is the term we apply to this human behaviour, but it's not unique to humans. Biologists use the term *forced copulation* for other animals. It is present throughout the animal kingdom, primarily among insects, reptiles and birds. It is far less common among mammals. But it does exist, conspicuously so within our taxonomic family, *Hominidae*—the great apes.

Of the five hominid species—orangutans, chimpanzees, humans, gorillas and bonobos—three commit what we, as humans, would call rape. Among orangutans, forced copulation is a normal mode of reproduction. Males chase females through the trees, abduct them and force them into coitus. It is not an anthropomorphic stretch to say it's scary and painful for the females. There is a well-documented case of a male orangutan raping a human, a woman who worked as a camp cook at an orangutan observation station in the Malaysian jungles.[19]

Field researchers estimate that about a third of chimpanzee sexual pairings are forced. More than this, chimps seem to use a long-term form of sexual violence that is strikingly analogous to human spousal abuse. Male chimpanzees often chronically batter fertile females. It's not rape, but it does seem to be a form of sexual coercion. Battered female chimps, like battered women, learn that fighting back is painful and dangerous and so, over time, they resign themselves to the situation. Among both chimps and orangutans, forced copulation is a more common behaviour among smaller, less socially dominant males. It seems to be a strategy used by males who are not especially winning mates.

While gorillas don't resort to forced sex — not exactly — males regularly kill the offspring of females they want to mate with — that is, if those infants have been sired by another male. Infanticide among gorillas is a form of sexual violence by proxy; the mother of the murdered infant reliably mates with the killer, the logic being that it is the only way to guarantee her next baby — *his* baby — will not be killed by him.[20]

Human rape seems to be present at some level in every society on Earth, including that of the Mbuti in the Congo and the Kalahari !Kung, which some anthropologists have argued are rape-free.[21] It's less clear whether rape has always been with us. The argument that patriarchal control of women began when we took up agriculture and began to accumulate wealth as a way of ensuring that men knew who their heirs were doesn't stand on especially strong legs. Particularly if you stop to consider that rape and violence against women is common among non-agricultural, non-agrarian hunter-gather societies such as the traditional Inuit. More to the point, patriarchal values didn't just appear out of thin air at the dawn of civilization. Cultural institutions — literature, art, agriculture, science — generally have their origins in organic human behaviour: language, visual-spatial problem solving, food acquisition, curiosity. The feminist evolutionary psychologist Barbara Smuts argues that early humans were likely only "mildly patriarchal" before the advent of agriculture, and that civilization acted as a sort of positive-feedback loop, amplifying, reinforcing and institutionalizing power differences that likely pre-existed in a milder form[22] — and which, presumably, can be mitigated through reverse social engineering.

One of the most compelling lines of evidence that men have always raped comes, counterintuitively, from studies of women's sexual arousal. It turns out that there are fundamental differences between how men and women react to sexually explicit material. In men, measuring their physiological response involves using a penis-cuff that measures erections; in women, it's done with a tampon-shaped instrument that measures blood circulation in the vaginal capillaries. Men show a direct match between their subjective sexual preference and their physiological response. So, for instance, a gay man will get harder when he sees two men having sex; a straight man will show a stronger response to hetero sex. Penises don't lie.

With women, the story is more complicated. There is not the same match between their sexual desires and their physiological response. Women are physiologically aroused by a whole constellation of sexual images, including of sexual violence and of other primates copulating. It's important to understand that this isn't the same as being turned on. The point is that there's a mismatch between women's desire—what they find erotic—and their physiological state. The most reasonable explanation for this is that it's a protective adaptation that allows women to respond to sexual information—any sexual information, even stuff they find scary and disturbing—with a state of physical readiness. Being aroused increases vaginal moisture, which decreases the chance of a vaginal tear during forced sex. This would have been an important adaptation since gynecological injuries threaten a woman's fertility, if not her life. That the female reproductive tract responds this way suggests it evolved under the pressure of unrelenting sexual attack.[23]

There are no obvious physical adaptations in men that facilitate rape, unless you consider the fact that men can maintain an erection when they are in the presence of—or are the cause of—someone in profound physical and/or psychological pain.[24] If men have in fact evolved to use rape as a reproductive strategy, then the adaptation lies in the shape of their mind, their ability to see their victims as objects, to turn callous or angry, to feel justified in what they do, to rationalize what is a form of torture. Or simply the uncanny ability to not think about it that much.

—

THE BLADE IS A flimsy knife stolen from his mother's cutlery drawer. He has no intention of using it. It's backup, something to force the point in case he can't get there on his own. That's what he tells himself.

He's been teetering on a precipice for weeks. Leaning out over the edge, considering it, imagining the final step, the leap, the irrevocable pull of gravity, and then backing away at the last moment.

Tonight, he feels ready.

Darrell sees her get off the bus. He's watched her a few times already. She's in her early twenties. Indian. Beautiful. He knows her usual route home and he runs ahead of her and waits. He's nervous. He has trouble standing still. This is crazy. His head is floating above it all, lofty, airy, removed, but his body has been consigned to the sea. It has been thrown overboard and hung with weights and drawn down into a murk as dense as liquid concrete, as dark as blood. The pressure in his chest is crushing. He feels as though he should crumple like a submarine in a low-budget movie. Instead, the pressure is doing to him what it does to minerals, crystallizing what is soft, transforming him into something hard and impenetrable.

She passes through a tunnel and out into the park. He runs up to her and says: "Hey, miss! Miss! I think you dropped some money. Back at the tunnel." It's November. He has a scarf over his mouth. The woman is hesitant. But Darrell looks like a child. He is extremely polite. Darrell, seeing her hesitate, plays up his innocence.

"I didn't want to touch it," he says. "I didn't want anyone to think I was trying to take it. I'll show you where it is."

She follows him towards the tunnel. Darrell can hardly breathe. *What do I do? What do I do now?* This is happening. He has both feet on the edge. He is leaning, leaning farther out.

He steps off.

At the mouth of the tunnel, it's as if someone flicks a switch and fear floods her senses. The woman must realize there is no money, that there never was. "Don't worry about the money," she says quickly. "Keep it." She turns to leave.

Darrell grabs her from behind. He waves the knife in her face. She does not struggle. She does exactly what he wants. She undresses in the autumn air. He cuts off her underwear. He tries to go down on her, but he doesn't know what he's doing. He forces her to go down on him. He's too wound up to really get into it. But still, he enjoys it. It's exciting, having sex for the first time. Watching himself. Watching her. It's exciting to see your plans in action.

He makes her lie down. He lies on top of her. He doesn't quite know what to do next. He tells her to put it in. There is litter all around, strewn on the pavement. The woman grabs a piece of plastic, a candy wrapper or something. It's dark and Darrell can't see exactly what it is, but he lets her put it over the head of his penis. When he enters her, the plastic folds and digs into his glans. It hurts. It feels like a blade.

He stops. He apologizes and pulls out.

He apologizes again as she gets dressed. She is conciliatory. She tells him not to worry about it. She tells him that now that she knows him, she can tell he's actually a really nice guy. She says something about how, under different circumstances, it could be different between them. He asks if she wants to meet again. She says no, but she is very nice about it. He escorts her through the dark, back towards the street, apologizing all the way.

"That was sort of my thing," Darrell tells me. "I always used to apologize afterwards."

The next day. A Monday. Fear covers him like a fog. He skips school. He doesn't leave the house. He listens for a knock on the door. Towards evening, when the police haven't burst into his bedroom, the fog begins to burn off—though it never fully lifts. He's been thinking about the woman all day, how she was so nice. How she had said the thing about how, under different circumstances, he could have maybe been her boyfriend. He didn't hurt her, not on purpose, at least; he didn't beat her or brutalize her. In a sense, he didn't even really force himself on her—not that badly.

Something he has planned has worked. That pumps him up. But he also has a niggling sense of dissatisfaction. He assumes it's because he didn't go all the way.

That night, he returns to the park. He walks along the paths in the dark, hoping to find the girl again. He wants to say hello now that she knows he's a nice guy. He's just going to talk to her. That's what he tells himself, though he's brought one of his mother's serrated steak knives along.

He's still waiting for her when he sees another woman. This one is slender too, with a nice figure. He's nervous, but less nervous than the night before.

He runs up behind the woman. He grabs her. He shows her the knife. He lies: he says he was forced to hurt his last victim. He says he doesn't want to hurt her too, so she should do exactly what he wants.

What he wants is for her to remove her clothes. Socks too. She is older than the girl from last night, but still sexy. He tells her to lie down. He's on top. Her legs are open. He tells her to put it inside her. This time it does not hurt him. This time he is going all the way. For a moment, the fall feels like flight. He ejaculates inside her.

He has done it, and yet the sense of disappointment hasn't lifted. As he watches her scramble to put on her clothes, a tremendous sense of shame washes over him. He begins to apologize. He is still apologizing as he walks her through the park towards the street.

It's on TV the next day. The two women have given similar descriptions, they've told the police about his apologies. The police are sure it's the same attacker. They've mobilized some sort of task force. Fear lances his lungs. It is hard to breathe. Back then he was religious, a Catholic. He asks the Lord for help breathing, for protection. He makes the sign of the cross.

At school, he glides down the hallways as though rolling on casters. People are looking at him funny. They know. No. They can't possibly know. People always look at him funny. That night, he goes to work. He goes door to door, talking politely to householders from the shadows of their porch, taking in the warm dinner smells wafting from their bright kitchens. He apologizes for interrupting their evening. He thanks them for their time. He goes straight home afterwards. He thinks about what he has done. It comes at him like a storm surge. The fear is too overwhelming to face head-on. He hides from it in his mind.

The next day, or maybe the day after that, he has the sudden realization that he dropped the steak knife in the park and left it there. The realization is like plunging your hand in ice water. It is so chilling that it's beyond what your senses can accurately register, and for a moment you think you've scalded yourself. He walks to the park in a state of alert and quiet horror. He's sure the police must have searched the scene by now—but somehow the knife is still there, hidden in the undergrowth.

He knows what he's done is wrong. It's enormous. It's bigger than the place in his mind where he puts the things he doesn't want to acknowledge. He's tried to stuff it in the corner, but it always manages to slip out. He's gone back to minding his own business. For a couple of weeks he's done nothing other than go from school to work to home. But while he's afraid to look at it, it is not afraid to look back. He can feel it watching him from the corner of his mind with its gigantic, unblinking cephalopod eye. It can see in the dark. It is comfortable in hidden places. It knows everything about him. It is far more powerful than whatever mental process he uses to tamp down unwanted facts. It's like trying to flush a leviathan down the toilet. You can try to stuff it down with the plunger, but the tentacles of self-knowledge will reach up from the depths and filth and seek out your insides.

Sometimes he'll be in class and he'll get a flash of excitement over having done something remarkable and terrible, something no one knows about. And it stirs, constricting his innards, making it hard to breathe. If Darrell is not careful, if he can't control this thing, it'll give him away. Already, people at school are starting to ask if he's all right. He is not himself, they say. He's moody. Whatever it is thrashing inside him, he thinks to himself, has to be separate from him. *I couldn't have done that*, he thinks. *That can't be me.*

—

IN ONE OF OUR phone interviews, I ask Darrell how he feels about women.

"Some people just hate women, period," he tells me. "I've seen lots of guys like that. I don't think I'm like that exactly because, when I know someone, I don't think of them that way. I never thought that way about the girls who were my friends. Not that there was a lot of them. But I thought of them more like family. I love my mother. I love my sisters. It wasn't about hating women, to answer your question, it was more my drive to have sex. My problem is more that I'm someone who shut off my empathy completely when I didn't know someone."

It's easy to think of misogyny as a deliberate policy men actively pen into their personal constitutions: resenting women, belittling them, harming them—all of it superheated by a conscious hatred. But evil burns cold, too. It doesn't always require hatred as its oxygen. What it requires most is a lack of caring, a certain neglect. You don't have to be a psychopath, entirely devoid of empathy, to fall into this.

Still, how is it a man with at least some capacity for empathy can be attracted to a woman's body and not really care about the person who inhabits that body? Part of the answer may be found in the male tendency to see parts where women see wholes.

Richard Wassersug became aware of his own tendency to objectify women when he was being treated for cancer several years ago. I first met Richard when I was a grad student at Dalhousie. He was a professor in the Department of Anatomy and Neurobiology where Lyana was going her graduate work. He was tall, bearded, affable and had a penchant for bow ties. He'd also taught a couple of sessions of a course I was taking. Other than that, I'd see him occasionally in a hallway. But while I was researching this book I came across an article he had written in which he identified himself as a eunuch.

Since my grad school days, Richard had been diagnosed with advanced prostate cancer. He had been treated with Lupron and then, after that, a few long courses of estradiol, a form of estrogen. Both drugs do the same thing in men, effectively shutting down the production of testosterone in the testes, which is the point: the cancerous prostate cells rely on testosterone to proliferate. (Incidentally, Lupron is sometimes taken by dangerous sexual offenders to bottom out their testosterone.) When I called him up to ask him about the article, Richard told me that he had always been prone to argument and easy to take offence, but while he was on Lupron, the drug had made him feel less combative. The hair on his head quit falling out, while the hair on the rest of his body thinned out. And the way he perceived women shifted.

"One of the most astonishing things," he said, "was this sense of: 'Oh my God. I should find every woman I know and apologize to them.'" Richard was used to doing what so many men do—habitually checking out a woman's "hip-to-waist ratio," as he puts it. "With lots of testosterone in me, women were sex objects as opposed to people. Thankfully I found out from my female friends that I wasn't as bad as I thought I had been," he said. "But in my own mind, it was suddenly clear that the same objectification was what led to male chauvinism."

After being on Lupron for a while, Richard realized he noticed the colour of his female colleagues' eyes. He felt that he was paying more attention to faces and facial expressions than bodies. Losing his testosterone helped him see people the way women tend to; women are generally better than men at interpreting expressions, presumably because they pay more attention to faces. (Violent male offenders on the other hand are often especially poor at this.) Richard still found women beautiful but he was more captivated by their overall presence than any particular body part. With this new gestalt appreciation of beauty, he began to find men attractive too. This was completely new to him. And there was an absence too: he felt none of the pressing, aching, feverish urge for sex he was used to feeling. He found that something of a relief.

When I last spoke with Richard, he was doing well. He had been off Lupron for several years and estradiol for several months. His "broadened sexual orientation" had shrunk back to its original heterosexual dimensions.

I asked him if the way he looked at women had changed too.

"Yeah," he said. "I'm checking out their bums more. And their torsos and waists. But now I'm aware I'm doing it."

I know that when I'm especially pent-up, I'm more prone to parsing women into their constituent parts, automatically scanning their bottoms and breasts, their calves, their clavicles, the drop of their décolletage. I imagine the colour and texture of their nipples, what their pubic hair is like. I wonder what they might look like naked. I think of their bodies in the same tight-frame close-ups that are the hallmark of a lot of porn. It is almost unconscious, this process. Almost, but not quite.

And when I look at porn, it's almost exclusively for this experience; it satisfies my desire to watch specific parts doing specific things. I'm a complete hypocrite. I tell myself I'm an ethical consumer, but I'm more like a vegan who keeps falling off the bacon wagon. I feel okay about some porn—the stuff that isn't tailor-made for frat-house date-rapists, stuff that's less disjointed, comprising fewer close-up shots of waxed mounds being bonked into submission. But if I really want to get off, if I want fast physical release, none of that matters much. A few uninterrupted minutes staring at the back half of a woman is generally all I need—or, in that moment, want.

I don't feel great about this. I know the porn industry is mostly gross and sad. I know it caters to my—to men's—tendency to see women in parts. And yet, while I'm doing it, while I'm sitting in front of my computer, I don't especially care. I tell myself I'm not hurting anyone, that I only look at free clips, that I'm not actively supporting the porn industry and its general shittiness towards women, that it doesn't influence the way I see my wife or other women, that it doesn't contribute to some tiny, undetected spot of inner coldness somewhere inside me.

I believe this to be true.

Would I recognize it if it wasn't?

—

DARRELL'S THIRD ATTEMPT is a total nightmare.

He has returned to the tunnel, the site of his first attack. It's late. He has a kitchen knife. He comes up behind a woman and grabs her the way he did the other women. But this one is different. The sight of the knife is a flame and she is a firecracker and she goes off in his face. He isn't sure what's happening. He's losing his balance. She grabs for the knife. She is kicking and screaming. She's stronger than he expected, way stronger. He's fighting her for the knife. He is totally unprepared for resistance. They're on the ground. They're rolling around in the dark and, holy fuck, she's making so much noise, yelling for help, yelping, crying. They're hidden from view, but the street is close. Even this late, the street is busy enough that someone's bound to hear. Jesus Christ. She's so loud.

"I'm sorry," he says. "I'm sorry. Quit yelling. Just quit yelling! I'll go. I'll leave you alone if you just quit yelling."

She keeps screaming.

"I promise you I'll walk away. Just shut the fuck up," he hisses. He's not sure she even hears him. The terror that washes through him is enough to make him sick. It is worse than the body shock he got turning the page in the paper and seeing the police sketch of himself, the stiff, two-dimensional portrait that looked nothing like him and exactly like him at the same time. *I gotta go. I gotta go. I gotta fucking go.* He's not sure if he's saying it aloud or to himself. She is like a siren, wailing in the cold night air. Without question, someone will come running any second. Suddenly he is unbearably angry. He has lost track of the knife. She will not let go of him. "SHUT THE FUCK UP!" He punches her in the ribs, hard—two, three, maybe four times. The blows knock the wind out of her.

He remembers thinking that it's the first time he's hit a woman. Somehow, among all the other things he's done, this stands out as a low-tide mark. While she's fighting for breath, he scrambles to his feet and sprints across the park.

Darrell wonders if he should be doing something different. It's not just that he botched the last attempt, it's that even after succeeding with the second woman, nothing really changed for him. The thing is, he honestly thought it would be better than it was. Not just the sex part, but everything. He thought it would make him better somehow—like, stronger, complete. But he is still the awkward, smelly kid. And now he is also, as the papers write, a serial offender.

He is walking through a park. A young mother is pushing her kid in a stroller. She's attractive. They pass one another and the thought pops into his head. Just like that, like a tranquilizer dart; one moment you're fine, the next you're clutching the back of your neck, looking around wide-eyed before it all goes dark. He shakes it off. He forces the thought back down to wherever it came from. That kind of crazy shit is too much. That's crossing a line even he's not willing to step over . . . he thinks. He hopes.

The bizarre and confusing thing—confusing to his family when he is finally arrested, confusing to me as I listen to him Sunday after Sunday, and probably most confusing to him—is that at some level he is a genuinely helpful and strangely sweet kid. Even as a burgeoning serial rapist, he's the kind of boy who helps old ladies across the street, who carries their groceries home for them. Literally.

He runs back to the woman. "Miss," he says. "Miss. You shouldn't be here. Don't you know there's been a bunch of attacks? Some guy has been attacking ladies around here." The woman stiffens as he tells her this. He turns and leaves her, and a few moments later he looks back. She's gone. He is relieved. He's the dragon slayer.

He is the dragon.

He tries paying for it. He still isn't sure how it's supposed to work. He's given the woman the money, a hundred and twenty bucks saved from his door-to-door work. He didn't know you could visit an escort at her apartment. He assumed they had to come to you in a limo or something, the way they do in the movies. She's just a normal lady, a little younger than his mom. He's waiting in her room while she gets ready in the bathroom. He stops and considers himself in front of the full-length mirror. He looks like a kid, a schoolboy. It's weird to see himself like this and consider the very un-childlike things he's been doing—the thing he's about to do with her, for instance. He can hear the shower running. He rummages through her coat and finds the tidy fold of bills he gave her when he arrived. She steps out of the bathroom just as he's pocketing the cash. She doesn't make a big deal out of it. She's seen this sort of thing a hundred times from a hundred neighbourhood punks. She tells him to hand back the money and then she leads him to the bed and tells him to lie down.

He remembers thinking it was cool, having sex, real sex. Still, it isn't quite as great, quite as transformative, as he had expected.

—

WE DON'T DO OURSELVES any favours by euphemizing sex.

If only it were only about making love.

It took a long time for Lyana and me to get pregnant—to stay pregnant, really. We could conceive, but Lyana would miscarry at about six weeks, before there was even a heartbeat. This happened for several years, over and over. We tried everything. Our sex life went from carefree and fun to something dictated by a rigid prescription of hormone shots, ovulation sticks and semen analyses. It became timed and scheduled, utilitarian and clinical. Sex became unsexy.

When we finally heard a tiny heartbeat, we quit having sex altogether. We treated Lyana's womb with reverence and superstition. We didn't want to anger it, further invoke its wrath. Then there was the delivery and her recovery and the first few months of parenthood. We slept apart a lot, both of us blind with fatigue.

We had a new life to care for, our tiny daughter. Lyana's hormonal system and reproductive tract had been through two years of serious medical manipulation. And yet I was overwhelmingly preoccupied with the fact I wasn't getting laid.

I did my best to keep my needs to myself, to not put more pressure on her. Masturbation is healthy and normal, but it's not an adequate long-term solution. Whatever immediate physical release you get, it's essentially the act of intensely imagining the thing you want most while never actually obtaining it. If this is your only option, after a while you're bound to become frantic. And I did.

It came out in weird, embarrassing ways. Over the months I became hypercritical of my own body. I became convinced I was deeply unattractive. I felt disgusting, and no amount of exercise or dressing well made me feel better. I'd feel sad walking down the street, passing beautiful women, thinking there was no longer any way I could interest them. I felt I had gone to seed. I started to worry about my penis size. This had never really concerned me before. It was a clichéd way to feel my own sense of diminishment.

I envied my single friends who were going out, picking up, getting laid. One of my friends had three women on the go. I envied my gay friends too, for the well-matched libidos they seemed to share with their partners. I felt I had come down in the world, like a man in rags. I thought back with regret on the women I could have had sex with when I was younger but had declined. It was like remembering needless waste during a time of destitution.

I began looking at other women more intently. I would think about having sex with them, more than I normally do, in a way I found intrusive—the way I did when I was fourteen, but without any of the naïveté. For the first time in my life, I really felt the constraints of monogamy. I came across an article about Ashley Madison, the online hookup site for people looking for discreet extramarital affairs. I found the site tasteless. Still, I wondered vaguely what it would be like, just ordering up a supposed no-strings-attached lay. The idea rolled around in my head for a few days like an empty beer bottle clinking away under the driver's seat. I was worried it was a sign of my sad lack of inner restraint. But it was more that I was curious about what other people did. And I would never ever, *ever* actually do anything like that—you know, cheat. It wasn't even really fair to call it a sexual fantasy. It was more like an intellectual experiment.

I was angry. Not all the time and not severely, but enough that it flared up a few times. I'd sulk. "I'm tired of having sex with my laptop," I'd say. Or: "You realize I'm fully dependent on you for sex, right?"

Though I'd been thinking about this non-stop for months, Lyana saw these as bolts of sudden and unprompted petulance. Some nights I had trouble falling asleep beside her. I resented her for not making our sex life more of a priority. Would it really kill her to sleep with me once a week? I thought. She knows I'm going mental. It's not like I'm hiding this from her. We're busy and tired, sure. But I still cook all the meals. It's not like fatigue gives me a get-out-of-jail-free card. I still have to attend to *her* biological needs. I deserve the same kind of consideration. I deserve sex. And of course, the more I pushed for it, the less Lyana felt like having it.

Sexual frustration makes it harder for me to be the man I want to be. It makes me a secret pig. It amplifies my tendency to objectify women. It helps me rationalize my sense of entitlement—that very male sense of being owed sex. And, when it gets bad enough, it can make me angry enough that I resent the woman I love.

I'll never sexually assault anyone, no matter how pent-up I get. I've never had that kind of fantasy. But I'd be lying if I said I don't understand how lust and resentment can circle around and meet one another. It makes me sad that this potential exists within me, that it's part of how I'm made. But it would be worse to deny it. It would allow it to grow in some unlit corner.

—

DARRELL'S GETTING WORSE. He's saved more money and tried another prostitute. But it didn't help. He's not thinking straight. He's taking stupid risks, blindly diving off the precipice into the void. It's broad daylight. It's sunny out and he's walking through the same park. It's warm. It is early winter, but swarms of midges have been led to believe it's spring. They'll be dead by nightfall.

People are clearly talking about him. It's no longer just paranoia. A few days ago, one of the kids from his old school came up to him and said someone saw him hanging out in the park where the first two women were attacked. There was something accusatory about the way the kid said it, like he knew something. And yet Darrell manages not to think too much about any of this.

The path leads downhill. In the middle distance, Darrell sees a woman in a parka. The jacket makes it hard for him to tell what she looks like. She seems shapely. He runs quietly towards her. He pulls out the knife and grabs her from behind. The blade is in her face. He tries to drag her from the path into the bushes. He does not recall her crying out. Her hood comes down and he sees her face and is caught off guard because she is not young at all. She is about sixty. This kills his desire for sex. She's too old. Way too old. While he's trying to figure out how to handle things, the woman reaches up and grabs the knife. It is instinctual and unthinking, and so she grabs the blade. He fights her for it and, in the process, slices her deeply.

"You're the wrong person," he's saying. "Give me back the knife and I'll go."

He has the knife and he runs. The woman clutches her hand to her chest.

—

WHAT IS IT WE'RE actually after when we're sexually frustrated?

It's a strange beast. It is a need cloaked inside another need. It appears as carnal desire, as a slavering, whipped-up, wild-eyed thing, all sinew and muscle, champing at the air that surrounds it, feeding off the frenzy it creates, humping anything, everything it rubs up against. But what it actually hungers for is different and more mysterious.

After several months of my own frantic petulance, of Lyana's physical exhaustion and lack of interest, the sexual impasse broke the way ice floes break. One moment it was eternal winter; the next it was an entirely different season. We had put our daughter down. We were on the couch. Lyana was lying down. I was sitting. I had brought it up again. Lyana, again, didn't have it in her. We felt broken and misaligned. It would never happen. This was how a bright marriage that once radiated heat from its own internal fusion dwindles into a dim and sexless dwarf star. We were so distant. We were circling around one another as sad and remote as the Earth and the moon. There was nothing else to say. I took her foot in my hand just to touch her, to make sure I still could, to make sure she wouldn't retract from me. Somewhere upriver there was the low groan of ice breaking. Slowly and almost without realizing it, we undressed.

The next morning, we woke up renewed and warm. We were glowing again, radiating energy. Later that day, I texted Lyana to say hi. I was about to thank her for the great sex, but then it struck me we hadn't actually had sex. We hadn't even tried. It hadn't been about that. We'd held one another, we kissed, we caressed, but we hadn't technically done anything sexual. And yet I was calm and happy and whole.

Sexual frustration is tricky, because while it often manifests itself as a purely physical need, it's often just as much about the need for connection, for real human contact. This is why masturbation, or fucking someone without caring, doesn't resolve it. Even if you get off, the emotional need continues to build. But because it expresses itself as a physical need, it creates a sort of priapic feedback loop. It's a beast you make more ravenous by feeding it what it asks for.

And this is why, if you believe sex to be purely physical, if you are emotionally stunted in some way, if you are afraid of your emotions or too concerned with being a tough guy, or you've never been taught that it's okay to have these feelings—the need for tenderness, to connect—you're bound to be perpetually and increasingly dissatisfied.

Sex is such a strong drive that it affects our perception of risk and consequence. Even if you're a fairly well-adjusted person, it can influence your short-term decision making. It can distort the world around you: who you want to have sex with; how you want to have sex with them; the parts of their body you want to have sex with. And above all, the urgency with which you want to have it.

If you pay attention only to the physical aspect of sexual frustration, if you are blind to your own emotions, you will keep trying to feed the beast what it asks for. And it will continue to demand more.

—

IT IS EASIER, he decides, to pay for sex than to take it. The problem is, it's not actually that easy paying for it either. Darrell is too broke to afford the escort again. He calls her anyway, the first one, the one who was cool when he tried to rip her off. He's thinking of ripping her off again, thinking about it the way he does, without acknowledging he's thinking about it. It's a terrible plan. He convinces her to come to his place—to his mother's house. His mom is working late. His younger sister is at a babysitter's. He's not sure when his other sister will be back; usually she's out late. He has a couple of hours at least. It's not even really rape, in a way—in the sense that this woman will have sex with anyone, providing they pay. The crime he is thinking of committing is closer to theft. He's stealing something he can't afford to pay for. Plus, she's putting herself in this position. She knows the risks.

The woman comes to the back door. Darrell leads her to his room. He walks to the kitchen. He's not sure quite what he has in mind. He's still deliberating whether he's actually going to do this when he returns to his bedroom with a large knife. The woman quotes a price.

Darrell pulls out the knife and says, "I guess this one will be free."

Immediately, the woman goes for her purse. Darrell drops the knife because he's not sure what she has in there—a blade of her own? pepper spray? a gun? He jumps her. She's on all fours on his bed, fighting him off while trying to rummage through the contents of her purse, which are now spread across his comforter. He jumps on her back. He has his arm around her shoulder and neck. He is pulling her off the bed and, in effect, choking her. He is pulling her hard enough that he abrades the side of her face and neck. But she is an exceptionally good fighter. Darrell realizes he can't take her, not without really hurting her—or her really hurting him. He lets go. He is apologizing and trying to help her pick up the stuff from her purse. Somewhere in all this, she has grabbed the knife. Darrell is not entirely sure how she got hold of it. She has her cellphone too. This is what she was looking for. She's making a call, speed-dialing someone, waving the knife at Darrell to keep him back. Within seconds, someone is hammering at the front door. It's her pimp. He's been waiting in a car outside.

Darrell's version of the story is that he let her out of the house as soon as her pimp showed up. The woman's version is different. In her legal testimony, she said that Darrell would not let her go; that when her companion showed up, she had to fight to make her way to the door; that her companion had to pull her past Darrell, who was blocking the way. Darrell and the woman agree that Darrell issued a steady stream of apologies the entire time.

The apologies have more to do with fear than with genuine contrition. He is awash in fear. Fear defines him the way salt defines the sea. It pours into him, filling the crevices of his mind with a briny metallic tang. It changes the way the room smells. He hears his heart, feels his pulse coursing through the arteries of his neck like ropes of blood.

He is outside. He's running. The pavement is cold beneath his feet. He's halfway to the house of a guy he knows before he realizes he isn't wearing shoes. When the police arrest him, he is inexplicably carrying a pair of handcuffs and a bungee cord. His socks are filthy.

He's twenty-seven when he gets out. This is February 2007. Kingston is a cold, grey place, especially the side of town he's on. The wind comes at you straight off the lake like a blade, sharp and impersonal. Parole is a tightrope walk. It's a single, straight line: a job washing pots at a local restaurant, a room at a boarding house, regular calls to his parole officer and mandatory attendance at the Salvation Army's Circle of Support and Accountability, a group for sex offenders. If you stray from the line, you fall. You fall far and you fall hard.

He feels all right at first, though the job's shitty. He's up to his elbows in greasy dishwater all night; he makes shit money, enough for shitty clothes and shitty food and rent for his shitty place. But it could be worse. The people at the restaurant are nice. There are a lot of students working there, good kids from Queen's University, slinging food part-time. Young men. Young women. He's not having any thoughts about the women he works with, which is a good sign.

When he was inside, he progressed through an intensive therapy programme. He tried to take it to heart. He didn't deny what he had done or blame his victims like some of the other men. He knows what objectifying women is. He knows what sexual entitlement is. He knows what distorted thinking is.

He goes to the Salvation Army group regularly. He calls his parole officer more often than he has to. Soon he's got a pass to stay out late if he's working.

The kids at the restaurant are only a few years younger than he is, but they're from another world, a planet with more oxygen and sunshine. They're energetic. They're buoyant. They have plans and the capacity to carry out those plans. Darrell's never been that way. There's a pane of glass between his life and theirs. He will never be able to pass through it.

He gets to know another guy who served time for rape. The guy's bitter. People read the paper, the guy reminds Darrell. He had an okay job too, just like Darrell. Things started out all right for him too. He was working as a grocery bagger, but then the uptight housewives start to recognize him and before long someone speaks to the manager and because the manager is a pussy he ends up getting shit-canned.

Darrell is getting skittish, because he's pretty sure people are starting to recognize him too. He's getting looks from people on the street. He wonders how long it will be before the nice kids at the restaurant learn what he's done.

He's walking home from work one night and a cab pulls up at the curb. A girl gets out. She's slender and attractive. She's wearing a short skirt despite it being cold enough to crack steel. Darrell knows she's a hooker on the way to a job. He's not sure how he knows—he just does. Something about the way she carries herself. It makes him think about women in a way he hasn't for a while. Seeing her gives him that sense of leaning out over empty space.

The most important habit for Darrell to maintain is being honest about his feelings when talking to the people at the Salvation Army group. He still goes. He still talks to the people there, the upright citizens who are there to help him walk the line. But now he doesn't tell them what's on his mind. There's no place there for the things he's thinking. They wouldn't understand.

Here's the way he sees it: a normal relationship is impossible. There's zero chance he'll find a girlfriend. What do you do—tell her on the first date, by the way, I did ten years for serial rape? Withhold that information from her until someone else lets the cat out of the bag, which they inevitably will? Let her find out when someone hands her an old newspaper clipping? On the other hand, seeing prostitutes would mean violating his parole. So, pragmatically speaking, sex is not an option, which is kind of like saying food or water or oxygen are not an option.

The bigger issue is this: maybe, deep down, Darrell doesn't really want a girlfriend. Maybe he's only into taking what he can't have. Maybe sex is only sexy for him when it involves physical force.

—

I'VE MET MEN LIKE THIS, men who are different from Darrell in the sense they're not criminals but for whom sex without the prospect of violence is like an egg without salt.

Zack is polite, engaging and articulate. He is short, fit and gregarious. He keeps his hair, which is receding, cropped close and often wears a newsboy or a baseball cap. He dresses in nice jeans and crisp T-shirts and sports the thick five-o'clock shadow that is *de rigueur* among hip men in the downtown neighbourhood where he lives and works. He is an excellent conversationalist. You cannot tell anything about his sexual proclivities by looking at him.

He does have a tell in some of the work he does. Not his landscapes or the bread-and-butter multimedia pieces you'll find in galleries in Boston, Chicago and Los Angeles, and in the lobby of one of Toronto's tonier hotels—but in a smaller, private collection, a series of portraits of young men. Each of these men is handsome. They are fit and statuesque. Usually they are shirtless. I envy these men their gracile bodies. They are each wounded in some way—the kind of injuries you get in a fight: a black eye, a laceration over the cheekbone, a broken nose.

They are — the paintings and the men they portray — physically charged and slightly menacing. They are also extremely attractive.

I met Zack a couple of years ago at a large outdoor exhibit held by local artists in Trinity Bellwoods Park, a sprawling public green near my old apartment. His paintings stood out because, besides being visually arresting, they were at odds with much of the other work on display, which were pieces designed to complement hip dining room sets and modern condominium living. I asked Zack what motivated him to paint them. He told me he had been in an accident with his father a few years earlier; his father had been driving and had struck his head against the steering wheel. The image of his dad, bleeding, stuck with Zack and started him, he told me, on "an exploration of the juxtaposition between male vulnerability and brutality." The phrase sounded like the sort of thing you might write on a grant application; it didn't fit with the glowering sexual energy of the portraits. Whatever the deal with his father and the car accident, I decided, there was something more behind those paintings.

I took Zack's card and later sent him some of the material I had written for this book, descriptions of my own violent outbursts and alpha-male fantasies. We talked over the phone. We met for coffee. We got along easily. Eventually, he opened up about his sex life. We sat in his studio, the front room of a large Victorian brownstone littered with big canvases in various states of completion, and he told me about the first time he kidnapped someone and forced him into sexual submission.

Zack and Bradley have had a beer. They've been hanging out on the main floor with their housemates, Frank, Aaron and Tim. (I'm not using anyone's real name here, by the way.) They've all been decompressing, letting the adrenalin boil off. They're in a good mood. They're laughing and relieved and amazed because their plan has worked. None of the neighbours saw them haul the blond man out of the van and into the house. He is in the basement now. Zack and Bradley have constructed a room to hold him. They've painted the walls black and boarded up the windows. They've laid down a plank for him to sleep on. There is a blanket and a pillow. There is a strong lock on the door.

The straight boys—Frank, Aaron and Tim—have no further interest in the man. The abduction was fun. It was like a fraternity prank, a good way to blow off steam. But the rest of the plan, the sex stuff, doesn't appeal to them. They stay upstairs and drink. It's Friday night. Someone cranks the sound system.

Bradley is eager to get started. Zack tells him they need to wait. The blond man is still too freaked out. He is lying on the floor in his cell, still tied up, blindfolded and gagged. When Zack opens the door, the man flinches and scuttles in blind crustacean fear. He's physically frightened. You can't fake this kind of fear. Zack likes this. It's exciting. It is also kind of frightening. His own heart is racing.

They check on the man again a short while later. Upstairs, the straight boys are now drunk. The sound system is driving the bass lines of punk rock down into the foundation of the house. The basement ceiling is trembling. The man is trembling too, but less severely than he has been. Zack approaches him and removes the gag.

"What the fuck is happening?" gasps the man. He has electrical tape over his eyes. Zack doesn't answer. Instead, he forces a stick between the man's teeth, like a dog with a bone.

"Don't let go of this," Zack says. He returns upstairs.

Forty-five minutes later, the man is still holding the stick in his mouth. He's drooling. He has quit shaking. Zack and Bradley sit him up in a chair. They replace the duct tape on his wrists and ankles with shackles.

"We're not going to untie you," says Zack. "But we're not going to hurt you. We're sane, okay?"

The man looks deeply skeptical.

Bradley is the bad cop. The stick comes out of the guy's mouth. Bradley's cock comes out of his pants. He's pushing it at the man's mouth like he's trying to force-feed him a banana. The man moves his head back and forth, trying to avoid Bradley's penis. His mouth is clamped shut.

"C'mon," Bradley insists. "Open up. It's just my dick."

Zack wonders if maybe they ought to give the guy a little more time to get his bearings. But maybe Bradley's approach is better. Maybe it's like taking off a Band-Aid or getting into cold water—best done in one fell swoop.

Now Bradley's cock is in the man's mouth. Bradley is holding the back of the guy's head. The man is shackled to the chair. There is no movement he can make to avoid what's being done to him. This is what does it for Zack: the struggle, watching the man squirm and try to resist. How much of it, Zack wonders, is real resistance and how much of it is an act? Zack is torn because, while he doesn't want to hurt the man, not really—at least not severely—he very much relishes the idea that the struggle is real. It makes him hard.

They didn't know whether they'd get any responses to the ad they'd taken out in a local alternative paper. This was in 1992, before Internet hookups. The ad read:

*Looking for a guy, 18–25, who wants to be raped at knifepoint and held captive for the weekend.*

Inside a week, their rented post-office box was crammed with mail. They exchanged letters with a few men, finally agreeing on this guy, the guy in the basement—Cam. They wrote Cam and agreed on a time and place for the abduction.

Cam remains cuffed and blindfolded the entire weekend. On Saturday, they mummify him in plastic drop sheets as though they're preparing to dump his body in the river. He cannot budge. It is hard for him to breathe. Zack finds this particularly erotic. He rubs himself against the plastic cocoon and gets off. They unwrap Cam. Later in the day, Zack and Bradley tell Cam they're going to tattoo him. Zack has an electrical engraving set, which makes a menacing buzz. They press it to Cam's skin, where it vibrates convincingly. This freaks Cam out. "Wait!" he yells. "Are you fucking serious? Are you really tattooing me?" They slap Cam and punch him in the stomach—though, admittedly, they pull their punches. They beat him off until he ejaculates.

Zack and Bradley have purchased two rescue cages at an army surplus store. These are old military field stretchers built into protective metal frames. Zack has modified them. He and Bradley stand Cam inside one of the cages and close the other over him, clamshell-style. They chain the two halves shut. There is barely enough space for Cam to move. Bradley starts beating the cage with a metal pipe. "We're going to fuck you up, faggot!" he yells. He is wailing on the metal frame. It makes a tremendous racket inside the small room. The pipe is extremely close to Cam's skull. Bradley has worked himself into a frenzy. He is hitting the cage over and over again. The metal begins to buckle. Cam is cringing and shuddering inside. His face is inches away from the pipe. Bradley is in a froth. Zack tells Bradley to chill, and he does.

Zack brings simple meals to Cam every few hours—scrambled eggs, soup, sandwiches—but Cam eats very little. Zack suspects this is because Cam is highly stressed, despite being there of his own volition. Living out a fantasy can be as awkward as meeting a famous person: There isn't quite the chemistry you imagined. He is shorter than you thought. He has halitosis.

Zack is experiencing a touch of this. It's a lot of work, having a captive, keeping him safe and fed and clean, even if he is ostensibly your slave. Zack is at odds with himself. He wants to hurt Cam, but he doesn't *really* want to hurt Cam. His libido wants him to cross a line his conscience won't allow him to cross. It's a bit like holding a newborn and wanting to bite it. You would never actually hurt it, not if you're sane. But you might think about it. You wonder if this is what the nutjobs who actually kill their children experience. It can be a little disconcerting. The weekend is supposed to be about mutual satisfaction. Zack genuinely wants Cam to enjoy himself. But what satisfies Zack— lighting up Cam with fear and keeping him lit—is a little too intense for Cam. When they ease up so Cam can relax and enjoy himself, the thrill flickers and dims for Zack. This is disconcerting too.

The weekend with Cam took place the summer Zack graduated from university. Since then, he's done this sort of thing maybe a half-dozen times. It's worth mentioning that Cam wrote Zack and Bradley, requesting a repeat of the weekend. Zack didn't follow through with Cam again but he does still do this sort of thing. He now arranges such encounters online. He's been both the abductor and the captive. His prospective partners—if that's the right word—will leave a note on the door to assure Zack he has the right house. Zack will sneak in and find his victim in the kitchen or bedroom. Alternatively, there will be a blindfold and a pair of handcuffs waiting for him. Zack will slip the blindfold on and cuff himself and sit there, waiting. Sometimes it takes quite a long time for the homeowner to find him. And the wait can become unbearable. This is part of the thrill. Sometimes the man, whoever he turns out to be, will come up behind Zack, as silent as fog, and clamp a hand over his mouth and tear the shirt off his back and throw him to the ground and tie him up as if he were a yearling calf being gelded.

Recently, Zack took an overnight bus to St. Louis, Missouri, to be held captive by a man he had never met. It does not escape him that these kinds of scenarios have the potential to drift towards the horrific and uncontrollable. He is otherwise a rational creature.

These urges—to dominate, to use physical force, to humiliate, hurt and make suffer, and, in turn, to be made to suffer—are as irreducible, as fundamental to his sense of eroticism, as his attraction to other men.

We have labels for this kind of thing. Clearly, Zack is into BDSM, the catch-all term preferred by aficionados that includes, but is not limited to, bondage, domination, sexual sadism and masochism. Until recently, all of these proclivities were listed in the *Diagnostic and Statistical Manual of Mental Disorders* as paraphilias, the contemporary term for sexual deviances.

Increasingly, the majority of paraphilias are viewed as harmless sexual idiosyncrasies, variations of normal sexual interest—within psychiatry and also in mainstream society. As our understanding of sexual diversity becomes more expansive and inclusive, most paraphilias are now following the trajectory of earlier so-called deviations such as homo- and bisexuality. The catch, of course, is that some paraphilias are truly harmful, either to the person with the desire, as in the case of auto-erotic asphyxiation, or to the object of that desire, as in the case of biastophilia—arousal from raping a non-consenting stranger. The most current edition of the DSM takes this into account by differentiating between benign paraphilias and the newly minted and more menacing category of *paraphilic disorders*.

There's a genuine need for this sort of differentiation. No matter how accepting of sexual diversity we grow, the rainbow will never—and *should* never—welcome all colours. But therein lies a challenge. Much of the rationale behind accepting diverse sexual orientations is that many of them are inherent. This is certainly the case with homo- and bisexuality. Getting Zack to like women is never going to happen. Like a lot of gay guys desperate to fit in, he dated girls in high school. We've solved this problem—at least in the civilized pockets of the world where LGBT rights are starting to flourish—by simply getting over being freaked out by non-hetero, non-vanilla sexuality and removing those orientations from the medically sanctioned lists of moral offences.

But it's not quite so clear what to do in cases where sexual desires *are* legitimately harmful. The most salient and relevant example is pedophilia. For the longest time an attraction to children was presumed to be the result of childhood trauma—or just plain moral depravity. More and more, however, it too seems to be a sexual orientation, something that comes on with puberty and remains unchanged—and unchangeable—throughout a person's life. Something like one to five percent of men are thought to be sexually attracted to children. Often men who have these desires don't want to have them—a state psychiatrists refer to as *ego-dystonic*. There are several biological correlates—differences in cortical white matter, for instance; a slightly lower IQ—which suggests pedophiles are born, not made.[25] If pedophilia is in fact a sexual orientation, it is almost exclusive to males. There are very few female pedophiles. In fact, paraphilias in general are far more common in men than in women.

If you consider how common it was, until quite recently, for grown men to take child brides—even in so-called advanced nations—it's clear that the view that pedophilia is a repugnant and immoral attraction is a contemporary one.[26] There are a couple of implications of this relatively recent change in thinking that are worth considering. First, it supports the idea that we can make broad changes to how a society views a certain kind of sexual predilection, whether or not it is biologically inherent. The other thing that's worth thinking about, though, is that while social condemnation makes it harder for men to victimize children, it hasn't taken away their desire to do so—it has simply driven it underground. Or, more precisely, into the benthic zones of the Internet.

After a lot of hunting, I found a social worker in Nova Scotia who referred me to a client of his, a construction worker in his fifties who has served time for molesting his own pre-adolescent daughter.

This man—I'll call him Joshua—is a sort of poster child for reformed pedophiles. I wouldn't necessarily have believed this if it had come only from him. But he has been the subject of peer-reviewed case stud-ies,[27] and the social worker who put us in touch with one another vouched that Joshua is doing precisely what it takes to control his urges. As Joshua explained to me, much of this work involves meeting regu-larly with other convicted pedophiles in a sort of AA-like support group where the men can talk openly about their sexual urges. Joshua is now one of the leaders of this group. The core tenet of the meeting is much the same as AA: before you can control the urge, you must first own up to it and recognize that it is bigger than you.

One of the challenges of running this group, Joshua told me, is that it's difficult to coordinate and maintain the meetings. Like AA, the men hold their gatherings in schools and community centres. When the people in charge of these institutions eventually find out who attends the meetings, Joshua and the other men are no longer welcome. It's an understandable reaction—I'm not sure I would feel any differently. But it's not doing anything to help these men keep themselves in check.

We're at a point where we are starting to recognize the inherent nature of pedophilia at some level, but we're still not comfortable facing what that means head-on. Evil may originate in our desires, but it is action, not thought, that does the damage. If there is a way of inter-rupting thoughts and emotions to prevent them from becoming actions, it's worth considering a different tactic—one that is not based entirely on moralistic repulsion.

Combatting a harmful sexual orientation probably takes a two-pronged approach. One line of attack needs to focus on the societal factors that support it—child marriage, for example—while the other addresses the biological factors—i.e., sexual attraction to children and personal impulse control. Neither approach is likely to succeed alone. No matter how socially vilified pedophiles are, they continue to secretly harm kids. And unless there is some modicum of social support for those pedophiles who genuinely want to control their inherent desires, their own attempts to govern their sex drive will likely be as unsuccess-ful as the alcoholic who, despite his best intentions, does not have an AA group to attend.

—

ZACK PUT ME IN TOUCH with his friend Tim. Tim is in his late forties. He's an architect at a respectable Manhattan firm. He asked me not to use his real name. He worries that if his colleagues find out what he's into, it would destroy his professional reputation. He's probably right.

The first time Tim "juiced," as he calls it, he made the mistake of doing it at his apartment. He didn't realize how messy things could get, even with all the precautions. He and his partner had pushed the furniture against the walls. They had draped plastic drop sheets to prevent splatter and stains. They started out nearly naked, sporting the kind of briefs professional wrestlers wear. Tim had secreted on himself—I forgot to ask where exactly—a razor blade. They started out wrestling, doing their best to pull off sleepers and half nelsons and leg locks. Tim knows these moves. He has been a fan of professional wrestling since he was a boy. Even then, watching it on TV gave him a proto-sexual tingle. In high school he wanted to try out for the school wrestling team but was convinced he'd get a hard-on during practice.

Tim's partner began to dominate. Tim stopped the action. He pulled out the razor and nicked himself just above the hairline the way the pros do, though not nearly as deftly. The first time, jacked up on adrenalin, he sank the blade in too deep. Soon he had a slick of blood running down the side of his face and over his sternum. He and his partner were covered in blood. Blood on the floor. Blood on the plastic sheeting. Drying blood, sticky in the creases of their necks and elbows. Blood like oil mixing with the sweat of their bodies. They stopped again and took photos of themselves. They started up again. Tim lost enough blood that he became light-headed. Eventually, the wrestling moves turned into close-quarter fondling. The nature of the struggle changed. The briefs came off.

For some, BDSM has little to do with a specific physical act—or any physical act. A friend of mine is a mild-mannered, middle-aged divorcee who works as a programme coordinator at a community centre. When he found out what I was writing about, he told me about his sex life on condition of anonymity. I would never have pegged him for the type. His relationships consist of short-term hookups he finds on S&M chat sites. For a while he was dating a woman who was an extreme submissive. One of the things that got her off was being forced to sleep in a large dog kennel and calling my friend "master." She was able to reach orgasm, according to my friend, solely by being bossed around and verbally humiliated. In the end, this was too much even for him, and they split up.

It's worth asking what's behind these desires, the impulses and fetishes that fit under the umbrella term BDSM, partly because they represent the most common kind of sexual paraphilia.

About 15 percent of American men and 11 percent of women have dabbled in some form of BDSM. The number gets higher depending on what definition you use. Nearly 40 percent of men in the general population have fantasies about tying someone up[28] and apparently about half of us enjoy biting or being bitten.[29] A quick tour of any porn aggregate site makes it clear that BDSM is one of—if not *the*—most common kink in mainstream pornography, accounting for about 17 percent of mainstream porn scenarios. Artistically speaking, neither the Marquis de Sade nor Georges Bataille invented anything new. Sadomasochistic art—both writings and imagery—dates back to medieval India and pre-Confucian China. And while you might dismiss the artistic merits of the *Fifty Shades of Grey* series, it's harder to dismiss its immense popularity. It has sold over a hundred million copies, been translated into fifty-three languages and holds the record as the fastest-selling paperbacks of all time.

BDSM is enormous and startling in the array of sexual acts it encompasses. It's easy to get lost in the variety, in the permutations and combinations of the nitty-gritty, of parts-doing-things-to-other-parts. But there's a single, binding commonality, a bigger picture worth pondering: all BDSM, regardless of the specific sex act, is characterized by the same desire—to use power and domination to supercharge sex, more often than not by employing physical violence, or the threat thereof.

I'm not suggesting BDSM is a biological predisposition. That would be missing what is arguably the most important point: the specific manifestations of BDSM—the whips, chains, sex-swings, ball-gags, PVC suits—are all clearly cultural inventions. In fact, BDSM is, by definition, a culture or, if you want to split hairs, a collection of subcultures. And, like any culture, there are agreed-upon norms and values. Bondage clubs aren't exactly the Ladies' Auxiliary or the Elks Lodge, but if members stray far enough from the agreed-upon norms, they will quickly find themselves on the outs. The most important norm—what differentiates BDSM from straight-up sexual torture—is the central tenet of mutual consent. I suspect BDSM is enjoying its current renaissance because its many vocal supporters have done a good job promoting this. Mutual consent, they argue, puts power in the hands of the submissive. Done properly, they insist, it's not about sexual violence or patriarchal power, but precisely the opposite: a transgressive deconstruction of these things. Serious BDSM kind of weirds me out. But I've met enough otherwise good, kind people who are into it that I believe this. But, of course, it's not true of everyone.

*Question:* What's the difference between a dom who doesn't care about mutual consent and a genuine sexual sadist?

*Answer:* Nothing.

My point is that BDSM is a culture that has been invented to negotiate a common and potentially dangerous desire. BDSM is not the desire; it is a set of controls we have invented to mitigate the danger imposed by the desire.

It's interesting to consider that in bonobos, the only great ape species that doesn't show any form of sexual violence, sex is still a way of negotiating power. Sex is commonly used among bonobos for social bonding, but also, importantly, as a means of diffusing aggressive tension. Individual bonobos will literally swoop in and intervene in a confrontation by fucking the tension away.

Power and sex seem to have co-evolved in humans and in the other great ape species. In humans, they form two sides of a Möbius strip. You start out on one side, thinking about sex, for instance, and suddenly you find yourself negotiating power. Likewise, you aim for power—for money, status, wealth, social respect—and suddenly you find yourself leveraging those assets to acquire sex. There's truth to the feminist argument that rape is about power. I expect that's because sex and power are inextricably conjoined, and always have been.

It's worth considering whether or not one of the cultural changes we need in order to reduce rape is an acknowledgement that there's something in men's psychological makeup, something that, while not inevitable, is inherent and can be triggered more easily than we'd like to admit. Maybe we need an approach that is more akin to BDSM, some way of subverting the urge rather than denying it outright.

—

DARRELL, ONCE AGAIN, has been trying to deal with his urges by buying sex. He is on the phone with one of the girls who's been coming to see him at his crummy Kingston apartment. She tells him she doesn't want to see him anymore. He offers her more money, even though he doesn't really have any. He's already blown what little he'd saved on the dozen or so girls he's been with in the past couple of months. The girl on the phone says it's not a matter of money. One of the other girls has told her she had a bad experience with him; she's told all the girls. He wasn't exactly violent, but he was a prick. He bossed her around, told her to take her clothes off like he was a drill sergeant. He insisted on having sex without a condom. That's a serious no-no. He was rough, too, and he insisted on paying by cheque, which is definitely not on the menu when it comes to paying for sex. The girls all know about him now. He's blacklisted. The girl on the phone tells him not to call back.

He's still going to the Salvation Army group, but he hasn't told them about the hookers. He's been telling them everything's fine, which is the same thing he's been telling the detective constable in charge of his parole. He visits him that morning and says everything is going just great. Afterwards, he thinks about calling his sister, because everything is not going great. Things are pretty fucked, actually. He can feel it, stirring inside him again. There's something inevitable about it. That's what he tells himself. He thinks about his sister and he's got his phone in his hand ready to call her. *Fuck it*, he thinks. Instead, he calls the number of a masseuse he knows, even though he's got no money.

He's at her place now, the masseuse. She's from Korea. He tells her he can have her deported if she doesn't do what he wants. She tells him to get out. He pulls a knife. He tells her to get undressed. She fights back hard enough that she rips out one of her toenails in the struggle.

He rapes her on the massage table as she tries desperately to get away. He chokes her unconscious twice, like an MMA fighter, but he does it brutally and clumsily. He ends up squeezing her head and bruising her face in a way that immediately gives her two black eyes. Now it looks as though he's punched her. When it's over, he tells her to shower. He watches to make sure she cleans herself well and gets rid of the evidence. He takes the cotton cover off the massage table and sets it on fire in the middle of her living room. It chars her carpet. He wipes down the massage table and the rest of the room with bleach. The whole time, she's shaking.

Partway through the bleach trick, he stops to consider exactly what he's doing. He considers what he's going to have to do to get away. He already knows it's a lost cause. He knew that before he did it. He knows how badly he's fucked up. He knows how messed up he is. He pictures running to his apartment, grabbing his things, robbing a store, grabbing some cash, getting on a train and heading to Toronto, heading out west. But there's no point. He has no will to go on. The cops would catch him. More to the point, there's no running from what he is.

He calls his sister. He tells her what he's done, that he's fucked up, that there's something wrong with him, that even when he knows something is wrong, he does it. He doesn't know why he didn't call her before, why he didn't call someone in the Salvation Army group. He's a monster, he tells his sister. He's evil. His sister tells him she loves him. It's a weird thing to hear at that moment. It catches him off guard. Suddenly he's crying. He's done a bad thing, she tells him. He's made a mistake, but he's still a good person inside. He still has the ability to be good, but right now he has to do the right thing. Does he know what the right thing is? He does, he tells her, through the mucus and tears gathering in the back of his throat. He knows the right thing is to call the cops on himself. That's right, his sister tells him. When you get off the phone with me, you have to call the police. She tells him again that she loves him. She says she is there for him, that she always will be. He hangs up.

He tells the cops there's been an assault. He can't bring himself to say *rape*. He warns them that when they arrive they'll see the woman has two black eyes, that it'll look as though he hit her in the face, but that's not what happened. There was a struggle, but he didn't hit her. He doesn't hit women.

When he got out after serving his time, everyone warned him. They told him to walk the line, otherwise he'd never get out again. A second go in the pen meant no more safety nets, no more parole, no more counselling, no more second chances. It meant he'd be a piece of shit, dumped and flushed. Even his lawyer told him the best-case scenario for a repeat offence would be him getting out when he is a very, very old man. They hammered this into his head.

He'd nodded. He'd said, "Yes, sir," and "Yes, ma'am," and he meant it. He really did. He knew they weren't shitting him, and he thought he wasn't shitting them.

He thinks about this in the back of the cruiser. At the apartment, the cops have interviewed the woman. They've gathered evidence. By the time he's led into the station, the charges have been upgraded from assault to sexual assault.

In her ruling, the judge overseeing the hearing points out that Darrell has had the best, most intensive psychological counselling the correctional system can provide. He is smart, she says, his intelligence above average. He's had everything at his disposal—the training, the mental horsepower—to stop himself, and yet he hasn't. Three forensic psychiatrists have been brought in. They all agree: Darrell has "a preference for sex with non-consenting adult females." Despite this, they also all agree he is capable of empathy, that he is not a psychopath. It is, as he has told me, more a matter of him turning off his empathy as he sees fit, which is why, in the end, the judge designates him a dangerous sexual offender—meaning he'll be a very old man before he ever sees the outside of a prison again.

In her decision, she writes: "The evidence is nothing more than mere hope that he can be treated at all."

At some level, he has always known this. He knew it from the moment he saw the girl get out of the cab. Maybe he knew it from the moment he stepped out of prison. In some ways, it's easier to give in to it. Maybe it comes down to laziness after all, because, as his sister said, at some level he is a good person. At least, he wants to be good. But goodness needs resolve and strength. Goodness must be an active agent, a proactive sensibility, a constant watching gaze. If you're too lazy, too self-centred, too self-defeating, then probably you need to have that gaze imposed upon you.

—

TO GET TO THE SHU, you drive across flat farmland towards a series of low buildings the colour of thunderclouds. The road leading to the prison is bolt-straight and roughly the length of an airport runway. It's like looking down the barrel of a rifle. At the end of the road, a slender communications tower marks the X of the SHU like a giant pin on a map. All around, the trees have been cut down. There is an infinity of grass swaying in the wind. There is no approaching the place or leaving without being in clear view of guard towers and cameras. Beyond the prison grounds are further expanses of agricultural land that go on forever, fields of crops and fields in fallow.

I waited in an uncomfortable chair. I signed my name and clipped on a badge. I emptied my pockets, shed my jacket and passed through detectors. I stood in front of the Plexiglas and waited while a guard took forever to read something off a clipboard. Finally he looked up and told me visiting hours had been cancelled for the morning and to come back that afternoon. I had to bow down and put my ear to the battered metal grille to hear him. He said the place was under lockdown.

"What happened?" I asked.

The guard shrugged.

"Do you think it will be over by this afternoon?"

He shrugged again and went back to reading the clipboard.

I slept fitfully in my car in the shadow of the watchtower. I woke up anxious and went for a drive.

In the afternoon, I was let in. I was led into a six-by-eight room. Darrell sat on the other side of a thick pane of Plexiglas. He nodded at me and grinned slightly. I wasn't sure how to greet him, so I put a fist against the glass and he gave me a virtual bump.

I had to lean in to hear him. My side of the booth was lined with old carpeting, a sort of grey, wiry Astroturf that covered every surface.

It smelled like the aftermath of a flood and left red welts on my arms when I brushed against it. There was an old phone cradle on the wall but no handset. We spoke to one another through a stainless steel grate that conducted almost no sound. Whenever Darrell leaned back in his chair, his voice faded to nothing. It was like watching someone mouth words from the bottom of a swimming pool. We leaned on our elbows, our foreheads nearly touching the Plexiglas so we didn't have to shout. Through the wall, I could hear a woman bellowing in French three booths down.

Darrell was wearing sweatpants and a white T-shirt. I could see the thick keloids running down the length of his forearms.

"Those are from where you . . ." I nodded towards his arms. He had told me about the scars already, over the phone.

He nodded back.

If you're going to kill yourself, you need to concentrate on the tissue near the wrist, where the vessels are close to the surface, not quite so high on the forearm. Darrell had missed the vital real estate on each arm by about an inch. He had taken a lot of pills, so things had got pretty jumbled by the time he started cutting.

Partly because of the pills but also because of his state of mind at the time, he has trouble explaining exactly what happened. And because of this, when he first told me about it, I couldn't decide whether I believed him, whether it was a real attempt or whether I was more sympathetic with the official take: that it had been a histrionic episode of self-pity.

He remembers the period leading up to it like this:

He was back in the pen, but not yet consigned to the SHU. He had a job in the prison kitchen. He was working long hours. When he wasn't in the kitchen, he was at the gym. He hoped working out might help him sleep. He had been to the prison shrink, but after reoffending, he was now low-priority. There wasn't much point in him using up therapy sessions that might benefit other men. Instead, the doc gave him a prescription for sleeping pills.

Part of his motivation for working out so hard was self-protection. None of the other guys on his range knew he was a sex offender. Yet. This was the main reason he was having so much trouble sleeping. They were bound to find out. Word always got out. Plus, while he was on parole, he had talked to some journalists for a piece on sexual offenders. He had agreed to a filmed interview. He wasn't sure if the piece had aired yet. There was always a TV on. Every time he left for work or the gym, he was certain the show would come on in his absence and he'd be returning to a range of men waiting to cave in his skull. He got big. He tried his best to look tough. He could do dozens of chin-ups and countless push-ups.

In the SHU, there's not much opportunity to work out. He gets an hour in the yard if it's decent out and the place isn't locked down. There's no equipment to speak of, other than a chin-up bar. The men aren't allowed to have weights. On top of that, he's got into the habit of watching too much TV. His stomach protrudes slightly under his T-shirt. His face is round and cherubic. He's let himself grow a beard and short little dreads, which, because his hair is receding, look like a jagged halo radiating from his crown. He now wears glasses. He looks more like a poet than a prisoner.

"If I ever get placed back in the general population again," he tells me, "I'll have to get back in good shape."

There's very little chance of either of those things happening.

When he arrived back in the pen, in the general population, he felt beaten down—not the way the other inmates did, complaining that they were victims of their childhood or poverty or racism. He felt defeated by himself, by the things about himself he never quite understood. He saved up his sleeping pills.

"At the time," he told me, "I was lost in my thoughts, I didn't think about hope. I had this mentality that if I end my life, then I'll make someone suffer before I go."

He took the pills all at once. It was late. The kitchen was empty. He raided the pantry. He knew it would bring in a guard. He remembers the guard coming in, but then things start to get choppy and disjointed, like a film with thirty-second segments spliced out. The guard is a woman. There's a broken broom handle on the floor. Maybe Darrell put it there. She sees the broom handle. She picks it up. He walks over to her. He is in front of her before he realizes it, as if he has materialized there. He yanks the broom handle out of her hands. He remembers being angry. Angry in general. Angry at this woman for picking up the broom handle, insinuating by doing so that she sees him as a threat, that he might use it as a weapon. Angry at himself too, because, let's be honest, that was probably his plan. He's having trouble keeping that plan straight. He has his hands on her. There is a washroom off the kitchen, towards the back. They have materialized in there as if they've been beamed in from the *Enterprise*. He is trying to pull her to the ground. He isn't thinking about sex. As far as he remembers, he's just angry. He has her in a corner, against the tiles. He is holding her in a sort of sloppy headlock while they fight for the broom handle. And then, according to him, he is thinking, *Fuck it. Fuck it. What's the point?* And he lets her go and she scrambles for her panic button. He remembers apologizing as she charges out of the bathroom to get reinforcements. He has hurt her, bruised her face, he thinks. He is in the kitchen. He has locked and barricaded the door. He has a razor. He is cutting his arm open. It is like butterflying a pork tenderloin. He cuts deep and hard until he sees pink, and there is a moment before the pink of his flesh is flooded with red so dark it looks like motor oil, and then there is blood all over him. In one arm he feels the snap of a tendon as it recoils towards the inner elbow. He is sticky. He is saying sorry. He is saying it aloud. It is echoing off the tiles. Or maybe he is saying it to himself and it is echoing in the dark of his head. There is blood on his hands, down his front. He has smeared it across the wall. He can read it as he lies on the floor.

On the wall he has written in blood: *I'm sorry*.

So many Sundays have gone by between me applying for this visit and the prison authorities granting it that I've already done all the serious interviewing over the phone. Our visit is mostly small talk, along with me getting a physical sense of the man I've known only as a hushed voice over a bad phone line.

Once he had recovered enough, Darrell was shipped here. He's been in the SHU for more than five years now. Other than his lawyer and me, no one has been to visit him.

"My mom works a lot," he says by way of an explanation. She manages a clothing store in Toronto.

He speaks with his younger sister, the one now in college, twice a week. She's the only person he has regular contact with. His uncle wants him to call, but Darrell can't bring himself to do it. "Mostly," he tells me, "because of the shame of what I've done."

His sister recently spent a weekend in New York City with her friends.

"She's a lot more social than me." Darrell says this with some satisfaction. He's happy she's getting an education, seeing a bit of the world.

"I taught her to ride a bike," he says. It's as if he had forgotten this for a long time and it has just now struck him. "I don't know if she'd remember that." He smiles. It is a beautiful smile. It has no business being here, in the SHU, on his face. It doesn't make sense. It is the kind of smile you hope your son will grow up to have, gentle and warm. It's impossibly strange that this is the smile of a serial rapist.

"Do you ever talk to her about what you've done?" I ask.

The smiles fades. "No," he says. "We don't really get into that. She tends to be a little too easy on me."

"Do you ever think about something happening to her?" I ask. "Someone doing to her what you did to other women?"

"All the time," he says. "That would be my worst nightmare. I would die if anything like that happened to my sister. I'm surrounded by guys like that, so I think about it a lot. The weird thing is, whenever I hear about a rapist, I'm like: 'I should snap his neck.' Then I'm like: 'Oh, wait. That's me.'"

—

# CHAPTER FOUR

# THE BLACK BOX

IN HIS FANTASY, the killer finds true love.

In his head, it is like this: He is driving down a country road, the kind of gravel road he drove down when he was a young man, when he was free, when he didn't yet understand what he was.

In the fantasy, it is early summer. It is perfect. It is night. The killer is alone in the uterine dark of his car. There is a thunderstorm. He takes a corner too quickly and the tires skid on the gravel and the car is in the ditch and when he comes to, there is a beautiful girl. She is milky and young and she has red hair. The killer has bumped his head in the fantasy, and magically, it is now the olden days. It is a time before the killer was born, a time that calms him to think about. A time when people still had morals and neighbours were neighbourly and love was wholesome.

This girl, the milky girl with auburn hair and red lips, she is wholesome. And in his fantasy, the killer, he is wholesome too. The girl lives with her parents in a nearby farmhouse. The bump to the killer's head is bad, but not that bad. It is the sort of injury you long for as a child. The kind that bleeds delicately beneath a lock of hair on your forehead and gets you attention but is not disfiguring or especially painful.

The girl takes the killer to the farmhouse where her parents live. The parents are stern but loving. They sense the attraction between the killer and the young girl whose skin is like fresh milk. But they understand young love and they trust their daughter because they know they have raised her to be wholesome. And they know the killer is wholesome too. They know because he is respectful and polite. He stays in a guest room and in the morning the mother has prepared breakfast. They all eat together, and before they eat, they pray.

The fantasy is a novel, or a partly finished novel, that the killer has written while in the hospital. He has been in this hospital nearly forty years. He will never get out, although every year he goes before a review board and petitions to be transferred to a lower-security facility. This too is a fantasy.

You know from the first chapter that the girl with the milky skin will marry the killer in the end. Their love is a thing that is simple and pure, like fields of clover blowing in the country wind. The killer's fantasy, all of it, is simple and pure. It is warm and cozy, like a blanket.

If the fantasy were a painting, it would be a piece by the late Thomas Kinkade, the Painter of Light™. Kinkade, like the killer, had a troubled past; in Kinkade's case, the problem was drink. Like the killer, he found redemption in Christ and turned his attention entirely to wholesome things. The subjects of his paintings embody that wholesomeness: quaint lakeside cottages, country homes surrounded by summer gardens in bloom; safe suburban houses in an America that loves children and God and neighbourly Sunday dinners. In the paintings by Thomas Kinkade, Painter of Light™, there is the same saccharine warmth that permeates the killer's fantasy, symbolized visually by the glow— Kinkade's trademarked light—emanating from the windows of the lakeside cottage and country homes and safe suburban houses. In Kinkade's paintings, there are rarely people. If there are, they are small and not fully realized. The characters in the killer's fantasy are like this: small and not fully realized, and good. And maybe that's why the killer likes his fantasy so much; in reality, being wholesome and good is confusing and not at all simple. Especially for someone like him.

He lives in a building made of red brick and grey stone, which sits heavy as a grudge at the top of a hill. It is surrounded by oak trees, birch and maple too. Below lies a deep bay, an inlet off Lake Huron. In the summer the water is the dark blue of deep sleep. The hills beyond are lush and green. It's an enviable place to live, provided you're not locked up forever atop a hill. The Oak Ridge facility, as it is known, is one of several buildings that make up the Waypoint Mental Health Centre, a provincial psychiatric hospital in Ontario's cottage country. Oak Ridge sits apart from the other buildings on the Waypoint campus. It doesn't look much like the generic, fluorescent-lit bastions of modern health care, or like the other buildings on the grounds. Architecture evokes adjectives, and Oak Ridge, a Depression-era building originally called the Criminally Insane Building, still evokes the words *crazy* and *dangerous*.

It is a maximum-security facility. To get in and out, you must pass through a series of barred doors, opened and closed in succession by large uniformed men. Inside are other men; men who have hurt and killed people in blind, psychotic breaks—men, for instance, who have asphyxiated babies by forcing their erect penis down the infant's throat. The majority of these men are not wholly responsible for the things they've done, although the things they've done are so horrific that it's emotionally difficult to exculpate them. Many of these men, once they are medicated and stabilized, realize what they've done and awake to a long season in hell.

They are ill. There is something wrong with them, with their brains. They are not right in the head. Many of these men do not possess normal IQs. Most have poor coping skills and low emotional intelligence. Many of them have been abused. They are, in one way or another, broken creatures and, if allowed back into the world, pose a considerable risk. So they wander the tiled halls of the Oak Ridge building in rumpled clothing, medicated, overweight, shuffling, not making eye contact. Or making too much.

But the killer is different. When I meet him, he's wearing a canary-yellow western shirt with pearlescent snaps and a cornflower-blue tie. He is polite. He is astutely concerned with other people's perceptions of him. He values esteem, although it may be that he conflates esteem and attention. Even though he has grown obese over the years, he is attentive to his appearance. He has carefully combed back his hair. There's a shiny pen in the breast pocket of his shirt and his glasses are free of fingerprints.

The killer is not crazy, exactly. He is not normal either, though that's not so obvious. If I didn't know about the things he had done, I wouldn't necessarily suspect him of any of it. He speaks like a normal man. He laughs at jokes and is reasonably pleasant, like someone's shut-in uncle.

But if you know enough about him, if you spend enough time talking to him, it slowly becomes apparent that the man you're speaking with is actually a projection of someone wholesome cobbled together by someone who doesn't quite understand the concept.

Behind the projection of this man, there is another man.

The killer has encouraged me to name him. Maybe he hopes it will bode well for him the next time he goes before the review board. He likes the idea that by talking to me, he is helping society understand why men like him kill, and that this contribution will be recognized. It makes him feel that he is giving back to society.

Giving back to society is important to the killer. When I first met him, he had a thick photo album tucked under his arm. He took me through it, page by page. Inside were photographs of things he had crafted in the hospital wood shop. He is remarkably good with his hands. He's made rocking horses and toy chests, which he donated to the local Kiwanis Club or Rotary Club for their Christmas auctions. He says he has raised $28,000 for charity in this way. Also, he sponsors several kids through the Christian Children's Fund and has sent money to the children's families. He sees these children as his own.

The killer prefers to meet in the hospital chapel, the Spiritual Care Centre, a tired fluorescent-lit room with a stand-up piano, several orphaned church pews and an assortment of interfaith posters. The killer was raised Pentecostal and so he always believed in God, but he couldn't connect with Him properly because he—the killer—was illiterate. When he first came to the hospital, he taught himself to read so he could understand the dirty stories in *Hustler*. But then he turned to the Bible. The killer still reads the Bible for at least an hour every day. One of his biggest regrets is that the women he killed may not have had a chance to accept Christ into their lives and so they may not have been washed of their sins. He prays for them. The killer has been washed of his sins because he has accepted Christ as his saviour. The killer believes he will go to heaven when he dies.

In addition to agreeing to be interviewed, the killer has also lent me several VHS tapes from the early 1990s that document a set of structured interviews with a staff psychologist. These tapes are extremely informative. On them, the killer talks at length about his marriage, his early childhood, his sex life and masturbation practices. His motivation for lending me the tapes is the same as his motivation for consenting to a series of interviews: he wants to give back to society.

Maybe the killer is right. Maybe his candour *can* help us understand his behaviour, but it's also true that he'd enjoy seeing his name in print. It feels wrong to use his name. It doesn't sit right in the pit of my stomach. The families of the dead women are still out there, and every time they see the killer's name in print, they relive the death of their daughter or sister or wife. The killer doesn't understand this — or, if he does, it is only in an abstract sense. He doesn't get the weight of these things in his gut.

Just to give you a sense of this, one time the killer was being questioned before attending his yearly review board hearing. A member of the panel asked the killer how he felt about the women he had killed.

"They're spilt milk," he said.

The panel member asked the killer to clarify himself.

The killer said, "They're like spilt milk. It happened in the past. There's no use crying over it." He didn't say this to be flippant or purposefully cruel. After all, he was trying to get transferred; he wanted to make a good impression. But he does not care about the women he killed, nor does he possess the capacity to fake that he does.

The killer is like this about everyone, even people who are — or ought to be — dear to him. The hospital's Director of Spiritual Care, Glenn Robitaille, told me this story:

The killer's son died suddenly one weekend several years ago. The following Monday, Glenn, unaware of the death, casually asked the killer how his weekend had been.

"Oh, pretty good," the killer replied, equally casually. "I watched some old movies. My son died. I played cards with some of the other patients." A few seconds went by, during which Glenn tried to process what the killer had said. Without missing a beat, the killer continued: "By the way, I have a good sermon idea for you."

That's the way he feels about the people closest to him. Emotionally speaking, old movies, card games, liturgical thoughts and the death of one's child are all on an equal footing.

This is not to say he doesn't have emotions. It's just that all of the killer's emotions revolve entirely around him. It is sad in name only when something terrible happens to someone else. However, the killer genuinely feels sad about his current situation, about being locked up. Most likely it will irritate the killer that I keep referring to him in a generic sense. It bothers him that people think of him solely as a killer, that in the past the press had given him a macabre nickname. He has changed a lot, he tells me. He has grown in the hospital. He is more aware of his feelings and emotions now. He has coping mechanisms. Besides, he has done a lot of other stuff since he's been hospitalized. He mentions his charity work again, the rocking horses and the toy chests and the girls he's adopted. He thinks it's clear he's changed. He mentions the book he's writing—not the novel, but another book. A children's book with the working title *Susie Visits the Zoo*.

The premise is that Susie, a young girl, feels awkward. Susie has body-image issues. That's a common problem in today's world, the killer tells me. If children could only know that they were accepted and loved for the way God made them, it would save them a lot of emotional pain. In the book, Susie goes to the zoo and learns important emotional lessons from the animals. She tells the hippopotamus she feels fat. The hippo says: "I'm fat too, but I like being fat because it helps me stay buoyant." Susie sees the giraffe and says, "My nose is too big." And the giraffe says: "You think you've got a big *nose*? Look at my neck. It's huge. But it helps me reach up high and eat all the leaves." Susie continues through the entire animal kingdom, through pages and pages of the animal kingdom, through the entire Ark, it seems. The killer has come up with dozens and dozens of animal-based emotional lessons, which he has written out in his precise, clear cursive in a spiral notebook. He reads each one aloud. This takes a long time. The killer is hopeful I can help him find a publisher for the children's book. And for his novel, once it's finished.

We have a lot of expectations about serial killers, and the way they're supposed to make us feel. But the killer is not Hannibal Lecter. He is not Dexter. He is not Patricia Highsmith's Thomas Ripley or Bret Easton Ellis's Patrick Bateman. He does not possess a sleek and magnetic confidence, a certain maleficent poise. While I was preparing to interview the killer, I was apprehensive. I was afraid he would have the ability to hypnotize me, like Kaa, the python in the Disney version of *The Jungle Book*. That he would slither around me with seductive words and mesmerize me with his eyes and try to swallow me whole. But the killer does not give me the shivers. I do not find myself frozen in the headlights of his presence. Nor do I find him intimidating. Often, I find my attention drifting while he talks. The killer, to be perfectly honest, can be a bit of a bore.

Still, there is something about him.

There is a test conceptualized in the postwar years by Alan Turing, the father of modern computing and artificial intelligence. The Turing test is a philosophical question that asks: how can we know whether a machine has achieved human-like intelligence? Turing suggested this solution: if a machine is capable of making another human believe that it, the machine, is human, then the machine can be said to have passed the Turing test. The killer makes you feel precisely the other way. You know he's a real person. It's clear he's a flesh-and-blood *Homo sapiens*. But listening to him talk about his emotions and the emotions of others, or reading aloud his lessons in emotional well-being and self-esteem, you have the distinct feeling he is reciting sophisticated command functions from a file named something like *c://emotions/human/emulator*.

Even though he is not a machine, the killer doesn't quite pass the Turing test.

He is one very disturbed and very violent psychopath. This is what is wrong with him, by the way: technically, he is a clinical psychopath. Along with men like Jeffrey Dahmer and Paul Bernardo, the killer is a poster child for just how abhorrently psychopaths can behave. But while a serial killer is almost certain to be a psychopath, serial killers aren't representative of psychopaths on the whole. People who do terrible things—things like kill people for the thrill of it—tend to get caught. They get put through batteries of standardized tests. They meet with psychiatrists and psychologists and psychometricians and are given official diagnoses. They end up in places like this.

But psychopaths come in various packages. If the experts are right, most go undetected because they aren't criminals, nor are they necessarily violent. Supposedly, there are a lot of non-criminal psychopaths out there. High-functioning psychopaths can hold perfectly respectable jobs in perfectly respectable fields: finance, medicine, law, government. There are self-help books that argue you can get ahead in business by emulating the cold, self-centred amorality of psychopaths. There's clearly something to that. The experts think that about one to three percent of the general population are psychopathic. That means there are, at a minimum, something like 5.3 million psychopaths in North America, a little less than the population of the city I live in. That's something like 700 million psychopaths worldwide, about the total population of Europe at the beginning of this century. That's a lot of people. It means there's a good chance we all know a psychopath, probably more than one. Sometimes they are very close to us and it takes us a long time before we realize they don't pass the Turing test.

I think about this from time to time, about these numbers, about the fact that popular culture largely gets them wrong, that they're like stealth bombers, undetected unless they cause spectacular destruction. I think about this stuff whenever I wonder if maybe the hunch I have is correct. I've never been sure. I probably never will be. I suppose that's part of my fascination with the killer. He's sort of a gauge. I'm trying to get close to him. I'm trying to feel him out. I want to see what it's like to be near him. I want to know if it feels familiar in any way.

—

LATE IN HIGH SCHOOL, a former friend of my mother's invited me into her living room. I was there to pick up my brother, who was playing with this woman's son. Her falling out with my mom was recent. Friendships with my mother were often turbulent and short-lived. This woman sat me down and poured me a glass of wine.

"Tell me what's wrong with your mother," she said. She said it with the kind of protective concern adults reserve for teens who are coping with their parents' divorce or the sudden death of a sibling. It was a shock to me, but also a relief, because until then I didn't really think anyone other than my brother and father could see past my mother's facade. Still, I didn't quite know what to say to this woman. I didn't have a clear answer. I still don't. I suspect I never will. I've been looking for that answer a long time.

For years, I didn't speak to my mother or talk much about her. I still don't, not really. I wasn't expecting to write about her. It's something that just happened when I started writing about the killer, when I asked myself why exactly I was so interested in him and in psychopaths in general.

I'm aware I sound like one of those men with mommy issues. And I suppose that's true, though not in any clichéd sense. If you spoke with anyone in my family—my mother's mother, her sister, her late father, my brother and father, my mother's other ex-husband and boyfriends— they'd all say there is clearly something not right with her, some slippery thing that retreats to the deep when examined directly, something that has gone undiagnosed since before I was born.

For the moment, let's just say that once you know her well enough, being around her can, at times, make you feel the way you might if you were awoken by the sound of coyotes in the night hills and realized you'd left the front door ajar.

There's really only one reliable way to tell if someone is an actual psychopath, and that is for a qualified and unbiased professional to administer a standardized test in conjunction with a series of in-depth interviews. The most commonly used and, arguably, the most reliable of these tests is the Hare Psychopathy Checklist. It's a deceptively simple tool: a list of twenty traits that, taken together, are extremely good at encapsulating psychopathic behaviour.* Roughly speaking, a psychopath is someone who has a specific emotional and behavioural profile; someone who can appear charming and affable but who is in fact entirely self-centred, emotionally shallow, callous, remorseless, unempathetic and highly manipulative.

I have spent a lot of time studying the Hare Checklist. I've gone to conferences where forensic professionals learn to administer the test. I've

---

* The twenty items of the Hare Psychopathy Checklist Revised are: glib, superficial charm; grandiosity; need for stimulation/prone to boredom; pathological lying; cunning and manipulative; lack of remorse; callousness; poor behavioural controls; impulsiveness; irresponsibility; denial; parasitic lifestyle; sexual promiscuity; early behavioural problems; lack of realistic long-term goals; failure to accept responsibility for one's actions; many short-term marital relationships; juvenile delinquency; revocation of conditional release; criminal versatility.

talked to Robert Hare, the Canadian forensic psychologist who has spent his career developing the test and who has been one of the most influential thinkers on the concept of psychopathy. But in no way am I qualified to diagnose anyone as a psychopath, especially someone close to me.

The biggest problem, of course, is that I am profoundly biased. For a long time, I reviled my mother. I no longer feel that way, but for many years I was happy to call her any name that summed up my frustration and loathing. And fear. That's the other thing: even into my late teens, I was terrified of her. Not always. But there were times. If she was on edge—and she was often, unpredictably, on edge—her anger could reach a thundering, house-shaking peak. The air around her seemed to shimmer the way a superheated engine boils the surrounding atmosphere. It made me freeze in my tracks. When I was eleven or twelve, she used to have me do the household ironing, massive heaps of it. If I was slower than she expected, which I always was, she would berate me so intensely I feared she might pick up the iron and hold it sizzling to my cheek. She never did this. She never even threatened it. It was more that I felt she could. The idea seemed to hover between us, an invisible iron floating on the shimmering, boiling updraft of her rage. It could be I was making this up. I've always been oversensitive and imaginative. But a few years ago my brother, who as a young boy burned the sole of his foot while sleeping in front of the fireplace, told me (without knowing about my ironing fears) that he has a vague memory of being startled awake in sudden and inexplicable pain, having just set his foot against the hot grate. He says our mother was sitting at his feet, looking at him impassively in the dark. Like me, my brother quit talking to her years ago.

I wasn't physically afraid of my mother so much as scared of the emotional space that surrounded her. There was a deadness to it. Not always. Not even most of the time. She could be charming, vivacious, funny. But when she got worked up, hers was a cold and unstoppable anger. There's that thing sharks do when they're going in for the kill: they slide a translucent protective membrane over their eyes. Their eyes become opaque and impenetrable. When she was angry, my mother looked like this— unfeeling, depthless. If I was in the basement, ironing while watching TV, something I was not allowed to do because it caused me to dawdle, the sound of her feet on the floorboards overhead would tie my stomach in a sick knot and take my breath away. There were times, in her rage, when my mother seemed to me not quite human.

Even if I weren't biased, and even if I *were* appropriately trained in administering the Psychopathy Checklist, I'm not sure it would help me figure out my mother.

From a purely utilitarian point of view, the Psychopathy Checklist—or PCL-R in the lingo (the R stands for Revised)—is extremely reliable at predicting whether a criminal will reoffend once they've been released. Hare started to develop the test in the 1970s, as a young researcher working as a prison psychologist in British Columbia. He was influenced by the work of the American psychiatrist Hervey Cleckley, who, three decades earlier, had written a book called *The Mask of Sanity*. In that book, Cleckley solidified a nebulous concept that had been floating around correctional and psychiatric institutions for decades: that there exists a taxon of criminal best characterized as constitutionally evil. These men—and they were almost always men—started their criminal careers early in life, often in early adolescence, and were responsible for a disproportionate number of the very worst, most violent kinds of crimes. They were not crazies, delusional nutters or the mentally feeble. These were men who were goal-directed. They hurt and killed, manipulated and coerced with the intention of profiting. They were after money or power or sex—or sometimes just the thrill of hurting someone. When caught, they were utterly remorseless, even if they were capable of superficially mimicking remorse.

With Cleckley's work in mind, Hare came up with a standardized description of psychopathic behaviour that he fleshed out with a super-abundance of interviews he and his colleagues had conducted with psychopathic prisoners. Hare's description evolved into the PCL-R, an imago against which to compare potential contenders.

To be considered a psychopath, you must attain a score of 30 out of a possible 40 points on the test—40 points representing the ultimate and idealized psychopath. The Checklist is an extremely useful tool for identifying the most dangerous and recalcitrant criminals. It is currently the gold standard among professionals in law enforcement, the justice system and forensic psychology.

However, because it was derived exclusively from Hare's work with male criminal psychopaths, it may not fully embody the traits found in female psychopaths. It's hard to know for sure, because we don't know as much about female psychopaths as we do male. The ratio of male to female psychopaths is quite high—in some studies, as high as twenty to one. Female psychopaths tend to have lower overall scores on the PCL-R; specifically, they score lower on the items that describe violent and anti-social behaviour.

Male psychopaths are clearly more violent, given the relative rarity of female serial killers as just one example. Or it could be—and there's an intriguing debate on the matter—that the big difference between male and female psychopaths isn't one of numbers or severity, but of manifestation. We may have developed different labels for male and female psychopaths because male and female psychopaths behave differently. Psychopathy in women may look more like other forms of mental illness. Psychopathy is traditionally categorized as a personality disorder. Borderline personality disorder, a behavioural profile that is much more common among women than men, and which has many of the same attributes as psychopathy, may be how psychopathy presents in females.[1]

—

THE KILLER ISN'T SO KEEN to talk about his own diagnosis. He does tell me he scores 26 on the Psychopathy Checklist. That's a high score (by comparison, I score somewhere between 2 and 6) but not quite high enough to be considered a clinical psychopath. The hospital staff won't confirm what the killer's precise score is, just that it's somewhere between 30 and 40, bona fide psychopath territory. I ask the killer what he makes of this.

"When you get to the Psychopath Checklist," the killer says, "I don't think it's worth the paper it's written on. They're using statistics. Statistics say: 'He is round.' So they're going to force him into a round hole, even though he's a square peg. You put a label on me and you haven't gotten to know me. I have a problem with this label because they're telling me that they don't want to get to know me. I don't see myself as a psychopath. I see myself as a schizophrenic with very strong psychopathic tendencies. I see myself as a very sensitive schizophrenic. A schizophrenic person runs on feelings and a psychopath runs on logic."

The killer shows no signs of schizophrenia. This self-diagnosis is another of the killer's fantasies. The killer's official diagnosis remains his albatross, try as he might to remove it through sophistry. Schizophrenia appeals to the killer because people with the disease are not held responsible for the things they do. There is the case of Vince Li, a forty-three-year-old paranoid schizophrenic who decapitated a fellow Greyhound passenger in 2008 on an overnight trip between Edmonton and Winnipeg. Li thought he was the Second Coming of Christ and that the man he killed, a stranger, was a space alien. He was found not criminally responsible. After being treated at a high-security mental health hospital in Manitoba, Li, who has since changed his name, is now on a daily dose of antipsychotics and has been deemed safe enough to live on his own. The killer is aware of cases like this. It is hard for him to bear that a man like Li has some measure of freedom while he, the killer, remains locked up.

The thinking on psychopaths has changed a lot since the killer was admitted to Oak Ridge. When he first arrived here, Robert Hare hadn't yet devised his test. Psychopathy was still a relatively loose term that had come into use in the late nineteenth century and meant, essentially, anyone who was off their rocker. Hervey Cleckley's book affixed a more stringent set of criteria to the label. But it was still assumed that, behind the mask of sanity, psychopaths were in some way insane.

More and more, that seems not to be the case. Psychopaths do not fulfill several of the criteria for mental illness. They are, for instance, perfectly able to tell the difference between right and wrong. They can choose to behave co-operatively and pro-socially when it's in their best interest. You can reason with a psychopath. They're good at sizing up and selecting vulnerable victims, and adept at evading justice.

There are some compelling physiological differences between psychopaths and the rest of us, differences in hard wiring that are present from a very young age. They have lower resting heart rates. They do not startle easily. They seem to experience less fear in general and are resistant to classical fear conditioning. That is, if you pair a loud noise or a shock with an innocuous stimulus such as a gentle tone, the rest of us will eventually show a rise in heart rate and skin conductance when we hear just that gentle tone. Not so much with psychopaths. Nor do they seem to find social stressors—reprimands or public embarrassment—all that unpleasant. They have abnormalities when it comes to identifying and experiencing emotions, say if you show them pictures of faces in agony or fear. These traits are correlated with anatomical and physiological differences in the amygdala and brain areas involved in processing emotions. Some researchers think this is the root cause of psychopathic behaviour. The human conscience, they argue, is the cumulative result of the countless episodes of reprimand and fear conditioning we're exposed to as children—"Don't do that! You'll hurt someone!" But if those reprimands don't stir some negative emotion within you in the first place, that foundation can never be laid. Some researchers think of psychopathy—especially non-criminal, non-violent psychopathy—as a deficit in emotional processing. But still, all this does not add up to mental illness, because most psychopaths function quite well.

That's the thing about mental illness: it completely messes up your life. Crazy people don't do so well. Left on their own, they take poor care of themselves. They get sick. They become malnourished. They expose themselves to the elements. They kill themselves. They die from accidents and overdoses and altercations. They are plagued by their own thoughts and emotions. Madness is a form of suffering. Psychopaths, by contrast, are the *cause* of other people's suffering.

Psychopathy is not associated with low IQ or any other correlate of mental illness—brain injury, birth trauma or neuro-developmental issues. And, importantly, psychopaths use violence to get what they want—their aggression is instrumental. In this respect especially, their behaviour is not insane, but predatory and parasitic.

This is how the late Marnie Rice and Grant Harris viewed psychopathy. Together, Rice and Harris oversaw Oak Ridge's research unit for twenty-five years.[2] Their theories on the nature of psychopathy are highly influential in the fields of forensic psychology and psychiatry. At the heart of their research are two simple questions: what exactly is the nature of psychopathy, and what can be done about it? They argued that psychopathy is an evolved behavioural niche. "Most humans are wired for reciprocal altruism," Harris explained. "But there's an opportunity for a small minority of humans to be aggressive cheaters by pretending they're like us."

Rice and Harris conceived of psychopathy as "an alternate life strategy." A strategy that profits from parasitic relationships, deception, greed and the use of force. The very worst psychopaths—the violent criminals—get caught, but most don't. They alienate people. They might get fired and have to move from town to town, but in one very important measure, psychopaths are extremely successful. They start having sex younger than non-psychopaths. They have more partners and, at least as far as male psychopaths are concerned, they have significantly more offspring than men with other psychiatric problems. Moreover, psychopathy and extreme anti-social behaviour is highly heritable.

In other words, psychopathy looks a lot more like a functional personality trait than a mental illness. "Hypothetically," Grant Harris told me, " this is a viable life strategy."

Rice and Harris argued that psychopathy is an example of balanced selection—a form of evolution that allows a small number of people to carry traits that are harmful to the majority of the population. Just as a parasite can infect and weaken a host indefinitely if it does not full-out kill it, a relatively small percentage of psychopaths can get away with breaking the social contract in perpetuity.

Psychopaths are social cheaters who are adept at pretending they're like us to get what they want. The killer has been caught and can no longer pretend to be normal. But he can, using skills inherent to the psychopath—lying, manipulation—attempt to pass himself off as a different, less blameworthy kind of killer. He is not crazy, not the way he wants to believe. Not the way he wants others to believe.

—

MY MOTHER HAS BEEN hospitalized a few times in short-stay psychiatric wards. Once, shortly after I was born, she took a rifle out of the closet (my parents were living on a farm in Alberta, in bear country) and said incoherent things about the Second Coming of the Lord and threatened to kill me. It happened again when I was in elementary school.

Not the gunplay or the messianic rambling. This time I found her on the front steps early in the morning in her nightgown. We were living on the east coast by then. She had called an ambulance. She told me that if she didn't live, she wanted to make sure I knew she loved me. Later, when I was finishing high school, one of her post-divorce relationships started to fall apart and she checked herself into the psych ward. I had been there the week before after a friend of mine had made a feeble attempt at suicide. I'd visited my friend every day. My mother knew this and, given that she and I had been fighting, it felt to me at the time that her hospitalization was like a checkmate move that forced me into a caregiver's position. My mother's then boyfriend wouldn't come to see her in the hospital. I felt guilty and so I visited her every day.

These episodes have always resulted in unclear and non-specific diagnoses. Mostly they've been filed under the ambiguous term "nervous breakdown," although her first breakdown—the one when I was an infant—was diagnosed as some sort of schizophrenic break. That didn't pan out, because it quickly became clear she didn't have schizophrenia. My mother contends it was a bad postpartum depression and that the rural doctors were simply incompetent. That could very well be. My father to this day feels she was toying with him and the doctors. That makes him sound like a heel, but there's every chance he's right.

My mother has been diagnosed with several disorders and potential disorders—physical ailments—that have never been confirmed. My mother loves nothing more than a meaty session with a doctor, discussing the possibility of some serious medical condition. In the waiting phase, when it's possible that she's actually afflicted, the prospect of being sick seems to fill her with a sort of anticipatory ecstasy. After my brother's birth, she was diagnosed with possible multiple sclerosis (which it wasn't, though she did suffer from double vision for a time); later, it was chronic fatigue syndrome; and all along, sundry allergies and food sensitivities, though my mother can and does eat everything. When she did have a job, she missed countless days fighting off infections whose only symptom seemed to be a need to sleep in.

She was so big on allergies for a while that she had my brother tested despite the fact he showed no symptoms whatsoever. For a time in grade school, she limited my brother more or less to rice cakes, miso soup and tofu. I used to provision him with candy bars like a gun-runner for the Resistance. To this day, he has no sign of food allergies. With me, she used my bad grades to shop me around to child psychologists, alternately presenting me as an underachieving wunderkind or a deadbeat depressive. Neither was true. But it gained her an audience with these high priests of the human psyche and, at least in my mother's mind, admiration for her psychological acumen and motherly concern.

There have been other strange things that passed as soon as she received the commensurate attention. Once, my mother, my brother and I were disembarking from a plane. I was about sixteen at the time. We had been visiting my mother's family in Oregon. We were walking up the accordion ramp into the terminal when my mother leaned against the wall and started uttering nonsense, like an evangelist speaking in tongues. People stopped and stared. Someone offered some help with my mother's carry-on. And just as the Holy Spirit comes and goes, the fit passed and my mother was fine.

Another time, she took my brother and a friend of his to see a matinee. After the movie, on the way to the car, she started babbling in the parking lot, asking for her mother. "When can I see my mommy? Are you my mommy?" she asked my brother and his friend. My brother, who was about twelve at the time, said it was like watching bad acting. Within a few minutes, she was fine again.

If you doubt my mother's capacity or desire to do strange things solely for attention and the pleasure of manipulation, let me tell you a story.

I was seventeen. My brother was eight. My parents had been divorced for about a year and a half. My father was paying a hefty alimony and living in a threadbare rental unit nearby. My mother remained in our family home. She had always been a profligate spender, despite never having held down a job for long. She was constantly buying new furniture, clothes, art, stereo equipment. The money got low and so she sold our home and bought a smaller townhouse.

Before the deal had been signed, she started sleeping with the townhouse's previous owner, whom she'd met over the transaction. He was selling the house because of his own divorce and she let him stay on in the house. He continued living there for several years, over my and my brother's protestations. The man had a young child, a boy who was a few years younger than my brother. This poor kid was the pawn in a miserable custody battle between the man and his ex-wife. There were three bedrooms in the townhouse. My mother and her boyfriend slept in the master bedroom, leaving two rooms for three kids. My mom wanted my brother to bunk with the other boy, who was only there every other weekend. She said it would make them feel like brothers.

Mike was young enough that the move had upset him tremendously. Living with this new man and his son upset both of us. And so, to make sure Mike had his own space, I moved my bed into the unfinished basement, where my mom's new boyfriend made beer. I slept next to the washer and dryer in a dim concrete space that smelled of yeast and empties. My mother used to wake me in the morning by starting a load of washing. Once I was awake, she'd tell me to go back to sleep, the washer hissing and whirring a few feet from my head.

Shortly after the unhappy bedroom arrangements had been settled, Mike started freaking out because his favourite toys kept disappearing from his room and reappearing in the new kid's room. He accused the kid of stealing them. During this period, Mike and I were shuttling between my mother's house and my father's, week on, week off. We were like gypsies, constantly moving, transporting our clothing and school work and whatever comforts we relied on from one place to the next in old laundry baskets. Mike's toys weren't just toys. His little plastic action heroes—Ghostbusters and G.I. Joes and Teenage Mutant Ninja Turtles—were a physical constant in his life, denizens of an imaginary world he retreated to for comfort. He carried them with him everywhere. My mother knew this. She would promise Mike a new, much-desired action figure and then renege on the deal because of some peccadillo of his, like leaving a dirty cereal bowl in front of the TV. This would work Mike into a desperate frenzy.

Anyway, it turned out my mother had been smuggling Mike's toys into the new kid's room. When I found out—I can't remember how any longer, I think maybe she told me—I confronted her. She told me she had done it to try to encourage the boys to share and get along. I didn't buy it. My mother had studied early childhood education when she was younger. She once ran an ESL daycare and helped operate a rural family resource centre. She knew exactly what made little kids tick. And how to mess up their diminutive and fragile works.

You wouldn't know any of this from meeting her. Unless you knew her well, you'd think her charming and vivacious, a free spirit. You might even think there's something wrong with me for saying these things about her. At the very least, you'd probably think I'm bitterly unsympathetic towards a woman who's been suffering, on and off, from a mental illness that isn't her fault. I've spent a lot of time worrying about that too.

It's common for family members of crazy people to feel that their loved one's behaviour is designed to harm them. Kids feel this way especially, because a damaged or hurting parent can't offer the security of unconditional love. It could be that I am looking to blame my mother unduly. But it could also be that, behind the problems my mother has been diagnosed with, there is a different sort of problem. She is exquisitely intelligent, and as I got older I started to wonder wether she might be exhibiting a more deftly crafted version of what the killer is trying to convince me of: that he is not fully responsible for his actions because he is crazy.

If pressed, I can probably come up with only about a dozen specific instances that clearly illustrate my mom's strange behaviour. That's part of growing up in Crazy Town — you take bad behaviour for granted because it's not unusual. You don't remember it especially well because it doesn't stand out as especially strange. It's only later, when you start to compare your life with the rest of the world, that you start to wonder why everyone else's normal appears a little off-kilter to you; when you start to question why you feel at ease in situations you know are a little fucked; when you start to realize you feel a touch vertiginous and slightly suspicious among the well-adjusted inhabitants of the world.

Most of my memories of my mother have drifted down to some inaccessible seabed where they have settled into sludge. I can dredge up what's down there, but the memories have become a sticky, indeterminate mass. I can bring up the feelings, but not their original form. And whatever's down there is a volatile substance. For a long time I couldn't talk about my mother without becoming incredibly angry. I could never tell whether my mom was actually as manipulative as I felt she was. I lacked hard evidence. I worried I was just being precious. That's part of the indignity of psychological abuse: it erodes your trust in yourself. You end up thinking you're just being weak.

—

IT'S EASY TO GROW accustomed to the killer. You'd think it would be impossible to forget that he murdered three young women. But the opposite is true—you have to remind yourself constantly. As Hannah Arendt discovered at the Eichmann trials, evil often schlepps along, frumpy and dull.

The killer has requested I bring him a Big Mac and fries on this visit. The Big Mac and fries are cold by the time I arrive at the hospital. The special sauce sits, gelatinous and vaguely seminal, on his lips and masticated Big Mac comes out from a gap where he has lost a tooth. Eating is a great source of sensory stimulation when you're locked away, and may be one of the few sources of sensory stimulation that pleases the killer. For years he has been taking Lupron, a drug that severely reduces the amount of circulating testosterone in the bloodstream, and keeps his sex drive, as well as his aggression, in check. He tells me he hasn't masturbated since 1991. During the period when he was killing young women, he was masturbating fifteen, sometimes twenty times a day. The weight gain is a side effect of the Lupron, as well as of all the eating. On the plus side, the killer has smoother skin and thicker and glossier hair than most men his age.

Before the killer will tell me the details of the murders, he says I need to know some things that will help me understand why he did what he did.

The killer was depressed as a child, he says. He didn't get enough love from his mother and father. When he was an infant, he was kept on sheets of old newspaper laid out on the floor. When he was a teenager, he says, his mother used to see him coming down the street and cross the road so she wouldn't have to look at him. Once a week, she would strap a broomstick between his shoulder blades so he would learn not to slouch. The killer tells me he had to do all the chores on the family farm. The killer only attended school until the eighth grade, he explains, because his father wanted him to go to work. His father, he says, was a "Victorian man"—that is, a man who kept to himself, who never talked about his emotions, and who was a quick and violent disciplinarian. The killer says his parents took in two foster children, two girls, when he was an infant. The girls were removed from the home by the authorities, he tells me, because his father was being violent with them.

The killer has an older brother. Occasionally the older brother visits him in the hospital. The killer tells me his brother used to beat him when they were kids. Twice, according to the killer, his brother hit him with an iron poker. Sometimes the brother would throw a hatchet at the killer. The killer says this as though he's remembering some light-hearted tomfoolery, which makes it hard to know whether he's telling the truth. Sometimes, too, the brother would make the killer hold a spoon between his teeth and shoot the spoon out of the killer's mouth. Luckily, the killer chuckles, his brother was a good shot. All of this, as I say, is the killer's version of events.

The killer believes his childhood forced him to develop into a timid, withdrawn person. The lack of unconditional love drove him further into himself, he says. He says he didn't express his emotions to anyone and began to withdraw into a fantasy world. He used to think about torturing and shooting his older brother. In his fantasy world, he always came out on top. In his fantasy, he wasn't shy or timid. In real life, the killer was a polite kid. As far as he knows, he acted normally. Sometimes he would go to the neighbours' farm and help them with work. He liked contributing, helping people out. It made him feel important. Sometimes he'd find one of his mother's old dresses and masturbate in it and then burn it. Sometimes, when he was alone on his own farm, he'd throw boiling water on cats. Or throw them off the roof of the barn. The killer likes cats, he explains, it's just that when they mewl, the sound gets to him. "Meow, meow, meow!" he mimics, then chuckles. "It drives me crazy, and when that happens, I just lose it with them. It's just a spur-of-the-moment thing, I guess. I just can't stand meowing."

The killer is probably right. Probably, being abused didn't help. The evidence is pretty solid that if you grow up with abuse, you're more likely to be violent yourself. Their upbringing may be one of the major differences between non-criminal psychopaths and violent psychopaths.

My mother's parents were both pacifists. My grandfather fought with the US Army at Monte Cassino in Italy during the Second World War. His friend died in his arms with guts spilling out of his belly, and after that my grandfather couldn't abide the thought of doing anyone harm. He'd see a kid playing with a toy gun and shake his head. "If they had any idea what that was really about," he'd say, "they'd snap those damned things in half." On the weekends and in the summer, my grandparents escaped Los Angeles, where they lived, and hiked in the Sierra Nevada and San Jacinto Mountains with the Nature Friends, their lefty hiking group. They were the original granola peaceniks, the predecessors of the Beats and the hippies, for which, as my mother's son, I'm probably extremely lucky.

The other thing the killer wants me to understand is what was happening with his wife at the time of the murders. In the shadowy place from where his fantasies emerge, his wife is tied up in the killings. This comes up over and over again in my interviews with him and also in the VHS interviews. He doesn't go so far as to say that she played a role in them. Not criminally speaking. But the killer blames her for his emotional state during the period when he was killing young women. Not that it's fair to blame her, the wife—the killer is clear on that point. It wouldn't be *technically* right to blame her for the murders. The killer is responsible for his own actions, he says. But, still, his wife is definitely an important part of the picture in the sense that she magnified a problem that was already there.

"If I had a decent marriage," the killer tells me, "chances are the Jekyll would never have come out." The killer means Mr. Hyde, but he hasn't read Robert Louis Stevenson's novella and so he's mixed up which one is the bad guy. The killer hasn't read any Shakespeare either because, if he had, I'm pretty sure he'd have made an allusion to Lady Macbeth by now.

The killer says his wife, like his childhood family, did not provide him with the love and respect he needed. She withheld sex. The killer had to work two jobs to pay their bills and to satisfy her material desires. Also, the killer suffered from a sense of sexual inadequacy. He says he was unable to satisfy his wife's sexual desires. That is how he understands the fact that his wife cheated on him. She had a boyfriend, an itinerant farm labourer who came to the area during the tobacco harvest. The killer loved his wife so much, he says, that he put up with this. In fact, on a few occasions, the killer chauffeured his wife and her boyfriend around town, to bars and the bingo hall. When the wife wanted to write a letter to her boyfriend, the killer helped her. He dictated what she ought to write, like a misguided Cyrano de Bergerac. He did this, he tells me, because he needed her love so badly. He felt that if he drove her and her boyfriend around and helped her compose a nice love letter, she'd eventually understand how much he loved her and reciprocate his feelings.

As far as he is concerned, the abuse from his wife drove him further into his fantasy world and so, really, if we're talking about moral responsibility here, it's not fair to pin everything entirely on him.

He first killed a woman in March 1974, at night. He and his wife had a place in town. Their son was an infant. Their daughter hadn't been born yet. The killer went out to get tickets for a hockey pool and was walking along the train tracks near his home. He makes sure to mention that this took place during a period of intense marital discord. He had no intention of killing, he says—though he did have a pocket knife on him. I ask him why he was carrying a knife if he wasn't planning on using it. "I always carried a knife," the killer tells me. He saw a young woman walking ahead of him, silhouetted against the night. He could tell it was a young woman because of her shape. He followed that shape. The shape was carrying a pizza box. It had gone for takeout.

The killer was in his own little world, he says, this fantasy world of his, as he approached her. He was thinking about how lonely he was, how bad things were with his wife. He wasn't thinking about killing at all, he tells me, but about sex and love and emotional closeness. As he came nearer to the shape of the woman, he was thinking about having sex with her. It was already happening in his head. He was very close to her now, thinking about sex. He reached out. He grabbed her by the shoulder and spun her around. The woman screamed.

Only now, asserts the killer, does he realize he knows the woman. She is someone from the neighbourhood, someone he says hello to on the street. She recognizes him too. The killer panics. In telling this story, the killer is entirely focused on his own emotional state and how he is lost somewhere between fantasy and reality. In the fantasy, he has already had sex with the girl, forcing himself on her. "Technically," he tells me, "I hadn't done anything wrong." But in his head, the deed is done. He has already raped her. And because of this, he says, and because she can identify him, he starts choking her. It wasn't that he was angry, he maintains. "I was in a state of panic."

He drags the woman to the ground. She is fighting so hard that one of her shoes comes off. Then the killer pulls out his knife.

I ask what he's thinking when he does this.

He says he doesn't remember, because he was in a delusional state. "In the police report, they said that it was obvious that this person"— the killer means himself—"was in a panicked state." What he means is that the slashing was not done in a calm and calculating way, but savagely and quickly. The killer is keenly concerned with getting across the idea that this was not a premeditated act, that he did not kill for the thrill of it but because he was trapped, cornered and surprised like a caged animal. He found himself *in medias res* and was forced, by the exigencies of the situation, to do what he did. That is the point he is trying to get across.

In October 1975, he killed again.

The killer and his wife were in the process of filing for divorce. This was his wife's decision. The killer was heartbroken, he tells me. He had been discussing the breakup with a friend of his, the young woman who was about to become his second victim, who had told him he could always talk to her if he needed someone to turn to during this difficult time. She lived on a farm with her husband. On the way into the city to meet with a divorce lawyer, he stopped by her farm. She was home alone.

They had danced together at parties, the killer and this woman. She trusted him. She put aside her housework and let him into her house. They spoke about the killer's divorce for about fifteen minutes, sitting in the living room. The woman comforted the killer and gave him a pep talk. Things will get better, she said. You deserve better. The killer says he felt close to the woman. He felt warmth. "My sex drive was high," he tells me. He thanked the woman and got up to leave. As the woman was walking him to the kitchen door to say goodbye, he turned and grabbed her and drove her down onto the kitchen floor.

He recalls her crying beneath him. He undoes her pants. The woman tries bargaining. The killer begins to rape her. She is in pain and making a lot of noise. The killer stops.

"Her crying brought me back to reality to a certain degree," he says. "So I panicked. Fear stepped in again. People were going to find out that I did something I shouldn't be doing, so I had to protect myself. I started to strangle her. I took a shoelace and tied it around her throat. She was making these weird gurgling sounds and it freaked me out. There was a butcher knife on the counter and I got up and took it and slit her throat because I realized from my first offence that it works— that if you cut the throat and they're dead, they stop all these noises."

Afterwards, the killer cleaned himself up and walked to his car and drove to his lawyer's office to discuss the divorce. On the way there, he pulled over. He was overcome by the shakes. He had to sit by the side of the road until his hands quit shaking.

If I understand the killer correctly, his wife and family hadn't given him the love he needed—he needed an extra amount of love. And because love equated to sex in his mind, it was only logical that when he was lonely and in need of love, he wanted to have sex with someone. And because his wife was having sex with another man and not him, he found other women to have sex with—because he needed to feel loved. And because the difference between thought and action was sometimes lost on the killer back then, the killings weren't premeditated or anything. It's not like he sat down and worked out a plan. They were bad, obviously. They were wrong, for sure. Because murder is wrong. But it's not like he was planning them logically. It was more like he awoke from a bad dream and found himself in the middle of doing terrible things, things he didn't understand himself.

My intention, in asking the killer to take me through the killings, was to get a sense of what he had been thinking and feeling. I wanted the killer to take me into the black box of his mind. After several interviews, I see that this is wishful thinking. Inside the black box, there is another black box, equally impenetrable.

I wonder if the killer perceives his own inner life this way—if, sub-jectively, when he looks inward, he sees black box after black box after black box. Maybe he is as opaque to himself as he is to me. It's possible that introspection and self-understanding require some inward turn of empathy, a capacity he can't extend to others let alone himself. Maybe when he turns his mind's eye in on itself, it's like looking into a pair of mirrors that face one another. Maybe there is nothing there but empty space, reflected back and forth forever. Perhaps the killer creates stories simply so there is something to behold. Maybe that is why his explana-tions of his real-world behaviour sound as hollow and unconvincing as his fantasies.

Or maybe he's just lying.

The killer has a living victim.

She lives in a small bachelor unit in a rundown public housing building not far from where the killer kidnapped her all those years ago. Elaine Anton is in her late fifties. She's had a hard life. It was hard even before the killer made his attempt on her life, and it shows. She's wear-ing a tank top, sitting with her elbows on a tiny round table in her small apartment. There are dozens of scars running up her left arm, from wrist to shoulder. They were originally thin slices, but the scars have expanded over the years as her arms thickened. They now look like eyelids. Dozens and dozens of eyes that don't want to open.

As a girl, she was sent to an institution that specialized in the "reform of troubled girls." Many of them, like Elaine, were Aboriginal. The head-master used to call her down to his office to rape her. She was thirteen at the time. A lot of girls got called down to the headmaster's office. He had a system, a rotating list or something. The other girls taught Elaine to cut herself. A good, deep cut to your arm meant a trip to the hospital for stitches and an overnight psychiatric evaluation. It was painful, but it bought you a reprieve from the greater pain of the headmaster.

By the time Elaine encountered the headmaster, she had already been raped more times than she could count. The assaults started when she was five. Two of her uncles put her in a sleeping bag and took turns. Between seven and twelve, she was raped at least once a month by one of these men. (Both of these uncles are now dead.) When she was twelve, she gave birth to a boy. Children's Aid then put her in a facility, ostensibly for her protection. There, she was raped by one of the male staff. When she started "acting out" at the facility—rather, acting the way you would if you were being sexually tortured: withdrawn, rebellious, aggressive—she was given to the headmaster.

Elaine survived by retreating to a place inside where these men couldn't reach her. On some level, she still felt the pain, but being in that place at least allowed her to gather her wits. When it comes down to it, this is what saved her from the killer.

Halloween, 1975. Elaine was twenty years old and seven months pregnant. She was hitchhiking at the edge of town. She was alone in the dark.

The killer, who at this point had already killed twice—the last time, just over a week earlier—rolled up in a van and offered her a lift.

Elaine turned him down. She had a bad feeling.

"Why don't you just hop in," the killer insisted. "I'll take you for a coffee. If you want a ride after that, I'll take you there. If not, I'll take you back to town."

Elaine said no, but the killer got out and muscled her into the van. The killer had been doing farm work his entire life. Before he became the fat, slow-moving man he is now, he was a stocky powerhouse. Elaine tried to escape through the passenger door, but the killer had planned ahead: the interior handle was snapped off. He told Elaine to sit in the passenger seat. She obeyed. There was no other option. He talked as he drove. Just small talk, like everything was hunky-dory, like it was perfectly normal to pull a woman into your van and drive off into the dark.

The killer assured Elaine he was just going to take her for coffee. Clearly, he was lying. Elaine knew how men talked to you before they hurt you. Her mind was racing. She kept looking for an out. She hoped maybe the killer would make a pretence of stopping at a doughnut shop for coffee. It might give her a chance to run. But he kept driving. He drove down an empty country road. Past an abandoned church. Past dark fields that disappeared beyond the headlights. Elaine knew where they were going. They were driving to the end of the world. To oblivion. To the end of her life.

The killer turned onto a narrow side road and then onto an even more remote road that was bumpy and rutted and unused. The killer stopped the van. He killed the engine. It was so quiet. There were tall pine trees lining the road. Immense dark trunks. A phalanx of giants standing guard. Merciless and impassive.

The killer was holding a butcher's knife. Elaine remembers him saying: "That's the last ride you take. I'm going to rape you. Then I'm going to kill you." It was surreal, the way he said it, like a line from a B-movie.

Then he was on top of her. She was on her back on the floor of the van, looking up, out of the windows, concentrating on the underside of the big pine trees, on their dark bodies rising up like plumes of ash into the night. Dark bodies against a darker sky. She searched for that place in her mind where she could think, where she could establish an opening move in whatever was about to come.

After the killer came, he pulled the knife off the dash and held it to her throat. He asked her if she had any last words.

Elaine said, "Why would you kill me?" A question required a response. A response was the beginning of a conversation.

"Because you'll talk," said the killer. "Then I'll have to go to jail for the rest of my life."

"But I've been raped before," Elaine said. "No one's ever gone to jail. I've never told the cops. I hate them. They wouldn't believe me anyway."

The killer considered this. Elaine asked him if she could smoke. He allowed her to pull a cigarette from her pack. When she was done, she asked if she could have another. Then another. Chain-smoking kept her alive. That and their shared hatred of the police. She played that up, trying to make the killer feel as though she were an ally. When she ran out of smokes, she asked if she could have one of his. He handed her the package. She was making progress. But then the killer nicked her with the knife, an accident, she thought. She felt a drop of blood roll down her cheek, heavy and slow. She watched the way the killer regarded the blood. His eyes changed. It excited him, she could tell. For a moment, she was convinced the sight of blood had doomed her, that that single drop was about to unleash a frenzy. But the killer remained still and Elaine kept talking, as though being raped hadn't phased her, as though the knife didn't make her want to piss herself. It was like he was on drugs, she said. It was like he was listening super-intensely but also like he wasn't listening at all.

"It's hard to explain if you haven't experienced it," Elaine told me, "but it was as if I wasn't talking to anybody."

She asked the killer if he had a family. Yes, he said. He had a wife and two young kids. He had got into a fight with his wife that evening. That's why he was out driving around. That seemed to change something, talking about his family. It broke the spell. Elaine felt that she was talking to a real person for the first time.

After an hour or two of this—Elaine still isn't sure how much time passed—the killer put the knife away and started up the van. He drove back to the highway and pulled over at a rest stop. Elaine was relieved to be bathed in the jaundiced glow of sodium lights, to hear the dull roar of trucks along the highway. The killer handed her a small black phone book and told her to write down her number. She thought about giving him a fake one but felt lying could be dangerous. They walked towards a phone booth. The killer had the blade against Elaine's spine. The killer told Elaine to dial the number. The killer took the receiver. Elaine could hear her mother's muffled voice on the other end of the line. The killer asked to speak to Elaine. Elaine heard her mother, telling him Elaine wasn't home. The killer thanked Elaine's mother.

"It's a good thing you gave me the right number," the killer said. "I would have killed you right here."

They drove back to town. The killer was more relaxed. When they were a block from Elaine's house, she told the killer to stop. She pointed to a house and said, "That's where I live." The killer turned to her and said: "I know how to get hold of you now. I'm going to check and make sure you're not talking to the cops."

The house that Elaine pointed to was not her house. The killer let her out of the van. She took a few steps. She could feel him behind her, watching. Her skin was crawling. The need to run was an urge she couldn't resist. It welled up in her, like the need to vomit. She broke into a hot sprint. She ran blindly through people's backyards. She ran wildly, in a wet, panicked frenzy, across the railway tracks, until she stood breathless and retching in her mother's backyard. She stayed there, hunched over, panting until she could breathe normally. It took forever. She was afraid to move. Eventually, she crept into the house and crawled into bed and lay there awake until the sun came up.

"Nah. That ain't quite right."

That's what the killer says when I tell him what Elaine has told me. He shakes his head and says again, "That ain't quite right.

"She was hitchhiking," the killer says. "I picked her up. We were driving along, chatting. She had broken up with her boyfriend and was feeling down and I think we consoled each other because I was going through the same thing. The more we talked, the closer I felt to her. The more I identified with her and the more she identified with me. So then I pulled down this abandoned road and told her I wanted to have sex. And we had sex."

"Was the sex consensual?" I ask.

"If you're talking about in my head, then yes."

"What about outside your head?"

"When you look at the reality of the situation, this is somebody you don't know and never met. You're in a van and you don't know where the hell you are. Now, is it consensual? Even if she says yes? No."

This is as close as the killer will come to admitting he raped Elaine. He has learned through years of counselling to say that what he did with Elaine was not consensual.

"Elaine has a different version of events," says the killer. The killer says Elaine was perfectly willing to get in the van. He doesn't mention the knife. He says after they had sex he drove her to a party in a nearby town. They partied together and had a good time, then Elaine asked for a ride back home. And that, he says, is how their relationship started. That's how the killer sees things with Elaine: as a relationship.

The morning after the killer attacked her, Elaine was scheduled to work. She had a job cleaning hotel rooms. She called in sick and walked to one of the downtown hotel bars. She knew she shouldn't be drinking because of the baby, but still. She sat at the bar, wired on adrenalin, her thoughts smeared and incoherent from lack of sleep. It was comforting, sinking into the dim fug of a smoky bar. Men were drinking and talking all around her. Their voices mingled with the music that played. The noise helped drown the high-voltage hum inside her head. She had a beer in front of her; her intention was to make it the first of many. Next to her, a man sidled up to the bar. Elaine wasn't really paying attention. The man said, "I didn't get a chance to buy you a drink last night. I'll buy you one now." Elaine's stomach turned over and she had to make a conscious effort not to shit herself.

The killer was perched on the stool next to her, smiling. After she took off on her wild sprint, he had driven to a nearby pay phone and called Elaine's mother again. Posing as a friend, he got the real address. He waited in his van down the street and, in the morning, followed Elaine to the hotel bar.

The killer bought Elaine a beer and she drank it because it was a drink and, despite the fact that it came from this man, right now another drink was what she needed more than oxygen even. He told her he was glad she hadn't gone to the cops. Elaine nodded listlessly, the way you do when a bad fever comes on. She told the killer she had to go. She walked to another hotel—she can't remember which one—and ordered another beer. And then another. And another, until she sank to a place where there was no noise or light or memory.

The killer continued to stalk Elaine. Some mornings she'd step out into the winter air and, from her mother's porch, see the gas fumes of the killer's idling engine. He'd be waiting in his vehicle. He'd force her to go on what he called dates, which consisted of forced sex and an implied threat of execution. Sometimes Elaine managed to put him off, but just as often she felt compelled to go.

"I made sure that I went out with him enough times to keep him at bay," she told me. The killer had threatened to kill her entire family if she ever went to the cops. She felt the killer was close to snapping, that he was growing more and more tense. Each time the killer raped her, Elaine thought it might be the last time, that this time he would kill her afterwards.

In January 1976, about two and a half months after the killer first attacked her, Elaine gave birth to her second child, another boy. The child was sick, and mother and son remained in the hospital. This gave Elaine a reprieve from the killer. She came up with a plan. She convinced her boyfriend, the father of the child, they ought to move to Hamilton, Ontario. He could get work at the steel mill. They could make a new start, raise the baby right. She hadn't mentioned the killer to her boyfriend. She had told her mother that she needed to get away from the killer, though she didn't mention that he had raped her and threatened to kill her entire family. Her mother thought the killer was just another guy who was a little too interested in her daughter. She agreed that it was best for Elaine to leave town. She promised not to tell anyone where her daughter had moved.

In the killer's mind, it's different. In his mind, things between them were ideal for a time. "I thought it was a nice relationship," the killer says. In the killer's mind, he was going to help Elaine raise her unborn child. He says he helped her pick out furniture for the baby's room. He says he intended on moving in with her. In the killer's mind, he broke up with Elaine when her boyfriend, the man whose child she was carrying, got jealous.

"You're saying you voluntarily broke up with Elaine?" I ask the killer.

"That's my recollection."

"Did you love her?" I ask.

The killer gazes somewhere just above my head. "Yeah." He nods. "To a certain degree. But you must remember, I have a fairy-tale version of love and marriage."

—

ROBERT HARE'S PSYCHOPATHY TEST is only so helpful; you also need to talk to people who know the person being tested. This is a point Hare himself stresses. Some psychopathic traits are, by definition, tricky to pin down without some sort of external triangulation. For much of her life, especially when she was younger, my mother managed to keep the people in her life isolated from one another—or at least managed to keep the stories she told each person separate in a way that made it hard to compare notes. In doing so, she influenced how her family and friends perceived one another. And so, for most of *my* life, I assumed only my father, my brother and I had any real insight into my mother's nature. For years I had no idea my mother's own family, her parents and her sister, who all lived on the west coast, found her difficult too. As a child, my mother could be unsettling. My aunt, two years younger than her, told me a few years ago that she grew up in fear of my mother. Older kids often pick on their younger siblings, my mom added her own unique twists. When she was seven or eight, she emptied a box of Sun-Maid raisins and filled it with her pet rabbit's turds and gave them to my aunt. That's kind of funny. But my mother kept insisting the turds were actually raisins and, through an act of precocious brainwashing, forced my aunt to eat a few.

In her teens, my mother had wild and violent screaming tantrums that perplexed and frightened her parents. Later in life, while visiting her family on the west coast, my middle-aged mother still threw tantrums. During a disagreement, she once kicked her mother out of the car and left her by the side of the road in Oregon. My grandmother was in her eighties at the time, legally blind and walking with a cane. My aunt now makes sure that when my mother visits, she's never left alone with my grandmother. And my grandmother does not want to be left alone with her daughter because she frightens her.

Something changed as my mother moved into late middle age. Her ability to control information began to slip. Maybe it was part of aging, losing her edge. Part of it, too, was that I had started talking to people.

I had tried this before—talking to people about her behaviour. It often ended up just making me look bad. When I was in my early twenties, my mother married again. This was her second legal marriage. (Although it was never legal, she had considered herself married to the townhouse man, who she eventually dumped.) The alimony from my father was running out, including the additional tuition money my mother insisted he contribute so she could pursue a second university degree. She'd actually spent that money on new furniture, clothes, stereo equipment and, at least on one occasion, one of her boyfriends.

The new husband was steady and stable. He was a university professor with a good income and health benefits. He was a gentle and generous man but he had had a rough childhood. His parents were alcoholics. They fought constantly. For a couple years he was in and out of foster homes while his mother was being treated for tuberculosis. I mention this to explain that I don't think he had much experience with healthy relationships and that my mother, who is highly adept at spotting these sorts of deficits in people, knew it. The professor, although thoughtful and caring, tended to be withdrawn and reserved—not the kind of man my mother was generally attracted to. He lived in a different city, and when my mother was deciding whether to move in with him, she told me she wasn't in love with him but that he was a good provider.

I told the professor this and predicted that my mother would likely leave him within a couple of years, which I'm sure came across as spiteful and malicious. My mother told the professor I was lashing out because I was still angry about my parents' divorce, which, understandably, he believed.

A few years passed. I was speaking to my mother less and less, avoiding her calls as much as possible, putting off holiday visits. Every interaction was awkward and increasingly strange. Once, while visiting Lyana and me in Halifax, my mother told us she was counselling one of her neighbours, a woman who, at fifty-something, was still a virgin. My mom was big on becoming a counsellor at the time. She had folded herself into her new husband's life. She had enrolled in a graduate programme in his department, where she could study for free—although she never finished the degree. The virginal neighbour was dating a man and had confided in my mother that she wanted to finally take the plunge, but was worried it would hurt. My mother gave her some technical advice. My mom explained this to us while kneeling on our living room floor, simulating the woman-on-top position. I asked her to stop. She ignored me and went on to explain how she told her neighbour to just "take in a little at a time." I asked her again, really, please, to stop. She demonstrated that you could make little Os with your pelvis in just this way. She thought Lyana, as a medical student, would be interested and might be able to counsel her future patients. I told her to stop three or four more times. When she finally did, she looked at me with a touch of triumph, knowing she had embarrassed me in front of my girlfriend.

In the mid-2000s, my mother's elderly aunt—my grandfather's older sister—was dying. She had moved from New York City to a Florida nursing home a number of years earlier, far from her immediate family. When my mother found out her aunt was in palliative care, she flew to Florida. It was odd, because my mother, who grew up in LA, hadn't been particularly close to her east coast aunt. We had visited her once, when I was five. My mom stayed in Florida for a few weeks, until her aunt died. While she was there, she moved her aunt to a different facility and she helped make some final arrangements. She told me she felt privileged to be using her counselling skills in an end-of-life scenario. I don't know precisely what that privilege entailed or how much influence my mother had over her dying aunt, but my mom came back from Florida having inherited a substantial share of her aunt's estate. Several of my mother's relatives were confused and appalled by this development.

Shortly after she returned from Florida, my mother found a cottage and a plot of land in Tobermory, a peninsula on Georgian Bay famed for clear, cut-glass waters and Group of Seven landscapes. She wanted to buy it and turn it into a bed and breakfast. Her husband urged her to use the inheritance to help pay down their mortgage. He had bought a modest house after they got married and had been paying the bills on his own because my mother wasn't working. But my mother insisted on buying the Tobermory property and he acquiesced. Shortly after the deal went through, I got a call from the professor: my mother had cheated on him with another couple. When I asked her about this, she told me she had actually only been sleeping with the man but, for whatever reason, believed the professor would feel less betrayed if he thought it had been a ménage à trois.

I spent an hour or so on the phone with the professor, who was distraught. In addition to the sting of cuckoldry, my mother's rage had knocked him off his feet. When he had confronted her, she had exploded. I don't know the exact details of their argument, but he was spooked.

"If this is what you and your brother grew up with," he said, "I understand why you have so much trouble with your mother. It's not normal. She's not the person I thought she was. She totally used me. She's scary."

A few months later, I got a call from a man I had never met. He introduced himself by telling me he had been seeing my mother. He was a retired RCMP officer. He didn't quite know how to start the conversation. He was calling, he said, because he felt he needed to speak with someone in my mother's family. What he was going to tell me might sound odd, and it might be hard to believe, but he said my mother had assaulted him. She had been arrested and he wasn't sure whether he ought to press charges or not.

I wondered if this was the guy my mother was sleeping with behind the professor's back.

In any case, they had been seeing one other for several months. Things had been going swimmingly, he thought. But he had noticed my mother's plans for the bed and breakfast weren't going anywhere. It just seemed to be a bunch of talk. He knew she had been studying to be a counselor and was close to completing her degree. One day while they were at her Tobermory cottage, he had told my mom she ought to finish what she started. He felt as though they knew one another well enough by this point that he could say that; it was the kind of thing you needed to talk about if you were going to be in a long-term relationship. But it set my mother off. She picked up a coffee carafe and shattered it over his head. He ran out and got in his car. She followed him with a canoe paddle and smashed his rear window. She was laughing at him, he said, as he peeled out of the driveway.

He didn't end up pressing charges. I think he just needed to talk. I spoke to my mother shortly after he called. She told me he had tried to rape her and she had defended herself. She said the cops didn't believe her. I understood why. I told her what her boyfriend had told me, about her not finishing her degree, about the perpetual delays with the bed and breakfast. "That's none of his goddamn business!" she cried.

The last time I'd seen her—about eight years earlier—she came into the city to pick up my grandmother, who was visiting from Oregon. She had a friend drive her because she had lost her licence after she had driven her pickup off the road earlier that year. According to her, the doctor had taken away her licence for medical reasons because she had been diagnosed, she claimed, with some sort of non-specific neurological disorder. My mother's plan was to take my grandmother to Tobermory for a couple of weeks. My grandmother was then in her mid-eighties. It made me nervous, because my mother was acting especially strange. And because her boyfriend at the time was a recovering opiate addict.

She and my grandmother spent the night with us. We went out for Tibetan food. My mother talked the whole time, dominating the conversation with a firehose monologue that made it impossible for any of us to say anything. She told us she had been accepted into the local indigenous community. Her new boyfriend lived on a reserve and his mother was teaching my mom "the old ways," the shamanistic traditions. When we got back to our apartment, my mother abruptly passed out, sunny side up, on our hardwood floor.

In the morning, I came out of my bedroom to make coffee. Our apartment was open-concept, with a large granite kitchen island in the middle of the main area. My mother had one of her feet on the counter and her head was bent over her knee. She was doing a hurdler's stretch. She didn't have any pants on. Or underwear. My grandmother, blind as a mole, sat on the couch, oblivious.

"Good morning," said my mother, as if impersonating a Georgia O'Keeffe painting in the middle of her son's kitchen was perfectly kosher. She wore that smile she got whenever she succeeded in making me uncomfortable.

My grandmother called from my mother's place one evening about a week later.

"I think I need some help," she said. My mother had left her alone in the cottage. She had been gone a couple of days. It was getting cold, and my grandmother's vision made it hard for her to find her way around. She was deeply anxious. My mother had woken her in the middle of the night and said something cryptic, something about following a falling star over the horizon. Then she had disappeared with her boyfriend. "I'm afraid she might try to kill herself," my grandmother said. "She's acting strange. I think she might be on drugs."

I wasn't worried about suicide. My mother had never followed through on that threat. I told my grandmother not to worry, that I'd come get her. It was a four-hour drive, so I called the local police and asked them to check in on her. I explained the situation. The officer I spoke with knew my mom and her new boyfriend.

"Your mother's boyfriend has quite a reputation up here," the cop told me.

Lyana's father drove us to Tobermory. I could barely talk. I was livid. And embarrassed. And awed—it was remarkable one person could act like a collapsing star, pulling in my grandmother, me, my wife, my father-in-law, the local police. I called my grandmother to check up on her. The police had been by. They were very nice, she said. But halfway there, I got a sinking feeling. I was worried my mother would come home and my grandmother would tell her I was on the way, that the cops were involved. I had seen what her temper could be like in such situations. I felt the invisible iron shimmering in front of me again, the heat of it. And that was the whole point, I was convinced. For some inconceivable reason, she enjoyed this sort of thing, a grand game of cat and mouse.

She used to do a similar thing to my brother, especially after I moved in with my father when I was sixteen or seventeen and was no longer around to protect him. She'd promise Mike something—a toy, an activity, a sweet—and never come through. Her specialty was promising whatever it was to neighbourhood kids too, but then withholding it only from my brother, ostensibly because he'd been bad. Mike would throw a tantrum and call my father or me. My mother would explain coolly over the phone that Mike was having a meltdown over nothing. It tied us up in knots. My father used to talk about trying for full custody, but decided the collateral damage to Mike of the custody battle would be too severe. During this time, I used to have nightmares about my brother, about not being able to protect him. I'd find him, in my sleep, bleeding at the bottom of a flight of stairs. Or I'd be swimming across a lake at night. He'd be on my back, hanging on, his arms slippery around my neck. I had to get us across this dark dream lake. Halfway to safety, Mike would lose his grip and sink into the inky water. I'd dive down, blind, grasping, unable to find him. I'd wake up in a breathless panic. It was the same feeling I had when I was listening to him on the other end of the line, crying and screaming and me unable to do anything. For a time this seemed to happen more frequently on the weekends my father was out of town, visiting his girlfriend (now my stepmother) in Montreal. My mother knew how protective I was of Mike, and with stunts like these she could torture both of us in one deft stroke.

One weekend, I got a frenzied call from Mike. Furious, I drove to my mother's house. I had had it. I was going to take Mike back to my father's place, custody rights be damned. When I got there, my mother stood in my way. I told her to move.

"What are you going to do?" She laughed. "What are *you* going to do? What are *you* going to do?" She said this over and over, jabbing me in the chest with a finger each time.

I stood stock-still, like a member of the Ceremonial Guard. Then she dug her nail into my cheek. It broke the skin. She was laughing. I realized that if she provoked me into hitting her, Mike would be lost. She'd have all the proof she needed that my father was a bad influence. I turned around and left. She followed me out into the street. "You were a mistake!" she yelled after me. My mother's neighbours came out of their townhouses, startled by her shrieks. "You *were* a big mistake!"

I drove away. I could see her in the rear-view mirror. She was standing in the middle of the street, giving me the finger. About a block later, I punched a spiderweb into my windshield. I looked in the rear-view mirror again. There was a crescent moon of blood on my cheek from her fingernail.

As we drove towards my grandmother that night, I could taste a rising tide of bile in the back of my mouth. My cellphone rang. It was the officer again. He sounded weird. He said everything was fine, but he was going to take my grandmother to a local hospital. No, there was nothing wrong with her. She was perfectly fine, he said. It's just that he didn't feel comfortable leaving her at my mother's house and thought the station wasn't a good place for her to wait for us. She'd be more comfortable at the hospital. I asked what had happened. He said that he had dropped in on my grandmother again to find that my mother had come back with her boyfriend.

"I don't know what's wrong with your mother," he said, and told me he'd never seen anyone that angry before. "I mean, she was worked up. No offence, but she isn't right in the head. She called me every name in the book." When he told her he was taking my grandmother into his custody, she got right in his face. "I mean chest to chest," he said. "I thought she was going to hit me. I've never seen anything like it. To be honest, it freaked me out. Your mother's got a very, very serious temper."

—

I WAS WALKING ACROSS the Waypoint campus, across a long expanse of grass, with Glenn Robitaille, heading back to his office. He'd sat in on the interview in which the killer told me about his crimes.

Glenn said, "You know, there's a reason he gets the shakes after he kills. He got a huge adrenalin rush. He got off on it. I don't know if he fully understands that aspect of himself. I don't think he likes talking about it."

The killer will talk about it, but only obliquely. When he was younger, he fought a couple of times, but fighting made the killer uneasy. "I knew there was a rage in me that scared the hell out of me," he has told me. "I didn't want anything to do with it."

I believe this rage is central to understanding why he killed, what motivated him. But it's hard to get at. It's another black box.

In June 1976, the killer murdered his third and final victim. She was younger than the other two women. She was still in high school. He found her trying to hitch a ride in front of the local police station. She wanted to go swimming and was looking for a lift to her family cottage. The killer had a job driving a rendering truck at the time. This entailed driving around the county disposing of dead and sick farm animals. Sometimes the killer had to dispatch one of the animals himself. Sometimes he had to flay the flesh off the bone. He had a long, thin knife for this purpose.

"We were chatting quite nicely," the killer tells me. "I was feeling a lot of warmth from her and I started to have fantasies about her." The killer drove down a side road. He drove to an abandoned farm where a farmhouse had burned down a long time ago. Its foundation was still there, a forgotten atoll among a sea of tall grass. This is where he raped the girl.

"She was the only one of my victims that I had a climax with," he told me. By "victims" he meant the women he had killed. Afterwards, the killer was getting dressed. The girl was lying on the ground. The killer remembers her saying: "What a dirty thing we done." Then the killer doesn't remember anything. Then he remembers coming to and being out of breath. He was dizzy and nauseous, as if he had just sprinted. He had destroyed the girl's body. He remembers the exhaustion, the fact that he had brutalized her so severely he could barely stand up afterwards. But he says he doesn't remember doing it. He says the rage took over his mind.

The killer slashed at the girl's genitals with the knife he used on animals. I ask him if he remembers doing that.

"Yes," he says.

"Why did you do it?"

"Probably I was angry at the act itself."

"Why were you angry?" I want to know. "Can you take me through what you were feeling when you were killing her?"

"I can't," says the killer.

"Why not?"

"I've tried numerous times over the years. I even tried it with Glenn, and he's been the easiest person to talk to about it. There's so much anger and rage that I can't focus. You just can't get in touch with it."

I once spoke to a man who had broken his neck as a teenager. He lost the use of his limbs and all sensation below his neck—or most of it. Some filaments of nervous tissue were spared and were still capable of transmitting faint messages from the far outposts of his peripheral nervous system. The physical sensation felt more like an emotion, more like a sense of psychological unease. If, for instance, he was sitting on a blanket and the blanket was bunched up under his buttock, or if his foot was twisted at an awkward angle, he wouldn't *feel* it; he'd just know something was wrong. Eventually he came to recognize that the signal came from his body, not his mind. Later in life, he realized he could still have sex because, although his penis didn't transmit sensation to his brain, it could still get aroused on its own. He couldn't feel it or control it, but he could watch it throwing its own private party, like an exiled aristocrat still holding court.

With the help of Viagra, he and his girlfriend developed a robust sex life. It was physically satisfying for her, but for him, because of the lack of sensation, it was primarily an act of emotional intimacy. One time, though, they were having sex and he felt a profound wave of unease building up inside him, a sort of non-specific anxiety, and then suddenly a flood of relief, as though he had been given good news after expecting the worst. He had ejaculated, something he hadn't thought possible. Subjectively, his orgasm was nearly indistinguishable from sitting on a lumpy blanket or having his foot twisted at a strange angle. Only the faintest of signals had reached his brain. It was hard to tell pleasure from pain.

I think the killer might be something like this.

There is an aspect of rage that is analogous to lust. Rage begets rage. It spawns itself. It builds up like clouds looming on the horizon. It causes a discomfort that is not entirely unpleasant, that is pendulous and heavy and can take the place of an emptiness if you are feeling empty. When you are full this way, it is pleasant to think about satisfying that rage. The more you think about it, the more it grows. The more it grows, the stronger the desire to think about it. It is an itch at first, then a tingle, then a pulsation, then a throbbing.

I mean this as an analogy, but I wonder if it is not metaphorical for the killer. I wonder if the tumescent buildup of rage is hard for him to distinguish from the buildup of his sexual feelings. He has trouble feeling the emotions you and I do, but he feels something, and I wonder if maybe the signals are so dim they're nearly impossible for him to differentiate.

One of the theories that's been put forth to explain the cycle of killing unique to serial killers is that it is an act of self-relief. The idea is that the internal state of such men—a low-arousal state, marked by a low heart rate, low fear, low anxiety—is not pleasant. We think of psychopaths as cool operators. Calm and unruffled. But subjectively, a low-arousal state feels gross. It's the way you feel after vegging in front of the TV all day. It makes your skin crawl; it makes you angry and unfocused and edgy, and leaves you chomping at some internal bit in a way that feels deeply unsettling. You need to do something to shake the feeling—take a jog or meet with a friend or get laid.

The theory is that psychopaths have trouble shaking this feeling, because the run-of-the-mill stimulation that kick-starts the rest of us doesn't work for them. They need profoundly intense stimulation to jolt them out of their funk. Even non-homicidal psychopaths seem to crave ultra-stimulation: constant sex, drugs, driving recklessly, thrill-seeking in general. Many psychopaths die through acts of misadventure.[3] And a lot of the anti-social behaviour psychopaths excel at seems to be a form of thrill-seeking.

Perhaps this is what the killer's murders were about: piggybacking two powerful stimuli—murderous rage and sex—in order to get a strong-enough signal to feel something. Serial killers often report exactly this kind of buildup prior to a murder, and a corresponding sense of peace and calm afterwards. With no empathy to speak of, what do they care that breaking out of their funk requires destroying another human being? The killings may have been one of the few ways the killer had of experiencing sensual pleasure. What I find spooky is that, as horrid as it is, this alone is not the trait that differentiates us from psychopaths.

Something like 75 percent of men and 60 percent of women—normal men and women—have had at least one homicidal fantasy.[4] Almost always this is because they're angry at someone. Many of us have a habit of carrying around our anger, nurturing it, creating a place for it within us and letting it grow. It can be intensely pleasurable to think of doing terrible things to people once in a while. I know that's true of me. In the sense of being common, it is a normal emotional state.

We don't like to acknowledge it in ourselves, but human cruelty came from somewhere. Some evolutionary psychologists have speculated that it evolved out of the complex set of emotions endogenous to predators.[5] The act of killing requires the motivation to kill. And because killing evolved in animals that didn't have the capacity for rational thought and planning, the act had to be self-rewarding, the way lust is self-rewarding—as a behaviour that is motivated purely to satisfy a form of desire. As monstrous as we feel about our own blood lust, it may very well exist—along with the pleasure we take in thinking about it, watching it and fantasizing about it—because it is an emotion that evolved for utilitarian purposes.

Often, just as I'm falling asleep, I see strange things. Usually they are benign and amorphous: bright, phosphorescent shapes, shifting geometrical designs, wormholes, lysergic colours and kaleidoscopic visions. More rarely I see faces or bizarre, alien landscapes. This occurs right at the brink of unconsciousness, when I have no control over what I see. Sometimes I see pornographic images—detailed images of penetration, wet, lurid. I don't find these erotic, though, which is strange, because when I choose to look at porn, it's precisely because these kinds of images turn me on. I don't feel anything towards these quasi-hallucinations at all, actually, other than a sort of detached curiosity. Occasionally I see terrible things: rabid animals, ghoulish monsters, decomposing bodies—the denizens of worlds created by Stephen King or H.P. Lovecraft. More infrequently, I see people being hacked apart, their abdomens splayed open like nightmarish blossoms. I see bombs tearing people's heads off, blood erupting in ropy geysers, people being tortured. These aren't nightmares. I'm still awake—or mostly awake. And they aren't at all terrifying in the moment. They are soothing, in a way, because they're a guarantee that sleep is coming. But I find it disturbing that these things are right there, just below the mantle of my consciousness. And I find it sort of spooky that I can be relaxed and even comforted by them.

This has been happening since I was a kid. For a long time I was afraid to tell anyone. I thought they were a sign of some internal defect I had inherited from my mother. I now understand that this sort of thing is common, that it is not tied to any form of insanity. The clinical term is *hypnogogia*, or *hypnogogic hallucination*. My sister-in-law experiences the same thing, Hieronymus Bosch imagery included. We have both taken comfort in the fact that we aren't alone in our horror-film reveries. Several writers have written about their own hypnogogic hallucinations. Edgar Allan Poe drew inspiration from his. I now believe it's the belfry of my mind releasing the bats from my unconsciousness, all the things I don't want to acknowledge during the day.

And that's another thing: even if you don't have the capacity to screen your own endogenous horror show, humans have always had a huge appetite for scary stories, horror movies, true-crime novels. Since the publication of *The Mask of Sanity*, there has been a growing taste for stories specifically about serial killers. And it may be a coincidence, but since the PCL-R has come into widespread use and our understanding of psychopathic behaviour has grown more sophisticated, this sub-genre of fiction—the psychopathic serial killer as protagonist—has exploded: *Silence of the Lambs*, *Dexter*, *The Bates Motel*, *American Psycho*, *House of Cards* and *Hannibal*, not to mention video games like *Grand Theft Auto* that let you create vicarious chaos through psychopathic (or at least seriously sociopathic) avatars. It makes sense in a way; the concept of psychopathy has been called one of the most important psychological constructs of the twentieth century.[6] But it isn't just that we want to know about the things psychopaths do from an objective standpoint; we are unaccountably enamoured of crawling inside their heads.

There is a strange Wonderland symmetry between our fantasy lives, the killer's and my own. Here I am, a member of the film-going, Netflix-watching, book-reading public, someone who enjoys using his empathic imagination to immerse himself in the mind of a serial predator. In front of me is the genuine article, who, in his spare time, enjoys creating for himself a fantasy life of love and compassion and neutered wholesomeness. It is like sitting in front of the looking glass, wondering what it's like on the other side, only to catch a glimpse of some shadowy inhabitant looking back, wondering the same thing.

Every era has its monsters—the faces we give to the fears we have about ourselves at the time. Morally speaking, psychopaths are monsters; they do monstrous things. But as a matter of fact, as biological organisms, they are not. They did not emerge from the swamp or the crypt or from the depths of intergalactic space. And whatever genetic or neural differences underlie the psychopath's lack of empathy, whatever the behavioural and emotional differences from "ordinary" folks, they *are* human. You might argue—and some do—that the capacity for empathy is, by definition, what makes us human. But that's being overly generous and wilfully forgetful.

It's pretty clear that we—the straitlaced, empathetic citizens of Planet Upright—are perfectly capable of merciless blood lust. History is punctuated with regular episodes of predatory and targeted slaughter: Rwanda, Kosovo, Cambodia, Germany, the Ottoman Empire, the Indian Wars, the Crusades, the sack of Jericho—perhaps even the disappearance of our Neanderthal cousins. The mass scale of industrial killing is a relatively new thing, but we've been killing one another since before we learned to put pen to paper.

You can argue that genocide is the result of propaganda and politics, and, certainly, you'd have a point. But mass atrocities are possible only because we have an inherent knack for dehumanizing other categories of people. "Dehumanization" is simply another way of describing the selective elimination of empathy. Once empathy is gone—something that happens with very little prompting—the emotional draw of violence seems to be an immediate corollary. It isn't that some surface nicety gets stripped away and our true brutality is exposed. Empathy and remorselessness are *both* inherent. And so is the capacity to toggle between these two states. And that's the issue.

There is some switch within us that allows us to kill and enjoy killing. There is plenty of historical testimony vouching for the fact that patent non-psychopaths enjoy getting their hands dirty—bloody, in fact. On the whole, we can be as creatively sadistic as any serial killer. We have it within us to get a sensual thrill from the act of killing. Under the right circumstances, many of us—far, far more than the meagre one to three percent of the population that fits Hare's criterion for psychopathy— can make this switch and then, weirdly, after a hard day's work of spilling blood, go home and kiss our wives and children. I find this more chilling than the notion that a tiny subsection of the human population exists permanently in this state. Psychopaths may be constitutionally cruel, but at least they are constant.

I'm not saying we're all psychopaths. The psychopath's blood lust is wholly self-centred, looking out for number one; the non-psychopath's blood lust is fundamentally, and paradoxically, pro-social—looking after your own. I'm just pointing out that, despite the revulsion we feel towards men like the killer, despite the fact that we prefer to think of him as an inhuman monster, there are some parallels between him and the rest of us. I think we know this at some level, and I think this is why we are so fascinated with the monstrosity of psychopaths. There is something familiar there. The longer you look in the mirror, the less alien that shadowy inhabitant seems.

—

THAT NIGHT, ON THE long drive to Tobermory, I realized I didn't want to go to the hospital where my grandmother was waiting. I wanted to go to my mother's house. I wanted to throttle her. It was the same feeling I had had standing there as a teenager in her old house while she pressed her fingernail into my cheek. I told Lyana and my father-in-law how I was feeling. I told them I was glad they were there, that I wasn't driving. I was afraid I would have driven myself to her house.

After that, I cut her off completely. She'd send birthday and Christmas cards and I'd toss them out, unopened. I'm sure it looked spiteful. It probably was. But it was also pragmatic. Like the killer, my own rage scared the hell out of me. I decided my mother was dead to me because, if I didn't do it figuratively, I'd continue to wish it were the case literally.

For years I had been trying to solve a puzzle. It was an obsession of mine, figuring out to what extent she was the pilot of her own actions, where she sat on the continuum between delusional insanity and conscious malice. Part of it was that I wanted to know what lay inside myself. Starting in my early teens, I felt there was something constitutionally rotten about me, a little spot that would continue to spread until the whole was corrupted. I couldn't see the point in much . . . in school, in the future.

I looked down on the kids my age who innocently enjoyed life. They were naive and foolish. I was unmotivated and lazy. I watched too much TV and smoked too much weed, which I swiped from the townhouse guy with the kid. I found a bag of it in his filing cabinet and stole fistfuls. I'd smoke a joint before school and another at lunch. I wandered the halls like a mellow zombie. Sometimes I'd sniff rubber cement in my mother's basement until my vision blurred and my lips felt numb. I'd sneak out of my father's house in the middle of the night and break into the public pool and sit in the turquoise water. When I was eighteen, I lost my virginity with my best friend's girlfriend. I knew it was wrong, but the idea of friends seemed pointless. All long-term things ended anyway. I wasn't purposefully malicious. But I was definitely self-centred and a little fucked up.

By nineteen, I was sick of who I was. I set about remaking myself, like an alternate version of Jay Gatsby, one who strove for mental and emotional solvency rather than fiscal success. I staked out hard lines, the borders of this new kingdom. And I prepared to defend those borders. I gave up drinking and weed. I quit watching TV. I read. I enrolled in a couple of part-time courses at the local university. I began working out with a proselytizer's fervour. I took part-time jobs. I volunteered to teach kids with Down's syndrome at a local high school. I held myself accountable. I did not tolerate personal weakness, self-pity, malingering, lack of follow-through, laziness, disingenuousness. Subconsciously, I excised all semblance of my mother. I wasn't aware that was what I was doing at the time, but it's clear to me now. Like her, I excelled in the visual arts; I gave up painting and drawing, my favourite pastimes and the only set of skills I had much pride in at the time. I gave myself close-cropped haircuts for years because I have my mother's fine, slightly wavy hair. I couldn't bear the resemblance when I looked in the mirror.

A corollary of my new no-bullshit policy was that I was profoundly intolerant of bullshit in others. I stood on the parapets of this new city-state of mine, hyper-vigilant and uncompromising. I would not tolerate breaches. I would not stand for manipulation or bullying. I mounted a watch and armed it and gave it permission to engage at the least sign of provocation. The one trait of my mother's I allowed to remain was my temper. It became a jumpy thing, like the fine needle of a seismometer.

—

ELAINE ANTON RECENTLY graduated from the University of Western Ontario with an undergraduate degree in sociology. It's a huge achievement, in part because, while she was studying, she was also kicking crystal meth. At school, she took a course on serial killers taught by a sessional lecturer named Kim Luton. The two women have since become friends. When I showed up at Elaine's apartment, Kim, a small, energetic woman with short, cloud-white hair and electric-blue eyes, met us there with a box of doughnuts and hung around until she was sure I was trustworthy.

The funny thing, Elaine told me, was that, until she started talking to Kim, the whole experience with the killer had become unreal to her. Elaine now has three grown daughters as well as her two sons. She had told her kids about the killer and they believed she had been raped and attacked, but she could tell they were skeptical about the other details.

"For the last thirty-eight years, my kids have sort of said: 'Yeah, she got abducted by a real killer, but he probably wasn't going to kill her.' I don't think they believed that I was ever in danger with him."

This, along with all the time that's passed and the strange, otherworldly state of mind in which it all took place, formed a capsule around the memories, like a cyst. When she started talking about it with Kim, the cyst burst.

"If this were a year ago," Elaine told me, "I would probably be crying and not be able to carry on the conversation."

For years, Elaine lived in fear the killer would eventually be released. She suffered from PTSD. She'd see someone who looked like him and freeze in the middle of the street. In 2006, the killer applied for transfer to a medium-security facility in downtown Toronto, where patients have access to the surrounding neighbourhood—my old neighbourhood, coincidentally. Remarkably, the Provincial Review Board recommended his release from Oak Ridge. Elaine was convinced the killer would find her and murder her as he had promised, especially since she had talked to the cops after all and helped put him away.

Back in 1976, when the Ontario Provincial Police had begun investigating the killer, they found Elaine's mother's phone number in the killer's black book and eventually tracked down Elaine. She testified against the killer, but before she did, she had the investigating officers swear he'd never get out. Now it looked as though he might.

The staff at Oak Ridge refused to comply with the transfer order. They felt the killer was too big a risk. The killer's lawyer brought the case before the Ontario Superior Court, but in the end the court backed Oak Ridge's position. The judge chastised the review board, pointing out that the killer himself admitted that part of the reason he wanted a transfer was that it would allow him access to women.

The case left Elaine shaken. "I kept thinking there had to be a way to deal with him and not let him have so much power over my life. I thought if I could meet with him and then talk to someone [at Oak Ridge] who would assure me that he isn't going to get out, that would make me feel a lot better."

A couple of years ago, Elaine wrote a letter to the killer. She wanted to meet. Kim Luton and Glenn Robitaille arranged the meeting. The killer was excited. He told patients and staff that his long-time girlfriend was visiting. He wanted permission to take Elaine to another building on campus, to the cafeteria where staff have their lunch. He wanted to make it a romantic, fairy-tale date. Instead, he met with Elaine under the fluorescent lights in the Spiritual Care Centre of the Oak Ridge facility.

Elaine told me she found herself surprisingly composed during the meeting. "I got to talk for about thirty minutes, just basically summing up my life, that it wasn't a happy place to be but that when I met him it was even a less happy place. I said: 'I never held this against you. I never hated you. I forgave you a long, long time ago. That's what I came here to tell you. The best thing that you can do for these women — you can't un-kill them, you can't un-rape me — the best thing you can do for these women is to continue to be a model prisoner and not cause any harm in the prison.'

"I didn't go in there with harsh words," Elaine said. "I didn't feel anger towards him. After seeing him, you almost get this pity."

Elaine's equanimity was lost on the killer. He kept referring to her as his girlfriend. Elaine brought the killer a mug and a shirt that turned out to be too small for him. They were peace offerings. The killer saw them as the kind of gifts a girlfriend brings to her boyfriend. At one point, Glenn had to interrupt. "I know you *believe* she was your girlfriend," Glenn told him, "but the truth is, she was just trying to survive. She has never wanted a relationship with you."

Glenn had also asked the killer to leave the photo album with pictures of his woodwork in his room, but the killer couldn't resist talking about himself. Halfway through the meeting, he got up and fetched the album to show Elaine. It didn't bother her. She had said what she had come to say.

On the way back home, Kim drove. Elaine fell into a deep, dreamless sleep. She slept for two hours and came to in an entirely different landscape. "When I awoke," she told me, "I turned to Kim and said: 'Kim, I feel so good! I feel like I'm two feet taller now.'"

—

IT HAD NOW BEEN several years since I had been in touch with my mother. Life without her had been calmer and better. Or maybe it was that I was calmer and better. I was certainly less angry. It was a physical relief not having to deal with her. I felt lighter and more free. It was the feeling you get in the spring when you leave the house without a coat and reflexively turn back to get it and then realize you don't need it after all. I thought about keeping things that way, never contacting her again. But avoiding what makes you angry isn't the same as mastering your anger. I decided it was time to see her again.

A subtle diplomatic thaw developed. We began communicating through the back channels of my aunt and grandmother, and eventually started sending e-mails. It seemed like the right time to visit. My mother was about to move to British Columbia. She had come to an arrangement with an elderly man who was too incapacitated with rheumatic arthritis to manage his isolated homestead any longer. She was going to learn to run the place—plant and harvest, make preserves and butcher—in exchange for room and board. There was also the possibility, she said, of inheriting the land. The old man had no family.

She wrote that she was self-conscious about seeing me. She had put on weight, she said. A great deal of it. It was one of the side effects of lithium. She told me she had been diagnosed in the last year with yet another disorder: bipolar.

This was part of my decision too. I was curious. Understanding the nature of my mother's psychological problems has preoccupied me for so long that naming what it really is has become a bit of a white whale. I would probably follow her over the edge of the world if I thought I could learn something definite about what makes her tick. I wondered if she knew this. In any case, I wanted to see what she was like on lithium. Part of me wondered too if she was even taking it.

I was cynical, but it wasn't entirely implausible that she might actually have bipolar disorder. It shares some similarities with major personality disorders: mood swings, manipulativeness, bizarre behaviour. It was possible that her so-called chronic fatigue syndrome was in fact the depressive phase of bipolar and that her nasty behaviour was part of the manic phase.

My aunt flew in from Oregon. She had made the journey to Ontario in order to drive my mother cross-country to the Rockies. My mom had eventually got her licence back, but she wanted her sister to drive her because she said her chronic fatigue made being on the road for more than a couple of hours at a time impossible.

My aunt spent the night with Lyana and me in the city. The next day, I drove her north to meet my mother at a bed and breakfast. It was a three-and-a-half-hour drive. On the way, my aunt brought me up to speed on the details of my mother's life. The alimony payments from the professor had come to an end. She had never got the bed and breakfast up and running, despite living a stone's throw from two popular national parks. She had split up with the recovering addict. She had run out of money and had to sell the Tobermory property. She'd moved into a small retirement community in a minuscule town where she had no real friends, no community, no resources. She was desperate to get out of there.

My aunt, now in her early sixties, had become fairly Zen about my mother. She knew her sister was volatile, mercenary and manipulative. But after a life of avoiding my mother, of getting wound up and freaked out whenever there was a family gathering, my aunt had started to take it all in stride. Now that there was a seemingly clear diagnosis, she felt she knew how to interpret my mother's behaviour. She could finally quit taking it personally.

"Your mom is a really sick person," she told me.

The other reason my aunt took on the long drive west was that she wanted to see exactly what my mother was getting herself into. Committing yourself to the back-breaking work of running a homestead at retirement age, especially when you can't drive for more than an hour or two at a time, seemed so quixotic it bordered on delusional. My aunt also found it uncanny that my mother was banking on inheriting the man's property. It was, my aunt feared, a measure of my mother's desperation.

Apparently, my mother had spent several months talking to my aunt about how she planned to commit suicide. She would call on weekends, often taking up two or three hours at a time. My aunt, who is a retired public health nurse, told me her strategy had been to stall my mother by discussing in exquisite detail the most painless and effective ways to do the deed. It worked. My mother seemed more interested in talking about it than doing it. She called every weekend for several months, until finally she seemed to lose interest in the idea of her own death—coincidentally, around the same time she had secured the position at the old man's homestead. These conversations wrung out my aunt, and although she did her best to appear cool, she was highly distressed by them.

We were twenty minutes away from the bed and breakfast where we were meeting my mother. My aunt asked me how I was feeling.

"A little nervous," I told her, "but calm."

"I get that feeling in the pit of my stomach," she said. "Like, you never quite know what you're in for."

Then we were there. It was true—my mother had put on a lot of weight. She was friendly and I think genuinely happy to see me. Her move meant a lot of downsizing. She had brought me a few things she thought I'd like, including a picture of my grandfather at the summit of the Grand Teton, when he was my age and still scaling mountains. I hugged her and it made me feel unsettled, as if I was doing something wrong.

Her bunions were bad, and one of her fingers was twisted and arthritic. She had trouble getting up a short flight of stairs. The three of us had dinner in a local pub. We each had a beer. My mother was subdued. There was none of the firehose speech. When I told her my brother now had a child, that she was a grandmother, she cried.

Seeing your parent in terrible shape after an absence of years is like visiting a ruined monument. It reminds you what time does to all empires, no matter how powerful or despotic. You can't help but be a victim of a strange brand of nostalgia, the way old Russians pine for their Soviet past. It made me feel small to have been so angry at her, to have cut her off so completely. She was pitiful. The three of us went for a walk along the water. It was early spring. All the pleasure craft were in dry dock and there were no leaves on the trees.

I wanted to believe it was bipolar. It was easier that way. I was less angry believing it was true.

—

ON ONE OF THE OLD VHS tapes, the Oak Ridge psychologist asks the killer about his masturbation habits. Among his other fantasies, the killer used to think about having sex with his daughter.

The killer told his daughter about these fantasies. This was maybe twenty years ago, during a visit when she was in her late teens.

"How did she react when you told her?" I ask.

"Oh, very favourably," he says. He tells me it was good for their relationship. He says his daughter wanted him to come live with her when he got out of the hospital, that she would take care of him.

This is a fantasy too, of course. His daughter hasn't had contact with him for years. The staff at Oak Ridge tell me she is normal, intelligent and, miraculously, well-adjusted. She wants nothing to do with her father. She has changed her last name.

I thought about getting in touch with the killer's daughter. But she has put that distance between her father and herself for good reason, and it felt wrong to impose myself on her. Still, I wonder what she says when people ask what she's doing for the holidays or, as people some-times innocently do, whether she's close to her father. I'm curious how she navigates those moments. Maybe it's more clear-cut if your parent is a convicted murderer. Part of me envies her that—not the fact that her father is a psychopathic serial killer, but the simplicity of the label. The distance she has put between herself and her father doesn't require an explanation. Not to others, not to herself.

—

I SAW MY MOTHER again a few months later, in Oregon. My cousin was getting married and I decided to go. I had always avoided visiting my mother's family if I knew she was going to be there. I had missed out on a lot of family gatherings that way. Whatever was wrong with her, what-ever effect it had on me, I didn't want to let it interfere with my other relationships any longer.

I had read a lot about bipolar since seeing her in the spring. I was skeptical. The mood swings associated with bipolar disorder don't tend to turn on a dime, as hers have done. Her kind of mercurial mood swings—which can vary from minute to minute, as opposed to weeks or months—seem to me to be far more indicative of a major personal-ity disorder. The other serious consideration was that, while my mother wasn't currently exhibiting signs of mania or depression, she could still act in ways that seemed sadistic and manipulative.

The wedding was held at a campground overlooking the Columbia River Gorge. It was high summer and the days lasted forever. At night there were campfires among the pines. The river was wide and proceeded slowly and majestically towards the Pacific. My aunt, as mother of the bride, was busy with wedding preparations and so my mother was in charge of taking care of my grandmother. My aunt believed that with her presumed bi-polar condition under control, my mom would have a new-found ability to treat her mother decently. The two of them were sharing a motel room in a small town close to the campground.

My aunt and cousin had planned a family barbecue for the day before the wedding. My grandmother, who was now ninety, completely blind, reliant on a walker and, at times, a wheelchair, was looking forward to it. She felt it was one of the last times she would have all her family gathered in one place before she died.

We arrived early to make preparations. Guests started showing up around noon. I saw family members I hadn't seen in years. The kids swam. We grilled hamburgers and hot dogs. A couple of hours went by, and my mother still hadn't shown up with my grandmother. We had called several times, but she didn't answer.

"What a surprise," said my uncle.

I ran into town in my uncle's old pickup truck to grab some beer and ice. The motel where my mother and grandmother were staying was just down the highway. I sat in the cab and watched the river for a while. I could go get my grandmother and bring her to the barbecue. But I also knew what my mother was doing. I had a good idea why she was so late. She was deftly killing two birds with a single stone: extinguishing my grandmother's joy and sabotaging my cousin's barbecue. I felt she knew that someone—probably me—would eventually come and get my grandmother. I knew that this was what I should do, but I wasn't sure I could do it without getting angry. I thought of my old car and the spider-web I had punched into the windshield. I thought of the rage I had felt driving up to Tobermory that night. I drove back to the barbecue alone.

She called as things were breaking up and people were carrying empty coolers towards the parking lot.

"Are you all still there?" she asked. She sounded innocent and breathless, as if she had mistakenly overslept.

"You knew what time this ended," I said.

"You have no idea what it's like!" she spat back. "Taking care of my mother. She's *extremely* demanding."

That was a patent lie. My grandmother, an intrepid and seasoned traveller, was still taking cross-country flights by herself, packing a

peanut butter and banana sandwich in her purse in case of an unex-
pected layover. She had once hiked the foothills of pre-Soviet
Afghanistan. She is the very model of self-reliance.

I could feel the heat of my mother's malice, the phone pressed to my
face like an iron.

The wedding took place among columns of Douglas firs. The reception was held outside a venerable park building made of stone. The
band were all old hippies, friends of my aunt's. My younger cousin had
rendered an entire pig into pulled pork and had baked an enormous
cake that he cut into thick slabs and served off paper plates. There were
garbage cans full of ice and bottled beer. I went from table to table,
catching up with people I hadn't seen in years. My mother followed me
around all evening. She wanted to talk, she said. I kept avoiding her.
She came up once and put her arm around me. It made my skin crawl.

—

THE KILLER HAS SINCE been transferred to a new building on the
other end of the Waypoint campus. The Oak Ridge facility has recently
been torn down. All that remains of it is a dust heap at the top of the hill.
The stone gate leading to the old facility remains, as do the oak trees.

The new building is polished and bright. It looks like the bridge of
the Starship *Enterprise*. There are no bars. There are no steel doors or
tiled corridors. Everything is locked and unlocked by a sophisticated
electronic system. The killer likes his new room because it has a
window facing the blue waters of the lake.

The new Spiritual Care Centre is clean and airy. It has glass doors
that open onto a fenced-in courtyard. Saplings have been planted
there. In another ten years they'll provide a shady place for the killer to
contemplate his existence. There is a small area for Muslim patients to
perform ablutions and there are plans to build a sweat lodge.

I bring the killer a Moleskine notebook. He disregards it. It does not
capture his interest. I tell him that many famous writers have used
them, thinking that will make him appreciate it. He told me he hasn't
been working on his novel. He is busy with other plans. He pulls out a
laminated letter he's sent to the Royal Canadian Mint. He's written to

suggest the government issue a special hundred-dollar coin to com-memorate the end of the First World War. In return he's gotten a cour-teous but generic reply. He also wants my help organizing indigenous groups across the country for a Remembrance Day ceremony. His idea is to coordinate a live drumming event that would start in Newfoundland and move across the country in a wave, east to west, ending in British Columbia. He is working on another book, a collection of yet-to-be-written essays by inmates and prisoners. He has mocked up a dust jacket. The book is provisionally entitled *The Freedom of War*. And he has another children's book on the go: an anti-bullying endeavour involving a beaver, a hawk, a giraffe and a gorilla. We shake hands and he lumbers down the newly constructed corridor that still smells of fresh paint and industrial adhesives.

Glenn walks me out of the building towards the parking lot. Along the way, he says, "I think he genuinely feels that if he comes up with enough Good Samaritan projects, he'll eventually balance out the bad stuff."

—

I'VE SPENT A LOT OF time thinking about my mother, obviously. And I've spent a lot of time thinking about whether I ought to publish what I've been thinking about her.

I know she'll read this eventually. And I know what I've written will make her uncomfortable. That sits on me, heavy and sad. I wish her no harm. In fact, I wish her happiness. Or at least contentment—though I have trouble imagining things working out in such a way she'll ever be content.

But I also know that if I hadn't written this, hadn't tried my hardest to understand the reasons for her behavior and the tenor of her emo-tional life—and how she has influenced my behavior and *my* emo-tional life—I would never have arrived at a place where I could wish that she was happy, or content.

As I've said, I didn't set out to write about her. When I conceived this project, I didn't even set out to write much about myself. I envisioned a dispassionate, research-heavy book about the objective realities of male violence. Yeah, I knew I had some issues, but, not being a thug or rapist or killer, I felt my own story would be fairly incidental to the endeavor. I figured I'd add personal anecdotes only to flavour the academic research and the reporting.

But writing is a funny business. Ray Bradbury said of the process: "Your intuition knows what to write." The novelist Patrick O'Brien argued that "a book can be represented as a conversation with one's demon." Looking back on it now, as this thing gets ready to go to press, my best guess is that in deciding to write this book, my intuition was urging me to have that conversation. My demon, as I've come to understand, is fear.

Yes, I have White Hat Syndrome. Yes, I want to make the world a better place by confronting—no, let's be honest—by vanquishing the people I find threatening, domineering, manipulative and sadistic. But that white hat sits atop an angry head. And beneath that anger is a twitchy and hyper-vigilant person who is overly attuned to threatening sounds in the underbrush. It's hard for me to think I ever would have—ever could have—come to this understanding of myself without writing about my mother.

And it's difficult for me to conceive how this book would work to help us better understand the inner workings of other violent men, if I was not honest about the origins of my own rage and violence.

I've told you the very worst of my mother's traits. This is because they have, over time, come to define how I see her, how I feel about her. I believe they reveal something essential about who she is. I believe that she came into the world like this and that she probably can't be fixed. I don't know what to call it. It is another black box.

Whatever the cause of her behaviour, I have trouble thinking of her as a good person. Although I think she may want to be one. The killer is right: no label captures everything. We are infinitely complex. Within all of us there are the seeds of our unrealized selves, the persons we wish to be or fantasize about being.

It would be disingenuous if I didn't also tell you some of the good things my mother did. And it would be unfair to her, because there were, after all, many of them, though maybe not quite enough to balance the ledger.

My earliest memories are made of these good things: We are in a meadow. We are walking hand in hand. She is holding me close. I am sick as a small child. I have a terrific fever and my mother brings her filly into the kitchen of the farmhouse where I am sitting, and the horse nuzzles me with its velvet nose. It is summer and during a thunderstorm my mother lets me run naked through the garden in the rain.

These good things are like the tiny moons of Jupiter. There are scores of them, all orbiting a larger churning mass. They are real, these places. They are their own isolated worlds. I can visit them, but they are hard to arrive at because the gravity of what lies below has more sway. They are brilliant and crystalline in their passage through the firmament. They are alluring and otherworldly. And they are a pleasure for me to behold. I can alight on them, but only for a moment. They are too small to settle upon. These are my fantasy worlds.

In my fantasy, it is early summer. It is perfect. I am still very young. There is a thunderstorm. And in the thunderstorm I am running naked through a garden in the rain while lightning strikes the distant earth. My mother is there and she is young and she is laughing. And I am not angry.

CHAPTER FIVE

—

# THE PEN AND THE SWORD

MY FRIEND JEFF WAS KILLED while serving in a war zone. He didn't have a dark lust for spilling blood or a need to physically dominate. He never carried himself as if he was spoiling for a fight. It's true he worked for a time as a bouncer, but only to make money for school. And anyway, he had a reputation for settling things diplomatically. He'd talk to guys. He wasn't interested in throwing punches. He wasn't a tamped-down ball of rage waiting for an excuse to go off.

He didn't need to hold a gun to feel like a man. He wasn't prone to knee-jerk patriotism. He was beyond pat explanations. He read deeply and widely: Foucault, Nietzsche, Hegel, Marshall McLuhan. He was a student of Buddhism. He listened to public radio and enjoyed the melancholy guitar of Ry Cooder.

The word you hear associated most often with him is *quiet*. That's the word everyone who knew him uses—his mother and father, his girlfriend, his friends and colleagues. As in: quiet and gentle. Or quiet and thoughtful. Quiet and funny. Quiet and strong.

That's how I remember him too: quiet as a lake at sunrise. Quiet as the dawn.

As a kid, he was especially close to his grandmother. When he was older, he wrote her letters from his university dorm telling her how much he missed her. He was a grad student when she died, a full-grown man in his late twenties. Still, he was heartbroken.

He loved his parents. He loved his sister. He loved his girlfriend,

Sylvie. He wrote her letters from his dorm too. She worked as an airline attendant. They lived in different cities, and spent long stretches apart. The university gym was full of dewy coeds in the flush of youth. When he worked out, he'd pull the brim of his ball cap low. He went to the gym to work out, not stare at girls.

Years later, he and Sylvie had a child together, a boy they named Ry—after the guitarist. When he was at home on leave, he held Ry against his heart and rocked him gently. He changed his son's diapers. He fed him. He babbled and sang to him.

I like to think that in those moments, the few he had, he transmitted something to his son that drifted down and formed a sedimental layer beneath language or memory or consciousness. I like to think the wordless quiet of those early moments with his father is stored away somewhere in the deepest regions of the boy's being. But this may be something I'm making up because the alternative is too sad to contemplate.

When Jeff looked at you, it wasn't immediately clear what he was thinking. Partly because he was so quiet, but also because he had a squint like a silver-screen gunslinger. This wasn't an affectation. It was just the way his skull was constructed, the way the muscles of his face naturally sat over the bone, the way the skin lay over those muscles. His smile started off as a smirk then veered at the last second into a warm, unguarded thing. When it happened, it felt as if he was giving you a gift.

I found him intimidating at first. This was before we met, when I was at the end of my undergrad and Jeff was at the end of his master's degree. It was the gunslinger thing, I think. I'd see him in the gym every day, doing weights. He was a few years older than me and more physically developed. He looked as though he had been punishing his body with biblical tasks: chopping down a forest by hand, carving a mountain pass with a hammer and chisel. I saw in him—in the way he carried himself, in his physicality—a tremendous discipline, the physical manifestation of extraordinary commitment and focus.

So I'm not sure I would have spoken to him. There's a good chance I would have kept to myself. But he approached me while I was doing single-hand cable rows and asked me what I was training for. The way that half smirk hung there, I thought maybe he was calling me out, suggesting I didn't know what I was doing. But then the smirk made its last-second turn. He smiled and held out his hand and we shook.

I remember the word he used: *training*. Not "exercise." Not "working out." Training implied preparation for something. It implied forward motion. It implied a goal. And it implied that he had noticed me and recognized in me someone who had what it took to fulfill some serious purpose.

He didn't join the military just to join. He wasn't like that. His natural habitat was the space inside his head. When you hung out with him, there'd come a time when it was clear he was ready to be alone again. He was never rude, but something subtle in his demeanour told you he was preparing to pull back within himself.

For a long stretch, through his teens and into his early twenties, he felt the military was for suckers. He was anti-establishment. He listened to punk and metal. There are old photos of him in high school dressed like a rocker, with long hair, sleeveless shirts. His dad was a military man. Maybe it was the inevitable form of teenage rebellion.

He had trouble getting through basic training because he had to bunk with men younger and dumber than him, and because it meant having to give up his autonomy. He was used to doing his own thing.

This, all of this, was the central paradox of his decision. Because, really, if you're not prone to violence; if you don't grow up wanting to be G.I. Joe; if you're not a natural-born killer; if you're a lover, not a fighter; if you're committed to your intellectual development and not prone to reflexive expressions of nationalism—if you are not okay with unquestioning obedience, then why?

Why *would* you want to enlist?

Here is who I was back when I met Jeff: I was the edge that could not stop sharpening itself.

Like him, I had been a poor high school student. Like him, I transformed myself into something new. Jeff dropped out in his last year and later had to make up the credits in adult night school before he could move on, part-time, to university. I got high and drank and daydreamed and received my high school diploma with completely unremarkable grades. After high school, Jeff moved with his family from Winnipeg to Ottawa. He got a series of go-nowhere jobs: stocking shelves, working airport security. He flirted with the idea of becoming a stockbroker. I drove out west and did casual labour on farms and feedlots. Then I came back to Ottawa, where I had grown up, and enrolled in university, part-time at first. By the time I got there, Jeff was close to finishing his undergrad. He was killing it: getting straight As, hitting the gym every day.

I had taken some of my father's books out west with me: poetry and novels, essays and philosophy. I read with the secret conviction the universe had embedded in them messages I was meant to find. That conviction spawned an equally mystical theory: that if you are not content with who you are, you can make yourself into something new. You can break yourself down and build yourself back up into something pure. According to this theory, I was a dull slug of pig iron, a raw, unformed thing that needed to be heated white-hot, hammered flat and honed. The theory presented a promise: that with hard work and discipline, I could shape the raw, dull thing into something sharp and tempered. I could forge myself into an exceptional tool and, as that tool, craft a new and more perfect world.

That prospect shimmered in the distance. I returned east and set out after it.

I studied. I read. I went to class. I listened. I took notes. I didn't drink or get high. I ate wholesome foods. I didn't play euchre or sit aimlessly for hours in coffee shops. I didn't go to keggers, concerts, clubs or house parties. I sat at tables alone and read. I stayed up all night sweating out papers.

I was the anvil and I was the hammer and the slug of iron, slowly heating itself from black to red, from red to white. The gym was the forge. I went every day, sometimes twice a day. I went when I was tired. I went when I was ill. I lay on the benches and brought the weights down and lifted them up and brought them back down again, over and over. I stayed for hours at a time. I was not strong at first. I was constantly sore. When I got used to the pain, I decreased my calories. Winter came. I started jogging. My lungs were soft and pink and not used to the work. The cold air jabbed my alveoli like the tip of a straightened coat hanger. I felt nauseous. I tasted bile. I pushed past it. The fat melted away like flux. My joints and sinews came to the surface. I grew stronger. I grew faster. When I ran, my lungs now burned, but like the holy fire that cleanses. Over the joints and sinews, muscle grew. I increased my calories. Those calories turned into more muscle.

Sometimes, when I had exercised as much as I could, when I had finished all my assignments and couldn't read any more, I'd take long walks to clear my head. I'd walk through my neighbourhood at night, along the quiet streets lined with brick houses and beneath the willows that lined the canal.

I felt it all signified something: the brick houses, the willows, the canal. Life in general. I felt as though I was walking on a movie set constructed just for me. I felt the universe transmitting a message at a frequency just beyond my hearing. I felt there was some grand meaning I couldn't grasp. Not quite yet.

Sometimes, when I slept, I dreamt about it.

I dreamt I was lacing up my boots, that I was in a hurry. I am in a basement apartment that has recently been abandoned. Empty tin cans on the table; naked coat hangers in the closet. Outside the window, three boys I know from high school are crouched on the grass like dogs. They are pressed up against the window, dressed in mismatched uniforms. I'm in a uniform of some sort too.

They're trying to tell me something through the glass, but I can't make it out. I'm not sure if I'm on their side or not. I'm not sure what the sides are, exactly. They are yelling at me. They pound on the window. A high-frequency hiss fills the room and makes it difficult to understand them. My arms quit working. I'm having trouble tying my laces. I look down at my hands. I can't move them. They're like the hands of a statue. I try to look back at the boys, but I can't move my head either, only my eyes. Their mouths are wide, like the mouths of striking serpents. The loud hiss grows louder. I clue in too late: it's the sound of poison gas issuing from the back of their throats.

In another dream, I'm with a group of young men. We're hiding in the attic of an empty house in the far reaches of an abandoned subdivision. We're waiting for something. We take great pains to remain quiet. We take turns on lookout. Eventually we see them: black government cars rolling along the asphalt. They stop in front of the house. There is one black guy among us. I turn to him and hand him a backpack. There are several days' worth of supplies in the bag. He and I move to the far side of the attic. It is night. Out the window, we can make out a tree line across a field as dark and wide as the sea.

"If you can make it to the trees," I tell him, "you'll be okay. We'll hold them off for you." But as I say this, I have the sinking realization we have no weapons. Down on the street, I hear the doors of the cars opening and then closing again.

In another dream from this time, I am riding down a muddy mountain road on a military motorbike while peasants march single file in the opposite direction. They are fleeing something I have been sent to deal with. In yet another, I am standing with a group of children. In one direction, a desert stretches to the horizon. We turn the other way to face an endless field of grain. A stealth bomber is making slow turns overheard.

I had dreams like this every month or two, from my late teens into my early thirties. They were always vaguely paramilitary. There were never recurring characters or places, but the mood was always the same. There was always a vague threat and the vague sense that I was supposed to stop that threat. They appealed to me because, as vague as the threat was, it was clear to me I was capable of stopping it.

Whenever I had a dream like this, I'd wake up and write it down. They were like fragments of a lost scroll. I felt if I could piece together enough of them, I'd be able to decipher some larger meaning.

Early on in my undergrad, before I met Jeff, I toyed with the idea of enlisting in the Ceremonial Guard, the red-uniformed foot soldiers who patrol Parliament Hill. A woman who worked at the gym and who, for a while, I had a crush on was part of the regiment. She thought it might be a good fit for me.

The idea of standing stock-still, sweating beneath a bearskin hat while tourists snapped photos, didn't appeal to me. And I wasn't keen on giving up my personal freedom. But you had to pass basic training to make the cut and I liked the thought of that. Rumour had it that, as a Parliamentary Guard, if you fainted in the heat, you were expected to drop like a plank and absorb the shock with the bridge of your nose. I liked that too. I liked the idea of a harder anvil, a heavier hammer.

But here is who I was *not* back then: I was not someone who would have joined anything. My final act as a high school student was to spit on the floor of my school before I walked out the door. I was tired of people telling me what to do, what to think. I wasn't about to subject myself to yet another form of institutional authority just as I was starting to gain a sense of myself. And so I was puzzled by the war dreams, by finding the idea of subjecting myself to a military regimen appealing. Even if it was just a fantasy.

—

IF THERE'S SUCH A THING as an accepted view on the origins of war, it's that it is humanity's own doing, a consequence of stepping from the Eden of our hunter-gatherer past into the artifice of civilization: agriculture and husbandry, trade and lucre and the institutions that grew up to protect them. While they made men rich and powerful, they created inequality. And this in turn sparked wars between men who, with their new wealth, raised great armies so that they could conquer one another and grow richer and more powerful still. Since man was supposedly created mild and loving, powerful kings and nations had to seduce young men with heroic tales of combat and sacrifice so that their hearts would be hardened enough to kill and die for a cause.

Or something like that.

The view that war is an invention, a cultural artifact and not a behaviour rooted in our evolutionary past, is nearly sacrosanct within the social sciences. It is the official position of public institutions as storied as the United Nations and the American Psychological Association.[1] This notion arose from ethnographic studies of hunter-gatherer warfare done in the late nineteenth and early twentieth centuries. A lot of what those early ethnographers observed was ceremonial: tribal warriors formally pre-arranging where a battle would take place, elaborate battledress that was more form than function, and, in some cases, battle lines set up just beyond the effective range of bows and spears. Hunter-gatherer warfare didn't meet the contemporary definition of battle. In the eyes of those studying it, it seemed ragtag and disorganized, not a grandly orchestrated event in which killing was done with earnest efficiency. And so they concluded that war before civilization was primitive and unserious and illegitimate—primarily a symbolic affair.

But the dismissal of hunter-gatherer warfare as somehow not real neglects a couple of vital points. First, while it's true hunter-gatherer battles weren't exactly Omaha Beach, they *were* lethal. Though they were usually called off after only a few men had been killed or seriously injured, they were small to begin with, and so the number of men killed could exceed the proportion killed in modern battle.[2]

The bigger point is that comparing modern battle with so-called primitive battle is comparing apples with red herrings. Formal battles are the pinnacle of modern warfare, its highest form, so to speak. But that's not the case in non-state societies. Battles among hunter-gatherers are fairly infrequent. There's a more common and, cumulatively, a more deadly form of fighting: the raid.

In the classic hunter-gatherer assault, a small group of men sneak into enemy territory, creep up on an unsuspecting villager, gut him and then run off again. Or they thrust spears through the walls of a hut or, alternatively, set the hut on fire and butcher those who try to escape. Most of the time, raiding looks more like a drive-by shooting or an Appalachian feud than what modern folk think of as war. But this was how we waged war for most of our history. Especially our prehistory.[3]

Archaeological digs clearly show that groups of early humans killed one another well before the advent of civilization. Buried in prehistoric graves are the skeletal remains of people done in by blunt-force trauma and projectiles. The archaeological record also shows that prehistoric raids occasionally took a grander and more terrifying form: large-scale massacres. In addition to picking off one another one by one in raids, ancient humans slaughtered one another *en masse* in surprise attacks that targeted men, women and children.

Some of the earliest complex human settlements were built with defence in mind. They were surrounded by walls and trenches, their peripheries littered with arrowheads and spear tips embedded in the bones of men they had been designed to defend against. Warrior culture, from what we can tell, is as old as human culture—and as pervasive.

Modern militaries put a lot of work into selling themselves to the governments that fund them and to the general populace. The marketing wizards behind the US Army's most famous slogan—*Be All You Can Be*—knew what they were doing. If you want to entice young people to join, convince them you can forge them into the thing they want to be. Military propaganda has far-reaching influence on the stories we tell ourselves. It's naive to think otherwise. But it's equally naive to overlook the fact that those kinds of stories—Gilgamesh, the *Mahabhrata*, the *Iliad*—resonated with us long before the advent of the military-industrial complex.

If you accept the definition of warfare as groups of humans organizing themselves to kill one another or, alternatively, to mount an organized defence against such attacks, it's clear we've been doing this for a long time. It's a distinct possibility that our ancestral species were already doing this to one another as they stepped out of the Pliocene and into the Pleistocene. Groups of humans may very well have been killing one another since before they were, technically speaking, human.

It's hard to imagine this hasn't shaped our psychology somehow.

—

WE'D SNEAK OUT OF our parents' houses and wander the streets of our subdivision at night. We dressed in black. We wore hoodies or balaclavas or our mothers' handkerchiefs tied bandit-style over our noses. We carried weapons. At the time, ninjas were hugely popular. My friend ordered a pair of steel *sai* from an ad in the back of *Karate* magazine, the short hand-held tridents designed to defend against samurai swords; they're the favoured weapon of the Teenage Mutant Ninja Turtle, Raphael. They were incredibly low-quality. One of them snapped in half shortly after they arrived. One of my friends wore his dad's camping machete in a canvas sheath tied to his thigh. I made a pair of equally low-quality nunchuks. I practised swinging them Bruce Lee–style in the basement but kept hitting myself in the back of the head. We pocketed our parents' lighters and matches, cans of aerosol hairspray, bottles of rubbing alcohol, WD-40 and whatever other low-grade volatiles we could get our hands on.

We called our excursions "night missions." For a while they were the culminating event of a sleepover, the whole reason to have a sleepover in the first place. At some point, sitting in someone's basement rec room watching VHS movies and gorging ourselves on Oreos and Doritos was no longer enough.

We'd wait until one or two in the morning. We'd shimmy out the basement window onto the cool lawn. Sometimes just two of us. Sometimes three. A few times we arranged to meet other boys in the wide field behind the high school. This was before anyone had a cellphone. We'd wait in a gully to see if the others would show, listening for sounds, watching for movement in the shadows.

We hopped fences and ran through people's yards. We hid in hedges. A few times we egged people's houses or toilet-papered their shrubbery. We'd try to pry street signs from their posts. We knocked over mailboxes. We'd steal safety barricades and set up roadblocks and then hide and wait for a confused driver to stop. Then one of us would holler and we'd all run. Or we'd throw rocks. One of my friends eventually got a paintball gun. One night he opened fire on a car. The driver got out and sprinted after us. We lost him in the dark. We hid in the hedges with our hearts racing, trying to control our breathing.

My ninja friend got hold of a copy of *The Anarchist's Cookbook* and soon considered himself an explosives expert. He made bombs out of whatever household ingredients he could find—spaghetti sauce jars filled with match heads and batteries. He'd light them in the middle of a park and we'd run for cover under the trees. We'd watch them sputter and smoke, and then abandon them when it was clear they weren't going to blow.

Once, I brought a bottle of nail polish remover. I soaked two rags with it and tied one to each end of a stick and lit them on fire and twirled the flaming stick like something you might see at Burning Man. This was in front of my high school. Someone must have called the cops. A cruiser snuck up on us and blasted us with its high beams. My friends took off at a sprint. I leapt into the bushes planted around the periphery of the school and held my breath. My ninja friend had told us that when you're trying to remain unseen, it's important to keep your eyes shut because people can feel when they're being watched. I knew this was bullshit, but I did it anyway. Maybe there was something to it. The cops didn't find me.

We did this for a couple of summers running, when I was fifteen and sixteen, or maybe sixteen and seventeen. It wasn't malicious, any of it. We weren't mean kids. We weren't out to hurt people or terrorize them. We weren't out to pick fights. I don't think I ever did it again after the incident with the police car. A few of my friends kept it up for a while. Eventually, the guy with the paintball gun got picked up by the cops for jumping up and down on a parked car. He ended up having to do a short stint of community service.

We got a little older. We gained some social capital. We started getting invited to parties. It got easier to get booze. We started dating girls and making out in our parents' basement rec rooms. There was less incentive to break out of them and roam around in the dark.

—

FOR MOST OF OUR HISTORY, we assumed we were unique as a species, that we were the only one that killed its own. Murder and especially warfare were assumed to be the unique purview of human beings. The fact that we're so good at it, and so often relish it, seemed a sign that humans had deviated from the natural order somewhere along the way.

Then, in 1974, Hilali Matama witnessed something that turned that assumption on its head. Matama was a researcher studying chimpanzees with Jane Goodall's group in Gombe Stream National Park, Tanzania. She was following a group of chimpanzees—five young males and one young, childless female—through the jungle. The chimps were behaving oddly, not the way a typical food-gathering party does. They were quiet and seemed extraordinarily focused. She trailed them over the border into the neighbouring chimp troop's territory. This was unusual too. The party quietly advanced on a solitary, healthy male feeding in a tree. They took him by surprise in a coordinated attack, and pulled him to the ground. The five males bit him, stoned him and beat him to a pulp. The female circled the fight, screaming and hooting. Then the attackers ran off, back to their turf, leaving their victim for dead.[4]

Matama had just seen a chimpanzee raid. At the time, she didn't know what to make of it. At this point, the study of chimps in their natural environment was only a few years old and no one had seen anything like it before. A few weeks later, she observed another raid. A year later, it happened again. By late 1977, raiding parties from the first troop had killed all of the adult males and one of the senior females in the neighbouring territory. Most of the females from the conquered group fled. A few were integrated into the invading troop. In three years of raiding, a community of chimps had been exterminated and their territory, its food sources and several breeding females had been appropriated by the conquering force. Since then, chimp raids have been observed in Tanzania's Mahale Mountains National Park, in Senegal's Niokolo-Koba National Park, in the Taï National Park of Ivory Coast and in Uganda's Kibale National Park. Primatologists now describe such episodes as an evolved behavioural strategy.

Here's what we understand about chimp raids: They are aggressive assaults, not defensive. They are almost entirely a male affair. And they are especially beneficial to the males of the conquering force. The resulting land grabs translate into an eventual increase in male reproductive capacity; more land and food means a larger carrying capacity, which means more mates for breeding males. (A male chimp can increase his bloodline with every new mate, whereas a female's reproductive capacity is limited by gestational period and by the time and effort it takes to raise an infant to quasi-independence.)

Chimps are a patrilocal species; genetically related males remain in their birthplace while females leave to mate outside the group. In terms of reproductive success, it's in the best interest of male chimps to initiate raids. A troop that is good at raiding is especially efficient at propagating the DNA of its related male members.

Here's what chimps understand about all this: sweet fuck-all. Chimps are clever creatures, but they don't have the capacity to understand the long-term consequences of what they're doing. They don't raid because they're tactical wizards intent on empire building. In terms of intentionality, the researchers who study them believe the animals are more or less out to enjoy themselves. From all accounts, raiding seems to be an exciting adventure, an electrifying form of thrill-seeking.

For chimps, war is not a conceptual thing; it's an emotional state. Chimps are not disputing ideological positions or responding to a political situation. They do not hate one another's gods. Chimps raid because it confers an evolutionary advantage. But from a chimp's perspective, that advantage is an incidental consequence. Their intentional goal, if it's even fair to call it that, is to get a kick.

It's easy to want to make comparisons between chimp raiding and human raiding, just as it's easy to want to anthropomorphize chimps in general. But then, nature has done most of the anthropomorphizing for us. Chimps share more than 99 percent of our DNA. Like chimpanzees, early humans were likely patrilocal; most human societies still are.[5] And we're the only two species in the animal kingdom that form male coalitions in order to eliminate members of the same species. And, not to overstate the obvious, we both arose from a common evolutionary ancestor.

Before there were weapons or tactics, ranks or manoeuvres, before there was language or politics or religion or ideology, there was a *feeling* that led to raiding. If chimp warfare is the result of an evolved emotional state, as close evolutionary relatives—and as a warring species ourselves—do we share that state? And if we do, how does it manifest itself in our species?

What if, because it arose in us before we evolved language and self-awareness, it remains, some unnamed thing in the shadows of our consciousness?

What if, on occasion, it emerges from the shadows and catches us by surprise?

—

VANCOUVER'S DOWNTOWN CORE was glutted. There were more than a hundred thousand people on the streets, maybe a hundred and fifty thousand—this in a city of just over half a million. There was a giant screen in the middle of a public square. A sea of people had amassed beneath it to watch the final game of the Stanley Cup playoffs. The Vancouver Canucks were tied in the series with the Boston Bruins. This was June 2011. The Canucks were expected to take the series. They had made two Stanley Cup runs, once in 1982 and again in '94. They had faltered both times. This was their chance to make up for it.

The city was electric with hope, but that energy had started to crackle with a dangerous charge. The streets were full of young men, their faces painted blue and green. A lot of them were drunk. By the middle of the third period, Boston was ahead 3–0. It was clear Vancouver wouldn't recover. The crowd began lobbing empties at the giant screen.

Before the game was over, the cops started getting calls. Fights were breaking out across the city. Clusters of young men were flipping cars. A cop car on fire. An officer down. More vehicles burning. Columns of smoke rose up out of the canyons between office towers. The officer in charge of controlling the riot later compared it to a giant game of Whac-A-Mole: they'd squelch one uprising and another one would pop up a few blocks over. There was no epicentre, no single source of instigation. It was organic. It was like the fires that smoulder underground for years and then flare up unexpectedly in the middle of a peaceful village.

The fights grew more serious. One group got a guy to the ground and began kicking him in the head; there were stabbings; somewhere, a gun went off. Street fights snowballed into gang rumbles; the rumbles turned into mobs; and the mobs grew powerful. They swarmed fire-fighters. The police bombed them with pepper spray and tear gas, but the mobs were too big. The men who composed them pulled their shirts over their faces and marched forward into the city to burn more cars. They set Dumpsters and portable toilets alight. They tore down fences and smashed windows. Men and women looted stores and burned Boston flags. It was one of the worst riots in North American sporting history.

Sports riots are common, especially during high-stakes playoffs; something like half of all championship-level events in North America result in some sort of violence. In Canada, hockey riots have been espe-cially destructive. Vancouver wasn't new to them. The city rioted during its 1994 playoff loss to the New York Rangers. As common as sports riots are, predicting them—predicting any riot, really—is little more than augury. Some experts have come up with contributing factors, things like a long series; a high-stakes game; a high-density urban gathering; a close game; and a large group of young, usually white, men.[6] As descriptors, these are spot-on. But as an explanation, they're tautological. It is a bit like answering the question "Why do people bake cakes?" by listing the main ingredients—flour, sugar, milk, eggs, baking powder. It brings you closer to the what, but it does nothing to address the why. It doesn't help us understand what's going on in the minds of the otherwise normal men who, for the most part, make up the ranks of a violent mob. It's a description of the fuel that burns, but it doesn't help us understand the spark that sets it alight in the first place.

In the 2011 Vancouver riot, about 140 people were injured. There were millions of dollars in damage. Initially, the mayor blamed it on a small number of hooligans and anarchists. But that wasn't accurate. More than a hundred people were arrested that night. In the weeks that followed, the police scoured hundreds of hours of video footage and more than a million photos. They eventually laid over 1,200 charges against more than 350 people. It was natural to blame a group of outsiders, a malicious band of others. But for the most part, these were the city's own. They weren't hooligans or sociopaths. Most of them, under normal circumstances, weren't violent. The riot was not an attack on the city by barbarian invaders. It was a form of internal combustion.

One of the riot photos went viral and is now infamous: it's a shot of a rangy blond kid in a Canucks jersey crouched next to a cop car. There's a rag—maybe it's a shirt—stuffed into the cruiser's gas tank. The kid's lighting it.

He was a seventeen-year-old high school student named Nathan Kotylak. He came from a good family. His dad is a surgeon. At the time, he was in his last year of high school. He had a scholarship to the University of Calgary. He was also a rising star on the junior national water polo team. A few days after being outed on Facebook, Kotylak turned himself in to the cops and made a televised apology.

"There is no excuse for my behaviour," he read from a prepared statement; he was flanked by his mom and dad. "It does not reflect the values my family or my community raised me to live by." Halfway through, the kid broke down. "For reasons I cannot explain," he continued, sobbing, "I went from being a spectator to becoming part of the mob mentality that swept through many members of the crowd."

The city was furious. Kotylak became its pariah dog. The family got death threats. They had to leave home for a while. The police appealed to residents not to resort to vigilante justice.

I called Kotylak's lawyer. I wanted to speak with the kid. I wrote him a letter. The lawyer promised me he'd pass it on. But I didn't hear back, and I wasn't surprised. The family was taking too much heat—and not just for the flaming-car stunt. The apology had pissed people off too. There were a lot of skeptics who thought it was just a clever PR move, a way of mitigating an inevitable sentence.

But I believed Kotylak. I think he probably *was* sorry. More to the point, I believe he genuinely couldn't explain what overcame him. I don't think anyone can, not really. Not the mayor or the police or the enraged citizenry. Not even the academic experts. And not the young men who feel this emotion well up inside them and then, only after they've unleashed it, look in amazement at the destruction they've wrought.

I've tried to imagine what kind of explanation I would have given my parents, or the cops, had I been caught twirling that flaming baton in front of my high school. I wouldn't have been able to explain it. I still can't, not rationally. But I do remember the feeling.

I still feel a touch of it when I visit the place where I lived as a teenager, walking along the vast manicured stretches, through the empty soccer fields and school grounds, under the hum of high-tension wires, or pedalling along the meandering roads and cul-de-sacs of residential subdivisions, the pristine and unimaginative architecture of isolationism. I feel a touch of what I used to feel slouching through the parking lots of strip malls where shop owners warned us not to loiter; in the creosote stench of asphalt baking in the sun; lingering in the parks that no longer served our recreational needs, under the trees buzzing with cicadas.

As an adult, it's easy to discount this kind of teen angst. We tend to look back and covet those vast stretches of time because as busy adults we forget the way it actually felt, the emptiness pulling at you the way the vacuum of space pulls at the thin metal skin of a space capsule, the aimlessness that gives rise to restlessness. The need to do something. To be something. To take part in something.

It doesn't really matter what that something is.

—

JEFF HAD HIS AIMLESS period before he dropped out of high school. He skipped classes, drank, got high. He got picked up by the cops once for shoplifting munchies from a 7-Eleven with a group of buddies. But by the time he and I met, it mattered very much to him—to me too— precisely what that something was.

Because we didn't know what we were looking for, we could only talk about it obliquely. We had both done some martial arts. We both leaned towards Eastern mysticism. I introduced Jeff to a translation of Lao-tzu's *Tao-te Ching*. I liked lines like: "The name that can be named is not the eternal name." He introduced me to *The Book of Five Rings*, a seventeenth-century Zen tract by the samurai master Musashi Miyamoto. He liked lines like: "The warrior's way is the two-fold path of pen and sword. Polish the two-fold spirit and sharpen the two-fold gaze. Then you will come to think of things in a wide sense and, taking the void as the Way, you will see the Way as void."

Jeff had the kanji symbol for *void* tattooed on his deltoid. I had the Chinese symbol for *Tao* tattooed over my heart. I couldn't name the eternal name. Jeff couldn't quite explain what the void was. But we could feel them. They pulled at our insides.

Back then, feeling was everything. It flew into my chest like a burning arrow when I was about twenty. The arrow became a needle and twitched inside me like a compass trying to find north. I'd have my weird paramilitary dreams and it would spin and tremble inside me as though I were passing through the Bermuda Triangle.

It was the singular thing guiding me, this feeling, the pull towards a pure and unknown purpose that hovered out there, shimmering on the horizon, vague and alluring.

Until I met Jeff, I assumed I was the only one who truly felt the burning arrow, the twitching needle, the pull of the pure quest. But before we even spoke, I understood he must feel it too. And, if anything, that he was closer to reaching it, whatever it was.

Jeff searched for it in the books he had piled in his dorm room. He had piles of them checked out of the library. He had stacked them in wobbly towers like a miniature city built by Dr. Seuss. I think he was already getting sick of them back then, towards the end of his master's degree.

I made a joke once, something like: "A little light reading?"

He looked at the teetering piles and let out a sigh that sounded like a switchblade going into the sidewall of a tire.

He searched for it in the gym too. I remember working out with him, burning out our limbs until they were like frayed ropes. Jeff nodded towards the stationary bikes.

"This is the best part," he said. He pulled the brim of his cap over his eyes and leaned over the handlebars and dropped his chin towards his chest.

I made jokes like: "Wanna race?" and "Ever get the feeling you're going nowhere in life?"

He smiled, but his eyes were closed. He was quiet and focused, entering the space you can create by burning the anxiety out of your system through physical exhaustion. He was turning his cranium into an empty vault, like the rotunda of a temple. And in that emptiness, I think it began to take form.

Around that time, we joined a boxing gym.

I remember the cold floor beneath my sock feet on the first night and the smell of the place: wet concrete and rotting sweat socks. The milky fluorescent light and the clickety-click of skipping ropes on linoleum. I remember Jeff trying to get the hang of it, laughing at himself when the rope caught on his toes. The flat smack of gloves on the leather bags in the next room where the fighters trained. The wet hiss of their breath as they threw punches, the bell chopping the evening into two-minute intervals. I remember how difficult it was to do the simple things correctly at first.

The two old guys who ran the place stuck us in front of a wall of mirrors and made us practise the basics until we were numb with repetition. For weeks we shuffled in and out. We threw jabs until our shoulders burned and the burn became so intense we couldn't feel it any longer. We reminded one another to look down our arms as if we were sighting a rifle, to corkscrew our fist at the last moment, to keep our hands up and our chin down.

When we were ready, the coach put us in the ring with an old work-horse, a guy who was about the age I am now. He was thick in the middle. His trunk and gloves were old and faded. I went first. I was trim and strong. For a second I felt a flush of confidence, because I looked like a weapon unsheathed. But then the workhorse hit me and the room sounded the way it sounds when you dunk your head under-water, and I spent the rest of the round avoiding getting knocked into darkness. I was stiff and halting and bewildered. I was no worse than anyone sparring for the first time, but I didn't feel that way. I felt as though my core had been exposed for everyone to see, and that I was still that dull slug of pig iron.

Probably I would have done what most guys do: kept that feeling of inadequacy to myself, tamped it down, kept working until I got good enough in the ring I could convince myself the feeling wasn't there. But then it was Jeff's turn. He was sitting on a bench outside the ring. He looked as if he'd already won the fight. I would have laid money down that he was immune to physical insecurities. I was helping him lace up his gloves, joking around, pretending I hadn't felt like a gazelle running from the jaws of a lion just a few minutes earlier. He looked up at me and said, "Fuck, man. I'm really nervous."

I remember the two of us sitting on the bus afterwards, wrung out, spread across the rear seats like dishrags left out to dry. Jeff raised his chin at me and said: "It feels weird, doesn't it?" He meant lacing up the gloves, putting on the boxing boots, going through the drills, getting in the ring. "It feels like playing dress-up. You ever feel that way?"

"All the time," I said.

"Fake it till you make it." He grinned.

From the outside, boxing seems like a contest between two people. But for the fighter, it can be an almost solipsistic experience. Your opponent is a concern, obviously. But to deal with that concern, you first have to deal with the more immediate problem, the thing that's jamming its elbow into your windpipe and trying to suffocate you: your own fear.

Boxing isn't just about beating people up. It's a way of working past fear. To do this, you have to let that fear wash into your lungs and fill your pores. You have to let it press itself against the delicate membranes of your eyes and seep into your ear canals and nostrils. You have to become a willing receptacle. By not resisting it, you take away its fulcrum. Only then — and I've only ever experienced this for a moment or two at a time — will you find the bewilderment washed away and your fear rendered void.

The elusive shimmer stayed out there awhile, shimmering. Sometimes I'd draw closer to it. Sometimes its edges seemed to coalesce, but they'd always dissolve again. Over time, the sum total of my movement was away from it — or it away from me.

It took me a while to understand this. I'd taken it for granted that if I put in the work, made myself into that perfect tool, fate would lift me in her hands and put me to good use. But partway through my undergrad, the click-clack of anticipation began to turn to a rattling anxiety.

Shortly after we started boxing, Jeff and I went out to watch the Tyson–Holyfield fight — the famous one where Mike Tyson took a bite of Evander Holyfield's ear. This was about halfway through my degree. I remember watching the fight with a vague and unfamiliar sense of envy. I didn't want to be a fighter. Still, I wanted what Tyson and Holyfield had: the sense that everything you did — every workout, every meal, what you read and watched and thought, who made up your social circle, the amount of sleep you got each night, your dreams — all added up to something. Something that *meant* something. Watching that fight was the first time it occurred to me that I might never find that purpose.

By the end of school, I was in tip-top shape. I had top-notch grades. I had been volunteering and working part-time while I finished my studies. On paper, I was a go-getter. But I had made no plan to actually go get anything. I hadn't yet applied to grad school. I had no real interest in a career. All around me, people were embarking on their first real job or professional school or an advanced degree. Shortly after that, they'd be on to their first marriage, their first mortgage. Most of the time I was still convinced there was something better out there for me. But my final year of school came to an end and fate hadn't touched me. I felt the way you do when your luggage fails to arrive at the airport. You stick it out by the carousel, watching everyone leave with their bags. You try to convince yourself yours will be along any moment. But you know it's lost.

Classes had ended. Exams were almost over. Jeff and I worked out one last time. He was headed to Halifax to start his doctorate. We shook hands and said goodbye. I got on my bike. I had told Jeff earlier how I was feeling. He was walking away, over one of the immense campus lawns. He turned back and called out to me.

"You just need a walkabout," he said. "It's cool, man. Some of us zigzag."

I got a job tending bar and waiting tables. My shifts ended early in the morning. I trained less and less. It was the hours, I told myself. Plus, I wasn't making enough to afford a gym membership. Really, though, it was that training had become exercise. I no longer felt it was taking me anywhere. I told myself I'd start up again in earnest once I recalibrated the needle.

I had trouble sleeping. I'd wake just before dawn with a dull ache under my ribs. I went to the doctor. He wrote me a prescription for ulcer medication.

Reading was one of the few things that gave me relief from this anxiety. I'd read something good and live inside the book. While I lived there, I could feel it: a path towards the shimmer laid out in words. I'd finish the book and the path would disappear and I'd be alone with myself again, horizonless, wound up like a watch spring.

I thought maybe the solution was to create my own path. I started writing short stories. I didn't have the skill to finish any of them. They tied themselves into knots I wasn't able to undo. The knot inside my stomach grew tighter, too.

I put a lot of work into one story in particular, about a girl from Sarajevo. I eventually threw the story away, but the research became an obsession and the obsession became a distraction and another form of relief.

The Siege of Sarajevo had come to an end a couple of years earlier. The city was still recovering. The survivors had started telling their stories. I romanticized the siege the way you can romanticize poverty if you've never experienced it. I saw it as a tragic situation that nonetheless allowed people of strong character to make themselves more noble. A fire that tempers you and turns you into something pure.

I read everything I could get my hands on. I read about Vedran Smailović, the musician who played his cello in the bombed-out ruins of the city, despite the snipers hidden in the surrounding hills. I read about the staff of *Oslobođenje*, the city's daily paper, who— despite their offices being a favourite target of Serbian mortar units— managed to publish an edition nearly every day of the three-year siege. I read about everyday people who helped secure water, food and medicine for elderly neighbours and expectant mothers. I read about the raging parties that sprang up organically during lulls in the bombardment. They were better than any peacetime celebration; in war, you can drink and dance and fuck like it's the end of the world, because it sort of is. Small, ordinary acts of living had extraordinary meaning in that context.

Years later, I came across a passage by the American journalist Chris Hedges, who had reported from Sarajevo, among other places. "The enduring attraction of war," he wrote,

> *is that even with its destruction and carnage, it gives us what we long for in life. It can give us a reason for living. Only when we are in the midst of conflict does the shallowness of much of our lives become apparent. It gives us resolve, a cause. It allows us to be noble. And those who have the least means in their lives, the impoverished refugee in Gaza, the disenfranchised North African immigrant in France, even the legion of young who live in the splendid indolence and safety of the industrialized world are all susceptible to war's appeal.* [7]

I was one of those youths living in splendid indolence. At night, I'd walk home from work along the empty streets. I'd pass slumbering homes and picture them with their facades blown out, their bedrooms exposed like an architectural cutaway. I envisioned myself thriving in an environment in which suburbia and cubicles and the workaday routine had been rendered irrelevant. I pictured myself armed and resisting the forces that surrounded the city; facing the gangs that ruled the black market; facing elaborate hardships in order to secure powdered milk for my neighbours' children; helping smuggle elderly people out of the city. I imagined myself a household name, someone the young women of the city talked about among themselves. Every day would be a physical challenge and, precisely because of that challenge, full of the meaning my actual days were lacking.

There was something appealing about the fantasy of a broken world. It was something to build up again, something to make more perfect.

A friend of mine joined the local police force after he graduated. We had worked out together nearly every morning for the first couple of years of our undergrad. We'd farted in front of one another and showered together after the gym and made dick jokes and eaten bagged lunches and talked about girls. After my buddy graduated, when I was bartending and he was a rookie constable, he'd occasionally stop by my apartment. He'd bound up the stairs in his black uniform, gun on his hip. He'd rest his hands on his belt. He seemed somehow more solid, more present in the world. I asked him what being a cop was like. He invited me on patrol. Before his night shift, we worked out together at the gym in the downtown police station. I was still strong from training and I threw weights around like they were made of foam rubber. It felt as though the two of us were preparing for battle. It felt good.

That night, we raced down the empty freeway, lit up, sirens blaring purely for fun. We got called to a domestic. Another cruiser arrived at the same time. My friend and his colleague pulled a guy out of the house and arrested him on his front lawn while I stood by and watched.

I pictured myself capturing murderers and rapists and pedophiles. I pictured myself bounding up stairs with a gun strapped to my hip. I pictured myself pulling wife-beaters out of their houses and subduing them on the dark grass of their own front lawns. I liked the idea of putting myself in danger's way, working out in the police gym, training again with real purpose.

I started jogging regularly. I did more push-ups and sit-ups. I took the physical test—a short run and a series of simple exercises. I took the mental aptitude test too. I passed both. I had to wait a couple of months until the next stage of the process, a series of interviews. The anxiety reverted back to anticipation. For a time, the needle seemed to centre itself.

There was a regular at the bar, a small, innocuous man who wore Oxford shirts and wire-rimmed glasses. He was soft-spoken and perpetually alert. He only ever drank a half-pint at a time. He often stepped away from the bar and took discreet calls on his cellphone. It was understood by the bar staff that he had some role with national intelligence. I thought about this path too, and while I was waiting to hear back from the police, I put in an application to the Canadian Security Intelligence Service.

I got a letter from the police. The city had put a freeze on hiring because of a budgetary issue. The letter encouraged me to continue with the application process once the freeze was over. But suddenly I didn't want to. The idea of being a cop fluttered down to Earth and landed at my feet, dull and unspectacular. It was like the feeling you get when you've been with the wrong person and you suddenly realize you have nothing in common but the desire to be wanted — equal parts disappointment and relief.

Shortly after that, I got a letter from the intelligence service encouraging me to continue with my application. I was no longer interested in that either.

At the bar, something was off with the intelligence agent. The cuffs and collar of his shirt had started to wear through. His jacket was shiny at the shoulders and elbows. One night, a lens fell out of his glasses and landed on the bar and spun for a moment like a silver dollar. He picked it up and put it back in its frame unfazed, as if it happened all the time. He started paying for his drinks with fistfuls of dimes. It became clear he wasn't with the government, that we had allowed his delusion to become our collective fantasy, that he probably didn't even have a job. One of the women I worked with realized his cellphone wasn't actually a cellphone but a small cordless handset, the kind of home phone that needs a signal from a base station. Once I clued in, I couldn't help but watch. He'd act for all the world as if he was getting a call, but the little LED never lit up. The phone was incapable of getting a signal, but it didn't matter to him. He still waited for the calls, certain the universe was sending him messages, convinced he was part of some special plan.

My girlfriend was applying to grad school in Halifax. I sent in an application too. We were both accepted. They offered us scholarships. It seemed stupid to turn down that kind of opportunity.

It wasn't a grand purpose. But it was something.

Jeff and I had lost touch. It had been about a year and a half, maybe two, since we had seen one another. Neither of us were the type to call or e-mail. I had sort of forgotten he was on the east coast.

When I bumped into him again, he was still searching for his purpose. That hadn't changed. But something had. You could see it in his eyes. They were deeper now, and darker. They were embers that had singed twin pits into his skull.

My girlfriend and I were walking through Point Pleasant Park, by the water's edge in Halifax, taking in the last of summer before classes began. Jeff was standing alone, leaning against his bike. I looked up and saw him giving me that half smirk of his.

In early November, he invited me to his folks' house, telling me they were having a little family get-together. He was living in their basement. At some point his mother brought out a cake and the room broke out in "Happy Birthday." It was Jeff's thirtieth.

I looked at him and shrugged, as if to say: "Why didn't you tell me?"

He shrugged back and grinned as if to say: "I didn't want to make a big deal out of it."

It was clearly a big deal for his parents. They were glowing like ships' lanterns, beaming with pride for their son. They had invited some of their own friends. When we toasted him, one of his parents' friends turned to Jeff and raised his glass and said something like: "You're in the very prime of your life!" Jeff smiled as though this was an embarrassing thought.

His girlfriend, Sylvie, had brought one of her friends. I think his parents were glad I had come, but it didn't have much to do with me. I think they were just happy he had invited a friend. He had been spending too much time alone.

He was still searching for it in books—or had been until recently. The way of the pen had begun to feel like a dead end. His academic career had started so well, full of hope and momentum. For a while it seemed as if he had charted an unwavering line to the horizon. But then, imperceptibly, academia imposed its own oblique angle. Slowly, it led him off course and into the doldrums. He told me he was having trouble concentrating. He couldn't write. His readings felt useless and irrelevant. There were books scattered across the floor of his bedroom, splayed open like birds shot in mid-flight.

He grew frustrated. He was depressed. He had digestive trouble. He had trouble sleeping. He started going to the Buddhist temple near his parents' house. He met with one of the monks regularly. He shaved his head and took up meditation. He told me he was learning how to empty his mind rather than fill it.

But still, he was training, pushing himself hard. Too hard, probably. He would wake up and do hundreds of squats, hundreds of push-ups. He'd hit the gym and do weights. He ran most days. Five, seven, sometimes ten kilometres. He was still boxing. We sparred once. I hadn't boxed in at least a year. He was fluid and composed. He threw punches and kicks like he was dealing cards, tossing them lightly and effortlessly in my direction. He ducked and slipped and changed direction the way an octopus moves through water. His breath came easy. Mine was ragged. I staggered to the end of the round.

It was a busy time. We saw one another infrequently. We went surfing together in the late summer of the next year. It was one of the last times we hung out. The circles under his eyes were darker than ever. We got longboards from an ex-navy guy who rented gear out of a cube van that smelled of hash oil. The ocean was so cold it made my legs ache like I had a case of shin splints. The water was the colour of slate. The waves weren't high and we were both inexperienced, so mostly we just bobbed and talked and pissed in our wetsuits to keep warm. We lay on the boards and looked up at the sky. It was the same grey as the sea. Jeff said, "I could stay out here forever." He was shivering slightly and his lips were the colour of the water. I had this weird feeling that he might not come back ashore. I could picture him paddling out in the North Atlantic, heading for the horizon. And then, immediately, I felt stupid for thinking that, as if I was being overly dramatic.

Now it doesn't feel that way. He *had* been eyeing the horizon. For some time, I think. That summer, the shimmering thing ceased to be just a shimmer. It finally resolved itself into a clear and definite purpose.

We got together a couple of weeks after that. He looked as though he had stepped out from under an immense weight.

It was a warm day in late August. It had been summer long enough you could almost believe it would continue forever. We had a barbecue in his parents' backyard. We drank a beer with his dad. The day stretched on and on. I left in the late afternoon. The Buddhist temple was on the way to my place and Jeff walked me partway home, across the wide green expanse of the Halifax Commons. There were cicadas in the trees and kids playing and, in the distance, the occasional metallic clink of someone hitting a run with an aluminum bat.

We were halfway across the Commons when Jeff told me that he had put his doctorate on hold. "I've enlisted," he said.

He had been with the reserves for about a year, he told me. He hadn't mentioned this before. He'd joined because it got him out of the house, because it paid and he was sick of being broke. But mostly, because it gave him a sense of purpose. He had decided on the infantry. If that went well, he said, he'd try for the JTF—the Joint Task Force, Canada's elite special forces.

On that walk, I also told Jeff about my own decision. Grad school wasn't going any better for me than it had for him. I had an absentee supervisor. My experiments weren't working. The equipment I was using kept breaking down. What was supposed to take two years was taking me three. I failed a stats class because I hadn't studied for an exam. This was unlike me. It pointed to a bigger issue—that I was in high orbit, unattached to the world I was supposed to be immersed in. I could feel myself pulled further and further out.

I was enrolled in a PhD programme. I told Jeff that afternoon what I had recently told my supervisor—that I'd be leaving the department after getting my master's degree, that I was going to become a journalist.

At the time, I thought of that walk like this: The two of us had come to that particular spot on that particular afternoon along a similar path. And then we parted ways where that path split, both of us moving out into the world, following our respective strengths towards our respective destinies.

But I think I actually felt the way I had watching the Holyfield–Tyson fight—the same mix of envy and sadness. Not wanting to be a soldier any more than I wanted to be a professional fighter but still aching for the seriousness of it. Greatness had brushed past me, continuing on to a place I'd never go.

The last thing I said to him, aside from goodbye, was that the military was lucky to have him; that it would be a better institution with him as part of it; and that if there were more guys like him serving in the world's standing armies, the planet would be a better, safer place.

Several years after he was killed, I talked on the phone with Jeff's father, Russ, about his son's decision to enlist. I got nervous before I dialed, worried I'd be plucking the sutures from an unhealed wound. But Russ was glad to talk. He told me it was how he kept Jeff close—talking about him, listening to the memories of people who knew his boy. And besides, he saw no point in tiptoeing around Jeff's death. It wasn't the kind of wound that would ever heal, not really.

Jeff always had a thing about looking after people, Russ told me. "Especially when it came to his friends. He was not a big guy in the sense of being heavy and thick-boned. But his height gave him that sense he could protect those who were smaller, male and female."

One time, when he was younger, Jeff was out with some friends at a bar. One of the guys he was with said the wrong thing to the wrong guy. The guy's friends gathered around Jeff's buddy like a pack of dogs. Jeff waded right in. He didn't say anything. He just stood there, doing his best Clint Eastwood. Back then, he didn't really know how to fight. There's no way he could have taken on a half-dozen guys.

"He told me his knees were quivering," Russ said. "He almost had to go home and change his pants." Still, it worked. "He was able to stare down those guys. He had that protective instinct all through his teenage years and into adulthood."

That instinct guided him to the military, but it wasn't the only thing at work. To think soldiers enlist solely to protect the weak and innocent, that they're not also in it to some degree for themselves, is like thinking people have sex solely because they want to become parents. Jeff was drawn to the army for the same reason he was drawn to the boxing ring. He liked the idea of testing himself. He liked the prospect of toughening up by facing danger. He liked the thrill and the adventure.

Russ and I talked about that too. Russ had recently retired a major, after a thirty-year career spent, unusually, in all three branches of the military. "The military and the police force," Russ said, "are the two places where you can go and exercise that desire most males carry— learning how to deal with violence, perpetrating violence—and yet do it legally. In a controlled way. In a way that's sanctioned by society."

I'm not suggesting Jeff's desire to protect others wasn't genuine, that it was a pretence so he could get some kicks. That's not what Russ meant either. The desire to protect others, especially friends and family, is one of the most genuine motivations we have. Yet it is fundamentally self-serving. It's hard to see how we could have survived as a species without developing some sort of defensive strategies—especially if raiding was as common among our lineage as the archaeological and anthropological evidence suggests. Protecting those close to us was tantamount to protecting our own bloodline.

In a creature without claws, horns, fangs, which stands on its hind limbs and exposes its vulnerable organs to the world yet lacks the impressive strength of our fellow primates, any defensive adaptations would have to depend on the faculties at which we excel: namely our capacity to make tools and our ability to organize ourselves in complex, cohesive social units that allow us to wield those tools. Success depended on the willing desire to be part of this sort of group—and, vitally, on the belief you were doing the right thing by putting yourself at risk, potentially dying for others.

There's a reason the proportion of men volunteering to fight in hunter-gatherer societies was higher than the proportion of men serving in modern armies—even with conscription.[8] And there's a reason being a good warrior was so highly regarded among traditional cultures: the warrior was vital to the society he was part of. It's easy to look back on traditional warrior culture and do a contemporary version of what nineteenth-century ethnographers did, dismissing it as primitive, as promoting savage and patriarchal values. But for most of our existence on Earth, being good at fighting was a matter of life and death.

Without young men's desire to deal with and perpetrate violence, it would be just about impossible to muster an effective force. The thing that makes being a warrior so dangerous—its potential for extreme violence—is precisely the thing that draws people to it. And the risk warriors are willing to take on behalf of their groups depends on a psychological prerequisite: finding that risk attractive.

It's fairly easy to accept we might have developed a set of emotions and drives that helped us coordinate our collective behaviour in such a way as to protect ourselves. It's less pleasant to entertain the possibility that we developed as an aggressive species bent on expansionism, like our chimp cousins. But then you have to ask the obvious question: who were we defending ourselves from? The obvious answer is other humans.

The unpleasant fact is that, while there is a clear ethical difference between launching an attack and defending against that attack, there isn't much of a utilitarian difference. In either case, winning pays off in terms of reproductive success; losing is a clear dead end for your bloodline. In terms of survival, there is little difference between the altruistic motivation (protecting the people around you through collective violence) and the self-centred (advancing the collective interest through violence).

To function reliably, an army depends on a basic exchange: armies need warriors, and warriors need a noble cause. That cause, quite possibly without exception, is the call to protect one's own—nation and homeland, people and kin. To the young men who heed the call, it feels like a self-evident proposition.

But I think about this: how the young men who make up those armies, the older men commanding those young men, and the government in control of all of them can genuinely believe they are protecting their kin and loved ones from some potentially terrible enemy, some monstrous force, even while they are advancing across a border, even while they are killing innocent women and children, even when they are clearly the monstrous force people need protecting from.

—

IN THE SUMMER OF 1954, Muzafer Sherif took twenty-two boys from their family homes in Oklahoma City and transported them into the wilderness of Robbers Cave State Park.

The boys believed they were attending summer camp, but the camp was a ruse. The staff were trained observers fastidiously collecting data. This was during the early days of social psychology research, when the ethical constraints on such studies were subordinate to intriguing experimental questions, such as: what happens when you allow two groups of boys to form their own societies and those societies are then placed in proximity to one another with minimal intervention? Coincidentally, 1954 was also the year William Golding published *Lord of the Flies*, which asked the same question in a fictional context and came to a similar conclusion.

Sherif, who was then a professor of psychology at the University of Oklahoma, selected his boys with great care—and with their parents' blessings. None of the kids had met. They were all of the same class (middle), religion (Protestant), race (Caucasian) and age (eleven). They all came from stable families; they all had decent grades, average intelligence, and an emotional disposition that, in the idiom of the era, was described as "well-adjusted." These boys loved baseball, fishing, canoeing and making forts. They were, in a word, completely normal—or at least completely representative of the norms of mid-century America.

The boys were randomly divided into two groups. With some careful planning the two groups remained unaware of one another throughout the first week. The boys in each group bonded over cookouts and canoe trips, swimming and wilderness hikes. Each group formed its own social mores and internal hierarchies and soon shared inside jokes and manners of speech.

Once it was clear the groups had gelled, the boys were informed that they were not alone in the woods, that there was another group nearby. Immediately, each team wanted to challenge the other to a game of baseball. Even before the two groups met, boys from one were calling boys from the other racist epithets.

The next phase of the experiment consisted of a series of supposedly friendly contests—baseball, tug-of-war. The matches were grim and tense. The name-calling grew more varied and constant. When they weren't competing against one another, the boys focused their collective efforts on making team flags and T-shirts. The two groups invented derogatory chants to insult one another. They captured and destroyed one another's flags, burning them and tearing them to shreds. They went on night missions and raided one another's cabins. They stole and wrecked one another's belongings. They physically threatened one another. The members of one group, fearing reprisal from the other after raiding its cabin, filled their socks with stones to use as blackjacks. Fist fights broke out.

The outcome of the contests was rigged in favour of one of the groups. When the winner was announced, things escalated. The two tiny armies faced one another in two parallel lines reminiscent of inter-village tribal warfare, a confrontation that devolved into wrestling and fisticuffs. The staff had to intervene, which they did immediately. Sherif had already attempted to run two similar experiments; both had to be prematurely shut down because the boys grew too hostile.

Throughout the experiment, the two groups were given opportunities to hang out and let things cool down. They wanted nothing to do with that idea. They held one another in bitter contempt. Boys literally held their noses at the sight of members of the other group. They refused to eat together. Each group felt the other was morally inferior, full of weak and dissolute characters, and was certain of the inherent superiority and moral supremacy of its own members. Each boy felt proud to belong to his group, despite the fact he had been placed there by chance alone, despite the fact the two groups were, in reality, as indistinguishable as two neighbouring slices of Wonder bread.

Sherif's work inspired a long line of experiments. For the most part, they are less dramatic. Most of them take place in laboratory settings. But what they lack in drama, they make up for in insight. It is precisely because they are so contrived that they're so fascinating. You can, for instance, randomly divide people into two groups by having them flip a coin or randomly assigning them different-coloured T-shirts to wear, you can divide them into groups based on eye colour or hair colour or any other superficial trait, and they will consistently and predictably develop an in-group bias. In these experiments, subjects consistently feel that members of their group are better than members of the opposing group. They tend to see members of the other group as the homogenous and slightly inferior Other.

Even if you don't give these newly formed groups a reason to compete, they'll find one. There's no need to introduce antipathy. In most cases it grows naturally, the way algae come to cloud a clean pool of water. The spores are there from the very start.[9]

—

IT WASN'T THE ROUTINE that got to Jeff after he enlisted. It wasn't the 0500 wake-up calls, the pre-dawn workouts. It wasn't the bedsheets that needed to be folded crisp as origami cranes, the uniforms steamrolled flat and the boots mirror-shined, the place-for-everything-and-everything-in-its-place obsessive-compulsiveness of barrack life. It wasn't the shin-shattering drills on polished concrete, on cracked asphalt; the thirteen-kilometre forced marches in the sun or rain, or the obstacle course, the wall climbs, or having to survive in the woods, getting bitten to fuck by mosquitoes and blackflies, barely sleeping for a hundred and twenty hours straight. Or the push-ups, or sit-ups, or weights. He had signed up for all that.

What got to him were the other men. They weren't bad guys, really. They weren't exceptionally nasty or sadistic. But they were younger than him, and unthinking, and they did what most young men automatically do when you put them in that kind of environment—an environment specifically designed to do this to young men: they coalesced like beads of mercury and merged into a singular body. And as the singular body, they thought the same thoughts, spoke the same way, shared the same mannerisms and inside jokes and linguistic tics.

"It felt weird to him to be part of a group," Sylvie told me. (She and I spoke once over the phone years after he had been killed.) Barrack life meant Jeff no longer had access to his natural environment, which was his inner life. To be in a place where you eat and sleep and shit together meant it was impossible for him to pull inside himself, something he had always needed to do. When he tried, the singular body did what it does when you refuse to willingly merge with it: it made being outside it as uncomfortable as possible. For instance, when the singular body wanted to go out and watch local girls peel off their underwear for money, it insisted Jeff join it. And when Jeff declined, the singular body whispered among its constituent parts that he must be a faggot or something.

Sylvie told me the only fight he ever got in—the only serious fight, other than the scuffles he broke up as a bouncer—was during basic training.

When they got to the point where they were allowed to leave the base, recruits would head for town. There was a bar there—there's probably a bar like this near every military base in the world—a local spot that survives mainly thanks to the steady stream of recruits desperate to pour as much liquor down their throats as possible during their brief R&R. Anyway, Jeff brought Sylvie there once when he was on leave, and she saw him notice a guy at the bar, some local guy. His hackles went up. He told Sylvie they needed to get out of there. It was obvious something had gone on between Jeff and the guy, though Jeff didn't say anything at the time. "I just remember Jeff pulling me out of there," Sylvie said.

Later on, she asked him who that guy was. Jeff told her he had gone out with the singular body one night, making an effort to be part of the group. The singular body got loaded that night. It got loud and sloppy and arrogant and obnoxious.

The townies had formed their own singular body. The guy at the bar had been part of it. It had been drinking too. It had been waiting there, shit-talking the recruits for their shaved heads and Boy-Scouts-on-steroids camaraderie. Jeff wasn't sure exactly how it went down, but at one point he found himself applying a chokehold to one of the townies, his bicep on one carotid artery, his forearm on the other. The townie was headed towards darkness easy as snuffing out a candle when Jeff caught himself. *Oh my God*, he thought. *I can actually kill this guy.*

"It scared the shit out of him," Sylvie told me. "He got caught up in that group mentality. It was a huge reality check for him. He was like: 'This is not what I trained for.'"

—

I THINK JEFF WOULD have liked Christian Mesquida. Jeff was a scholar turned soldier. Mesquida is a soldier turned scholar. He started his academic career late, after, among other things, serving as a tank commander in NATO-occupied Germany in the late 1960s.

Mesquida is an evolutionary psychologist by training, but he likes to refer to himself as a polemologist. I hadn't come across the term until I met him. It was coined—from *polemos*, the ancient Greek word for war—shortly after the Second World War by Gaston Bouthoul and Louise Weiss, two French intellectuals who co-founded the now-defunct Institut de Polémologie.[10]

"Polemologists," Mesquida explained, "can be historians, political scientists, sociologists, biologists, anthropologists and even demographers, as long as they have an interest in making sense of the phenomenon we call war." A central tenet of Bouthoul's premise on war is the belief that there are "underlying regularities" that can explain the cause of all conflict, another reason Mesquida likes the word.

He is a slender man with a trim white beard and a strong French accent. Now in his sixties, he was born in Casablanca and raised in French Algeria. We met in 2012, a little over a year after the Arab Spring had sprung. Tunisia, Algeria and Egypt were still reeling. The entire Middle East and North Africa was a boiling cauldron of civil unrest. I had been covering these stories as a radio producer. Like most people following the early days of the uprisings, I had been captivated by how suddenly these movements sprang up and how quickly they spread.

Mesquida had been following the Arab Spring with professional interest too—but also with a sense of déjà vu. As a boy, he had witnessed an entirely different uprising in the Maghreb—the Algerian Revolution of the late fifties and sixties. "I saw people lying in the gutter with their heads blown off," he told me. We were sitting on a park bench near my place, watching a young couple languidly bat a tennis ball back and forth over the sagging net of a public court.

Broadly speaking, there are two approaches to trying to understand the causes of war. One way is to try to understand the specifics—to see the conflict between, say, Israel and Palestine as the result of a set of historical, political, ethnic, religious, geographical, institutional, economic and ideological circumstances. This approach depends on specialists using their specific analytical and theoretical armamentarium and can be a powerful, intuitive and fruitful way of studying conflict. In this view, the Israeli-Palestinian problem appears a fundamentally different beast from the war in Syria, gang wars in South Central Los Angeles, cartel wars in Mexico or the inter-tribal raids among pre-European Native Americans. Clearly, these conflicts differ from one another. And if you were to ask the men actually doing the killing what it was all about, they'd cite the specifics—the land grab, the repressive regime, an angry god—that, in their minds, justify the use of violence.

The other, less common—and less intuitive—approach is to look for commonalities, those "underlying regularities" among various forms of group violence. This is the purview of polemology.

"We spend so much time focusing on the causes of conflict," Mesquida explained. "That it's about Islam or about the economy or about Israel, when in fact it's also about something deeper. We need to begin to understand that the cause isn't always *the* cause. There's something inherent in group behaviour, especially with males. You give men a cause, a reason to team up—anything—and we'll run with it. And the thing about it, whatever that cause is, we feel it. You *feel* you're a good Muslim. You *feel* you're an important part of the football team. It's inherently rewarding, that feeling."

Mesquida had brought some reading material for me, a satchel of peer-reviewed papers, bar graphs, US State Department booklets and a few magazine articles citing his research. He took out a photograph of a group of Cambodian guerrillas trudging through the jungle carrying automatic rifles, kerchiefs hiding their faces. "We see Khmer Rouge. We see Zapatistas. We should be seeing young men. And, if they have a mask," he said, pointing to a kerchiefed guerrilla, "we know who's behind the mask. Violence has a sex and it has an age."

The theory is that young men, specifically men between fifteen and twenty-nine, are the tinder that ignites wars and civil conflict. Presumably, there is something about the psychological state of young men, some predisposition that makes them prone to participating in group conflict. When there are enough young men in a given population, this state of mind comes to define the state at large.

It's not a new idea. Researchers have been paying attention to the relationship between especially young populations—demographers use the term *youth bulge*—and warfare for a long time.[11] It's not a particularly surprising relationship either. Pick up a paper, scan a news site: the big conflicts tend to be in countries glutted with young men. Gaston Bouthoul referred to a country with a youth bulge as an "explosive structure," a sort of incendiary device "creating the right conditions for war."[12]

Mesquida's contribution was to better describe the inner workings of the incendiary device. To do this, he compared population data from 153 countries between 1991 and 2000, which captured about 99 percent of the human population at the time.

Mesquida confined his study to internal violence, what some researchers call low-intensity conflict—fighting within a nation, often between a state's legitimate forces and groups of young men intent on overthrowing or destabilizing it. It is the constant simmering conflict that defines much of the current geopolitical situation: civil strife, armed uprisings, insurgency, terrorism, cartel wars, tribal warfare and general warlordism. It is the kind of violence that defined much of the Arab Spring. More generally, such violence has been responsible for the majority of casualties—at the very minimum, twenty million—in the last half of the twentieth century and the first years of this one. If the experts are right, it will continue to be the most common form of conflict in decades to come.

Mesquida's overall goal was to see whether there was a correlation between the demographic makeup of nations and the intensity of conflict within them. There was. He found a clear pattern: countries with a large proportion of young men between fifteen and twenty-nine are at higher risk for internal conflict. As the proportion of young men in the general population goes up, so does the intensity of conflict—as measured by the number of casualties. He also discovered what seems to be a tipping point: countries in which young men account for less than 35 percent of the male population show little indication of internal conflict. But, of the 144 states in which young men accounted for more than 35 percent of the adult male population, only five were untouched by civil violence (Kuwait, Taiwan, Singapore, United Arab Emirates and Oman).[13]

Mesquida also showed the impact of youth bulges waxing and waning within a single country. As the demographic composition of a country changes, so does the intensity of internal violence: a country undergoing a baby boom is setting itself up for conflict, while a nation undergoing a demographic greying can probably look forward to a reasonably civil society. Mesquida points to Colombia, which, over the past century or so, has passed through three particularly deadly periods of internal strife.[14] During each of these periods, thousands of Colombians were killed. The country's overall population grew from four million at the turn of the last century to thirty-two million at the turn of this one. Yet Colombia's internal violence occurred specifically during periods when the proportion of young men in the population was disproportionately large.

It's worth thinking about what war actually accomplishes. Cities burn. Flags are struck down and replaced. Dictators get hung by their heels. Democratically elected governments get deposed. Borders change. Treaties are signed and reparations are made. More than all of this, though, war kills a lot of people. Among the casualties are an extremely high proportion of young men. And so war is, among other things, a brutal and efficient way of deflating a youth bulge, a way of burning up the charge inside the explosive structure.

Mesquida argues that the proportion of young men is the single most important factor in determining the severity of conflict in any nation. It is also, he believes, the most overlooked. Part of the reason it tends to be overlooked is that it's hard to differentiate between the impact of young males and the impact of other factors. Countries with young populations have a lot of other things going on—many of which are justifiable reasons for civil discontent: lower levels of education, illiteracy, a tendency towards non-democratic governance, higher levels of unemployment, poverty and economic disparity.

These last two factors—poverty and disparity—are often put forward as a major cause, if not *the* major cause, of conflict. Compare a map of countries with low income levels or high economic disparity to a map of countries with youth bulges and you'll find you're looking at virtually the same map. There is a long line of respectable studies that have found a predictable relationship between poverty and the severity of violence. Mesquida's own research supports this. But he has also teased apart the effects of poverty and the effects of a young demographic. He examined countries with similar per capita GDP and similar levels of disparity. Among these countries, the nations with a large proportion of young men had much more severe internal violence. Poverty and disparity are often flashpoints, the fuse that ignites social violence, as they were during the Arab Spring. But it is not simply the poor, but the minds of poor, desperately frustrated young men, that catch fire.

The idea is that young men are generally trying to make a future for themselves, the kind of future that makes them viable mates. However, having fewer resources than their older and more established counterparts—and with an extremely high proportion of other young men to compete with—violence starts to look appealing. The spoils of war, the honour of potential victory, the chance to dismantle a system that seems rigged against you are all goals worth taking a risk to achieve, especially if you band together with your brothers, cousins, childhood friends and other like-minded young men to wrest control of resources and power. Likewise, the risk of being killed or injured in combat is less horrifying when you have little to lose in the first place and no future to speak of. In many places it's the only feasible way to get a leg up, to become more attractive as a potential mate and, ultimately, achieve reproductive fitness. In his doctoral dissertation, Mesquida argues that "economically marginalized young men constitute what could be regarded as a warrior class within what would otherwise be peaceful societies."

"In the end," Mesquida told me, "the real culprit is human reproductive ecology. It is not the Americans or the Russians or the Viet Cong or the mujahedeen."

Few people, maybe least of all angry young men, link their immediate motivations to the long-term, highly abstract cost-benefit analysis of evolutionary psychology. But that is Mesquida's point—and, more generally, the point of an evolutionary perspective on war: we don't really understand why we fight, not the deep, underlying cause. Not the ultimate cause.

It reminds me of what cosmologists have found: that much of the mass that composes the universe is not subject to direct measure. Looking out at the cosmos with our instruments, we can detect the energy of the electromagnetic spectrum—visible light, X-rays, gamma and infrared.

And from this energy we can derive a picture of what's out there—the stars and galaxies and superclusters all expanding away from each other at some incomprehensibly fast rate. Though, in actuality, it's not incomprehensible; astrophysicists have, in fact, measured how quickly the universe is expanding.[15] The puzzling bit is that this rate of expansion doesn't make any sense—there's not nearly enough mass out there to explain the speed at which the universe is expanding. It would only be possible if there were way, way, way more matter out there—some invisible, undetectable source of mass—that our instruments cannot measure. That's precisely what physicists think is going on. They call this undetectable mass dark matter. The best analogy I've come across is that what we can detect with our instruments is like a drop of cream swirling about in a cup of invisible coffee. The cream is the known universe. The invisible coffee is the dark matter—the unknown, unquantified, undetectable stuff that explains our movement through the void.

When it comes to war, we focus on the visible things too, the things we can quantify and put a name to. The political, ethnic, historical, religious, economic and ideological causes are real. But Mesquida argues that they are part of a larger whole we are not especially adept at perceiving. Behind every cause, he believes, there is another cause, a dark matter that explains all conflict.

Mesquida first published his findings in 1996 as part of his doctoral work. (He had a late start as an academic and, even while getting his PhD, remained at his full-time job as a university librarian.) His findings initially got a lot of attention among policy-makers in orbit around Washington, DC. But then the attention slowly fizzled out.

I spoke with Richard Cincotta, a former Director of Social Science and Demographic Programs in the US National Intelligence Council's Long-Range Analysis Unit. Cincotta's primary research interest is the relationship between demographics and democracy. He is a big believer in the power of youth bulges to shape nations—for both good and bad—and he's a proponent of Mesquida's research. But, as Cincotta explained, it's often difficult to convince people who have spent their careers studying the specifics of a particular country's history to pan out and focus on the abstract data of population demographics and the seemingly non-sequitur topic of biological reproduction.

"In 2008," Cincotta recalled, "I was asked to give a lunchtime talk at a group assembled by the US State Department. It was on the future of the Middle East. Typically, in these meetings, State Department people sit around the outside and just listen. I showed up early and I knew I was in trouble because these guys were saying that the Middle East is what it is and will remain so for the foreseeable future.

"I stand up and say: 'Well, here's my theory, and this is what I see: I see not the Middle East but North Africa—particularly the Maghreb region—changing dramatically. Why? Because they've invested in family planning and they've got fertility down.' I was focused on North African states because, as a group, between 2010 and 2020, they would all move past the median age of twenty-five. So I figured one of them might be a liberal democracy by 2020. I pointed to them—I had a map—and that's what I said. And of course, as a group, they burst out into laughter—one of them [was laughing so hard] he was crying."

Three years after that lunchtime talk, the Maghreb was in turmoil. In 2015, Freedom House, the US non-governmental organization that monitors civil liberties around the world, rated Tunisia a liberal democracy—a fragile and fledgling one hatched by the kind of youth-driven civil uprising Mesquida's research predicts.

Still, there is a missing link in all this that I find both frustrating and compelling. Mesquida's work, and more generally the argument that large populations of young people are a force that shapes nations, makes sense. The data seems, from my inexpert perspective, solid. But, like studying the movement of the cosmos, you can really only see the effect of that force at a macro level. It suggests we too have some form of dark matter without being able to describe it.

But populations are comprised of individuals. If this dark matter is related to some aspect of our reproductive behaviour, some emotional timbre we've inherited as a species, then it ought to be present, at least in some latent form, in many, if not the majority of, young men. Even if you're not part of a youth bulge. No one really knows what that dark matter might look like, what it might feel like.

I have a suspicion it's a shimmering thing that pulls at young men, that makes them invest in their own physical abilities, in their fortune or social position, that tells them to attend to their surroundings, to prepare for the future, to wait for some special sign from the universe, to keep their senses on high alert for their grand cause.

Clearly, there are causes worth fighting for. But let's say for a moment that group conflict did originate as a behavioural strategy that benefited the reproductive fitness of a male kin-group. And let's say that the feeling of purpose young men get by being part of a group, by contributing to the advancement of their group's interest, *does* have its origins in a purely utilitarian behaviour—a behaviour that preceded moral concern, consciousness and reason, that developed in such a way that we found severing the bloodlines of other humans inherently rewarding because it meant ours could flourish. And let's say that being part of a group like this is so rewarding, so primal, it has the capacity to twist the more recently evolved faculties of logic and rationalism in a way that justifies group aggression.

That would be a dangerous feeling. It would allow us to see just about any cause that confers potential power, esteem or wealth as something righteous and pure. That kind of feeling would be capable of reshaping how you see the world and the ethical implications of your own actions. It would be powerful enough to refract the teachings of the Buddha so they could be used, as they have in Myanmar and Sri Lanka, to justify the killing and persecution of Muslims and Tamils. It could convert the teachings of Christ into a call for inquisitions, witch-burnings, crusades, and the persecution of Jews and homosexuals. It could distort Muhammad's words so that passages such as "What actions are most excellent? To gladden the heart of human beings, to feed the hungry, to help the afflicted, to lighten the sorrow of the sorrowful and remove the sufferings of the injured" could be interpreted as an edict to bomb crowded markets full of women and children.

Being a righteous warrior is noble on paper but dangerous in practice. As a young man infused with this feeling, how would you know whether your cause was actually righteous, whether you were actually fighting a just war?

Before he enlisted, Jeff spent a lot of time mulling over the paradox: his growing attraction to the way of the sword; his growing commitment to

Buddhist compassion. On that walk across the Commons, he told me he had come to the conclusion these things didn't have to contradict one another, that there are real threats in the world: groups of armed men wholeheartedly committed to killing innocent people in the name of their righteous cause. To allow this when you can stop it is to neglect your duty to alleviate suffering.

That walk, in late August 2001, is the last memory of any significance I have of the time before the attacks on the World Trade Center. Jeff swore his oath of allegiance on September 7. By the time he was in basic training, the USA had declared its War on Terror. By October, Canadian special forces had quietly deployed to Afghanistan. Early the next year, our regular infantry units were on the ground. That green afternoon now sits on the far side of a gulf torn open by a form of conflict that then seemed new and now seems like the new normal.

Jeff had an idealistic vision of what soldiering ought to be. And he had good reason to think that the Canadian Forces, with its history in peacekeeping and its humanitarian ethos, might be about as close as you can get to that ideal. So I stand by what I said to him that afternoon: the military was lucky to have him.

But it goes the other way too. He was lucky to be able to join that specific military. The scariest thing about the world is that it is full of armies. And those armies are full of young men. And each of those young men is full of some burning cause. Not all young men question their motivations the way Jeff did. Not all armies are created equal; not all causes are just.

Sometimes an army isn't even a real army; sometimes the cause it fights for makes absolutely no sense at all.

—

IN 2005, MAJOR LEAGUE SOCCER, North America's professional league, announced it was awarding a team to Toronto. This was during an expansionist push to make soccer a mainstream sport across the continent. The new team was going to be the league's thirteenth and Canada's first.

Until recently, neither Americans nor Canadians had much interest in soccer. It is not important to either nation's sense of identity, not the way hockey or the gridiron are. Soccer has been seen as boring and sort of effeminate. Professional soccer has no history to speak of and no real tradition in North America. The MLS is only about twenty years old. Many of its athletes, even its best, are either past their prime and on a step-down trajectory out of the European divisions or local players who aren't quite good enough to compete abroad.

Among Major League Soccer's twenty or so teams, the Toronto Football Club consistently sat at the bottom of the rankings for about a decade. In its first season, it failed to win a game. When I first was researching this chapter, it had yet to make it to the playoffs (that changed in 2016). By any objective measure, it shouldn't have been a source of pride.

The Red Patch Boys didn't seem to be troubled by this. The Red Patch Boys are the largest, most organized and most vocal of Toronto FC's official supporter groups. If you care to join them, they will welcome you into the Bunker. As long as you're cheering for Toronto.

The Bunker is what the Red Patch Boys call the two sections they occupy in the southeast corner of BMO stadium, Toronto FC's home pitch. Even if you're not a diehard, they will welcome you as long as you come to cheer and support. In the Bunker, you are part of the whole. In the Bunker, you can ride the ups of collective hope and the downs of collective despair. You can sail on the winds of victory and commiserate in defeat, because the whole is greater than the sum of its parts. In the Bunker, no man is an island, not if he's a Toronto fan.

The Bunker is packed each game, though the seats are rarely used. The official Red Patch mandate, to quote their club charter, is to "be the voice in the stands, filled with passion, pride and purpose for every minute of every game." This involves a lot of standing. Standing and chanting. Chanting and singing. Singing and waving of scarves and stomping of feet upon the metal flooring of the stands.

In the Bunker, you will find red pennants and flags. You will find large men pressed in tight as a Tokyo commute, wearing T-shirts that say *Toronto 'til I Die!* and red Adidas jackets with the Toronto Football Club motto on the back: *All For One*. You will find shirtless men in red body paint. Men beating on the enormous marching drum emblazoned with a stylized maple leaf, the Red Patch Boys' official logo. You will find yourself immersed in the fog of smoke bombs and flares, drowned in the noise of men chanting in unison to the beat of the drum in a tuneless baritone, crying, "THIS IS OUR HOUSE! THIS IS OUR HOUSE!"

Across the pitch, you will see the Montreal flags, blue and white, in the visitors' section. The Montreal team's supporters will be chanting: "ALLEZ! ALLEZ! ALLEZ!"

And you will hear men around you shout things back, like: "Speak English, you fucking cocksuckers!"

You will come to understand that the Red Patch Boys, which in a good year comprise over a thousand members, believe themselves to be a super-massive Voltron whose constituent pieces come together to make a singular body, which, as many of the Boys are fond of repeating, is the Toronto FC's twelfth player. If you stay in the Bunker long enough, you will begin to feel this. It feels like an invisible cord stretching from the stands to the pitch, like the long drogue of a military refuelling jet. Through this connection, the Red Patch Boys provide a high-octane feed to the players doing battle on the field below. This may sound a little overblown, but there's something to it. You can see how a Montreal player is rattled by it when he has a kick from the Red Patch Boys' corner. You can see that he feels the eyes of the singular body on him. It is a screaming, gesticulating body with hundreds of arms. It gnashes its jaws and bellows and throws plastic cups full of beer onto the pitch and sets off flares and sends a column of steam from its collective heat into the cool air. You can tell he finds it unnerving— that it is like being at the zoo and leaning against the pane of glass that separates you from an apex predator.

The singular body can work itself into a frothing mass when it gets going. And it can take a while for the frothing mass to subside. Sometimes, after a game, a writhing limb will break off and form its own cell. It will roam around the stadium parking lot, looking for fuel to keep itself at a boil. You might find it beneath the visitor section, holding its Toronto FC scarves aloft, while the Montreal Impact fans peer over the stadium's edge and attempt to drop streamers and beer down on it. The Toronto mob will chant, "THIS IS OUR HOUSE! THIS IS OUR HOUSE!" and one of them, an indistinguishable young man, pale and thin, will have both hands over his head, giving the

Montreal fans the double finger with such vigour his arms shake as if he were struggling to hold up a tremendous weight.

"You're the armpit of Canada!" he will yell. "Why don't you just separate?"

At that exact moment, a young family from Montreal might walk by, a mother and father and their two young kids, all wearing Impact jerseys. They will see this breakaway limb of the singular body, this writhing tentacle of hatred, and the father will instinctively reach out and put his hands on the shoulders of his children and pull them close.

And later, when the stadium grounds are mostly empty, after the Toronto supporters have dispersed and the stadium authorities feel it's safe to release the Montreal fans—they are typically held back for at least twenty minutes post-game because they too have formed a singular body, and their singular body also forms breakaway limbs—you may run into one of them. They may come around the corner, seven or eight young men, all in their early twenties, all wearing Impact paraphernalia, all looking for something. You can see it in the way they move, in the way their collective movement makes you feel. It is like watching dark clouds on the horizon in tornado country. You can see its multitude of electric eyes flashing like lightning. It is hypnotizing and slightly alluring, like watching a funnel cloud approach. It has its own inevitable motion. It has the power to lift you up and tear you to pieces. And if it gathers enough force, there is very little you can do to stop it.

Of course, you'll find some manifestation of the precursory buildup to group violence at almost any sporting event. And, to be clear, there has not yet been a real, full-fledged soccer riot within the MLS. But here is what is so peculiar about the scene in Toronto:

The Red Patch Boys predated the Toronto FC by almost a full year. Before the FC played a single game, before it had been given a name, before its roster had been worked out, before BMO Field—the stadium expressly built for it—was anywhere near completion, the Red Patch Boys were already a fully realized, fully functional group. Before Toronto had a soccer team, the yet-to-exist team had a full-fledged army of diehard fans.

In the year or so between the MLS announcing the franchise and the team's inaugural game, the men who would go on to form the Red

Patch Boys found one another on Internet chat groups. They staked out a local sports bar and designated it their official HQ. They held meetings. They appropriated a nickname given to the First Canadian Division, an infantry unit that fought in both world wars. Soldiers in the First wore a red patch on the shoulder of their uniform and had a reputation for being so tough that, during the Second World War, German soldiers took to calling them the Red Patch Devils. And, man, how the Red Patch Boys endeavour to live up to their namesake — to inspire that level of fear and awe in their rivals. They strive to be men who act purely and bravely in defence of something sacred, something unambiguously important. Something that means something.

They commissioned custom-made scarves and T-shirts. They had their flag custom-made too. They ordered their emblazoned marching drum. There are pictures of the founding members at the construction site, the skeletal infrastructure of BMO stadium rising behind them out of the frozen earth, gathered around their new, unblemished flag. The Red Patch Boys are all smiles. This belongs to us, say their smiles. This is our house.

By the time the FC played their first game, in early 2007, Jeff was already in Afghanistan. But he knew the neighbourhood of their new stadium since Sylvie's condo was within spitting distance of it and the lakeshore. I'd bet good money he went past it to run along the ribbon of asphalt that hugs Lake Ontario. On a good day, the city skyline reaches up like an ode to the future. The sailboats are a brilliant white against a two-tone blue — cobalt water, azure sky.

Coincidentally, Lyana and I moved to the neighbourhood the next year. We could just make out the green of the stadium's pitch from the roof of our building. Sometimes I wonder what Jeff would have made of what the Red Patch Boys started.

It's not as if they took to the streets and rioted like actual hooligans. Actual hooligans plan forays into their adversaries' territories and ambush fans of the opposing team and place them face down in the street, their mouths agape on the curb so that when they're kicked in the back of the skull, their jaw unhinges and their teeth shatter. At the height of English hooliganism, in the seventies and eighties, some of the more professional hooligan operations would leave calling cards behind that read: "Your head has just been rolled by the Portsmouth Skull Patrol." Real hooligans march en masse through foreign cities. They consider themselves a sort of paramilitary force, and sing racist, ultra-national songs. They burn things and start street brawls.

The Red Patch Boys are to real hooligans what knock-off absinthe is to the original wormwood concoction. They resemble the genuine article but, for the most part, are devoid of the noxious component that makes it so deleterious to public health. Still, it is fun to play at, and if you're a teensy bit prone to self-delusion, you can convince yourself in your play-acting that you are edgier and more risqué than you really are.

But mostly what the Red Patch Boys are interested in is sitting together, eating and drinking vast quantities while surrounded by sporting paraphernalia, and then marching together from the bar where they do this to the stadium, waving their flags, pounding their drum, singing their battle songs. They are not by any stretch of the imagination anywhere close to real hooligans. They simply dress the part.

And that's what Jeff missed out on seeing: a massive game of dress-up.

The FC's first season went unimaginably well. Not in terms of its performance—it was a hot mess—but in terms of its popularity. Season tickets evaporated. The stadium sold out every game, even though the team's owner, Maple Leaf Sports and Entertainment, which also owns the Toronto Maple Leafs and the Raptors, didn't initially have a bead on how to market the team. It took out a local TV ad in which inoffensive residents kicked a soccer ball to one another through the city's various neighbourhoods to a neutered hip-hop beat. The message was that soccer was a friendly sport that would tie us all together but wasn't anything to get especially worked up about.

By its second season, Maple Leaf Sports realized something organic was happening in the stands, best exemplified by the Red Patch Boys, something beyond just sports fans enjoying a new professional team. It recognized the singular body heaving and bellowing in the Bunker. It hired a heavyweight ad agency to come up with a new marketing strategy. The agency's execs had been to some FC matches and had seen the singular body in action. And so they did what any good adver-tiser does: they told a better version of the story Toronto FC fans were already telling themselves.

The new TV spot opened with a red banner fluttering in slow motion against a cloud of battlefield-grey smoke. The music is ultra-minimal-istic—a sustained note here and there; there is no other sound. There are a series of close-ups, all slo-mo, all silent: a statuesque white woman; a good-looking black guy with dreads. They are wearing FC jerseys. They have strips of red cloth tied around their arms and heads, and their faces are smeared with red-and-white war paint. Their mouths are open, yelling, suspended in a moment of intense emotion. Their eyes are serious and supremely focused. They are not smiling. They are concentrating intensely on what is taking place behind the camera, the contest on the field below.

A stentorian voice asks: "What is this call to glory so many pay heed?" It is the Voice of the Ages, the voice of Homer recounting the glory of the Trojan War; Henry the Fifth uniting his band of brothers at Agincourt.

There is a close-up of a lean white dude with close-cropped hair. He is also in war paint. The sleeves of his jersey have been cut off, exposing supremely defined biceps and triceps. He raises his arms skyward. He is yelling too, emitting a silent, slo-mo battle cry. He slowly leaps to his feet, surrounded by tendrils of smoke.

The Voice of the Ages continues: "This sacrifice for others where loyalty runs deep. For on this hallowed ground, red legions shall make it known: this is our house!"

The camera pans out to a medium shot of the crowd. The crowd jumps up in unison. Everyone in the stands is dressed in red and white. Everyone is equally fierce, their eyes equally steely. They are a tribe. This is a battle.

The Voice says: "Concede defeat and go home!"

Around the time this commercial started getting play, our neigh-bourhood became glutted on game days with newly minted soccer fans. The local restaurants and bars hung up red-and-white banners and *All For One* posters. The faces on the posters were beautiful and fierce and smeared with red-and-white war paint. The bars sold themselves as official Toronto FC headquarters. They introduced pre- and post-game drink specials. Beer and liquor distributors got in on it, positioning their products as official fuel for loyal TFC supporters. And so, on game days, our street was awash in tides of red and white, flooding the stadium and then, afterwards, washing back out, drunk on beer and, more meaningfully, being part of something.

These people were not violent or especially rude. They were, for the most part, good-natured and well-behaved. Still, I found it a little unnerving, how quickly and thoroughly a game of dress-up had spread through the city. How people took part in that game without understanding how that game tends to play out.

—

YOU MAY NOT HAVE heard of Muzafer Sherif or the Robbers Cave Experiment, but you almost certainly know what Philip Zimbardo did nearly twenty years later at Stanford University. It's arguably the most famous social psychology experiment ever conducted.

In the summer of 1971, Zimbardo, a newly tenured psychology professor, transformed a corridor in the basement of the university's psychology department into a prison block. With the help of the Palo Alto Police Department, Zimbardo had half of his volunteer subjects handcuffed and brought to the lock-up. The other half were assigned roles as guards.

The prisoners were stripped and dressed in smocks and slippers. They were locked in spartan rooms repurposed to look like cells, bars and all. The guards wore khaki uniforms and mirrored sunglasses. They were each issued a billy club and a whistle.

The experiment was meant to be a two-week study of the psychological effects of imprisonment. It had to be shut down after six days. This wasn't because it failed. If anything, it was overly successful.

After a brief period of collegial awkwardness, the young men took to their roles. The hostilities began shortly after that. The guards, having the authority and the weapons, quickly became physically oppressive and sadistic. The prisoners revolted. The guards clamped down, forcing the prisoners to do countless push-ups. They took away their beds and sprayed them with fire extinguishers. They forced them to piss and shit in buckets rather than giving them access to the washroom. They refused to empty the buckets. They lined them up in the hallways; they humiliated them, bullied them, belittled them and psychologically tortured them. The abuse grew especially bad at night, when the young men who had become the guards believed they weren't being monitored.

In 2003, when photos of American soldiers mistreating prisoners in Abu Ghraib prison were leaked, the parallels to Zimbardo's experiment were uncanny. It was as if the Stanford Prison Experiment were a play that had originally been staged in California in 1971 and was then restaged in 2003 Iraq.

Like the boys in the Robbers Cave Experiment, Zimbardo's men had been selected because they were perfectly average. Like the boys, they were arbitrarily assigned to groups. One of the key findings of the study—the one the experiment is most famous for, and one that continues to haunt many of the men who played guards—is that, every day, average people seem to have an inherent capacity to do nasty, violent things when they are placed in a position of authority. And they feel their behaviour is justified when the people they have authority over are members of a clearly defined group of rivals.

But what I find most disconcerting is that, unlike Muzafer Sherif's boys, the young men in Zimbardo's experiment *knew* they were taking part in a giant game of make-believe. Zimbardo even drank his own Kool-Aid and was acting the hard-nosed warden before he came to and called off the study.

That's the unnerving thing: when it comes to groups of men, there is no such thing as a game of dress-up. Somehow it always turns into something real.

—

JEFF FINISHED BASIC and started training as an infantry officer. Army life didn't get any easier. His commanding officer struck him as a stone-cold prick. Jeff transferred out of the programme along with eight other recruits. He switched over to artillery, which meant having to relearn mathematics he'd never had much of a handle on in the first place. It took a toll. He failed one of his courses.

A year after he enlisted, Jeff and Sylvie split up. I've never asked why. When Jeff told his family it was over, that's all he told them. So I assume, if he were still alive, he'd prefer to keep quiet about it.

When I was still chasing after the shimmer in my waking life, training like a soldier, dreaming of it at night, my assumption was that whatever my ultimate purpose turned out to be, it would be in the cause of justice or benevolence, and would involve the righting of wrongs. I wanted to make myself into a pure vessel so I could be entrusted with that kind of power.

But being pure meant being unencumbered. Early in university, before I met Jeff, I broke up with a woman I was seeing because I felt she was an impediment to my forward motion. During this period, I didn't spend much time with friends, either. I'd show up late and leave early, worried about my studies or getting enough sleep to train the next day. I purposefully kept myself from people. I had far to travel. I couldn't afford the extra payload relationships entailed. I was so miserable at times, I wept. Still, I felt it was worth it, that the misery and loneliness were hardships I had to endure for what I was trying to achieve, whatever that turned out to be.

There's a photo of me from back then, a snapshot taken at a family gathering that, I have to admit, I still find sort of appealing. I was twenty-two. It was the summer I felt closest to reaching the shimmering thing. In the photo, I am smiling, but my eyes are burning and feverish. It is the portrait of a zealot without a cause.

After I had finished grad school and started freelancing, my dreams changed. Jeff would have been somewhere in his officer's training.

Two of the dreams from this period have stuck with me. In one, I'm in a flat in what seems like 1940s France. I'm with a woman, someone I don't know in real life. We're playing a record, the music drifting out our open window into the night air. I look down into the street. A group of young men has gathered under a street lamp directly below us. They're wearing homemade uniforms, dark pants and light T-shirts. They have their hair cropped close. When they move, their muscles twitch beneath their shirts. They look up at me. I crack a nervous joke. They remain serious and aloof. Our flat casts a reddish light onto the cobblestones below. It occurs to me that the men may have mistaken the apartment for a brothel. I am suddenly paralyzed with fear for the woman I'm with. I'm afraid for myself too.

Down on the street, more men have gathered. I smile, trying to placate them, trying to make them believe I am sympathetic to their cause. I am overcome by a new worry: that they have interpreted my smile as an invitation, that they will be here any minute. I turn towards the woman, the fake smile still on my face. I whisper to her through clenched teeth that we need to leave now, through the back door.

In the other dream, I'm lying on my back. I'm naked. A woman I had a crush on in my first year of university is kneeling beside me. This is a real woman, someone I knew in waking life, though not well. She was originally from Afghanistan. I sat beside her in a first-year course on the history of Islam. This was in the mid-nineties. The Taliban had recently come to power. I first learned of them from her; she was part of a group of expats that handed out brochures in the student union building describing the public beatings, the soccer-stadium stonings, the rapes and executions.

In the dream, she and I are in a candlelit room. Her hair forms a tent over my face and chest, and smells of beeswax. I am dizzy with plea-sure. Then the light changes, becoming the harsh, unforgiving glare of a winter desert. We are lying in a shallow gully, naked and exposed. The dirt is baked hard as concrete. A phalanx of men stands over us, lining the edge of the gully. They're armed with automatic rifles, ban-doliers of ammo slung over their shoulders. One of them steps aside. Behind him is another man. This man is crouched behind a tripod mounted with a rotary cannon, a heavy weapon that spews hundreds of rounds in a few seconds.

The woman starts to crawl towards me on her hands and knees. I reach out for her. One of the men fires his assault rifle into the dirt next to her. She freezes. She is sobbing. I hear the whir of the cannon, its barrels spinning like a massive drill. I am trying to think of some way of saving her. The cannon lets out a brief burst of fire. The woman is torn open and flung onto her back, her knees bent awk-wardly beneath her. I am still trying to think what to do. Her torso is a pool of bloody tissue, but she is writhing and convulsing. I am shouting her name and crying and thinking I need to rewind the whole thing and do the something I cannot think of to save her, but then the man with the rotary cannon opens up on her again and her body disintegrates like overripe fruit flung against a wall. Then he opens up on her one final time. It is entirely gratuitous at this point, but the men are attempting to make a point by desecrating her body. One of them climbs down, dumps a jerry can over her remains and lights a match. What's left of her goes up in a sooty fireball that reeks of gasoline.

All my war dreams became saturated with this new anxiety. They were all still paramilitary-themed. They still teased me with some hidden meaning. They still felt interconnected, part of some lost scroll. I continued to write them down. But they had turned on me. In my dreams, I was no longer a young man pursuing his grand cause. The grand causes of other young men were now pursuing me.

I had thought myself special for wanting to be part of something great, for trying to be pure. I realized my desire was exceedingly common. More importantly, I realized that, for a great many young men, the lion's share of their enthusiasm isn't actually for the build-ing up of anything, but for the destruction that precedes the building up. In the eyes of many young men, these two are indistinguishable. The destruction is the fire that allows a forest new growth. It is the creation of a new surface on which to build a more perfect world, even if you never get around to building it.

Before I knew this in a way I could articulate, it came to find me in my dreams.

Things eventually picked up for Jeff, professionally speaking. He made up for the failed course and graduated top of his class, a lieutenant. He was then posted to the Canadian Forces base at Shilo, Manitoba. He trained diligently. He made captain. He earned his Airborne wings. He continued to punish himself with gruelling workouts. In his spare time, he sparred at the local boxing club. He had a reputation on base for being a mature, competent officer. He won his men over with his quiet humour and the example of his own dedication to work.

Things picked up for him personally too. He and Sylvie started seeing one another again in late 2004, after being apart for a couple of years. When he got leave, he'd visit her in Toronto. He asked her to move west so they could live together. She couldn't. She had her job. It didn't matter. They were old hands at long-distance.

Whatever darkness and solitude Jeff had been struggling through, he had made it. He told Sylvie a fog had lifted, that the way ahead seemed clear.[16]

He was put in charge of a troop within an artillery unit—C-Battery— at Shilo. His job was to prepare his soldiers for Afghanistan. Canada was part of the NATO-led security force whose job it was to scrub Taliban and al Qaeda fighters. Canadian Forces, especially its infantry, had played a major role in the offensive that deposed the Taliban in 2001. But Talib fighters still lingered in pockets, especially in the south of the country. The plan was to send C-Battery to Kandahar province sometime in 2006, where it would provide fire support for the infantry units.

The goal was to cleanse the area once and for all so reconstruction could begin in earnest. It was dangerous work. But it seemed worth the risk. There was genuine optimism that the country might be built into a real and lasting democracy. Kids were going to school and getting vaccines. Farmers were tending their fields. Women were safer. The public executions had stopped.

It was what Jeff wanted to be doing—protecting people who couldn't protect themselves, helping make the world a better place.

In Halifax, I met Lyana. We fell in love. We moved in together. We met one another's families and eventually got engaged. We had a wide social circle and promising careers. Life made more sense than it ever had. I felt for the first time I was more or less where I was supposed to be.

The shimmering thing had dipped out of sight and settled somewhere below the horizon. Still, I'd feel it from time to time: walking down the street on a spring day; eating with friends; at the seaside with Lyana. It would tug at me gently and ask me, uninvited, why I was wasting my life on trivial things, why I was neglecting my training and allowing my body to lie fallow.

I taught myself to do some version of what people who learn to cope with schizophrenia do: I tried my best to ignore it. I told myself it was a sort of inward mirage. I told myself that living a good life takes discipline too. A different form of discipline, a commitment to attend to the world around you—the actual world and not some made-up Platonic realm. Most importantly, it took discipline to not attend to the spot where the arrow once burned and the needle once twitched, even though it is an opening that does not close.

January 2006. Jeff and Sylvie were stronger than ever.

Jeff was stronger than ever too. He was thirty-six and still training daily. The figure of carved wood had transformed itself into steel. He had entered the Mountain Man competition the previous summer— the Canadian Forces' answer to the Ironman. He finished in the top 10 percent. Still, he wanted more. He had tempered himself. But he had yet to truly test himself.

I asked his father, Russ, if he got the sense Jeff was satisfied with his choice to become a soldier, if it gave him the sense of purpose he had been looking for.

"I think he enjoyed what he was doing," Russ told me. "He was satisfying a professional quest." But Russ also said that Jeff was starting to worry he might not actually get to Afghanistan. There's often a long line to get to the front line, especially in relatively small conflicts. Jeff was considering a re-muster, retraining in a field that would give him a better chance of combat. Russ arranged for Jeff to meet with a couple of former colleagues, guys in military intelligence.

Jeff put in his application and was accepted. His commanding officer at Shilo didn't want to see him go. He asked Jeff to remain with C-Battery and sweetened the deal by recommending Jeff for a training course to become a Forward Operations Officer—a FOO in militarese. The job entails calling in enemy coordinates to the artillery units behind you. This often means accompanying the infantry to the very tip of an assault. It means looking into the proverbial whites of your enemies' eyes. It means you are in the front line. It is a position of extreme danger.

It was too good an opportunity to pass up. Jeff stayed on. In February, he got the green light. He was told he'd be deployed in less than a year—a six-month rotation in Kandahar.

That same month, on Valentine's Day in fact,[17] he and Sylvie decided to try for a kid. The fact that he would soon deploy made

Sylvie feel sick. Jeff told her he had to go, that it was something he had to do. He told her that once it was over, he'd sign up for a desk job. He'd push for a transfer to Toronto. They'd get a place together. They'd do the things normal couples do, all the stuff they had missed out on—taking walks, going to Starbucks and Costco, waiting in line at IKEA and Walmart. It sounded nice to both of them. It sounded like heaven, actually.

Sylvie was pregnant within a month.

Ry was due in November 2006—three months before Jeff was scheduled to fly to Afghanistan. He was in intense training at Shilo when Sylvie called from Toronto a few days before her due date. The baby was breech. The doctor had scheduled an immediate C-section and Sylvie told Jeff she needed him there. He hustled for permission to leave. He was told he needed to concentrate on what was in front of him. He made ready to go AWOL, whatever the consequences—even if it might prevent him from being sent over. It didn't come to that. His commanding officer went to bat for him again. He got Jeff a pass. Jeff arrived in Toronto in time for the delivery.

Ry was healthy, Sylvie too. Jeff was lying beside her, the three of them crammed into a hospital bed, when he turned to Sylvie and said: "We have a purpose now. Can't you feel it?"

I know this only because Jeff's maternal aunt wrote about it in a book she published about him after he was killed. When I read what Jeff said to Sylvie, I had to put the book down because I was sobbing.

I called Sylvie to ask her about that. I asked her what she thought Jeff meant.

"I've always wondered the same thing," she said. "I know it's only a few words. I remember Jeff saying, 'Now there's a purpose,' and I thought it was a beautiful thing to say, but I always thought there was purpose before. I never heard Jeff say that about his quest to be a soldier. He was always incredibly proud of what he was doing. But, to me, this was on a deeper sort of level."

Lyana and I had moved from Halifax to Toronto in 2005. We got married. Our careers took off. Lyana started her medical residency. I got

freelance work at the national broadcaster in TV and radio. I won a journalism fellowship and spent the better part of a year working in London,
Spain, Australia and India writing for a prestigious publication. Lyana
joined me in India for close to six months. She volunteered at a couple
of hospitals in New Delhi. We travelled the country. We got lost together
in the crowds and the heat and the monsoon rains. We sat holding hands
at the Taj Mahal at moonrise. We slept in a stilted house in a jungle full
of tigers and elephants. We watched the sun rise over emerald rice patties
from a houseboat in Kerala. We fell in love all over again.

All that moving around seemed to settle something in me. I didn't
feel the pull of the shimmer at all.

We moved back to Toronto. We bought our condo—the one a few
minutes away from BMO stadium. I landed a permanent position as a
radio producer, covering science and current affairs. Lyana finished her
residency and began her practice. We started thinking about children.

We had no trouble getting pregnant; staying pregnant was the problem. Before there was even a heartbeat, the tiny thing inside Lyana
would sputter and go out. This happened several times over several
years. We tried schedules, ovulation sticks, hormones, pills, specialists.

We eventually tried in vitro fertilization. Lyana took hormones to
boost the number of follicles she made. I beat off in a room down the
hall from our doctor. The lab made a cocktail of our effluvia. In the
end, we ended up with one viable embryo, our one chance.

Lyana lay on a table in the procedure room, thick-tongued from
fentanyl, her feet in stirrups. I sat on a stool next to her, gowned and
masked, holding her hands, my forehead against hers. She was sweating. The doctor inserted a long, thin cannula. A moment later it
appeared on the ultrasound screen, dark and grainy, the kind of image
beamed back from a space probe. The embryo was a tiny white dot
inside the glass tube. The doctor slowly flushed the cannula with saline
solution and the bright spot moved down the tube and into the dark, a
single star hanging in the vault of Lyana's interior.

I had that feeling you get when you watch a rocket launch—the
momentary exhilaration that comes from witnessing a tremendous
force suddenly unleashed, hurtling itself towards some distant, unimaginable spot.

We waited two weeks. We tried not to think about it. When the time came, we bought a urine test. Lyana sat on the toilet. We waited a minute. It was negative, but the instructions said it could take up to three minutes. We waited a couple more minutes. I counted the drips from the sink faucet. It was still negative. We waited another five minutes, and then I threw it in the kitchen trash. Half an hour later, I dug it out again. It was still negative.

I thought about the tiny star and how it had felt for a moment as though we were on our way to some new place. Now it seemed different. It was still like looking at a star, but the way you look at a star from Earth: as something impossibly distant and forever beyond your reach.

It occurred to me that when we are younger, we believe we are the projectile, the thing that is intended to reach its mark. We aim at a distant target only to realize later, mid-flight, that we're not the projectile at all. We're the catapult. We are catapults flinging catapults forever into the future.

—

I WAS ON THE BUS to Montreal for two minutes before I wanted to get off again. I had a window seat, looking down on the Red Patch Boys as they loaded their flags and banners and their enormous marching drum into the undercarriage. It was seven thirty in the morning. I was nursing a coffee. Several of the Boys were suckling on king cans. I wasn't sure if they had just started drinking or had been at it all night. The sky was turning from salmon roe to glacial blue. The city was freezer-burned and hadn't yet started to thaw. It was March, still hockey season.

One of the Boys sauntered aboard wearing a blue-and-white Maple Leafs cap. Somewhere behind me, another Boy groaned like he had been kicked in the gonads. "Aaaawwwwgghhh!" he cried. "Aaaaawwwwggggghhhhh!" I turned around because I genuinely thought someone was hurt. But it was just a fleshy guy in his late forties, hamming it up. "Aaawwwgghh!" he moaned again. "A blue hat! A BLUE hat! Aaawwwggghhh!"

Blue and white are the colours of the Toronto Maple Leafs—the team the Red Patch Boys reflexively turn their allegiance towards during hockey season. But they're also the colours of the Boys' number one rival, the Montreal Impact. It was hockey season, but it was also the first day of soccer season. The groan was a parody of internal confusion: the shock a Red Patch Boy undergoes seeing one of his own wearing white and blue. The guy doing the groaning laughed. The guy in the Maple Leafs hat laughed too. But jokes usually make you laugh because they contain some grain of truth, and the truth at the heart of that joke wasn't especially funny.

I was wearing a brand new red-and-white Toronto Football Club scarf and T-shirt. I had never bought a single item of team paraphernalia in my life, but I bought these for this trip because, if you're not wearing red and white in a group of men who have pledged their allegiance to those colours, and if those men are drinking and things take a particular turn, it can very well end up being your gonads on the line.

We stopped at a mall near the nuclear power station in Pickering to pick up more Boys. One of them hauled himself onto the bus and then flung himself from seatback to seatback like a dying cephalopod, trying to work his way to the rear of the bus before he croaked. But there were beer coolers in the aisle, impeding his way. He sank onto one of them, assumed the airline safety posture, and puked into a plastic grocery bag. The bus filled up with the stench of beer vomit and masticated pizza.

By a quarter after nine, the smell of puke had been replaced by the bright, yeasty scent of freshly opened beer cans. Most of the Boys were drinking now. A DVD was playing on the overhead screens—interviews with some of the Toronto players and coaching staff. The volume had been muted and no one was paying attention.

A heavy-set guy in his mid-thirties stood up in the aisle, swaying as we moved down the highway. He was one of the capos, whose job is to rally the troops before a match—summon the super-Voltron of the singular body and keep it laser-focused throughout the game. His voice crackled through the PA system:

"Oh, when the Reds!" he sang. "Oh, when the Reds . . ."

The other Boys joined in:

"OH, WHEN THE REDS GO MARCHING IN!
I WANT TO BE PART OF THAT NUMBER!
OH, WHEN THE REDS GO MARCHING IN!"

I did not want to be part of that number. But it was too late for that now. Someone handed me a beer. I drank it quickly and took another. The Boys chanted for a while then grew quiet again. We were still hours away. I started to nod off. The guy behind me tapped me on the shoulder.

"When do we get to the Highway of Heroes?" he asked.

Whenever a Canadian soldier is killed abroad, the body is flown to the military base in Trenton, Ontario. Then it's driven the 170 kilometres west along the 401 to the coroner's office in Toronto. In the early 2000s, when Canadian soldiers started dying in Afghanistan, the overpasses that span the highway from Trenton to Toronto would spontaneously fill up with people, a lot of them firefighters, paramedics and cops—but also just regular citizens. They'd drape the red-and-white Canadian flag across the overpasses. They'd wave smaller flags and salute. The cops and firefighters would roll the cherries on their vehicles as the convoy passed beneath them. In 2007, the year Jeff was killed, the government officially designated the route the Highway of Heroes.

I told the guy behind me we were already on it.

"This right here?" he asked.

I nodded.

He sat back and looked out the window. The sky was corrugated steel. "Cool," he said. "That's so fuckin' cool."

—

I DIDN'T KNOW Jeff had been killed for several years. I was in India when it happened and not reading much news from home. Every once in a while I'd wonder how he was doing. But it had been a long time since that walk across the Commons.

It never occurred to me he might be in danger. I had run into his sister once, about a year after he had joined up, and had asked her how he was doing. She said fine. And so I sealed him off like that, like a snow globe in my mind. He stayed up there, on a shelf, undisturbed, fit, moving forward with purpose. Healthy. Whole. Perfectly fine.

I started thinking about him again when my life had become peachy, or ought to have been. When I had a good job and stylish condo, a loving partner, nice colleagues, interesting friends; when I had good food and good clothes and had seen some of the world; when I ought to have been optimistic and grateful. Instead, I'd get side-swiped by an intense emptiness. It hit me hardest in the mornings, walking to work, especially on airy summer mornings when the city was bright and people were moving with purpose, carving out the future, making the world a better, more sensible, more civilized place with their collective productivity. None of it—the future, the sensible, civilized productivity, a sense of purpose— meant much to me. They were things I wanted to feel but didn't. It was like a form of colour-blindness. I knew other people could perceive some vivid and attractive future, but I couldn't make it out.

I wasn't unhappy, exactly. I didn't have trouble getting out of bed or being motivated to go to work or see people. I was in constant motion. I made things: a bike, bookshelves, meals for friends and family. I renovated our condo. And I found those things satisfying. Just not as satisfying as I felt they ought to be.

When I started thinking of Jeff again, when life was good and gentle and inexplicably unsatisfying, this is what preoccupied me. Had I chosen a path that left a part of myself untested? I wanted to know whether Jeff had tested himself the way he had set out to do. And if he had, on the other side of that test, had he become content and whole?

I searched for him on Facebook. Facebook came back with a page called *In Memory of Jeff Francis*. I was confused. I scrolled and clicked for a while because I thought there was some mistake. The Internet is huge. His name isn't that rare. But there was no question. There were pictures of him. And pictures of Sylvie, and pictures of him holding Ry. It was Jeff.

The snow globe in my head fell to the floor and shattered.

—

WE DROVE OVER THE FARMLAND that marked the final stretch of Ontario. The fields were white tinged with rust. Outside, everything was frozen, but inside the bus, things were heating up. The Capo was back at the mic, leading the Boys through the Red Patch version of "Sloop John B."

"FOR-EVER WE LOVE YOU SO!" they sang. "THROUGH ALL OF THE HIGHS AND LOWS! THIS IS OUR CREST!"—some of the Boys pounded their chests like mountain gorillas—"AND THIS, *THIS* IS OUR HOME! WE WANT YOU TO KNOW! WE WANT YOU TO KNOW! FOR-EVER WE LOVE YOU—WE LOVE YOU T.O.!"

You can explain what goes on between the Red Patch Boys and Montreal supporters as the new face of an old sporting rivalry, an extension of a long-standing grudge played out in different eras between different teams: the Maple Leafs and the Canadiens; the Argos and Alouettes; the Blue Jays and Expos. You could explain the sporting rivalry as a manifestation of a more profound discord that has expressed itself in different ways between French and English Canada throughout their shared history: the chauvinist barbs; the referendums on separation; the occasional terrorist act; the repressive anglo policies; the drastic French language laws. You can look back to the Plains of Abraham when the British sacked the French at Quebec. Or further back, to the Hundred Years War. Or to the countless other wars in which the French and English hefted broadswords and shot arrows into one another's chests in the name of God. Or back into the foundational mists of the Norman Conquest. Before France was even France. Before the English were really English. You could explain the aggression and the rivalry as the cumulative result of historical momentum, something that began to flow long ago in the blood of battle and continues to trickle along in the sweat of physical competition. You wouldn't be wrong about any of this. But none of it explains what happened in Columbus, Ohio.

Montreal got a Major League Soccer team in 2012, five years after Toronto. During those five years, the only other MLS team anywhere near Toronto was Ohio's Columbus Crew. Since there wasn't yet another team in Canada, Columbus was touted as Toronto's main rival, even though there was nothing between the two cities—no history, no bad blood. Just polite indifference. But the MLS had a game to hype and seats to fill in both stadiums. It was relatively easy to bus the teams and their respective fans seven hours between the two cities.

The initial matches between the Toronto FC and the Columbus Crew were about as big-time as high school games, and only marginally more exciting. That didn't matter to the Toronto fans. For the 2009 season opener in Columbus, the TFC's third season, the Red Patch

Boys organized an army of about two thousand supporters. They travelled to Ohio in buses, drinking and singing and devouring the all-you-can-eat buffets at cut-rate travel hotels. They hired a single-prop plane to fly over the stadium trailing a banner that read GO YOU REDS! They jumped and bounced in the stands. They raised and lowered their arms and shook all over like Pentecostals receiving transmissions from the Holy Spirit. They held their FC scarves aloft like Charlton Heston revealing the stone tablets in *The Ten Commandments*. They sang themselves hoarse and threw smoke bombs down onto the pitch and tore out a section of the metal guard railing and threw it on the awning directly below their section and stomped so hard on the aluminum bleachers several had to be replaced.

After the game, the Toronto supporters were let out at the same time as the home-team crowd. The Toronto boys came out chanting: "C-R-E! W! SORRY EXCUSE FOR A FUCK-IN' CREW!" The Americans countered with: "U-S-A! U-S-A!" As the crowd flowed out of the stadium, the two groups mixed like the currents of merging rivers. A few of the Toronto guys waved their scarves and gave the Americans the finger and shouted things like: "You guys have to *pay* for medicine!" Some of the Columbus fans called the Canadians commies. A few of the boys dressed in red and white stepped up to the boys in black and yellow and started yelling, "Pussy!" and "Faggot!"—which inevitably drew in more black-and-yellow reinforcements. Which in turn drew more red-and-white reinforcements, until the crowd had divided itself along a front, where guys started to shove one another. One guy tried to grab another guy by the hair. Another guy tried to put a rival fan into a headlock while other, more sensible guys got between them and yelled, "Whoa! Whoa! Whoa! Let it go, man. Let it go!"

This was happening on an upper concourse. Down below, on the stadium grounds, there was a bigger problem. A few Columbus fans had been shaking hands with the fans from Toronto, giving one another big, back-slapping hugs. Then a couple of Toronto guys tried to grab one of the Columbus fans, all in good fun. Something changed. It was like what happens when you sprinkle iron filings on a magnet: suddenly there was a red-and-white cluster and a black-and-yellow cluster. Then the drums started in and the red-and-white flags and the black-and-yellow flags were waving. Guys flipped the bird back and forth and tried to grab one another's scarves. Toronto started singing "THIS IS OUR HOUSE!" over and over again and the Americans sang back "FUCK TO-RON-TO!" Within seconds, the two clusters grew to about fifty guys each. Then the cops showed up, wearing white caps like old-fashioned milkmen. A few security guards joined them. They knew what was about to go down.

At first, there's a space between the two crowds, a ten-foot gap maybe. And no contact, just the hoisting of scarves and waving of flags and hatchet-chopping of arms. But the crowds continue to grow until there is no longer a gap between them. The outer edges merge, and as they do, a current passes through the crowd and it moves as one organism, the way a school of fish turns on itself. And then it is like fry breaking the surface of the water—arms popping up and diving back down into the crowd as the boys exchange rapid punches. And then it changes again, as though a large predator has taken a lunge at that school of fish. In a matter of a second the crowd is gone, emptied out from the middle so that all that's left are a few confused men hiding their eyes in the crook of their elbows, coughing and spitting up mucus. The white hats have hit them with pepper spray.

We crossed into Quebec and onto the Autoroute du Souvenir, Quebec's version of the Highway of Heroes. We crossed the lead waters of the Ottawa River onto the western shore of the island of Montreal. The bus picked up speed. We were in the industrial outskirts now, three-quarters of an hour from the stadium.

The Capo was on the mic again. "Let's get into Montreal and *fucking wreck the place!*" he screamed.

The Boys broke out in: "LET'S GO FUCK-ING MEN-TAL! LET'S GO FUCK-ING MEN-TAL!"

I wondered whether any of them were actually up to a fight. I had done a quick inventory when I got on the bus. There was only one guy I thought might be good to go, a tall, raw-boned fellow with a heavy five o'clock shadow. He started off quiet, but the more he drank, the more he laughed—a caustic bark that made me uneasy. I was constantly aware that he was somewhere behind me, beyond my field of vision. There were maybe another half-dozen guys who might follow his lead.

But mostly it was just the Boys talking the talk. I'm not sure any of them knew this, though—that they were merely playing dress-up. In the safety of their warm cocoon, in the haze of their beer-induced confidence, some of them likely were convinced they were rumbling towards a rumble. Many of the Boys saw Columbus as a trial they had endured, an ambush on enemy turf. It became a story to tell themselves about themselves. In their minds, the Red Patch Boys had been in battle together. In their minds, they were an expeditionary force.

—

IT'S WORTH CONSIDERING that most groups of men who band together to fight for a cause no longer comprise blood kin.[18] And so it's also worth asking this: if it's no longer blood that holds us together in battle, what is it?

Humans have no built-in tricorder to determine whether we're related to the people around us. Instead, we have emotions. Spend enough time around someone you have something in common with and there's a good chance you'll grow close. The mechanism is mundane, but the effect is profound. This is what allows us to adopt children and love them as if they were our own offspring. It's why long-term friends eventually become extended family. Anthropologists sometimes call these kinds of relationships *fictive kin*. As far as our emotions are concerned, there's no discernible difference between blood kin and fictive. And for good reason.

For most of our history, familiarity was strongly correlated with shared blood. The people you grew up amongst, lived with, ate with, hunted with and faced danger with had a pretty good chance of being either genetically related to you or tied to you through marriage. Familiarity is a solid-enough proxy of consanguinity that kids who are not genetically related but grow up in close confines—say, children raised in a communal setting such as an Israeli kibbutz—tend to be less likely to be sexually attracted to one another later on in life than kids who were raised apart, despite the shared values and experience. This is called the Westermarck effect, after the Finnish anthropologist who discovered it, Edvard Westermarck. Presumably, it evolved as an emotional trait that helps us to avoid inbreeding.

Likewise, for most of our history, you could be fairly sure the people with whom you shared physical traits, who dressed like you and spoke the same language and sang the same songs, were members of your kin group. And so maybe it's not surprising we have a knee-jerk tendency to view a superficial trait—skin colour, an accent, a team jersey, a red flag—as sufficient criteria to divide ourselves into Us and Them.

Here is what very few men, least of all the Red Patch Boys, will put into words, likely because it smacks of homoeroticism: fighting is an act of physical intimacy. The only other physical acts that involve as much bodily contact and intense emotion are sex and child-rearing. It's a strange comparison, and I'm not suggesting they feel the same or are morally equivalent. But when men unite in battle, they develop an affection for one another that is as specific to that form of physical intimacy as eros is to lovers or filial love is to a child.

You might join a particular army because you believe in the cause that army stands for. But in the heat of battle, causes become abstractions that boil off amid the fear and confusion. What remains is more visceral: the desire to protect your band of brothers, even if, strictly speaking, they are not your blood.

—

IN JULY 2007, Jeff had been in Kandahar five months. He had one more to go. Ry was nine months old.

There was a mission in the works. A big one: eighty Canadian infantry soldiers, sixty Afghan—a sweep through a village suspected to be a Taliban stronghold. Jeff's commanding officer wanted Jeff and the rest of C-Battery atop a nearby mountain, a peak with a view of the village, from where Jeff could coordinate artillery strikes and gunships—if it came to that. Jeff was worried about the people he was supposed to be protecting.

Jeff looked over the maps and thought about the lay of the land, then paid a visit to his CO. He told his CO he was concerned. There were early morning fogs that rolled down through the valley. He'd be blind up on the mountain, looking down on grey wool. He suggested an alternative: he'd leave C-Battery on the peak and join the convoy. He'd ride with the infantry over the mine-infested roads, through the village and back, eyes wide, radio channels open, ready to call in fire from above. His CO liked the idea. He praised Jeff for his thoughtfulness and his commitment to the team. He gave him the go-ahead.

The mission was a dusty goose chase. There were no Talib in the village. No weapons cache. No ambush. Jeff rode back with five other guys, soldiers with Princess Patricia's Canadian Light Infantry. They travelled together in an RG-31 Nyala, a mine-resistant armoured vehicle that wasn't nearly resistant enough. It drove over a stack of buried anti-tank mines. The earth opened up. The air turned into a fountain of fire and sent the armoured vehicle nine storeys up into the atmosphere. Jeff and the other men were dead before it hit the ground again.

I try not to think about what a blast like that does to a body. I've looked it up and then, afterwards, tried to ignore what I learned. I like to think of my friend as broad, tall, strong. I like to think of the half smirk, the warm smile, the way the muscles of his face sat over the bone, the way the skin lay over those muscles. I try to keep him like that, all the parts together, the snow globe restored and back on the shelf in my mind.

There's another way I think of him too. Once, under laughing gas, I had my wisdom teeth extracted. The surgeon injected me with anaesthetic and then prodded my gums. Because I didn't react to that surface poke, she cut swiftly and deeply to the bone. The anaesthetic had only numbed the superficial tissue and I felt the knife enter the deeper layers with exquisite clarity. My eyes welled up and I let out an agonizing moan — except I didn't quite perceive the sensation as agony. The laughing gas distorted things so that, even though I was in pain, it felt as though it was happening at a distance. The surgeon immediately stuck me with more local.

On the way to the clinic, I had been listening to a podcast on mathematics in which the narrator had been explaining the origin of the number line. He suggested, as a way to visualize positive and negative integers, picturing an infinitely large sphere. Encircling the sphere like an equator is the number line, with zero facing you. To the right run the positive numbers, to the left the negative, both curving along their respective courses to that unreachable place on the far side, the point at which the infinitely positive and the infinitely negative meet. This is what I had been thinking of when the surgeon cut into me. In my befuddled agony, I pictured my pain as something situated along the negative line, some moderately high number that would continue to curve back higher and higher. Then the anaesthetic kicked in. The pain gave way to relief, and relief became pleasure. But in my head, under the gas, I thought of the pain as having continued along its course and out of sight towards the place where the infinitely negative merges with the infinitely positive and becomes something beyond either pleasure or pain.

I try to think of the blast that way: as an instantaneous journey through infinite pain to a place of infinite peace. And when I do, I can almost think of Jeff as having done what he set out to do: tracked it down, chased that shimmering thing to the horizon and grabbed hold of it. And then, like the proverbial angel, he struggled with it, the two of them falling over the edge and into the void.

—

THE BUS CRAWLED INTO Montreal's downtown core. Mount Royal rose from the heart of the city, its bosom covered in a bib of dirty snow. I could see the inclined tower of the Olympic stadium looming over the grounds below. A police cruiser pulled into the lane next to us.

"It's the Po-Po!" someone cried.

Another guy broke out in a bad version of N.W.A.: "Fuck the po-lice!" he sang. "Comin' straight from the underground!"

The other Boys joined in and made it into a chant: "FUCK THE PO-LICE! FUCK THE PO-LICE!" Several men were banging on the windows. The officers in the cruiser remained oblivious and eventually pulled away and took an off-ramp, moving on to something of real concern.

—

BEING CHILDLESS MEANT I could devote myself entirely to myself. To my hobbies and interests and personal ambitions, and to Lyana's.

We talked about travelling again, maybe starting a non-profit. I quit my job to write full-time. Lyana threw herself into her work. Each time she had got pregnant, the hope of what was to come grew inside her. And each time she miscarried, or when the IVF failed to take, that space remained inside her, silent and empty. Her work meant delivering children to other mothers. She never resented this. She never grew bitter or jealous. She told me about the joy and excitement of each new mother—and she was genuinely happy for them. But at night we curled up on the couch and gorged on TV, back-to-back episodes of a boilerplate sitcom—a group of sassy friends helping one another through life's ups and downs. Each down followed by a comedic up. Sometimes you need simple stories for complicated reasons. Lyana would cry while we watched.

We talked about adoption. We got on a list. We talked about trying again naturally, but Lyana needed a break. She had opened up too many rooms inside herself. She was afraid of creating more emptiness.

I started doing martial arts again, Brazilian jiu-jitsu, Jeff's favourite. It gave me something to look forward to every day. It gave me a touch of that old feeling of moving towards something. We went out. We ate with friends. We shopped. We improved our home.

Lyana's biological clock had been focused and insistent. It was different for me. As a childless adult, you hear people with kids say how having a kid changes everything. It can get annoying, because it seems to imply that all of your childless plans and ambitions are trivial and insubstantial compared with the sacred cause of raising one's offspring. But slowly I began to hope there might be something to this.

It was New Year's Day. We were at my in-laws' for a family dinner. It had been six months since we last tried IVF. Our two nephews, both of them toddlers, were playing on the floor. I thought of Lyana and me sitting around the same table in twenty years, still childless, still watching TV sitcoms at night.

I looked at her and said, "Why don't we try one more time?"

—

THE STADIUM GROUNDS were frozen. There were little mats of ice fused to the concrete walkways. The white paint of the stadium was peeling away in huge strips. Beneath was water-damaged concrete.

The idea was to march in as a cohesive unit, a united presence, a powerful force. I stood around while the Boys unpacked their flags and banners and drum. It was like watching a drunk tying to yank up his pants after being startled awake. The Boys milled around, forgetting where they had put things, then remembering. Their flags came undone and got caught in the wind and flapped in their faces. A group of us, a dozen or so, finally rallied and stood in a shivering cluster. The Boys broke out in a chant and began their march.

A group of Montreal fans walked by. "Montreal is first!" one of them shouted in a heavy French accent.

"Speak English!" one of the Boys yelled back.

The men's washroom in the visitors' section was jammed with red and white. Outside, there were lineups for beer. Inside, there were lineups for the urinals. A short, stocky guy in front of me was carrying a cowbell and had a pair of boxing gloves slung around his neck.

I looked down the row of pissing men. The guy who had puked on the bus was taking a leak. He had a plastic cup of beer resting atop his urinal. He schlepped over to the bay of sinks and threw water on his face.

One of the other guys at the sinks looked up at his own reflection and barked: "TIC-TAC-TABARNAC!"

The rest of the washroom bayed back automatically: "WHO THE FUCK'S THE IMPACT!?"

The line moved forward. I stood pissing next to the guy with the boxing gloves.

"You plan on using those?" I asked him.

He smiled. "Like they say in the UFC, this time it's personal."

—

I WANTED SOMETHING TO go down in Montreal, something like Columbus, for my own weird reasons. I had been training a lot over the past couple of years, sparring and conditioning and weights. I didn't look the way I did when I was younger. I was bulky and heavy, but I was fast and stronger than I'd ever been, and my conditioning was excellent. Training was different now too. It was no longer a way to get someplace magnificent. It was a thumb in the dyke holding back a vast emptiness.

It made me feel better about myself. On a good day, I'd walk down the street, past the clubs and bars, and the doormen would notice me, size me up and maybe nod. I wasn't ripped like a bodybuilder, but I was dense and I carried myself like I could handle myself. I felt I could.

I'd think about that quite a bit. Handling myself. I had been writing this book and training and doing little else except spending time with men whose dangerous desires had led them to some pretty bad places. I was, on the whole, a little less impulsive than I had been when I went after that purse snatcher or head-butted the guy on the subway. I told myself I was less inclined to start something. But the desire was still there. I enjoyed thinking about where I sat in the hierarchy of tough guys. Whenever I walked down the street, I scanned the crowds, categorizing the men around me into nice guys and bad guys; and then into guys I could take care of and guys who might take care of me.

I came out of the gym one night after sparring for a couple of hours. I felt good. The gym was on a busy street in Chinatown. There was a lot of traffic but few pedestrians. It was dark. I thought I heard the sound of breaking glass. I looked around but didn't see anything. I started to walk home. Then I heard it again, this time for sure.

I ran across the street, towards where I thought it was coming from. I felt a little flutter of excitement, like leaping off a precipice into the dark. Every muscle in my body was alive. My peripheral vision expanded. I was aware of cars approaching to my right and left simultaneously.

I got to the other side of the street and was standing in the gap between the hood of a parked car and the rear end of a minivan. The minivan had tinted windows. There was movement on its far side, someone pulling something out. Then he was standing in front of me. Both of us in the tight space between the parked car and the minivan. Traffic swished directly behind me. He was about a foot shorter than me. Somewhere in his forties, Asian. He was holding a backpack. He was looking directly at me. I was not particularly alarmed. I had slung my gym bag over my shoulder. I let go of it. It hit the ground behind me at the same time I hit him, a left jab that landed between his eye and his mouth, just to the right of his nose. I felt the skin give and the bone rise up to meet the bones of my knuckles and then spring back again. It sounded dull and earthy. He crumpled against the rear of the van. I caught him and brought him down on his back. I had the back of his head cupped in my right hand, his right sleeve in the vise of my left. My right knee was on his solar plexus. He tried to get up. I sank my weight down. His face went the sick purple of a bruise.

"You move," I said, "I do this." I took the pressure off. He gasped as if I had been holding him underwater. He tried to get up. I sank my weight back down. He let out a wet grunt as the air left him. He tried to take another breath. His eyes began to bulge. His tongue was like a creature trying to escape the anoxic environment—it shot out of his mouth and squirmed for air. I had maybe half my weight on him, placed just right. "Don't move," I said. "You understand?"

He nodded.

I took the pressure off. He gasped for air and started squirming again. His free hand wandered behind him. I thought maybe he was reaching for something in his rear pocket. By this time, I was starting to wonder what he had smashed the window with. I drove my knee into him and grabbed the back of his head and pulled it so that his chin touched his chest. I sank my knee in deeper. Panic washed over his face. His eyes moved left and right, looking for escape. He looked up at me. I'm fairly sure it occurred to him I could kill him if I wanted. It occurred to me. His mouth moved as if he was trying to say something, but there was no air for him to make a sound.

"Are you going to move?" I asked.

He was looking somewhere beyond me.

"Are you going to move?" I asked again.

He shook his head.

The cops had to lay newspaper in the back of their cruiser because he had shit his pants. They knew him. He was a regular in the lock-up. He had three stolen laptops in his backpack from his efforts that night.

While I was giving my statement to the cops, my friends from the gym came out and gathered across the street. They were laughing and yelling and giving me the thumbs-up. As I was walking away, one of the cops called me back. The owner of the van had come out of the restaurant. The cop nodded at me.

"You owe this guy a thank you," he said to the owner of the van. The guy shook my hand.

I told Lyana a redacted version when I got home. I told her I had been
minding my own business, that I had crossed the street and was stepping
onto the curb when I ran into the guy, chest to chest, and that I dropped
him out of fear—that I was worried he might have a weapon or try
pushing me out into traffic. I didn't mention hearing breaking glass or
trying to find out where the sound was coming from. Or crossing the
street with the flutter of excitement. I didn't tell her that I felt I had
been given a gift in the form of a man I could punch and get away with
punching. I told her I was glad I caught the guy but sorry I had had to
use force. I didn't tell her that, while I walked home, I felt satisfied with
myself, even though the guy was a lot smaller than me, even though he
was just a sad, petty thief and a crack addict. I didn't tell her that the
satisfaction washed over me like anaesthetic and for a few minutes I felt
buoyant with purpose.

—

THE RED PATCH BOYS were chanting and singing. They were jumping up and down in the visitors' section. I could feel the concrete floor
trembling beneath us. I had visions of stadium collapse, of being
crushed beneath slabs of cement, trapped among the bodies of several
thousand large men.

At the far end of the field, the Montreal supporters were displaying
blue-and-white striped banners, huge vertical columns that descended
thirty or forty feet from the upper stands into the section directly behind
Montreal's net. They looked like a cross between a Barnett Newman
painting and the banners at the Nuremberg rallies. An enormous hori-
zontal sign that spanned the front of their section read, in French:
"YESTERDAY TODAY AND FOREVER!"

The players stood in formation on the field below. The national
anthem crackled from the loudspeakers, tinny and distorted. Several of
the Toronto fans sang with their hands over their hearts. Throughout
the anthem, guys around me shouted: "FUUUUCK QUEBEC!"

I had an aisle seat, next to the stairs. There was a steady conveyor belt
of men making trips to the beer stands and back. The beer inside me had
gone flat. I was suddenly profoundly tired. More than anything, I wanted

to sit down and close my eyes—but I couldn't. Not in the Red Patch section. It would have been like taking off your pants during Mass.

Directly in front of and behind me, guys were waving flags. They fluttered all around me, brushing the top of my head. Towards the front of our section, someone had mounted a flag vertically between two parallel poles so it remained flat and legible to the Montreal fans across the field. It was a stylized fist with a raised middle finger. Below the fist, block letters read: "IMPACT MERDA!"

There was a ripple in the stands.

"What the fuck is this guy doing?" someone yelled.

"Get out!" someone else shouted.

I turned around. A man in his late fifties was walking down the stairs into our section. With him was a boy in his early teens. They were father and son, or maybe grandfather and grandson. They were wearing Impact scarves and the man also had a Montreal hat. He had a beer in each hand and came ambling down the stairs, the boy behind him. They were both looking around, as if trying to find their seats. I thought maybe the older guy had got drunk and forgot where they had been sitting. He seemed surprised by the sudden appearance of all the red and white in his section.

The Toronto fans had quit looking at the field and had turned around to see what all the fuss was about. The man and the boy slowly walked down the stairs. A thousand pairs of eyes followed them. They got to the front of the section and then turned around and slowly started walking back up the stairs. I wasn't sure whether they had made a mistake or whether it was an act of derring-do and, having counted coup, they were now headed back to their territory. The man was smiling nervously.

"That guy has balls!" someone near me said.

A woman behind me yelled, "Get him out!" She said it the way you might if you saw a blind person about to step out in traffic.

Someone yelled, "They send in their elderly and their children."

The man and the boy were nearly beside me when the guy next to me stepped out into the aisle and blocked their way. He had sat next to me on the bus, where he had been one of the more sober, more thoughtful guys. He was in his forties. He had several university degrees and a good job and a family. Now he stood there, not letting the man and boy pass. They tried to walk around him. He moved to the side and blocked their way again. They sidestepped. He blocked them again. Then he got out of their way and came back to his seat, looking up at the crowd, laughing, as though he were a matador and the old man a bull deserving pity.

A security guard came down the stairs and escorted the man and the boy out of our section.

Someone yelled after them: "FUCK YOU!"

—

WHEN OUR DAUGHTER was born, I rocked her and babbled to her. I sang to her and held her against my chest. I sat like this for hours while she lay on me in the unconscious drift of perfect sleep.

Neither Lyana nor I slept much. Part of this was the three-hour circadian rhythm of a newborn. Part of it was that sense of excitement you get from travelling to an exotic place, the pleasure of being transported somewhere fresh and unknown: being exhausted from the voyage but wired because you don't want to miss anything—the air and light and food and smells. My daughter slept on me while Lyana slept on the couch. I dozed, but not deeply enough to dream. I'd fall into a sort of twilight consciousness where words and images blurred.

I had spent the last couple of years writing about male violence. There were, as always, bad things on the news. Groups of young men killing for their cause. I pictured the three of us, me and Lyana and our new child, in an isolated cove where calm water lapped softly at a pebbled beach. It was night. Surrounding the cove were high cliff walls. The sky was clear. The stars were brilliant. Everything was gentle and soft. Soft and safe. And then I pictured Lyana and me standing on the shore while our daughter drifted gently a few feet from shore in a small bark, like Moses in his basket. We could reach out and touch her. But I knew, even just weeks into her life, we were already preparing her for the larger world. She would continue to drift out, slowly at first. We would continue to see her, to speak to her, to hold her. For a while, we would continue to be able to wade in when she needed help, swim out if she got in trouble. But eventually, she would move beyond the cove.

She would set her sights, as she should, on some distant thing, some place we could not go, a point on the horizon that was hers alone, across a vast ocean of possibility. And danger.

I would have liked to talk to Jeff about fatherhood. I didn't have the sort of epiphany when my daughter was born that he had had about Ry. I was captivated by her. I adored her. I was fully present as a parent, changing her, comforting her and, as she grew older, preparing her food and feeding her. But I wasn't hit by the same clear sense of purpose. At least not right away.

If her birth had been a voyage to some far-off land, I kept wondering when we might get back home and resume normal life, when I'd be able to concentrate on my work again, get back to the gym, see friends, get enough sleep to think straight. One of my best friends, the father of a four-year-old boy, told me he kept waiting for normal to return too, until one day he realized the five-thirty wake-ups, the diapers, the feeding, the constant vigilance and cleaning up were the new normal. That there was no going back. The thing he had previously called his life now sat in the corner of his new life, a steamer trunk of former ambitions, perpetually waiting to be unpacked.

I had to let go of jiu-jitsu. I barely got any exercise. I was so sleep deprived for a while I couldn't write comprehensible sentences. I walked through my neighbourhood pushing my daughter in her stroller. I was overweight and deconditioned, a writer who couldn't write, a man in middle age who had given up his day job, unshowered, in dirty clothes. I envied the young professionals, well-dressed, trim, flitting about me unencumbered on important excursions into the future. Fatherhood seemed like a cage that would not allow me to move forward with my life.

One afternoon, about four months after my daughter was born, I left a coffee shop where I had been trying to write for several hours. It was snowing big heavy flakes. I was crossing the street. I had the light. A car came through the intersection and made a left directly into my path. I jumped out of the way just as the driver slammed on the brakes. He came to a stop exactly where I had been standing. I was beside the driver's window, the side-view mirror resting against my hip. Traffic around us stopped. I couldn't make out the driver. There was too much snow. But I could tell he was avoiding looking at me. He started to pull away. I stepped back. He was still extremely close. I was suddenly livid. I turned on the ball of my foot and unleashed a left hook into the driver's side window. It evaporated.

"Fuck you," I said into the space where the window had been.

The driver was an older guy, my dad's age, somewhere in his mid-sixties. He was too stunned to say anything. I was surprised too. I had just wanted to rattle him. I hadn't intended to break the glass. I hadn't expected an old guy. I'd pictured a guy my age, my size. His mouth was open, speechless. There was a pebble of glass hanging on his lower lip like a speck of food. Beneath it, a tiny bead of blood. There was shattered glass across his lap too, piles of it, like someone had doused him in ice chips. There was a man next to him and someone in the back and, also in the back, a child's car seat. It was empty.

"You almost killed me," I said. I walked away. He drove off.

For a moment, I felt justified. I had righted a wrong. The city is full of aggressive drivers. Pedestrians are always getting hit. I hadn't hurt anyone. I had probably taught him a valuable lesson. I looked down at my hand. My knuckle was bleeding slightly. I thought about the blood on the guy's lip, the glass on his lap. I thought about the empty car seat. I thought about the glass going into his eye. Or the eye of whichever child sat in that car seat. I thought about my daughter in her car seat. I thought about all the possibilities in the world. All the danger. The vast ocean of it.

The car stopped down the street, at the next light. A man got out and marched down the sidewalk. There were a lot of pedestrians and he didn't seem to notice me. I thought about just going home. Then I thought about the driver, the look on his face. I worried he might have a heart attack. I kept seeing the pebble of glass on the guy's lip and the little bead of blood and the car seat.

I crossed the street and came alongside the car. There was a middle-aged woman in the back seat. She saw me before the driver did and started yelling and shaking her head. I crouched down beside the car, but I kept my distance. I put my hands up as if I was surrendering. She was still yelling. I made the time-out motion with my hands. I motioned to her to roll down the window. She shook her head. I put my hands together like I was praying. She rolled the window down a crack.

"Go away!" she said. "I'm scared of you. I don't want you to hurt me."

"I'm not going to hurt anyone," I said. "I wanted to apologize."

She rolled up her window and said something to the driver. He leaned over to roll down the passenger's window about a quarter of the way.

"I wanted to make sure you were okay," I said. "And to pay for your window."

"We already called the police," he said.

"Are you okay?" I asked.

He nodded and rolled up the window.

I stuck around, waiting for the cops. A few minutes later the guy who had marched down the sidewalk came back. I saw him from a distance. He saw me too. He was short and stocky, but he came at me directly. He was in his early fifties. His face was bright red.

I held my hands up in the surrender motion. "I wanted to make sure you guys were okay," I said. "I was an idiot. I didn't mean to smash the window."

The guy looked at me for a long second. Then he shrugged and his face changed. "Yeah," he said. "I've done that kind of shit before. I have a temper. He's not like that, though." He meant the driver. The woman in the back seat rolled down the window. "It's okay," the stocky guy told her. She rolled the window back up. She was his wife, the driver's sister.

It took the cops over an hour to get there. The temperature had dipped and the snow had accumulated and there were fender-benders across the city. I got coffee with the stocky guy and brought it back to the car. His wife wasn't talking to me, but the driver had relaxed. I asked about the car seat. He told me he drove his grandkids to and from school each day. I told him I had an infant daughter at home. I couldn't feel my feet. They were frozen. My arms and legs were tingling too, but not from the cold. The whole time, I was thinking about bail and hearings and a criminal record.

The cops showed up and talked to the driver for a long time. One of them questioned me. He was curt. I told him my side of things. I told him I had been an idiot. He listened to me for maybe thirty seconds. He walked away and said to the driver: "You can press charges if you want, in which case we'll arrest him." I thought about my daughter.

The driver shook his head.

I paid to have the window replaced. The driver sent me an invoice from the body shop. His name was Daniel. He had requested a used window to save me some money. I wrote him back to thank him. I apologized again.

"Don't blame yourself," he wrote back. "I understand sometimes people are under pressure from work or too tired, and do some unreasonable thing. Relax and play with your daughter."

—

MONTREAL GOT THE FIRST point on a penalty shot, thirty-three minutes into the game. The guys around me were saying how retarded the Montreal refs were. Forty-five minutes in, Montreal scored again. The frustration in our section turned to anger. On the field, Toronto tried to rally an offence. One of the shots hit Montreal's crossbar and ricocheted off. The Montreal fans were feeling supremely confident, bouncing up and down in their section like a pan of Jiffy Pop going off. Then the bouncing became coordinated. The Impact's fan section started the wave. It spread outward and raced counter-clockwise through the stands. A swell of blue-and-white pride surged towards us. It hit the seawall of our section and broke apart in a furious spray of red-and-white arms, middle fingers raised.

Toronto scored a penalty. There were twenty-two minutes left, enough time to make a comeback. Someone set off a flare a few rows behind us. Higher up, someone lit another one. Smoke came rolling around my shoulders and drifted down towards the field. All around me, the Boys were chanting and yelling and waving their flags. They were jumping up and down in unison. The ground was quaking under my feet again.

There were five minutes left. Directly behind me, someone lit another flare. The smoke was thick and scarlet. The Toronto fans pulled their scarves over their faces like an army of marauders. The clock ran out and the refs issued four minutes additional time. Toronto pushed but couldn't rally. The clock counted down. Toronto fans sent one-fingered semaphores towards Montreal. Montreal returned them. The whistle blew. Montreal fans kept cheering. The Boys continued to shoot disconsolate fingers towards the Montreal fans.

We were kept back about fifteen minutes as the rest of the stadium emptied out. The rear of our section looked down into the mezzanine. There was a crush of Toronto fans leaning over the balcony, taunting the Montreal fans below.

"MONTREAL'S A SHITHOLE!" they yelled, and "YOU'RE ALL SHITE!"—pronouncing *shit* the way they do in the UK, singing it the way preschoolers might. Another group of Toronto fans were chanting: "LET'S GO SU-PER-SEXE! LET'S GO SU-PER-SEXE!" Club Super Sexe is a Montreal landmark, the most famous of the many downtown strip joints along rue Sainte-Catherine.

I was one of the first back on board the bus. A few of the Boys were outside smoking. One of them was the tall, raw-boned fellow with the evil laugh.

A couple of Montreal fans strolled by. The tall guy said something to them. I couldn't hear it. One of the Montreal guys said something over his shoulder but kept on walking. The tall guy stepped towards them. The Montreal guys turned around. The raw-boned guy was much bigger than either of the Montreal fans. He stuck out his chin and spread his arms. It was a way of saying, "You want some of this?" The guys from Montreal kept walking. They saw the same thing I had seen, the thing simmering inside the tall guy. He called after them, and when they didn't respond, he flicked his cigarette into some dirty snow and got on the bus.

He looked at me. "Fuck-ing fag-gots," he said in a sing-song, and walked back to his seat.

—

HERE IS THE FINAL impossible-to-answer question I'll subject you to: if chimps are unaware of why they fight—unaware at the ultimate level of evolutionary utility, but also at a more proximal, subjective level—if they are devoid of the sort of rationalizations and justifications we deploy, our religion, politics, ideologies—what *is* the subjective feeling that prompts them to leave their troop and start a raid in the first place?

While they are on the raid, butchering some unwitting neighbour, they are, presumably, subject to the flutter of excitement that accompanies a covert and dangerous operation. But just before the

raid, what is it they feel? Presumably they don't raid on an empty stomach; or when their own troop is in danger; or when they're in the middle
of copulating; or sorting out intra-troop tensions. It is a need that seems
to come out of nowhere, something beyond the exigencies of mere survival. An alpha will commence a raid by, say, dragging a large branch
around and calling attention to himself with loud vocalizations. Other
chimps heed the call and follow him. They work themselves up. They
head into the forest and make their way towards enemy territory. The
impulse seems to arise in the middle of everyday activities, when things
are copacetic, when the chimps have everything they need to be content.
And so my question: is contentment not enough for chimps either? Are
they also seized by a relentless emptiness? Is that the shared grain of sand
evolution has placed under the eyelid of our genetic lineage—the thing
that bothers us, an itch that turns destructive when we try to scratch it?

Do chimps sometimes start wars to cure themselves of boredom?
Do we?[19]

—

WHEN OUR DAUGHTER WAS eight months old, Lyana went back to
work full-time. She started her own practice and was soon overworked,
setting up her clinic, hiring staff, buying equipment, recruiting patients.
It was a long commute for her and long days for both of us. I looked
after our daughter while she was gone and tried to write at night. It
didn't work very well—the working-at-night part. Sometimes I'd go
down to the parking garage and try to write in our car. Often I just
stared into the distance and tried to gather thoughts that never came.

One evening, I went to Walmart with my father-in-law. I had to get
diapers or new pyjamas or shampoo for the baby. We were standing in
line. The line was long and slow. I was one of the unwashed among the
great unwashed. A man in front of me was with his young son, buying
something for his boy, a video game or a console accessory. The cashier
scanned it. The man said the price wasn't right, that it was on sale.

The cashier said, "Sorry, sir. That's what came up."

The man pulled out a flyer. He pointed to the item he was purchas-
ing. "What does that say?"

"That's last week's flyer," the cashier said.

The man pointed at the flyer again. "What does it say here?"

"Sir," said the cashier, "I can't do anything about it. It's last week's flyer."

The man turned to the cashier serving the next line. He showed her the flyer. "What does that say?" he asked her. She looked puzzled.

"Sir—" began the first cashier.

The man cut her off. "All I'm asking—" He was growing louder. I felt the flutter in my stomach. My legs and arms were tingling. "All I'm asking is: what does this say? Can neither of you tell me? Can neither of you read?"

He was a big man. My height. Well over two hundred pounds. A few years older than me. Not in particularly good shape. I stepped up to him and said, "Friend. Why don't you bring it down a notch? They're just trying to do their job."

"All I'm asking," he repeated, "is what does this say?"

"Come on, man," I said. "You're being obnoxious."

"Who are you?" he asked. He was wearing glasses. Behind the lenses his eyes stopped moving like two fish suddenly aware of something beyond the aquarium.

"You're making a fool of yourself," I said.

"Who are you?" he asked again.

"Listen, man," I said. "They can't answer your question. Go to customer service. You're picking on two women who aren't allowed to talk back to you."

"All I'm asking—" he started.

"You're not asking anything. You're being an obnoxious prick."

"You're being a prick!"

"No," I said. "You're definitely the prick. I'm just letting you in on what everyone else here already knows." I motioned to the line behind us.

The two fish darted back and forth and then settled again on me. He leaned in close to my face.

"Don't be stupid," I said. "There's not a fucking thing you could do."

"Come on," my father-in-law said. "Let's go."

I remembered my daughter. I felt the eyes of everyone on me. I walked away.

"You're the prick," the man said to my back.

"Better than a coward." I opened and closed my hand at him, signifying he was all talk.

In the car, I asked my father-in-law not to mention any of it to Lyana.

Lyana and I took our daughter for a stroll down Queen Street West. It was high summer. The sidewalks were packed. Pop music blared out of the stores. The street was a happy confusion of sunglasses and young, tattooed limbs and pastel colours. We were singing to our daughter. She faced us in her stroller, laughing.

We stopped at a light. The sidewalk was jammed with pedestrians. We couldn't move. The stroller was embedded in the crowd like a freighter frozen into an ice floe. I made silly faces at my daughter. The crowd bucked sideways. A couple of squeegee kids, a young man and woman, muscled through it. There was shouting. Behind them came a middle-aged guy in a golf shirt, who was yelling at the squeegee kids. They had done something to his car. He had left it idling at the stoplight to pursue them. The squeegee-kid guy turned around and told the golf-shirt guy to fuck off. The middle-aged man lunged at him.

"No!" he yelled. "Fuck you!"

The squeegee kid didn't back off but stepped closer. The crowd bumped and swayed like a plane passing through turbulence. There was some contact between the young guy and the older guy. A hand on a shoulder maybe. A shirt collar in someone's fist.

I reached out and put my hand on one of their shoulders. "Guys," I said, "there's a baby right here."

They kept yelling at one another. I started to say something else when someone yanked hard at my arm. It was Lyana. She had pulled the stroller backwards, out of the crowd, and was now pulling at me.

"Get out of there!" she said. "Are you nuts?"

It hadn't occurred to me I was doing anything wrong. It didn't feel risky.

As we walked away, I tried explaining that I just wanted them to calm down and pay attention to what was around them.

"Do you really think putting your hands on them would calm them down?" Lyana asked. "You don't think that might escalate things? You of all people? You know how guys are when they get like that. Why do you have to get involved? It's not your fight! It had nothing to do with you!"

"It did," I said. I motioned to our daughter. "I didn't want them hurting her."

"Me neither," Lyana said. "So I *moved* her. Didn't you think about doing that? Getting out of the way. Don't you ever think about that? Honestly, it's like you think it's your mission to get involved with those kinds of things."

The three of us moved out of downtown that winter, to a rental unit on a quiet street in the north end of the city, at the end of the subway line, closer to Lyana's office. Her job and commute were eating at us. Our lives felt like a shoreline being gobbled up by a rising tide.

Lyana was still busy trying to keep her new practice on the rails. We hired a nanny to take care of our daughter during the day while I took care of packing, moving and setting up our new place. We had to renovate our condo so it could compete in Toronto's insane real estate market. I worked with the contractors—hard physical labour, tearing out tiles and tubs, ripping up flooring and laying new boards—pushing them to finish quickly so we could sell the place and I could get back to my real work. I kept discovering new levels of fatigue. I felt like one of those robotic subs that drifts down into the trenches of the ocean floor. The fatigue worked on my brain, compressing it into a minuscule, unthinking singularity, a black hole that swallowed up meaning and ambition. One night I was at a hardware store, paying for a shower stall that we were putting into the condo, and I couldn't remember how I got there. I genuinely thought I might be dreaming.

I was so busy trying to stay afloat in our new life, I literally didn't have a moment to write. My ambitions felt trapped in that streamer trunk tucked in the corner of my life. I thought about tossing it overboard and drowning them so they'd quit pestering me. I grew increasingly frustrated. I was angry most of the time. The littlest things set me off—a spill, stubbing my toe, running out of milk. After Lyana said living with me was like walking on eggshells, I bought an audio course on mindfulness.

Easter was coming. I took my daughter to the grocery store early one morning so Lyana could sleep in. She had just done an overnight shift at the hospital. There were foil balloons over the cash registers, bunnies and duckies and chickies, like miniature parade floats. My daughter pointed at them. "Boon!" she cried. "I want a boon!" I paid and pushed the cart, with her in it, under one of the balloons. She gazed up, enthralled.

Behind me, a loud and angry voice was yelling at someone. I turned around. There was a middle-aged man berating one of the guys at the customer service desk. His milk was rotten. He wanted a refund.

Did he have a receipt? the customer service guy asked.

No, he didn't have a goddamn receipt! He shouldn't need one. Smell the goddamn milk! He didn't care if it was the store's policy. He wanted fresh milk.

Something about the tone of his voice chipped away at the dense, unthinking black hole of my brain like a chisel. I walked over to him and told him to calm down.

"This guy's being a bully!" he cried. He meant the customer service guy, who looked impossibly bored, as if his life was defined by a long, though not especially cruel, hardship.

"You're being the bully," I said.

The sour-milk guy stepped back as if I had slapped him.

"In fact," I said, "you're being a fucking asshole."

His eyes popped open.

"You should get out of here," the customer service guy told me. "It's not your problem."

I suddenly realized I had left my daughter in the cart behind me. She was only a couple of steps away and strapped in, but my vision had closed in around the sour-milk guy and I had forgotten her for a moment. I turned around. She was sitting in the basket, still admiring the balloons.

—

THE BUS RIDE BACK from Montreal was quiet. Most of the Red Patch Boys were hungover. Many of them slept the entire trip. One of the guys asked me about this book. I told him it was a book on why men fight.

"It's because of pussification," he said.

I asked him what he meant.

"We're all pussies," he said. "Guys, I mean. Modern guys." He told me he had been listening to Joe Rogan's podcast. Rogan played Joe Garrelli the electrician on the 1990s sitcom *TalkRadio* and later hosted *Fear Factor*. These days he's better known as a UFC commentator. "It's like Joe says," the guy on the bus went on, "men can't be men anymore. He calls it 'the pussification of America.' It leads to all sorts of bad shit. Guys need an outlet. They need to be men."

"Is that what this is all about?" I asked him. "The road trip, cheering for your team? An outlet?"

"Totally. It's a way of getting it out of your system. It's harmless," he said. "Mostly harmless, anyway."

—

I SURPRISED MYSELF BY listening to the entire course on mindfulness. I played it in the car on the way back from working on the condo, and at night, while Lyana put our daughter down and I cleaned the kitchen. I am not religious. I am no longer given to mysticism the way I was when Jeff and I were swapping ancient Zen aphorisms. The Tao symbol on my chest has faded over the years.

But I liked the idea of having a discipline again. I liked the idea of training my mind to settle down and be with itself. I liked the metaphor: that the conscious mind is like silty water; that meditation is a way of calming the water so that the silt drifts to the bottom and the water clears and you can begin to make out what is really down there. I started meditating ten minutes a day, then twenty, and eventually thirty. Sometimes I did it twice a day. I did it when I was tired or sick.

There was no cross-legged epiphany. But I did grow slightly calmer. Lyana commented on it. I noticed things I hadn't noticed in a long time. The smell of snow. Birdsong in the morning. Certain angles of light. I noticed how on edge I am when I walk down the street. How I scan everyone. How I scan every car. How I am constantly on the lookout for threats, how I often confuse threats and mere annoyances. How I play out scenarios: if he does this, I'll do that. How so much of my life is taken up by a constant stream of situation-room briefings.

I started thinking about how we all have only a limited amount of attention. And time. I started thinking: if I am investing so much of myself paying attention to this, what am I missing out on?

Lately, I've been writing to my daughter. I want her to know something of me when I was still relatively young. Also, I worry I won't be with her as long as I hope. Every parent fears this, coming up against something that takes you out before your kid is grown. I worry that something might be a fight I start and can't finish.

Recently, I wrote this to her:

*We drove to our friends' house. Andrew and Diane have a small apartment with an enormous backyard, which feels, in the middle of summer, slightly magical. There was a table under an apple tree. The grass was soft. There were vegetables growing and flowers in bloom. Butterflies and bees and birds. There was a cicada singing in a tree. There was a cat named Daisy which you called "Daishy" and a spider you watched build its web.*

*You made everyone laugh by falling over and over on your bum. You're a ham. You know how to charm a crowd already. You ate Goldfish crackers and pasta and cherries and a few bites of lemon meringue pie off my plate. Andrew bought you bubbles, which you can now blow. Diane keeps herbs growing in a big clay pot. You tried basil, parsley, mint and rosemary. You loved the mint. You kept returning to the herb pot and taking more until I stopped you. I was worried you might get sick.*

*I made a sling out of a picnic blanket and lifted you up. You threw your head back and screamed with laughter. I knelt down and pretended to eat your tummy. I love your little teeth and your neck and cheeks when you laugh.*

*Everything was green and warm and lush. And, later, when it got dark, there were lights in the trees and lanterns in the grass. Your mother sat beside me, in a red-and-black dress with her dark hair falling against her neck in curls. I couldn't believe the beauty in my life.*

*We put you in pyjamas and drove home in the dark. There are huge tiger lilies growing under our front window. They are maybe five feet tall. The other day I lifted you up to the blossoms and pretended the giant orange flowers were trying to kiss you. We pulled into the driveway in the dark and you said: "I want to kiss the flowers!"*

One afternoon, while I was writing about Jeff, I took my clippers to my head and shaved the hair clean off. I'm not sure why exactly, other than it made me feel closer to him in the moment. Maybe it's also that I was trying to do what I had seen him do—empty my head of thoughts, make my cranium into a vault where I could seek clarity.

There is a Buddhist temple near our new home. I went there one evening to join a meditation group. I felt strange about going. I felt the way I did wearing the Toronto Football Club scarf and T-shirt—that I was submitting myself to the singular body and betraying my principles.

The space was beautiful, a grand, cavernous hall with an apse in which sat a large statue of the Buddha dressed in garlands and fruit and incense. The people were gentle and welcoming. We sat on cushions and meditated to the sound of a bell. We walked around the dim hall in silent contemplation. We recited together the five precepts of Buddhism, the personal vows to refrain from stealing, sexual misconduct, false speech, intoxication and, most importantly, harming living creatures. I recited these along with the group. But I did all these things from an inner distance, watching myself without really meaning any of it, going through the motions so I wouldn't offend people in their place of worship.

In my head, I was thinking that sometimes living things must be harmed. If, for instance, they are harming other living things under the pretence of some great and holy cause. Who stops that if everyone is a pacifist?

I woke sobbing.

In my dream, I was getting ready to go somewhere with my daughter, just the two of us. I had packed her backpack, the one we keep her diapers and snacks in. I opened the front door. There was a ladder running down to the ground, as though our house was an enormous tree house. We were a hundred feet up, at least. My stomach turned over. My daughter was standing on one of the high rungs, trying to climb down in that awkward, fumbling way of toddlers. She was oblivious to the danger. She looked up at me and smiled. I told her not to move. She didn't listen. I tried to distract her with her backpack. It looks like a cartoon hedgehog and she loves it. She reached out for it and fell backwards and hit the ground. I heard myself say: "She's gone." I prayed she was dead because the thought of her in pain was too much. She started convulsing, but I was too high to reach her or comfort her.

Maybe I read too much into my dreams, but I do think that sometimes, in their aimless course through the night, they stumble on some important fact we have failed to pay enough attention to.

Here is what I have not been paying enough attention to: there is a great risk I will do some small, thoughtless thing, something intended to protect her or protect the world at large, that will actually put her in danger.

I've always assumed the road to senseless violence and dangerous, rationalized destruction lay in allowing yourself to become part of a group. There is something to that, obviously. There's always a risk, no matter how righteous the cause, no matter the calibre of the people, that a group of men will make the group itself the cause and that nasty behaviour will follow.

But there are people who are capable of resisting this tendency, who have gazed inward and understood that this is part of what we are as a species—that groups of men are the original weapons of mass destruction. Like my lost friend, Jeff, they know that to be part of any grand cause, part of any group invested with the capacity to use force, requires a constant inner vigilance—a capacity to recognize when one is rationalizing violence, or seeking it as its own end, or dividing the world into Us and Them, or pursuing a cause because it fills some void inside oneself rather than a need in the world. Jeff was one of those people, and he made himself into a peaceful warrior.

That's not me. I assumed that my autonomy made me immune to becoming part of a destructive force. But there are other ways to get there. Here's the route I took: I believed I was exceptional, both in my quest to right the wrongs of the world and in my capacity to use physical force as a means of doing this. There's nothing wrong with wanting to make the world a safer place. But that was only my intention on paper. I have been as nimble as any zealot at using my "cause" as a justification for violence.

A while ago, a friend asked me what the scariest part of researching this book had been. I told him it was hanging with the Red Patch Boys.

Worse than the rapist? he wanted to know. Worse than the serial killer?

Yes, I said, because the Red Patch Boys represent the world's unthinking men, who pursue personal glory and petty thrills while fooling themselves into thinking they are emissaries of righteousness. They represent all men who are blind to their own destructive potential.

It took me a surprisingly long time to see that I've been blind too.

Beyond the safe cove of my present life, there is that ocean full of possibility and danger. My great fear is that the danger will find a way into the cove and harm my daughter. Or, when she is ready to leave the cove, that the ocean will be less full of possibility and more full of danger. And yet, when I am out there in the ocean, I actively seek that danger and stir it up in my tiny, middling way, telling myself I will quell it and thereby make the world safer. But it has never worked out like that. I have always escalated the danger. I have always made things more volatile, more violent than they already were. I seem unable to walk away from an accident without making it into an incident.

I have been lucky. But that's all it is: luck. I believe in the laws of probability. They say that, if you keep repeating risky behaviour, eventually the dice will roll against you. Your luck runs out.

My daughter will travel out into that ocean past the point where I can go. And part of me will go with her too. If I have been sending out ripples that make the waters more dangerous, do they eventually dissipate or do they mix with the other ripples and make the whole sea tumultuous and choppy? What happens if I continue to insult and threaten people, make people more angry and frustrated? Don't the waters get higher and more dangerous?

Of course, I could become Gandhi-like and chance still might sink her and all my hopes with her. But the laws of probability also say this:

if I am not contributing to the tumult, then she has a slightly better chance out there on the water.

I'm not saying we don't need protective forces, just that it's now clear to me that I'm not one. I have not made myself into a protective force, though I guess I've sort of fancied that I am one. But I don't have the right to use physical force, because I tend to use it for the wrong reasons. I inadvertently made myself into a sword, but I have no skill at wielding it.

The whole point of reciting those vows at the Buddhist temple was to commit a public act, to hold myself accountable before others. I didn't really have my heart in it that day, and I'm not sure I'll ever return there. I'm probably not likely to become religious or join a religious community. But I do think I need to take a vow of non-violence. I need some new purpose. And I definitely need some way of holding myself accountable before others. So here goes:

I cannot be the sword. I need to be the pen.

—

I NOTICED HIM FIRST in the deli section, trudging in a straight line towards me without actually seeing me. I stepped out of his way. His shorts were riding low, his polo shirt was riding up, exposing the white sag of flesh beneath. He was a little taller than me. About the same age. His clothes were expensive. So was his haircut. But his skin was rough — red and pebbled like painted asphalt. I heard him from a distance talking to the women behind the deli counter, bellowing but not angry, the kind of yelling you do when you're wearing headphones and have the music high. I turned to watch him. I realized he wasn't talking to the women behind the counter but to the store in general. He began laughing, and I felt the flutter. I felt the icy tingle in my arms and legs. I felt my heart pick up pace and my vision focus. I told myself to relax. He wasn't doing anything wrong. Maybe he was having a manic break. I moved on, searching for eggs or milk or frozen waffles.

I met Lyana at the cash. Our daughter was in the cart. They were in line behind him, the man with the expensive haircut. He was talking loudly now to the cashier, an older Asian woman.

He was saying: "*Domo arigato!* Right? *Domo arigato!* Right? Right?" He was smiling while he said it and brushing his expensive bangs out of his eyes.

The cashier was not smiling. "Actually," she said, "I'm Korean."

He said, "Oh! Right. Riiiight." Then he said again, "*Domo arigato! Domo arigato!*"

I felt my jaw clench and unclench. Lyana was saying something to me — something about the groceries. She was behind me and hadn't heard what was going on. I was too focussed on the guy in front of me to pay attention to what she was saying. I realized I was staring directly at him, waiting for him to make eye contact. He was a perfect target. He was being a racist asshole. He was my size. I had just cause. I had looked him over for vulnerabilities and felt confident I could get him to the ground if it came to that. Part of me very much wanted it to come to that.

My opening line slid into place like a pinball waiting to be launched: *Why are you being such a dick?* I felt my hand on the lever, testing the spring, pulling it back ever so slightly.

I didn't use my opening line. What I said instead was this:

"I'm sorry he was so rude." I said it to the cashier after the guy was out of earshot. "You must have to deal with a lot of jerks."

She shrugged. "He's drunk," she said. She'd smelled it on him. Lyana and the cashier were worried he was going to drive off and kill someone.

I followed him out to the parking lot. I saw him get in the driver's side of a Jeep. I thought about him speeding off and T-boning some family on the way to a picnic. My cause was even more just now. I thought about opening up the door of the Jeep and pulling the keys out of the ignition and maybe also pulling him out.

What I did instead was call 911 on my cellphone. I felt like a tattle-tale, involving the cops. I told myself that if I had any backbone I'd go over there and take care of it myself. I ignored myself and listened to the 911 attendant. She asked me to keep an eye on the guy in case he drove off. She'd need to know which direction he headed. "But sir," she said, "don't put yourself at risk. Make sure you stay at a safe distance."

I laughed. I told her I thought my days of putting myself at risk might be coming to an end. There was an awkward pause. Then she said, "Very well, sir."

The guy didn't go anywhere. He stayed in the Jeep, eating peanuts and throwing the shells out of the window. There was a dog in the car. He fed the dog peanuts too. A cop car rolled into the parking lot and slowly crept up behind the Jeep, blocking him in. Two cops got out. They talked to him. They were calm. He seemed calm. It was hard for me to be sure at a distance. They opened the door and got him out, cuffed his hands in front of him and walked him to the back seat of the cruiser.

The cops stuck around until another cruiser got there, along with an animal handler to deal with the dog. I walked over to the cops in the second cruiser and told them I had called it in. They made me give a statement. What I wanted to know, I told the officer taking down what I was saying, was whether the guy was actually messed up, whether I had made the right call. Her partner, a middle-aged guy, laughed.

"Oh yeah," he said. "You definitely made the right call."

We drove home. We gave our daughter dinner and then bathed her and sang to her and put her to bed.

Later, I went into her room and watched her sleep.

# ENDNOTES

## INTRODUCTION: THE DANGEROUS DESIRE

1. This is from Doris Lessing's 1986 collection of essays *Prisons We Choose to Live Inside* (originally the 1985 CBC Massey Lecture Series by the same name). I'm including a longer excerpt here because it's intensely wise:

And yet, while all these boilings and upheavals go on, at the same time, parallel, continues this other revolution: the quiet revolution, based on sober and accurate observation of ourselves, our behaviour, our capacities. In a thousand universities, laboratories, or in deliberately contrived research situations, information is being collected which could, if we decided to use it, transform the world we live in. But it means making that deliberate step into objectivity and away from wild emotionalism, deliberately choosing to see ourselves as, perhaps, a visitor from another planet might see us.

It means, and I hope that this won't sound too wild, choosing to laugh . . . The researchers of brain-washing and indoctrination discovered that people who knew how to laugh resisted best. The Turks, for instance . . . the soldiers who faced their torturers with laughter sometimes survived when others did not. Fanatics don't laugh at themselves; laughter is by definition heretical, unless used cruelly, turned outward against an opponent or enemy. Bigots can't laugh. True believers don't laugh. Their idea of laugher is a satirical cartoon pillorying an opposition person or idea. Tyrants and oppressors don't laugh at themselves, and don't tolerate laughter at themselves.

Laughter is a very powerful thing, and only the civilized, the liberated, the free person can laugh of herself, himself. (page 46)

2. World Health Organization, *World Report on Violence and Health* (Geneva: World Health Organization, 2002), www.who.int/violence_injury_prevention/violence/world _report/en/.

3. A more realistic estimate come from the National Health and Social Life Survey headed by Edward Laumann. The survey found that 54 percent of the men

interviewed said they think about sex every day or several times a day compared with 19 percent of women; 43 percent of men and 67 percent of women thought about it a few times per month or a few times per week; four percent of men and 14 percent of women thought about sex less than once a month.

See: E. O. Laumann, J. H. Gagnon, R. T. Michael, & S. Michaels, "National Health and Social Life Survey," (Chicago: University of Chicago and National Opinion Research Center, 1995).

4. J.S. Hyde, "Gender Differences in Aggression," in J.S. Hyde and M.C. Linn, eds., *The Psychology of Gender: Advances through Meta-Analysis* (Baltimore: Johns Hopkins University Press, 1986).

5. F.T. McAndrew, "The Interacting Roles of Testosterone and Challenges to Status in Human Male Aggression," *Aggression and Violent Behavior* 14 (2009): 330–35.

6. The misapplication of biology has a horrific past. One of the major concerns with a biological take on violence—one that deserves serious consideration—is that this kind of research not only has the potential to lead down a slippery slope into a nightmare of well-intentioned eugenics, it has already done so. There are clear historical precedents. Nazi Germany comes to mind, but you don't have to look so far abroad, nor so far back in time: the eugenic sterilization programmes of 1920s and '30s North America, which sought to eliminate the "socially inadequate" and "feeble-minded"; the tens of thousands of psychiatric lobotomies performed during the 1940s and '50s; the unnerving suggestion by zealous neurosurgeons of the 1960s and early '70s that psychosurgery could be used as a cost-effective way of transforming violent young criminals into responsible, well-adjusted citizens. This last one is an especially unnerving suggestion if you keep in mind that the "violent young criminals" of the 1965 Watts race riots or, more broadly speaking, the people behind the necessary social unrest that characterized the civil rights movement were largely, if not almost entirely, African-American.

Debra Niehoff discusses the unsavoury history of psychosurgery—including some of what I've just mentioned above—in her book *The Biology of Violence: How Understanding the Brain, Behavior, and Environment Can Break the Vicious Circle of Aggression* (New York: Simon & Schuster, 1999).

7. World Health Organization, *Violence Prevention: The Evidence* (Geneva: World Health Organization, 2009), www.who.int/violenceprevention/publication/en/ index.html.

## CHAPTER ONE: THE RIDE

1. World Health Organization, *Gender and Road Traffic Injuries* (Geneva: World Health Organization, 2002), http://www.who.int/gender-equity-rights/knowledge

/a85576/en/; and Road and Traffic Authority of New South Wales, *Road Traffic Accidents in New South Wales* (Haymarket, NSW: Road and Traffic Authority of New South Wales, Road Safety Branch, 2001), download available at http://road-safety.transport.nsw.gov.au/search_results_iframe.html?q=Road+traffic+accidents +in+New+South+Wales.+#gsc.tab=0&gsc.q=Road%20traffic%20accidents%20 in%20New%20South%20Wales.%20&gsc.page=1.

2. D.J. Kruger, "Sexual Selection and the Male:Female Mortality Ratio," *Evolutionary Psychology* 2 (2004): 66–85.

3. See, for instance, the chapter "Altercations and Honor" in Martin Daly and Margo Wilson's book *Homicide* (1988). I can't recommend this book highly enough.

4. You might expect that altercations were less likely to result in death before the advent of guns, but mortality rates from fights (along with pretty much everything else) have actually gone way, way down since the paleolithic. See Steven Pinker's *The Better Angels of Our Nature: Why Violence Has Declined* (New York: Penguin Group, 2012) and Lawrence Keeley's *War before Civilization: The Myth of the Peaceful Savage* (Oxford: Oxford University Press, 1996).

5. G. Hohmann and B. Fruth, "Intra- and Inter-sexual Aggression by Bonobos in the Context of Mating," *Behaviour* 140 (2003): 1389–1413.

6. See for instance: W.D. Lassek and S.J.C. Gaulin, "Costs and Benefits of Fat-Free Muscle Mass in Men: Relationship to Mating Success, Dietary Requirements, and Native Immunity," *Evolution and Human Behavior* 30 (2009) 322-28.

7. The most common measure of testosterone is circulating blood levels of the hormone, which are about seven times higher in men. This is lower than the amount men produce (around twenty times more than women) because men also metabolize more of the hormone than women. For an entertaining and informative read that explains the role testosterone plays in male behavior, check out James and Mary Dabbs' book: *Heroes, Rogues and Lovers: Testosterone and Behavior* (New York, NY: McGraw-Hill, 2000).

8. The idea being that anger is an inherent emotion that has evolved, among other things, as a means of solving conflicts. The more physically formidable a person is, the angrier they can afford to be—because they can back it up.
   See: A. Sell, J. Tooby, and L. Cosmides, "Formidability and the Logic of Human Anger," *Proceedings of the National Academy of Science* 106,35 (2009): 15073–15078.

9. See, for instance, M.I. Newman and R.A. Josephs, "Testosterone as a Personality Variable," *Journal of Research in Personality* 43 (2009): 258–59.

10. For a brief summary, see F.T. McAndrew, "The Interacting Roles of Testosterone and Challenges to Status in Human Male Aggression," *Aggression and Violent Behaviour* 14 (2009): 330–35 (specifically, section 3, "Societal Influences on Aggression: Cultures of Honor").

11. S.L. Ristvedt, R.A. Josephs, and S.H. Liening, "Endogenous Testosterone Levels Are Associated with Assessments of Unfavourable Health Information," *Psychology and Health* 4 (2012): 507–14.

12. For the sake of a nicely flowing sentence, I've modified this ever so slightly from the original, which appears in T.K. Shackelford, "An Evolutionary Psychological Perspective on Cultures of Honor," *Evolutionary Psychology* 3 (2005): 381–91. The original reads:

> Such cultures are particularly likely to develop where (1) a man's resource holdings can be thieved in full by other men and (2) the governing body is weak and nonexistent and thus cannot prevent or punish theft.

13. Nelson quit his bouncing job at the club as I was writing this book. For a while, he was working security overnight at a boutique hotel. He wore a suit. There were no more fights. He spent most nights tucked away in the security office, watching movies, listening to music and reading. Shortly after he turned forty, he got out of security entirely. He still gets asked to bounce at various clubs, but he politely turns down those requests. He makes his money as a personal trainer and playing music at venues across the city, hosting open-mic nights, doing session work and touring with one of his bands, The Celebration Army. I asked him if this meant he was finally getting more sleep.

"Nope," he said. "But I *am* getting more peaceful sleep."

I should also mention that Adam won his fight in China. He fought a few more times, winning most of them. Then he was hit with a series of injuries, including a torn ACL. It took him the better part of a year to recover from surgery. He got back in shape—better than before, even. He was more confident too, more sure of his skills. But then something happened. The ride petered out. The sense of exhilaration boiled off. Cutting weight started to get to him too.

"At one point I just lost passion for it," he told me.

By the time he read what I've written about him, he had been out of the fight game for a couple of years. "I guess I'm sort of where Nelson is now," he told me. He also winced reading about himself talking about making another guy his "bitch."

I had initially used Adam's real name. But now, because he's working full-time as an elementary-school teacher, he was worried about his students (and their parents) reading about him talking this way. "I think Seiji's quote about dominance is what I was trying to convey," Adam said. "For me it was very appealing to be able to use my technique and skill to dominate another trained athlete. That's more or less what I meant, except I used meathead language, as I tended to in the gym setting."

He and his girlfriend recently bought a house. "I want to have the family and kids," he told me, last time we spoke. "Fighting isn't conducive to that. Most of the time you don't get back what you put into it. I don't regret the journey at all though."

## CHAPTER TWO: THE MOUSE AND THE SERPENT

1. C.S. Widom, "The Cycle of Violence," *Science* 244, 4901 (1989): 160–66; also Michael Rutter, Henri Giller, and Ann Hagell, *Antisocial Behavior by Young People* (Cambridge University Press, 1998).

2. C.S. Widom, "Child Abuse, Neglect, and Witnessing Violence," in *Handbook of Antisocial Behavior*, ed. D.M. Stoff, J. Breiling, and J.D. Maser (New York: Wiley, 1997).

3. For a review of the research into XYY Syndrome, (which is also known as Jacob Syndrome after the British geneticist, Patricia Jacob, who did the first detailed genetic study of the disorder), including more recent studies that have found a link between aggression and an extra Y chromosome in men, see:

L. Re, and J.M. Birkhoff, "The 47,XYY Syndrome, 50 Years of Certainties and Doubts: A Systematic Review," *Aggression and Violent Behavior* 22 (2015): 9-17.

4. H.G. Brunner et al., "Abnormal Behavior Associated with a Point Mutation in the Structural Gene for Monoamine Oxidase A," *Science* 262 (1993): 578–80.

5. J.C. Shih, K. Chen, and M.J. Ridd, "Monoamine Oxidase: From Genes to Behavior," *Annual Review of Neuroscience* 22 (1999): 197–217, https://www.ncbi. nlm.nih.gov/pmc/articles/PMC2844879/; also O. Cases et al., "Aggressive Behavior and Altered Amounts of Brain Serotonin and Norepinephrine in Mice Lacking MAOA," *Science* 268 (1995): 1763–66.

6. A. Caspi et al., "Role of Genotype in the Cycle of Violence in Maltreated Children," *Science* 297 (2002): 851–54.

7. R. McDermott et al., "Monoamine Oxidase A Gene (MAOA) Predicts Behavioral Aggression following Provocation," *Proceedings of the National Academy of Sciences* 106, 7 (2009): 2118–23; and D. Gallardo-Pujol, A. Andrés-Pueyo, and A. Maydeu-Olivares, "MAOA Genotype, Social Exclusion and Aggression: An Experimental Test of a Gene–Environment Interaction," *Genes, Brain and Behavior* 12 (2013): 140–45.

8. R.L. Sjöberg et al., "A Non-additive Interaction of a Functional MAO-A VNTR and Testosterone Predicts Antisocial Behavior," *Neuropsychopharmacology* 33, 2 (2008): 425–30.

9. Just as there are different versions of the monoamine oxidase A gene, there are a couple of versions of the gene responsible for producing a molecule called the serotonin transporter. This is a protein that regulates the amount of serotonin in the nervous system. One version of the gene results in comparatively low—though still normal—levels of circulating serotonin. Several studies show that men who carry this version of the gene and who are raised in harsh environments are more prone to aggression and criminal behaviour (for example: A. Reif et al., "Nature and Nurture Predispose to Violent Behavior: Serotonergic Genes and Adverse Childhood Environment," *Neuropsychopharmacology* 32 (2007): 2375–83).

Another study showed that teenaged boys with this version tend to show higher levels of aggression, but only if they've been the victim of racial discrimination growing up (G.H. Brody et al., "Perceived Discrimination, Serotonin Transporter Linked Polymorphic Region Status, and the Development of Conduct Problems," *Developmental Psychopathology* 23, 2 (2013): 617–27).

Along the same lines, there are several versions of the gene responsible for the expression of dopamine receptors—these are molecules embedded in the surface of brain cells that respond to the neurotransmitter dopamine. A couple of studies have found that people who carry one version in particular are more likely to show conduct problems later in life, but only if they've been raised in harsh conditions (for example: G. Guo, M.E. Roettger, and T. Cai, "The Integration of Genetic Propensities into Social-Control Models of Delinquency and Violence among Male Youths," *American Sociological Review* 73, 4 (2008): 543–68).

10. R.L. Simons et al., "Social Adversity, Genetic Variation, Street Code, and Aggression: A Genetically Informed Model of Violent Behavior," *Youth Violence and Juvenile Justice* 10, 1 (2012): 3–24.

11. Ibid. Also see: J. Belsky and M. Pluess, "Beyond Diathesis Stress: Differential Susceptibility to Environmental Influences," *Psychological Bulletin* 135 (2009): 885–908.

12. S.Z. Sabol, S. Hu, and D. Hamer, "A Functional Polymorphism in the Monoamine Oxidase A Gene Promoter," *Human Genetics* 103 (1998): 273–79.

Also see: R.L. Simons et al., "Social Adversity, Genetic Variation, Street Code, and Aggression: A Genetically Informed Model of Violent Behavior," *Youth Violence and Juvenile Justice* 10, 1 (2012): 3–24.

13. See, for example: T.K. Newman et al., "Monoamine Oxidase A Gene Promoter Variation and Rearing Experience Influences Aggressive Behavior in Rhesus Monkeys," *Biological Psychiatry* 57, 2 (2005): 167–72.

14. See, for instance: S.W. Baron, L.W. Kennedy, and D.R. Forde, "Male Street Youths' Conflict: The Role of Background, Subcultural, and Situational Factors," *Justice Quarterly* 18, 4 (2001): 759–89.

15. E. Anderson, "The Code of the Streets," *Atlantic Monthly* (May 1994), https://www.theatlantic.com/magazine/archive/1994/05/the-code-of-the-streets/306601/.

16. R.L. Simons et al., "Social Adversity, Genetic Variation, Street Code, and Aggression: A Genetically Informed Model of Violent Behavior," *Youth Violence and Juvenile Justice* 10, 1 (2012): 3–24.

17. Ibid.

## CHAPTER THREE: THE LACUNA

1. See table 2.5 in M.C. Black et al., *The National Intimate Partner and Sexual Violence Survey: 2010 Summary Report* (Atlanta: National Center for Injury Prevention and Control, Centers for Disease Control and Prevention, 2011), https://www.cdc.gov/violenceprevention/nisvs/summaryreports.html.

2. The National Intimate Partner and Sexual Violence Survey found that 19.3 percent of women surveyed reported having been raped over the course of their lives. See:

M.J. Brieding, J. Chen, and M.C. Black, Intimate Partner Violence in the United States—2010. Atlanta, GA: National Center for Injury Prevention and Control, Centers for Disease Control and Prevention (2014)

Approximately 70 percent of rapists are known to their victims, according to the Rape, Abuse and Incest National Network. Forty-five percent of rapists are acquaintances; 25 percent are current or former partners. These data come from:

Department of Justice, Office if Justice Programs, Bureau of Justice Statistics, National Crime Victimization Survey, 2010-2014 (2015).

Sexual assault with a weapon is quite rare and accounts for only about seven percent of male and female sexual assault. See:

K.G. Weiss, "Male Sexual Victimization: Examining Men's Experiences of Rape and Sexual Assault." *Men and Masculinities*, 12, 3 (2010), 275-298.

3. This paragraph contains an amalgamation of such pursuits gathered from my own, uh, practice as well as from several of my close friends, who shall remain anonymous for the sake of continued friendship.

4. N.M. Malamuth, "Rape Proclivity among Males," *Journal of Social Issues* 37, 4 (1981): 138–57.

5. P. Federoff, "Sadism, Sadomasochism, Sex and Violence," *Canadian Journal of Psychiatry* 53, 10 (2008): 637–46.

6. Strangely, this was also true of the *women* polled; 25 percent thought women would secretly enjoy it too. C. Crepault, "Men's Erotic Fantasies," *Archives of Sexual Behavior* 9, 6 (1980): 565–81.

7. G.M. Petty Jr. and B. Dawson, "Sexual Aggression in Normal Men: Incidence, Beliefs, and Personality Characteristics," *Personality and Individual Differences* 10, 3 (1989): 355–62.

8. M.P. Koss, "Hidden Rape: Sexual Aggression and Victimization in a National Sample in Higher Education," in *Rape and Sexual Assault*, vol. II, ed. A.M. Burgess (New York: Garland Press, 1998), 3–25.

9. E. Fulu et al., "Prevalence of and Factors Associated with Male Perpetration of Intimate Partner of Violence: Findings from the UN Multi-country Cross-sectional Study on Men and Violence in Asia and the Pacific," *Lancet* 1, 4 (2013): 187–207, http://www.thelancet.com/journals/lancet/article/PIIS2214-109X(13)70074-3 /abstract.

10. E. Meier, "Child Rape in South Africa," *Pediatric Nursing* 28, 5 (2002): 532–34.

11. P. Federoff, "Sadism, Sadomasochism, Sex and Violence," *Canadian Journal of Psychiatry* 53, 10 (2008): 638.

12. Page 67 in Randy Thornhill and Craig T. Palmer's A *Natural History of Rape: Biological Basis of Sexual Coercion* (Cambridge, MA: MIT Press, 2000).

13. See, for instance: D.J. Parrott and A. Zeichner, "Effects of Trait Anger and Negative Attitudes Towards Women on Physical Assault in Dating Relationships," *Journal of Family Violence*, 18-5 (2003): 301-307.

14. J.S. Carroll et al., "Generation XXX: Pornography Acceptance and Use among Emerging Adults," *Journal of Adolescent Research* 23, 1 (2008), 6–30.

15. Peggy Reeves Sanday, *Fraternity Gang Rape* (New York: New York University Press, 1990), 40.

16. L. Stemple and I.H. Meyer, "The Sexual Victimization of Men in America: New Data Challenge Old Assumptions," *American Journal of Public Health* 104, 6 (2014) 19-26.

17. See, specifically, Figure 2 in:
L. Stemple, A. Flores and I.H. Meyer, "Sexual Victimization Perpetrated by Women: Federal Data Reveal Surprising Prevalence," *Aggression and Violent Behaviour* 34 (2017) 302-311

18. It's also worth pointing out that although, as I mentioned, women are raped far more than men and the perpetrators of those rapes are almost always men, women are also often the *perpetrators* of sexual violence. In one study around 28 percent of the perpetrators of sexual assault against men were female. And often female perpetrators use physical violence.
See: L. Stemple, A. Flores and I.H. Meyer, "Sexual Victimization Perpetrated by Women: Federal Data Reveal Surprising Prevalence," *Aggression and Violent Behaviour* 34 (2017) 302-311

19. This story is told in Biruté Galdikas's book *Reflections of Eden: My Years with the Orangutans of Borneo* (New York: Little, Brown, 1995).

20. For an in-depth understanding of primate sexual violence, *Demonic Males: Apes and the Origins of Human Violence* (1996) by Richard Wrangham and Dale Peterson is indispensable.

21. See, for instance, the chapter "A Question of Temperament" in Richard Wrangham and Dale Peterson's book *Demonic Males: Apes and the Origins of Human Violence.*

22. B. Smuts, "The Evolutionary Origins of Patriarchy," *Human Nature* 6, 1 (1995): 1–32; and B. Smuts, "Male Aggression against Women," *Human Nature* 3, 1 (1992): 1–44.

23. It also helps explain a phenomenon that has been used to rationalize rape: women sometimes, though it is extremely rare, experience sexual stimulation and even orgasm during rape—despite the fact that they find it horrifying and repulsive. This kind of thing has been used to justify the rape myth that at some level "women really want it." The biological evidence suggests a different and more

logical interpretation: that the sexual stimulation is a woman's reproductive tract doing what it can to protect itself against a violent attack.

24. This is a point made by the feminist evolutionary psychologist Margo Wilson:
> The very fact that men are able to maintain sexual arousal and copulate with an unwilling female requires an explanation, for such persistence without cooperation or encouragement is evidently not a universal of male sexual psychology in all animal species.

Margo Wilson, "Femicide: An Evolutionary Psychological Perspective," in *Feminism and Evolutionary Biology*, ed. Patricia Adair Gowaty (New York: Springer, 1997), 457–58.

25. M. Seto, "Is Pedophilia a Sexual Orientation?" *Archives of Sexual Behavior* 41, 1 (2012): 231–36.

26. Granted, it's probably (and, needless to say, hopefully) never been widely acceptable for men to have sex with extremely young children, but it certainly was common until quite recently across the Western world for a certain proportion of men to marry pre- and peri-pubescent girls. In several American states, preteens and young teens can—and sometimes still are—wed. (See: https://www.nytimes.com /2017/05/26/opinion/sunday/it-was-forced-on-me-child-marriage-in-the-us .html?_r=0.)

More broadly, child marriage is a practice that's still accepted across parts of South Asia, the Middle East and Africa. In addition, there are the Sambia of Papua New Guinea, a tribal society in which it is—or at least it traditionally was—socially sanctioned for boys as young as seven to give older tribal men fellatio until they were about fifteen, at which point they were initiated as men themselves and became the recipients of oral sex from other, younger boys.

27. T. Augusta-Scot, "Power, Control and Beyond: An Interview with Tod Augusta-Scot and a Client Who Perpetuated Sexual Abuse," *Journal of Systemic Therapies* 28, 2 (2009): 89–100.

28. P. Federoff, "Sadism, Sadomasochism, Sex and Violence," *Canadian Journal of Psychiatry* 53, 10 (2008): 637–46.

29. K. Kolmes, W. Stock, and C. Moser, "Investigating Bias in Psychotherapy with BDSM Clients," *Journal of Homosexuality* 50, 2–3 (2006): 301–24.

## CHAPTER FOUR: THE BLACK BOX

1. J. Sprague et al., "Borderline Personality as a Female Phenotypic Expression of Psychopathy?" *Personality Disorders* 3, 2 (2012): 127–39.

The DSM-IV diagnostic criteria* for Borderline Personality Disorder are:
1) frantic efforts to avoid real or imagined abandonment
2) a pattern of unstable and intense interpersonal relationships
3) identity disturbance: markedly and persistently unstable self-image or sense of self
4) impulsivity in at least two areas that are potentially self-damaging (e.g., spending, sex, substance abuse, reckless driving, binge eating)
5) recurrent suicidal behaviour, gestures, or threats
6) emotional instability (e.g., mood swings, irritability, or anxiety usually lasting a few hours and only rarely more than a few days)
7) chronic feelings of emptiness
8) inappropriate, intense anger or difficulty controlling anger
9) transient, stress-related paranoia or severe dissociative symptoms.

* There are actually newer criteria for Borderline Personality Disorder in the most recent edition (the DSM-5). However, for the general reader, this list is probably more comprehensible.

2. Marnie Rice and Grant Harris were world leaders in psychopathy research. While I was still writing this book, Grant died of a stroke. Shortly after that, Marnie committed suicide. I am extraordinarily grateful for their help researching this chapter, especially Marnie, who, in addition to facilitating the interviews I was conducting, lent me important research material. She also read, fact-checked and commented on this chapter. It was a pleasure to learn from her.

3. See, for instance: O. Vaurio et al., "Psychopathy and Mortality," *Journal of Forensic Sciences* (2017), doi:10.111 1/1556-4029.13566, http://onlinelibrary.wiley.com/doi /10.1111/1556-4029.13566/full.

4. "Seventy-six percent of 'normal' men have had at least one homicidal fantasy. For normal women the rate is a bit lower, at 62 percent." D.T. Kendrick and V. Sheets, "Homicidal Fantasies," *Ethology and Sociobiology* 14 (1993): 231–46.

5. V. Nell, "Cruelty's Rewards: The Gratifications of Perpetrators and Spectators," *Behavioral and Brain Sciences* 29 (2006): 211–57.

6. See, for instance: P. Babiak et al., "Psychopathy: An Important Forensic Concept

for the 21st Century," FBI *Law Enforcement Bulletin* (US Department of Justice) 81, 7 (2012): 3–13.

## CHAPTER FIVE: THE PEN AND THE SWORD

1. If there's an official position on the origins of human violence, it's probably best articulated in the UNESCO Seville Statement on Violence, a document drafted in the mid-1980s by a group of international scholars who, at the time, were understandably preoccupied with the threat of nuclear annihilation. The tenets of the Seville Statement are:

1. It is scientifically incorrect to say that we have inherited a tendency to make war from our animal ancestors.
2. It is scientifically incorrect to say that war or any other violent behaviour is genetically programmed into our human nature.
3. It is scientifically incorrect to say that in the course of human evolution there has been a selection for aggressive behaviour more than for other kinds of behaviour.
4. It is scientifically incorrect to say that humans have a "violent brain."
5. It is scientifically incorrect to say that war is caused by "instinct" or any single motivation.

Over the years, the Seville Statement has gained a lot of public support, including endorsement by the American Psychological Association and the United Nations. (And I'd personally argue that tenets 3 and 4 are accurate, while 5 is *sort of* accurate; there are few "single" motivations for any complex human behaviour.)

Part of why the Seville Statement is so attractive is that it presents an optimistic view; it suggests that ending war is possible, namely through creating more peaceful societies in which we all simply agree violence is bad. But I think it's optimism based on naïveté, if not willful ignorance.

I spoke with the lead author of the Seville Statement, David Adams, a former US government scientist turned full-time peace activist. Adams is clearly opposed to biological explanations of violence, but his main concern doesn't seem to be a scholarly debate about human behaviour. His goal is more pragmatic than that: stopping what he calls "the culture of war." He feels that understanding the biological underpinnings of human behaviour leads to pessimism and nihilism. Adams mentioned a study that found kids who believe that war is biologically determined are less likely to try for peace. This is an understandable concern; if you can't convince people that peace is possible, good luck getting them to change.

I was surprised to learn Adams doesn't actually object to the notion that we've evolved certain violent tendencies. He cited, as an example, the fact that monkeys slap their young for misbehaving, just as humans do. "This is a very old behaviour," Adams told me. "It's deeply ingrained and essentially human. I think it's one of the ways humans learn. I'm against maiming and killing. I'm not against physical punishment."

Adams started his anti-war activism studying the biological correlates of aggression, hoping it would help him figure out a way of stopping war. He gave up on this approach early on, not because he couldn't find a link between biology and aggression but because he felt *individual* aggression was "irrelevant to issues of war and peace." Things like anger, rage and spite, he argues, are beside the point.

"War isn't emotional," he told me. "Look at basic training. Basic training isn't emotional. It's about getting rid of emotions," especially empathy. As Adams sees it, wars are conducted from afar by calculating tacticians and fought close up by unquestioning automatons. War, he argues, is a complex societal activity, beyond the influence of individual desires.

I believe this is deeply fallacious. Certainly there are strategists with abacus minds sitting in the world's war rooms, but equally, there are hotheads. The more pertinent point is the situation on the ground right now; I don't understand how you can miss the sheer anger, the rage and resentment in Syria, Afghanistan, Iraq and Sudan, across the Maghreb—the hundreds of little factions across the world, thirsty for the blood of their respective enemies. I believe it's clear violent emotions *are* part of war. A major part.

2. Lawrence Keeley, *War before Civilization: The Myth of the Peaceful Savage* (Oxford: Oxford University Press, 1996). See, specifically, Figure 4.1.

3. Ibid.

4. For a detailed description of chimpanzee raids, including the one I've mentioned (and for some discussion on human raids too), see *Demonic Males: Apes and the Origins of Human Violence* (1996) by Richard Wrangham and Dale Peterson.

5. L.T. Rodseth et al., "The Human Community as a Primate Society," *Current Anthropology* 32 (1991): 221–54.

6. Jerry M. Lewis, an emeritus professor in sociology at Kent State, has proposed these as contributing factors to sports riots. See *Sport Fan Violence in North America* (Lanham, MD: Rowman & Littlefield, 2007).

7. This quote comes from the introductory chapter of Chris Hedges's book *War Is a Force That Gives Us Meaning* (New York: PublicAffairs, 2002).

8. Lawrence Keeley, *War before Civilization: The Myth of the Peaceful Savage* (Oxford: Oxford University Press, 1996). See Figure 2.1.

9. That said, one of the most fascinating (and optimistic) findings of the Robbers Cave experiment is that the two groups of boys *were* able to overcome the us-versus-them mentality—again through manipulation. Sherif and his colleagues designed a series of situations in which the two groups of boys had to work together to solve a series of common problems. (For instance, they were told a group of vandals had messed with the camp's water supply. The boys were thirsty at the time and highly motivated to fix the problem.) These superordinate goals brought down the psychological barriers between the two groups. In the end, boys from both groups made altruistic overtures; one group treated members of the other group to malted milks.

10. The term *polemology* was coined by Bouthoul and Weiss, but the idea wasn't theirs alone. Herbert Moller of Boston University published the same idea at around the same time—though it doesn't seem Bouthoul and Weiss were aware of Moller's work (and vice versa).

11. For example, Jack Goldstein's book *Revolution and Rebellion in the Early Modern World* (Berkeley: University of California Press, 1991).

12. G. Bouthoul, "De certains complexes et de la pyramide des ages," *Guerre et Paix* 3 (1968): 10–22.

13. C. Mesquida, "Resources, Mating, and Male Age Composition: An Evolutionary Psychology Perspective on Coalitional Aggression" (doctoral thesis, York University, Toronto, 2002), 166–67:

> What becomes evident is that below a certain "age distribution threshold", which seems to be located around 35% [that is, when 35 percent or less of the adult male population is between 15 and 29 years old], countries show no indication of violent conflict. When this threshold is reached, only 5 countries (Kuwait, Taiwan, Singapore, United Arab Emirates, and Oman) show no political violence. All the other countries beyond that threshold have experienced different levels of conflict severity during the 1990s.

14. The three periods of intense violence in Colombia have been: the War of a Thousand Days (1899–1902); La Violencia (1948–65); and the sporadic conflict between the government and farc, which started in the 1970s and which, as I write this, seems to be coming to an end.

15. The most accurate measure comes from NASA's Spitzer Space Telescope: roughly 75 kilometres per second, per megaparsec—a parsec being about 3.26 light years or 31 trillion kilometres; a megaparsec being a million parsecs. Point being: space is expanding all around us, in all directions. And it is accelerating. The farther out you look, the faster it is expanding. With each megaparsec that rate of expansion increases.

16. Jeff's aunt, Melanie Murray, wrote about her nephew in her book *For Your Tomorrow: The Way of an Unlikely Soldier* (Toronto: Random House Canada, 2011). I'm indebted to her for the book—it was an important resource. But also for her time and openness.

17. Ibid., page 131.

18. That said, there seems to be an intriguing preponderance of brothers among radicalized terrorists. See, for instance, "The Outsize Role of Brothers in Terrorist Plots," *New York Times*, March 23, 2016, https://www.nytimes.com/interactive/2016/03/23/world/brothers-terrorism.html.

19. Bertrand Russell probably would have agreed. In *The Conquest of Happiness*, he wrote:

> A wish to escape boredom is natural; indeed all races of mankind have displayed it as opportunity occurred . . . Wars, pogroms, and persecution have all been part of the flight from boredom; even quarrels with neighbours have been found better than nothing. Boredom is therefore a vital problem for the moralist, since at least half of the sins of mankind are caused by it.

# ACKNOWLEDGEMENTS

Thanks to my family, and above all, to Lyana for equal measures of love, faith, encouragement and patience. For shooing me away from the drain whenever I was circling it. For helping me see myself clearly in the first place. For your own courage, letting me write about us. For making me more whole and life more joyful.

Simone, my delight and hope. Thank you for your visits while I was making this. They kept me anchored and brought me much needed lightness. You are my great and true purpose.

My father, Jeff; my first—and most influential—writing instructor. A gentleman in every sense. This is the becoming.

Jeannette, thanks for suggesting journalism in the first place. And for my first real science lesson: osmosis.

Mike, for being the guy in my life who believes in a good idea *before* you see it. For your unending appetite for story. Also an ace at making fish tacos.

Laila and Mario. For your warmth, love and unquestioning support. Thank you for making me family.

My grandfather, Mike Fairless—a genuine huggy. My grandmother, Solvieg—blind and still painting naked in her late nineties. Your work sits above my desk reminding me that creation trumps despair. And my late grandfather, Nat, whose motto was, "Keep living and never stop loving."

Neena and Gary for their love and warmth.

Maxine Lee for her unfinished works and unmet literary ambitions.

A special thanks to my editor, Anne Collins. Your encouragement, guidance, faith, light touch, good humour and heroic patience were vital while I searched for my voice. Thank you for the space and time to come into my own.

Thanks to the rest of the team at Random House Canada, and the larger Penguin Random House Canada, for launching this into the big, bad world: Terri Nimmo, for the slick cover design. Deirdre Molina, my managing editor. John Sweet, for the meticulous copy edit. Sarah Jackson, editorial linchpin. Brittany Larkin, in production. My publicist, Scott Sellers. Matthew Sibiga, head of imprint sales—and Sarah Smith-Eivemark, marketing lead.

I owe a debt of gratitude to the men I've written about—those I've named and those who wished to remain anonymous. It takes courage to be honest.

Thanks also to Carol Off for championing this project from the beginning and, more importantly, for mentoring me as a journalist. Fierce, incisive, curious and compassionate. A privilege to work with. A pleasure to know.

Lee Steven Chappelle for showing me, by example, that the real tough guys have the *cajones* to deal with their own insecurities.

Stev'nn Hall, for his exquisite art.

Fanny Corpiz for magnificent child care.

Thank you to the friends I imposed this manuscript on, in successive drafts. Especially Chris Howden, Sophie Kohn, Mary Lynk, Kevin Ball and Sarah Giles. Thank you for your comments, suggestions and wonderful conversation. Thanks to Reza Yazdjerdi for the chats about group violence. Glenn Robitaille for your help setting up interviews, for reading, talking, for handing me suggested readings and general positivity. Diane Eros and Andrew Budziak for being lovely. Thanks also to Lynda Shorten, Robin Smythe, Michelle Parise, Cate Cochran, Elizabeth Bowie and Frances Cappe. Jennifer Moroz, thank you for handing me a copy of Anne Lamott's book at just the right time.

Thanks to those friends who made a special effort to get me out of my own head when I needed it most: Neil Acharya for the Gerrard Street paan runs, whiskey and the constant ego props. Nelson Sobral for the slaps, corny jokes and great music. Shah Franco. Aamir Sukhera and Ravi Subramanian. Ghazal Tehrani and Reza Yazdjerdi, Reza Sheikh and Elnaz Sheikh: thank you for the fine coffee and even finer company.

Thank you to the many researchers, scientists and thinkers who informed my research with conversation and feedback. This book is built upon the foundation of your collective work: Christian Mesquida, Martin Daly, Margo Wilson, Richard Wrangham, Marnie Rice, Grant Harris, Robert Hare, David Carrier, Robert Josephs, Jack Goldstone and Richard Cincotta.

I also spoke with a lot of people whose input didn't make it directly into the book but whose comments and ideas pushed me in the right direction and helped clarify my thoughts. Brenda Adams. Stewart Smith. Alex Butchart of the World Health Organization. Steven Porter. Alexandra Lysova. Daniel Krupp. Eric Kirsh of Jewish Family & Child. David Wiesenthal. Kate Graham. David Adams. Samantha Wells. Harriet McMillan. Bob Mann. Jennifer Bass

Thanks also to Andrea Sisca, Ehea Perego, Jehad Aliweiwi, Lailoma Ahmadzai, Daria Stadnik and Tameem Sharifi of Thorncliff Neighbourhood Office. Catriona Verner, Lydia Riva, Julian Gojer, Stewart Smith, Craig Penny, Patricia Mannion, Jeff Gauthier, Nick West, Will Eagle, Raquel Cader of Toronto Family Services. Phil Tobin. Alex Halkias, Seiji Sugiman-Marangos and Peter Lee. A special thanks to Russ Francis, Sylvie Secour and Melanie Murray. And Jeff—I hope Ry finds something of you in this.

# INDEX

DAEMON FAIRLESS is a writer and journalist with a master's degree in neuroscience, who has worked as a producer on CBC Radio's flagship current affairs show *As It Happens,* and as a print journalist for the science journal *Nature*. He lives in Toronto with his wife and daughter.